A WORLD IN TURMOIL

A WORLD IN TURMOIL

An Integrated Chronology of the Holocaust and World War II

Hershel Edelheit and
Abraham J. Edelheit

Bibliographies and Indexes in World History, Number 22

Greenwood Press
New York • *Westport, Connecticut* • *London*

Library of Congress Cataloging-in-Publication Data

Edelheit, Hershel.
  A world in turmoil : an integrated chronology of the Holocaust and
World War II / Hershel Edelheit and Abraham J. Edelheit.
      p.   cm.—(Bibliographies and indexes in world history, ISSN
0742-6852 ; no. 22)
  Includes bibliographical references and index.
  ISBN 0-313-28218-8 (alk. paper)
  1. Holocaust, Jewish (1939-1945)—Chronology. 2. World War,
1939-1945—Chronology. 3. Jews—Germany—History—1933-1945—
Chronology. 4. Holocaust survivors—History—Chronology.
I. Edelheit, Abraham J. II. Title. III. Series.
D804.3.E34   1991
940.53′18′0202—dc20   91-22265

British Library Cataloguing in Publication Data is available.

Library of Congress Catalog Card Number: 91-22265
ISBN: 0-313-28218-8
ISSN: 0742-6852

First published in 1991

Greenwood Press, 88 Post Road West, Westport, CT 06881
An imprint of Greenwood Publishing Group, Inc.

Printed in the United States of America

The paper used in this book complies with the
Permanent Paper Standard issued by the National
Information Standards Organization (Z39.48-1984).

10 9 8 7 6 5 4 3 2 1

"that the latest generation might know them, even the children that are to be born; that they may arise and relate them to their children"

{Psalms: LXXVIII, 6}

Dedicated to

Ann D. Edelheit
wife and mother

Contents

Preface

Momentous changes transpiring in Europe and the Middle East during the late 1980s and early 1990s—the collapse of communism, the renaissance of nationalism within the Russian empire, the end of the cold war, the reunification of Germany, and the Soviet Jewish exodus—reiterate the crucial importance of the 1930s and 1940s as a turning point in the history of our planet. However, the events that transpired over half a century ago were often bewildering: the chronological context of these events is often lost in broad generalizations of the history of sixteen historically significant years. Nevertheless, those events have shaped and molded our modern world and must be understood in order to comprehend current developments.

The 5,840 days between January 30, 1933 (the Nazi *Machtergreifung*) and May 14, 1948 (the establishment of the State of Israel) formed a most dynamic, fluid era. Of necessity this chronology concentrates on the most important and illuminating political and diplomatic events affecting world and Jewish history. Nevertheless, noteworthy cultural events have also been included, although on a more limited scale.

Within this context we have primarily concentrated on events in Europe and the Middle East; less emphasis is placed on Asia, Africa, and the Americas. The experiences of three countries in particular define this chronology: Nazi Germany, the United States of America, and the *Yishuv* (the Jewish community of pre-state Palestine). Nazi Germany declared itself a thousand year *Reich*, but the perpetrators of humanity's most heinous crimes were fated to rule only for twelve years. Along with Great

Britain and the Soviet Union, America, which sought to remain isolated from the tumultuous events in Europe, was fated to become one of the main partners in a grand coalition which destroyed Adolf Hitler's racial apocalypse. The *Yishuv*, Jewry's only true sanctuary, would, despite facing many dangers, crystallize into the reborn State of Israel. This chronology explains how, although not necessarily why, these events transpired.

To the extent possible dates have been verified and may be considered exact. In some cases verification has proved impossible, and these dates are given as approximations as close as possible to the actual events. In order to avoid confusing the reader, we have made no effort to distinguish exact dates from approximate ones. Since any number of events may conceivably have occurred on a single day, all such events have been cited as independent entries with the most important cited first. In some cases discrete events, such as conferences for example, continued past a single date. In these instances both the beginning and ending of the event are cited as a single entry. Similarly, battles and campaigns often lasted for days or months. In such cases, the opening of the campaign, key operations during the campaign, and/or the closing date of the operation are cited as separate entries. The same holds true for Nazi and collaborationist *aktionen* dedicated to the extermination of European Jewry. In addition to the dates of creation and liquidation of major, and many minor, ghettos and concentration camps, the dates of important intermediate *aktionen* have been included as independent entries. Readers interested in a specific locality, person, or subject are advised to use the appropriate index to follow entries on related topics. In general, avoided has been the temptation to include editorial comments on the events in order to let the facts speak for themselves. Where it was felt that a brief description would be too cryptic, however, explanatory comments were added. A glossary of foreign terms, bibliography and name, place, and subject indexes are also included.

The scope of this project required some assistance from others. We gratefully acknowledge the institutions and individuals who made our task a bit lighter: the librarians and staff of the New York Public Library Jewish Division, the Library of Congress, the Gelman Library at the George Washington University in Washington, D.C., the Central Zionist Archive in Jerusalem, and the Histadrut and Jabotinsky Institute archives in Tel Aviv. Individual thanks go to Rabbi Amos and Helen Edelheit who made this project possible in both the long and short terms. To Professor Randolph L. Braham of the City University of New York, to Dr. Luba K. Gurdus, Marc Rose and Chaim Wiener for their encouragement and assistance. We are especially indebted to Ms. Karin Vanderveer for her editorial assistance. Nevertheless, we alone bear responsibility for any errors contained herein.

Key to Abbreviations

{A}	Austria
{B/R SSR}	Belorussian Soviet Socialist Republic
{Bu}	Bulgaria
{Cz}	Czechoslovakia
{Est SSR}	Estonian Soviet Socialist Republic
{F}	France
{G}	Germany
{Gr}	Greece
{Ho}	Holland
{Hu}	Hungary
{I}	Italy
{Lat SSR}	Latvian Soviet Socialist Republic
{Lit}	Lithuania
{Lit SSR}	Lithuanian Soviet Socialist Republic
{Mold SSR}	Moldavian Soviet Socialist Republic
{P}	Poland
{Ru}	Rumania
{RFSSR}	Russian Federal Soviet Socialist Republic
{Slov}	Slovakia
{Uk SSR}	Ukrainian Soviet Socialist Republic
{Y}	Yugoslavia

Introduction: The World in 1933

It has been observed that the world as we know it today was born yesterday. In this way historians can account for the causality of events over a span of time and the events of one particular era can thus be placed into a relational historical perspective. If this is true, then it may safely be said that our world was created in 1933 on a winter's day in Berlin when *Reichspresident* Paul von Hindenburg invited Adolf Hitler, *Fuehrer* of the Nazi party, to create a coalition government for Germany. To be sure, however, January 30, 1933 was not itself created *ex nihilo*, but was the product of a series of events that must be viewed in historical context. However, January 30, 1933 does not only represent the culmination of one series of events relating to German history; that date was also the starting point for a new era of history, some of whose implications are still felt today. Moreover, the relevance of that pivotal event transcends German history to include the histories of virtually every country and national group in the world. Most particularly, Hitler's appointment to the chancellorship opened a new and important chapter in the history of the Jewish people.

The theme of this book is the unfolding of the Nazi regime, its quest for global domination, and its attempt to exterminate Jewry through the "Final Solution." To understand the context of the events, this essay will survey the relevant currents in European and Jewish history in the late nineteenth and early twentieth centuries.

GERMAN ILLIBERALISM

Few would deny that the origins of Nazism can be traced back to the ideological roots of radical illiberalism in *fin-de-siecle* France and Germany. Germany, it must be recalled, was not a united country for most of modern times. Only in 1871, as the result of a series of three wars fought (respectively) against Denmark, Austria-Hungary, and France, did a unified German state—the Second *Reich*—emerge.

Although itself caused by events of the previous century, the unification of Germany was the root cause of a number of new and significant developments in European social and intellectual history. Of special importance was the development of what historians have come to term "national egotism," or the idea that one's own nation represents the pinnacle of all that is good and pure. National egotism acted to justify national demands for respect from other nations as well as the nation's attempt to "find its place in the sun" through territorial expansion. National egotism, thus, also justified a jingoistic and militaristic form of hyper-patriotism. Paradoxically, the same roots of national egotism also created the sense of imperfection within certain elements of society, primarily the intelligentsia. Given the premise that the nation is perfect, a premise that flows naturally from an egotistical analysis of one's own nation, then the analyst must take pains to explain why mundane reality has continued— especially if one perceives the creation of a nation-state in messianic terms. These varied intellectual trends came to their head in Germany at the turn of the century. A group of so-called Germanic Critics saw the new *Reich* not as a worthy heir of the traditions of Teutonic greatness nor as the proper vehicle for expressing the national will of the German *volk*, but rather as a philistine state influenced by a foreign body that had been permitted to fester within the German body-politic: the Jews. As a result of these critics' activities, the best known of whom was Richard Wagner, antisemitism was introduced into both the political and cultural strata of German society.

It must be duly noted that national egotism was neither unique nor endemic to Germany. Indeed, virtually every European state experienced a similar development at the turn of the century, as did the United States. Nevertheless, these trends were most clearly defined in Germany and in France—especially in relation to the status of Jews. The reason why the trend was more muted in the Anglo-Saxon countries may be explained by three factors: the age and security of their institutions (the British Parliament, for example, dates its existence from the thirteenth century); by the existence of ever-expanding frontiers (the American West, British colonies in Africa and Asia) into which creative energies could be channeled; and by the general lack of violent social upheaval for most of the nineteenth century. Thus, England had not experienced any violent political upheavals (except in Ireland) after the Glorious Revolution (1688), while the American Civil War (1861–1865) resulted in the strengthening, rather than weakening, of the principles upon which the United States was founded. In the words of President Abraham Lincoln's Gettysburg Address: " . . . that government of the people, by the people, for the people, shall not perish from the Earth."

Germany, as already noted, was born in the midst of war, while the nineteenth century was also one of intense turmoil for the French nation. Thus, expectations of perfection, which could never be reached in a living human society, were transformed into goals to be implemented when the nation could be purged of foreign elements and become pristine and pure, just as it had been—or so the critics claimed—in the glorious past. Making matters more difficult, in the long-run, were four unusual features of the newly united Germany. First, Germany was unified as a political entity but not all Germans lived under the sovereignty of the *Kaiser*. Austria, Bohemia-Moravia, and Switzerland, all areas identified with German culture, remained outside of the new German state, which was dominated by Prussia. On the other hand, Germany did contain a significant non-German ethnic population, primarily composed of Poles in Silesia and a small but prominent Jewish minority. Added to these factors was the continuing territorial conflict with the French, who sought revenge for their defeat in 1870. Finally, the state created by Chancellor Otto von Bismarck and its foreign policy owed much to his own personal style of rule. In particular, Bismarck's system of contradictory defensive alliances with Austria (against Russia) and with Russia (against Austria), which was designed to thwart French revanchism, was undone when he was removed from office by *Kaiser* Wilhelm II in 1894.

NATIONS IN CRISIS AND CONFLICT

While the course of nineteenth century events unfolded in Germany, a similar development occurred in France. After the dramatic upheavals of the French Revolution (1789) and the rise and downfall of Napoleon Bonaparte (1793–1815), France had become a nation driven by deep internal divisions. These divisions were increased by the revolutions of 1830 and 1848, which almost completely disrupted French society. In the aftermath of the Franco-Prussian war (1870–1871) and the Paris Commune, an attempt by the populace of the capital to impose a "people's

government" on the state, matters became even worse. Although outwardly restabilized by the end of the century, the Third Republic, born
in the aftermath of the Commune, was still beset by numerous discordant
relationships: between workers and employers; between urban and rural
elements; between Monarchists, Bonapartists, and Republicans; and
between true Frenchmen and those perceived to be foreigners, once again
primarily Jews. These various trends may be seen as having come
together, with a passion, during the Dreyfus affair.

Captain Alfred Dreyfus—a French Jewish artillery officer -was falsely
accused of espionage in 1893 and was convicted and punished for that
crime by banishment to the French prison colony on Devil's Island.
Although continuing to profess his innocence, Dreyfus was widely
assumed guilty, even within the Franco-Jewish community. As the wheels
of justice slowly turned, however, it became increasingly clear that
Dreyfus was indeed innocent, the victim of an antisemitic officer corps
wishing to blame a scapegoat for failure on the battlefield in order to
avoid admitting defeat at the hands of a better-prepared enemy.

After years of advocacy by the pro-Dreyfusards justice was finally
served; in no small measure thanks to the efforts of the writer
Emile Zola, whose essay *J'accuse* forced the case to be reopened, and the
Socialist leader Jean Jaures, whose humanistic spirit was offended by the
very act of injustice. Nevertheless, the anti-Dreyfusards were not swept
away in defeat, but rather were forced underground. The position of those
opposed to reopening the case must also be kept in mind, for it indicates
much about the crisis of French society at the time. Many of the
anti-Dreyfusards were willing to admit, in the face of overwhelming
evidence, that Dreyfus could actually be innocent. Yet, they argued, the
best thing for France would be to continue the charade of his guilt so that
the army's reputation would remain untainted. For the anti-Dreyfusards,
as for the German critics, an imperfect society had to be brought to
apocalyptic perfection, even against its will.

Continental Europe's three other major states—Italy, Russia, and
Austria-Hungary—also suffered greatly in this era of social malaise. The
modern Italian state, created in the crucible of war during the 1860s and
finally unified (like Germany) in 1870, rapidly lost the enthusiasm of its
citizenry. Economically backward, in an era of rapid industrialization,
the young Italian state was not able to cope with the growing crisis of
unfulfilled expectations. Moreover, the untimely death of the father of
the Italian state, Count Camillio Cavour, left the reigns of government
in considerably less capable hands. Instead of trying to make much
needed reforms Italian politicians undertook a policy called *Trans-*

forismo, making changes in the facade of government to divert attention from the real needs of the people. In Russia, the Czarist regime tried to use a similar policy of obfuscation to divert attention from the real problems of an autarchy no longer able to maintain itself. Unlike Italy, however, where meaningless changes in government personnel were made to satisfy popular calls for reform, in Russia attention was diverted by creating a demonic internal enemy who had to be destroyed before perfection could be attained. As in Germany and France, the Russians chose the Jew as their quintessential definition of evil.

Austria-Hungary faced similar problems, compounded by the specific character of the dual monarchy. Previously one of the dominant forces in German (and hence all central European) affairs, Austria was defeated by the north German forces and entered a period of steady decline. Further-more, in the nineteenth century the Habsburg empire was an anomaly—a multi-national empire on a continent of nation-states. Whereas the diverse nature of the population had once been a source of strength, the fact that the Germans and Hungarians, two of the more than thirty nationalities represented in the population, possessed a modicum of national self-expression increased centrifugal forces that were tearing the empire apart. Three groups especially chafed under Habsburg rule: the Czechs, the Poles, and the Serbs. All sought independence from Habsburg rule, although the Czechs and Poles were willing, as an interim measure, to accept cultural and political autonomy. The Serbs, on the other hand, were not willing to remain part of the Habsburg empire and were a special security problem, since an independent Serbia existed and shared a common border with Austrian Serbia. Austria also experienced the rise of egotistical nationalism, although most ideological concepts similar to those current in Germany were used without any sincere belief. Vienna's mayor Karl Lueger offered an excellent example of this insincere use of ideas when he was catapulted to national prominence by promising to deal with the Jews. When elected, however, Lueger justified his weak actions against the Jewish population of the city by noting "I define who is a Jew."

Thus, a series of intertwined territorial conflicts were created while an increasingly vocal segment of the population sought war as a means of finding relief from the mundane world and righting what was wrong with government and society.

THE JEWISH PROBLEM

Coinciding with the rise of egotistical nationalism was the rise of a "Jewish problem" throughout Europe. Although the Jews were only a small minority of the European population—in 1939 only about 11 million Jews lived on the continent out of a total population of more than 500 million—the Jews became almost instantly identified with the worst elements of modern society. The reasons for this identification are clear and may be subsumed into three broad categories. First, Jews had traditionally been both demonized and victimized by Christian societies seeking a scapegoat for their imperfections. Martin Luther, the father of the Protestant Reformation, went so far as to suggest in 1543 a ten-point program for ridding Germany of the Jewish scourge. Second, although the Enlightenment of the seventeenth and eighteenth centuries reduced religious antisemitism to a fringe element, the philosophes nevertheless retained considerable antipathy toward Jews. This antipathy was partly rooted in the philosophes' critique of organized Christianity, which was seen as the ultimate victory of Judaism's morality over Greece's aesthetic sense. The philosophes' hatred of Jews, however, also contained a good proportion of traditional antisemitic rhetoric, paradoxically taken straight from the teachings of the same Christian church that the philosophes publicly scorned. This was especially true of Voltaire's condemnation of Jewish usury, but may also be discerned in the writings of other members of the French and German Enlightenment. Third, was the inescapable appearance of Jewish "success" in the modern world. Whereas Jews had previously been outsiders, they had been emancipated as a result of the changes in European politics in the eighteenth and nineteenth centuries and had now entered into the very bosom of European society. In the view of the aforementioned social critics, emancipation, which was supposed to lead to a disappearance of the Jews, had only resulted in the "Judaization" of society. In order to reach the millennium, the critics argued, society had to be "de-Judaized," i.e. returned to its pristine pre-Christian form by the creation of a "new" ghetto, through legislation strictly segregating Jews and protecting society at large from their harmful effects, and a return of the old pagan Nordic values. As already noted, the result of such agitation was that antisemitism became an element on the political agenda in Germany and France during the last decades of the nineteenth century.

Two additional elements were added to the new antisemitism over the course of the three decades between 1870 and 1900. One was the reorientation of antisemitism from religious to racial hatred. At this point in time it was no longer plausible to hate Jews because of their continuing adherence to their ancestral religion, as had been the case in the Middle Ages. Rather, antisemitism merged with the quasi-science of racism and the subsidiary ideology of Social Darwinism. It must be emphasized that most antisemites adopted racism because of their *a priori* antisemitism, and not vice versa. Nonetheless, they adopted an ideology that had developed over the nineteenth century and turned it into a eugenic science. In general, the racists argued, humanity was not a totality that originated from a common root. Rather they assumed the existence of different races, much like there are different breeds of animals linked by a common genus, with one, the aryan (Nordic) race, being superior and the others inferior. Society was seen as being ill from racial intermingling, whose prime result was the Jewish rise to prominence. Jews, however, were not merely a lower race—as Negroes and Orientals were viewed—but represented an anti-race. Jews were actually identified with bacilli or with cancers; just as the bacillus infects the victim so too had Jews infected European society. Just as the only response to physical disease is to attempt to exterminate the bacilli so too the only response to the crisis of European society was to eliminate the cause, the Jews.

This eugenic and quasi-scientific line of analysis seemed to gain considerable justification from the ideology of social-Darwinism. Essentially a distortion of Darwin, who rejected the relevance of his theories of evolution to mankind, social-Darwinists adopted the racists' worldview and turned it into an incontrovertible aspect of human society. According to this theory there is a struggle for survival among humans as among animals; similarly, only those worthy few survive to reproduce; finally social-Darwinism posits the idea that superior races ought to dominate the inferior races, if they do not eliminate them altogether. Thus, social-Darwinism could justify a variety of different specific ideologies, including militarism, imperialism, and antisemitism.

When combined with racism and social-Darwinism, antisemitism became a potent and potentially violent ideology. At the turn of the twentieth century a further justification was added to this ideology in the guise of the so-called Jewish conspiracy theory. As developed by the authors of *The Protocols of the Elders of Zion*, this theory holds that Jews seek world dominion, using both liberal capitalism and revolutionary socialism as tools to manipulate the political life of Europe. In addition, according to believers in this theory, Jewish financiers attempt to centralize control of Europe's finances. Together, the ultimate goal of this conspiracy, variously attributed to the Rothschilds, to the Bleichroders, and to Theodor Herzl, is to create and cement Jewish domination over the entire world.

The Jewish conspiracy theory may be seen as the ultimate development of the position of the German critics regarding the "Judaization" of society. However, one major difference existed. Whereas the critics held that society had already been "Judaized," since even Christianity (as then organized) represented the victory of Jewish morality, the conspiracy theorists held that the process of Judaization had not yet been completed. Regardless, both variant positions held that de-Judaization was still possible, if not morally imperative. Doing so, however, required the adoption of a conscious program designed to remove the Jews from all influential positions in politics, the economy, and culture and to encourage them to emigrate (preferably to Palestine). The creation of such a program itself required that antisemitism become the operative ideology of a government and resulted in the growth of antisemitic political parties as well as the rise of professional antisemitic rabble rousers.

In western Europe this antisemitic agitation, although intense at times, did not turn especially violent, emphasizing emigration and the creation of a "new" ghetto instead. In Czarist Russia, however, the new antisemitism did turn violent; especially during the years of upheaval after the assassination of Czar Alexander II (1881) and after the Russo-Japanese War (1903–1905). In both cases pogroms broke out. In 1881 the pogroms began in the Ukraine and spread north from there in an unsystematic way. Although not sponsored by the government, the pogroms did teach the Czarist administration that antisemitism could be manipulated for the benefit of the autocracy. The pogroms in 1903, however, were more systematic, and indeed were directly sponsored by the government which released the Black Hundreds (Cossaks). Antisemitism had, by then, been proved to be a convenient means to divert attention from Russia's real problems by blaming them on a scapegoat.

A similar process of scapegoating, on a smaller scale, may be seen in the 1911 Beilis trial. Not unlike the Dreyfus trial, this was a case of conscious distortion of justice. Mendel Beilis, a Jewish factory worker in Kiev, was accused of ritual murder when a young Christian boy was found killed. Eschewing a proper investigation, the local police authorities, on orders from the Interior Ministry, arrested Beilis and soon placed him on trial. Almost immediately the show-trial nature of the Beilis case became obvious, with the Russian prosecutors attempting to prove the truth of the traditional antisemitic accusation that Jews use the blood of Christians in the process of baking *matzoh* (unleavened bread used on the Passover festival). As with the Dreyfus trial, the Beilis case ended with the accused being cleared of all charges.

These various trends came together at the turn of the century to place European Jewry into a virtual state of siege. Yet, such a conclusion about antisemitism, while not wholly inaccurate, should also not be exaggerated. Despite the intense hatred elicited toward Jews in many circles, they were able to maintain a widely ramified social, economic, and intellectual life. Even in Russia, where pogroms and random expulsions of Jews from localities within the pale were the norm, Jewish communal life was never completely disrupted. The nineteenth century proved to be an era of great creativity for European Jewry and the contributions of Jews to the social and intellectual, life of Europe was not inconsiderable. However, Jews did sense a growing crisis, and were also affected by their generally nationalistic environment.

JEWISH RESPONSES TO CRISIS

In general, Jews responded to the crisis in one of four ways. In Germany, France, England, and America, Jews tried to become "invisible" by assimilating into their surroundings and abandoning the distinctive cultural and religious traits that were identified with Jewishness. Rather than identifying as Jews, these assimilators preferred to be citizens of the Mosaic faith or, at the best, Israelites and they denied any political or social connection between Jews living in different countries. Judaism, according to them, was only a religious community with no political overtones; there could be no world Jewish conspiracy since world Jewry did not exist.

Although there were Jews who advocated assimilation into the eastern European environment, their efforts were doomed to failure by the Czarist government. Unwilling to permit Jews to live in Russia as Jews, the Czarist autocracy also was unwilling to take the steps necessary to assimilate Jews. The result was a policy of brutal and violent repression coupled with scapegoating. The goal of this policy was to force Jews out of the Russian empire, and indeed millions of Jews left for western Europe, the Americas, and Palestine between 1881 and 1920. Rather than emphasize emancipation and assimilation, the three movements that became dominant in eastern Europe emphasized self-emancipation and Jewish identification: Folkism, Bundism, and Zionism.

The ideology of Folkism was developed in large part by the historian Simon Dubnow, and may be summarized thus: Jews, according to Dubnow, are indeed a nation and all Jews are connected by bonds of nationality. However, Jews are a spiritual nation and their national consciousness requires no specific territory. The upshot of Dubnow's position, which may also seem as a form of Diaspora Nationalism, was to emphasize the need for Jews to reorganize their communal structure on a regional and international scale while also attaining recognition of Jewry's right to cultural autonomy in eastern Europe.

While Folkism had no specific economic agenda, Bundism was a form of Jewish revolutionary socialist nationalism. Although the early founders of the Bund thought that Jewish nationalism was transitory in nature and that Jews were fated to assimilate out of existence after the advent of socialism, by the late 1890s most Bundists had adopted a position of unqualified advocacy of their form of diaspora nationalism. According to the Bundists, Jews are a nation whose destiny is to be an ever present minority in European society. Cultural and communal autonomy—the centerpiece of the Folkist agenda—would be necessary to guarantee Jewish national self-expression; however, true justice for the Jews could only be attained by overthrowing the capitalist system and its replacement by the type of socialist society predicted by Karl Marx. The Bund, therefore, exerted much of its energy on preparing Jews for revolutionary activity. Nevertheless, there were two potential inconsistencies to the Bundist approach, neither of which was apparent in the 1890s, and the second of which only became clear considerably later: the first was the issue of how other socialists responded to Jewish requests for autonomy. Shortly after the turn of the century a meeting of the Central Committee of the All Russian Social Democratic Party (held in Switzerland) rejected requests for autonomy from the Poles and the Bund, meaning that for the foreseeable future (at least) the main nationalist part of the Bundist agenda was unattainable even under the best circumstances. The second inconsistency was, however, even more basic to the problem posed by Bundist ideology: a nationalist party must *ipso facto* represent all elements of the national group, irrespective of their class consciousness. As a socialist revolutionary party, however, the Bund was committed to a policy of class warfare and the overthrow of all capitalists. Left unstated was the Bund's attitude toward Jewish capitalists, although the problem would not become apparent until after the 1917 Bolshevik revolution in Russia. In 1917 many Bundists defected to the ranks of the victorious Communist party and abandoned all pretense of a nationalistic orientation.

In contrast to both the Folkists and the Bundists, who retained a primary Jewish presence in the diaspora, Zionists despaired of a diaspora based solution to the Jewish problem. Based on the premise that Jews form a single nation and that a territorial base was needed to anchor world Jewry, Zionism set as its goal the creation of a renewed Jewish society in Palestine, Jewry's ancestral homeland. To be sure, Zionism was not a monolithic ideology, although all Zionists agreed on basic principles. Beyond that, issues including religion, cultural orientation, political activism, and economics divided Zionists into a multiplicity of political parties which often competed against one another in violent terms. Such disputes notwithstanding, Zionism did represent the movement for Jewish national rebirth and offered a clear solution to two problems—that of Jews seeking a safe haven and that of Judaism seeking an accommodation with contemporary modes of thought.

Unfortunately, the World Zionist Organization—formed by Herzl in 1897—was beset by a number of weaknesses, in addition to inter-party strife. First, Jews represented a minority of Palestine's population. Second, Zionism could not, initially, sway even a plurality of the diaspora Jewish communities. In western Europe assimilation seemed to offer a means of individual salvation, even if at the expense of national and religious identity. In eastern Europe, however, conditions were so unbearable that many Jews eschewed all ideologies and emigrated westward in the millions; among them were the approximately five million Jews who immigrated to the United States between 1880 and 1920. Then too, at least until the Balfour Declaration (1917) Zionism appeared to be an almost utopian dream with little chance of success; seeking a solution, rather than a *luftmensch*'s dream, most Jews turned to other solutions, mostly to revolutionary socialism, whether of the Bundist variety or not.

On the positive side, the World Zionist Organization [WZO] did manage to create the eventual conditions for Jewish statehood: a parliamentary body (the World Zionist Congress) was created and operated on the principle of democratic elections; fundraising agencies and a Zionist bank (the Anglo-Palestine Bank, now Bank *Leumi*) collected the money needed for development work and land purchase. Before World War I, Palestine's Jewish population increased to between 80,000 and 90,000, up from only 25,000 in 1880.

WORLD WAR I

As noted above, a social and political crisis of increasingly vast proportions developed in Europe at the turn of the century. Nevertheless, peace in Europe allowed for the outward facade of stability. When wars were fought, for example the Boer War (1899–1902), they were generally in far flung colonies and did not elicit more than a minor ripple in the social life of the countries involved. Only the Russo-Japanese War (1903–1905) does not fit this pattern. An abortive revolutionary upheaval, born in defeat, further weakened the Czarist autarchy, although in the end the principle of absolutist monarchy was upheld for the time being. No other European state suffered such turmoil as Russia, although again it must be emphasized that in most cases stability was just a facade.

One event changed the entire European picture irrevocably. For years Serbian nationalists on both sides of the border attempted to provoke Austria-Hungary into a war, confident that Russia would aid a fellow Slavic state in order to guarantee its interests in the Balkans against Austrian and German encroachment. However, such a war would inevitably escalate into a trans-European affair as a result of the alliance system that replaced Bismarck's system of defensive alliances to isolate France. Specifically, Europe was divided into two armed camps: the Central Powers—Germany, Austria-Hungary, and Ottoman Turkey—and the Triple Entente—France, Russia, and Great Britain. In 1914 Italy was allied to the Central Powers, although it switched sides before entering World War I on the side of the Entente in 1915. Each of the major blocs also controlled a number of client states, including Serbia, Rumania, and Bulgaria (the former two associated with the Entente, the latter with the Central Powers). The other states, especially Belgium, studiously avoided involvement with either alliance, hoping thereby to steer clear of any war. Belgium's neutrality was also the subject of a specific warning from the British, who made Belgium a *causi belli*.

It has been said that no war has ever been as well planned as World War I. Yet, at the same time no war has ever caught the combatants as unprepared over the long run as World War I. On a number of occasions between 1890 and 1914 war appeared imminent. Therefore, all of the European powers took the precaution of maintaining massive military capabilities, which resulted in an arms race of then astronomical proportions. The economic strain of such a system would have been enormous, however, and almost every country relied on a reserve force of trained men—conscription being mandatory in all European states but England —who would be called to the colors in an emergency. As was to be proved in 1914, however, this system of rapid deployment via road, rail, and telegraph had one flaw: once deployed the army could not be called back without threatening national security. Deployment, therefore, virtually sealed the fate of the soldiery; only a short war would prevent chaos.

On June 28, 1914 three assassins stalked Austrian Archduke Francis Ferdinand and his wife as they traveled in Sarajevo, a city in the Serbian sector of Austria-Hungary. Two of the assassins failed in their task, but the third assassin, Gabriel Princip, was indeed able to murder the royal couple. The Austrians, who suspected a plot by the Serbian intelligence service, demanded revenge. A diplomatic impasse ensued, with each side preparing for the worst. Austria-Hungary declared war on Serbia July

28 and within a week almost all of Europe was ablaze. The Germans pursued a pre-existing strategy, the so-called Schliefen Plan, designed to defeat France in a rapid campaign before Russia could fully deploy its military might. The Schliefen Plan, however, required traversing Belgium, which was invaded by German armies on August 4. Britain, which had guaranteed the territorial integrity of Belgium, was thus drawn into a war that was clearly avoidable.

The short war Europeans expected was not to be. Mobile combat soon gave way to trench warfare on the Western Front, as both sides suffered grievous losses in futile frontal assaults. Thereafter, machine guns, artillery, barbed wire, and poison gas ruled an essentially deadlocked battlefield. The Russians also became active, but their early offensive soon turned into a disaster and the Central Powers gained the initiative on this front as well. By 1917 both sides had attempted every possible gimmick: naval blockade, unrestricted submarine warfare, and aerial bombing. Then too, new fronts were opened. Italy joined the Entente in 1915, attacking its former allies in an attempt to retrieve Trieste, Fiume, and other parts of *Italia Irredentia*. The Italians were hampered, however, by the poor state of communications in the alpine front as well as by poor leadership and an army not fully prepared for war. Stalemate soon ensued on the southern front as on the western front. A British attempt to outflank the Central Powers by invading Turkey (which also would provide a supply route to Russia) failed in the crucible of the battle of Gallipoli. Although both sides were nearing exhaustion, the war continued and became more bloody.

In 1916 a new attempt was made to break the deadlock on the Western Front. The allies undertook a major offensive using a new military invention, the armored tank. The new weapon, however, did not prove decisive. As 1917 dawned the military situation remained deadlocked. In April the United States joined the Entente, goaded on by the Germans' renewal of unrestricted submarine warfare.

Of greater immediate importance were events in Russia. In March 1917 Czar Nicholas II abdicated; overnight Russia became a democratic state led by a provisional government under Alexander Kerensky. Kerensky attempted to transform Russia into a Western style democracy while remaining in the war. Both goals proved incompatible under the circumstances. Finally, in October (actually November, since the Russians still used the Gregorian Calendar) the Bolsheviks led by Vladimir I. Lenin seized power. In creating a one party state based on his interpretation of Marxism, Lenin was faced with numerous problems—civil war at home, continued fighting against the Germans, and an economy that had been reduced to shambles. In response, Lenin withdrew from the war against Germany, preferring to concentrate on his internal foes, and surrendered a large mass of territory to the Germans in the Treaty of Brest-Litovsk. For the next two years the Red Army, led by Leon Trotsky, fought the White counter-revolutionaries, finally emerging victorious at the end of 1919. Full control of the country was not restored until the early twenties, by which time Lenin had already created the institutions of a vast police state; these institutions would later form the core of Josef Stalin's terror apparatus and are one of the more unfortunate parts of the Leninist legacy to this day.

The entry of the United States into the war along with the increasingly successful Allied blockade of Germany finally brought the Central Powers to their knees. On November 11, 1918—the eleventh hour of the eleventh day of the eleventh month—the guns fell silent. That very day an armistice was signed which brought World War I to a military close, although peace negotiations took close to a year to complete. The war had been devastating. It has been estimated that ten million soldiers perished during the war. Many civilian casualties were also suffered as a result of the allied blockade, submarine attacks on civilian liners, aerial bombing raids, mass artillery bombardments, disease caused by poor sanitary conditions (especially in regard to the disposal of dead bodies), and starvation. The economic life of virtually every country in western and central Europe was shattered. Morale also was shattered among both the victors and the vanquished. More than anything else World War I destroyed the old world while also destroying the sense of optimism that had characterized European thought during the nineteenth century.

THE POLITICS OF WAR AND PEACE

As the First World War spread throughout Europe, Britain was led into a search for new allies to aid in the war against Germany and its allies. In particular, the failure of the Gallipoli operation led to the serious concern that Britain's position in the Middle East might be in danger. This concern led Britain into secret discussions with the French over partition of the Ottoman empire and culminated in the Sykes-Picot Agreement. To stir up opposition in the rear of the Ottoman lines the British sent T. E. Lawrence (better known as Lawrence of Arabia) to stir up an Arab revolt. To further fan the flames of the revolt Henry McMahon, British Minister Resident in Cairo, promised Emir Faisal that Britain would support—indeed would assist—creation of an Arab state in the Levant. Unfortunately, the British failed to inform the Arab leaders of the agreement with France, even though the idea of an independent Arab state contradicted the planned Anglo-French partition of Ottoman territories into British and French zones. Augmenting the problem (and in the broad view one of the main causes for the present Arab-Israeli conflict) was the Balfour Declaration issued on November 2, 1917. With the Balfour Declaration, His Majesty's Government committed itself to help fulfill the Zionist endeavor in Palestine. Again, however, the territory was already promised—or appeared to be promised—to the Arabs as part of the McMahon-Faisal Agreement. Thus, in the span of three years Britain laid the foundations for many of the complexities of the vexing Middle Eastern conflict that plagues the world until today.

The United States was yet another ally brought into the war in 1917. Although America entered the war as a response to the German announcement that the country would once again conduct a campaign of unrestricted submarine warfare, President Woodrow Wilson also sought to give the war a moral meaning. In his declaration of war Wilson elucidated fourteen points for which the United States was going to war. In general, these points called for a fair peace in addition to calling for a solution to the nationalities problem in eastern Europe. Interested in gaining American support, the Entente powers all officially accepted the fourteen points, although in practice they intended to undermine many (if not all) of Wilson's idealistic pronouncements. The Germans, however, believed that Wilson's fourteen points were a fair basis for negotiations and hoped to gain some advantages from allied idealism. They therefore requested an armistice which was concluded in November 1918. In 1919 peace negotiations began in Versailles, France. The French intention for revenge in addition to the narrow self interests of each allied state, all of which pressed their demands to the maximum, rendered Wilson's hope for a fair peace based on his fourteen points meaningless. Once the Treaty of Versailles emerged, little was left of the fourteen points except for Wilson's idea to create a League of Nations.

Instead of a peace without territorial gains France demanded the return of Alsace-Lorraine, Italy demanded Tyrol and other territories, and England seized Germany's African colonies. New countries were created in east-central Europe: Czechoslovakia, Poland, and Yugoslavia (created by fusing the independent states of Serbia, Montenegro, and Croatia). Additionally, Austria-Hungary was partitioned into two states without the Habsburg dynasty, which went into exile. In addition to territorial losses Germany was saddled with demands for massive reparations and was forced to considerably curtail its armed forces. The German army was to include only 100,000 troops with no tanks, heavy guns, or aircraft.

The German navy was to be reduced similarly to simply a coastal defense force with no battleships and no submarines. Naturally, many Germans saw the Treaty of Versailles as grossly unfair. Those who opposed the treaty viewed it as a betrayal, seeing the German signatories as traitors who stabbed Germany in the back.

If any consolation was to be drawn from the treaty, it would have been the League of Nations. Based on the idea of collective security, the League was supposed to replace war with negotiated settlements. The League had little power however. With no means to enforce decisions—save voluntary economic sanctions—and (especially) without the ability to mobilize forces to prevent or quell conflicts, the League rapidly degenerated into a debating society. The United States Senate's decision not to join the League further weakened the organization, since this decision was seen as a message that the country which originated the idea had no faith in it. Clearly, the war fought to "make the world safe for democracy" did not have its intended result. Conflict was not replaced by negotiations and, once again, some nations sought revenge for real or perceived grievances.

THE POSTWAR WORLD

Despite the weakness of the League of Nations the postwar era began with the fervent hope that the carnage of World War I would never be repeated. Many countries, including America, France, and England, began the process of slow but steady arms reduction. It seemed that stability had returned and with it the facade of civility that had been lost during the war. America, for example, "returned to normality" after its brief experience as a key player in international affairs. Although still interested in economic trends throughout the globe, America returned to a sense of isolation and of disinterest in other peoples' politics. Britain and France, too, returned to their imperial concerns, although the latter also maintained a watchful eye on Germany. Many French citizens were appalled at the thought that a new war might break out and fear led to paralysis such that, by the mid-twenties, the French no longer acted but rather reacted to events in other countries. Then too, many voices argued for the purge of foreign elements—i.e. Jews—from the French body in order to restore the nation to its vigor.

Political crisis during what some historians have termed the Devil's decade was not limited to western Europe; the successor states of eastern Europe also suffered from numerous problems: border disputes, national minorities demanding autonomy, economic hardship, and the weakness of democratic institutions being but a few of the many difficulties connected with the new state structure that replaced the German, Austrian, and Russian empires. Poland, for example, began to develop toward a democracy, but was soon side-tracked into the paternalistic dictatorship of Marshal Jozef Pilsudski. Antisemitism was also rife in interwar Poland. Jews faced intense economic discrimination and the threat of frequent, but fortunately not centrally organized violence. Furthermore, most avenues of escape were closed as country after country ceased to welcome new immigrants. Similar problems were experienced in other eastern European states including Yugoslavia, which was divided between Serbs and Croats, Rumania, and Hungary. In almost every case internal discord inevitably impacted negatively on the security of the local Jewish community although in most cases, unlike Poland, anti-Jewish violence was rare.

Born in the throes of the collapse of the Romanov empire, the creation of a provisional government, and the subsequent Bolshevik *coup d'etat*, the Soviet Union faced many problems that were similar to the successor states. The need for economic recovery was a foremost priority and led Lenin to advocate a temporary step back from pure Communism in the form of the New Economic Program [NEP]. In essence the NEP permitted a limited amount of profit taking in order to stimulate the economy; it is clear that the NEP was planned as only a temporary gesture, even though Lenin died before ending the experiment. Stalin, who succeeded Lenin in 1928, built on the police state that Lenin created, liquidating the NEP and embarking on a program of forced collectivization and industrial development. Resistance was met with the means of a modern totalitarian dictatorship. In the Ukraine, for example, food supplies were cut off to break resistance to collectivization; in the interim millions of innocents died or were murdered by the secret police.

The fate of the Jews in the Soviet Union was somewhat paradoxical. During the 1920s Russia was the only country in which antisemitism was outlawed. Yet, Stalin had a deep antipathy to Jews—many of whom formed a loyal opposition to his positions in the Communist party—which would become more pronounced during the 1930s and 1940s. Similarly, although all restrictions on Jewish residency rights and employment opportunities, which had existed during the Czarist regime, were removed, all traces of an independent Jewish culture were also eradicated. Jews, Stalin had long argued, were fated to assimilate out of existence and ought to be encouraged to do so. Any manifestation of Jewish nationalism, especially Zionism, was to be strongly discouraged. Here too, the paradox is clear: in seeking to uproot Zionism Stalin offered the

Jews an alternate Zion in the form of the Birobidjan Jewish Autonomous Region. Albeit, by decade's end Birobidjan was Jewish in name only; the majority of Soviet Jewry continued to reside in the European segments of the country, principally in the Ukraine, Crimea, and Belorussia.

For Zionists the postwar era represented a new era of building the newly established Jewish national home. In 1922 the League of Nations approved a mandate for Palestine that was granted to Great Britain. Antisemitism was not eliminated, however, nor did the creation of the Jewish State proceed smoothly. Two forms of nationalism, Jewish and Arab, came into being in the same region at nearly the same time. Although the conflict between Jews and Arabs was not inevitable, it has become one of the most difficult problems in the world today. In essence the Arabs attempted to liquidate the Jewish national home through local violence. The first Arab riots began in 1921; thereafter violence broke out again in 1929 and 1930. The 1929 riots belie the Arab claim that they only oppose Zionists; the main victims of Arab outrages were anti-Zionist members of Palestine's ultra-Orthodox community, primarily in the city of Hebron. Unfortunately, the conflict has continued to this day and appears no closer to resolution in 1991 than it did in 1920.

THE RISE OF FASCISM

The postwar political crisis was not limited to northern Europe, encompassing Italy and the Iberian republics as well. As already noted the *Risorgimento* left Italy in less than satisfactory condition both economically and politically, proving that unification could not solve all of a nation's problems. Many Italians felt that Italy should have gained greater compensation for its sacrifices during the war. In addition, there were those who dreamed of recreating the grand Roman empire. In reality Italy was riven by serious political divisions which the country's parliament was unable to solve effectively. As matters became worse, radical politicians increasingly advocated a *coup* to replace the ineffective government. In 1922 a little-known former Communist marched on Rome at the head of a private army of blackshirts—called the *Fasci di Combatimento*. Benito Mussolini was, at this time, consciously aping Julius Caesar and the immediate result was about the same: before the blackshirts reached Rome the government caved in and Mussolini was appointed prime minister. For the first time a fascist government took over and began to rule.

Initially, Mussolini was somewhat successful in creating an effective government. In the long run, however, his use of strong-arm tactics combined with the Fascist effort to uproot Italy's other traditional centers of power was not successful. Despite Fascist attempts, Italian society was not fully recast into the totalitarian state that Mussolini hoped to develop. Nevertheless, Mussolini's power base was secure for the 1920s, as was his role in international affairs. Such opposition as existed was swept aside with relative ease.

Despite the perception that radical antisemitism was primarily an ideological fixture of the political right, Mussolini's takeover did not initially alter the status of Italian Jewry. As Europe's oldest community Italian Jewry was well integrated into the Italian nation. As a result, antisemitism never became a mass movement in modern Italy and Jews did not become the butt for Italian frustrations. Jews were not turned into the scapegoats for an ill society and were thus able to participate fully in the Fascist movement; many did so although most remained outside of politics. Mussolini also played an important role on the world Jewish political scene. He was seen as a potential counterweight to Britain's colonial government in Palestine and was courted as a potential ally by such Zionist leaders as Chaim Weizmann, Zeev Jabotinsky, and Nahum Goldmann.

WEIMAR GERMANY

Although totalitarian movements had gained control of both the Soviet Union and Italy by the middle of the twenties, it was Germany that experienced the most concerted crisis in the aftermath of World War I. Many Germans felt that the Versailles treaty was unfair; these groups also claimed that Germany had been betrayed by its internal enemies. In the interim a republic was established, colloquially known as the Weimar Republic since the new constitution was drafted in Weimar. Ruled by a coalition of Social-Democrats and other left-center parties, Weimar was not established on a very secure foundation. In the earliest years of the republic, a Communist-inspired rebellion nearly overturned the democratic government. The rebellion was eventually suppressed, but the political cost to the republic was massive: the government was forced to call on right-wing paramilitary groups (*Freikorps* and *Stahlhelm*) to eliminate the rebellion. This decision would cost the republic in later years for these paramilitary groups could not be eliminated.

Germany stabilized briefly but again faced a crisis that almost shook the republic to its foundations in 1923 and 1924. Economic difficulties in Germany, brought about by an imbalance of trade after the French occupation of the German industrial centers in revenge for lax German payment of reparations, led to a massive inflation which sapped support for the republic. At this time an unknown rabble-rouser named Adolf Hitler led his *Nationalsozialistiche Deutsche Arbeiterpartei* [NSDAP] (the Nazi party) in an abortive putsch. The inflation was, however, only temporary; when economic stability returned, the Nazis lost what little support that they were able to amass. The right-wing activists were not, however, uprooted: Hitler served a nine month prison term for a crime that would have brought Communists under the headsman's axe. While in prison Hitler penned his vision for a Nazi future and later published the book under the title *Mein Kampf* (My Struggle). Therein he set out the new NSDAP strategy which was to use the Weimar Constitution, and especially the election laws, to undermine democracy and constitutional government.

For the most part Hitler's strategy was a failure during the mid-twenties. With the economy stabilized and steady political progress being made both at home and abroad, by chancellors such as Gustav Stresemann the Nazis could not strike root. The Nazis did maintain one advantage: their use of limited political violence and their mastery of *voelkisch* symbols were arrived in the form of the stock market crash in New York. The resulting depression destroyed all vestiges of economic stability in the United States and throughout the world.

Once again the Weimar Republic was beset by internal strife as both Nazis and Communists vied for control. This battle was played out on the streets, not in the voting booth and eventually the Storm Troopers [SA] gained the upper hand. The depression also splintered the already fragmented German party structure. In the *Reichstag* coalition governments rose and fell without a decisive majority being established. The republic briefly rallied in 1930 as a center-right coalition was created by Franz von Papen. This coalition was soon broken, however, and von Papen began to rule by decree. In elections held in June 1932 the NSDAP received 40 percent of the vote, becoming the largest party in the *Reichstag*, although Hitler still required a coalition to rule. Refusing to accept a coalition, Hitler demanded new elections, which were held in November. At this point the Nazis actually lost ground, tallying only 32 percent of the vote but still remaining the largest single party in the *Reichstag*. Intense negotiations finally led to Hitler's appointment as chancellor by President Paul von Hindenburg—heading a government that had a minority Nazi representation—on January 30, 1933.

Hitler's date with destiny, however, was to prove a source of turmoil and destruction of unparalleled proportions for the entire world.

1933

JANUARY

30 Adolf Hitler, *Nationalsozialistische deutsche Arbeiterpartei* [NSDAP] (National Socialist German Worker Party) leader, becomes chancellor of Germany upon invitation by *Reichs* President *Feldmarschall* Paul von Hindenburg.

30 *Juedische Jugendhilfe* (Jewish Youth Help) is founded.

30 Brown Shirts [SA] and Communists clash violently in streets throughout Germany. The SA celebrates Nazi accession to power with a giant torchlight parade through Berlin.

31 Edouard Daladier becomes premier of France.

31 Eamon De Valera wins in Irish Free State elections.

FEBRUARY

1 A decree Hitler obtains from von Hindenburg orders dissolution of the *Reichstag* (parliament). New elections are called for March 5.

1 Italy publishes the Fascist Ten Commandments.

2 Hitler bans all demonstrations, except those by the National Socialists.

2 The Geneva Disarmament Conference begins.

3 Hitler secretly addresses leaders of the German armed forces, outlining the aims of the new Germany.

5 Martial law is proclaimed over most of Rumania.

6 The Prussian *Landtag* (state legislature) is dissolved and its powers are transferred to the *Reichskomissariat* (State Commissariat), the civil administration of the central government in Berlin.

6 Socialists in England, Germany, France, Poland, Italy, Norway, and Holland call for cooperation between Social Democrats and Communists in the struggle against Nazism.

6 The Danish government prohibits strikes and lockouts.

7 Reorganization of the German Communist party [KPD] is called for by its chief, Ernst Thaelman, in preparation for clandestine operations in Germany.

7 A violent confrontation erupts between Arab and Jewish workers in Ramat ha-Sharon.

8 Egypt's King Fuad meets with World Zionist Organization [WZO] president Nahum Sokolow.

11 Large protest rally is staged in Tel Aviv by *Hitahdut ha-Zionim ha-Revisionistim* [HA-ZOHAR] (Union of Zionists-Revisionists) supporters.

12 Jews begin an exodus from Nazi Germany.

12 Arab bands uproot 10,000 saplings in the Nahalal wood.

14 Border hostilities break out between Peru and Colombia.

15 An assassination attempt is made on the United States president-elect, Franklin Delano Roosevelt, by Joseph Zangara, an Italian-born anarchist, in Miami, Florida; Chicago mayor, Anton J. Cermak, accompanying Roosevelt, is instead mortally wounded.

16 Czechoslovakia, Rumania, and Yugoslavia reorganize the Little Entente.

22 A joint conference committee is formed by the American Jewish Congress, American Jewish Committee, and *B'nai B'rith* (Sons of the Covenant) to examine the German situation.

23 Japanese forces occupy China north of the Great Wall.

24 *The Stahlhelm* (Steel Helmet), SA, and SS officially granted auxiliary police status.

25 Sir Arthur Wauchope, the British High Commissioner for Palestine, rejects Arab demands making sale of Arab lands to Jews illegal.

27 *The Reichstag* is set on fire; German Communists are accused.

28 Hitler, with von Hindenburg's approval, abrogates individuals' constitutional rights.

28 Under the decree "For the Protection of the People and the State," the SA and SS begin rounding up German Communists.

28 The League for Human Rights of Czechoslovakia issues an appeal on behalf of refugees fleeing Nazi Germany.

MARCH

1 Nazi Germany promulgates its decrees, "Provocation to Armed Conflict" and "Provocation to a General Strike."

3 An earthquake and accompanying tidal wave near Yokohama, Japan claims 3,000 lives.

4 Franklin Delano Roosevelt is inaugurated as thirty-second president of the United States of America.

4 Esterwegen, a concentration camp near Hannover, opens.

4 The Austrian parliament dissolves.

5 The Nazi slate wins 288 seats in the new *Reichstag:* Together with the 52 seats won by the Nationalists, the Nazi coalition gains a majority.

5 The SA, *Stahlhelm*, and *Schutzpolizei* (Protection Police) stage a mass victory parade in Berlin.

5 Roosevelt declares a four-day bank holiday to stop a run on banks and calls for a special session of Congress to deal with America's urgent economic problems.

6 An emergency decree proclaimed by the Nazis, For the Protection of the German People, restricts opposition press and information services.

6 Marshal Jozef Pilsudski sends Polish troops into Danzig, breaking a 1921 agreement that it remain a free city.

6 *Coup d'etat* in Greece.

7 Engelbert Dollfuss, the Austrian chancellor, assumes dictatorial powers.

8 Dollfuss suspends freedom of the press.

9 Heinrich Himmler becomes Munich's police president.

9 The U.S. Congress passes the Emergency Banking Relief Act, leading to establishment of the Federal Deposit Insurance Corporation [FDIC].

9 Japan withdraws from the League of Nations.

9/10   The SA sponsors a series of Anti-Jewish riots throughout Germany: KPD headquarters and Communist individuals are searched and attacked by German police.

10   An earthquake kills 123 people in southern California.

11   The United States agrees to participate in a League of Nations commission considering the Sino-Japanese dispute.

12   The SA stages incidents along the German-French border.

12   Roosevelt delivers his first "fireside chat."

13   The SA sponsors picket lines at county and district court entrances in Breslau, in order to prevent Jewish judges and lawyers access.

13   Dr. Josef Goebbels is appointed *Reich* (State) Minister for Public Enlightenment and Propaganda.

13   The Polish government demands unlimited emergency powers from *sejm* (the lower house of parliament), due to political conditions in Europe.

14   The KPD half-heartedly tries to establish an anti-Nazi coalition with the *Sozialdemokratische Partei Deutschland* [SPD] (German Social Democratic Party).

15   Brandenburg, a concentration camp near Berlin, opens.

16   Dr. Hjalmar Schacht is appointed president of the *Reichsbank*.

16   Belgium begins constructing fortifications along the Meuse River.

17   *Leibstandarte SS Adolf Hitler* is established as a 120-man bodyguard contingent of the SS, under Sepp Dietrich. SS-*Sonderkommandos* (special detachments) are established in all major cities of Germany.

17   Hitler speaks before the *Reichstag,* declaring himself a man of peace and international cooperation.

17   Poland protests Nazi mistreatment of Polish Jews in Germany.

18   Nazis arrest and beat Jews and Communists in Oehringen.

19   The Jewish War Veterans of America initiates an anti-Nazi boycott.

20   Goering orders the police to use force against hostile demonstrations.

20   The newly elected *Reichstag* gives Hitler full leadership power.

20   Jews of Vilna declare an anti-Nazi boycott.

20   The American Jewish Committee and *B'nai B'rith* together condemn Nazi Germany for denying German Jews their basic rights.

21 The new *Reichstag* opens in the Garrison Church at Potsdam with a solemn ceremony in front of the tomb of Frederick the Great. The German Communist Party is eliminated, giving Nazis the absolute majority in the new rubber-stamp parliament.

21 Nazis commit numerous vandalous acts against Jewish business establishments in Berlin.

21 Germany establishes special courts to prosecute political enemies.

21 *Sejm* gives the Polish government until November 1 the power to rule by decree.

22 *Konzentrationslager* [KL] Dachau opens near Munich as a concentration camp for political prisoners.

22 Rabbi Stephen S. Wise testifies before the U.S. House Immigration Committee.

22 The *Geheime Staatspolizei* [GESTAPO] (Secret State Police) searches Professor Einstein's Berlin apartment.

22 Stop Hitler Now, a rally at Madison Square Garden in New York City, attracts a crowd of more than 20,000 people.

23 *Reichsmarschall* Hermann Goering opens the first session of the new *Reichstag* and raises the problem of the anti-Nazi boycott.

23 *Ermaechtigungsgesetz* (rule by decree), the Enabling Act, passed by the *Reichstag* gives Nazis the legal right to incarcerate non-Nazi political leaders, among others.

23 Spain outlaws Fascist propaganda.

23 A joint delegation from the American Jewish Committee and the *B'nai B'rith* requests that Secretary of State Cordell Hull investigate German Jewry's precarious position.

24 The World Alliance for Combating Antisemitism calls for a boycott of German goods and services, to last until the Nazis stop persecuting German Jews.

25 The Bavarian Ministry of Justice replaces Jewish judges in disciplinary and criminal cases.

25 Goering publicly denies mistreatment of Jews and political opponents.

27 A mass anti-Nazi demonstration is held in New York City under American Jewish Congress sponsorship.

28 A large protest rally against German Jewish persecution is held in Tel Aviv.

28 The Conference of German Bishops on National Socialism opens in Fulda.

29 Roman Catholic bishops of Germany take a reconciliatory position toward Nazism.

30 President von Hindenburg tries to convince Hitler to cancel the projected Nazi boycott against German Jewish shops and businesses.

30 *Va'ad Leumi* (National Council) approves a protest resolution regarding the persecution of German Jewry.

30 The British House of Lords is the scene of an imposing demonstration against Nazi persecution of German Jews.

30 The American Committee on Religious Rights and Minorities sends an investigative committee to Germany consisting of leading Catholic, Protestant, and Jewish clergymen.

30 A telephone line linking London to Jerusalem begins operation.

31 *Schutzbund*, the Socialist uniformed defense force, is ordered disbanded by Austrian government.

31 The Civilian Conservation Corps is founded in the United States.

31 Establishment of KL Oranienburg, a concentration camp near Berlin.

APRIL

1 Prussian Jews are forbidden to act as notary publics.

1 Nazis declare a boycott against Jewish businesses and professionals: Armed black-clad SA men place themselves in front to Jewish-owned stores to prevent would-be customers from entering.

1 Himmler is appointed chief of the Bavarian Political Police.

1 SA troopers demolish the Mannheim synagogue's interior.

1 Pope Pius XI proclaims holy year.

4 Legislation of anti-Jewish laws begins in Germany.

4 Robert Weltsch publishes an article in the *Juedische Rundschau* under the headline banner, "Wear the Yellow Badge with Pride," in reaction to the Nazi boycott of Jewish businesses in Germany.

4 Chaim Arlosoroff meets with high commissioner; demands easier entry requirements for German Jews immigrating to Palestine.

5 An American airship falls into the sea, killing seventy-three people.

6 The Belgian Federation of Protestant Churches sharply protests the Nazi treatment of German Jews.

7 *Berufsbeamtengesetz* (Law for the Restoration of the Professional Civil Service) promulgated in Nazi Germany; thousands of Jews and German Communists in the civil service are fired from their jobs.

7 The Law Concerning Admission to the Legal Profession is published in Germany affecting Jewish judges, district attorneys, and lawyers.

7 *Reichsstatthaltergesetz* (Law concerning the State Governors) strips German states of their autonomous powers.

7 Switzerland denies "political fugitive" status to Jews fleeing Nazi Germany.

8 Zionist leaders, including Chaim Weizmann and Arlosoroff, meet Arab leaders from Transjordan at the King David Hotel in Jerusalem.

10 Wittmoor, a concentration camp near Hamburg, opens.

11 Administration of KL Dachau taken over by the SS.

12 A groundbreaking ceremony is held at the Daniel Sieff Research Center (Weizmann Institute) in Rehovot, Palestine.

12 The British cabinet considers the Jewish refugee question. A debate in the House of Lords considers the fate of German Jewry under the Nazis.

13 Nazi policies toward Jews are condemned during House of Commons debate.

14 Japan imitates the Nazis in an anti-Jewish drive in Tokyo.

14 Jerusalem's Hebrew University inaugurates its outdoor theater.

15 Osthofen, a concentration camp in Hessen, opens.

17 Uniformed members of *Brith Trumpeldor* [BETAR] (Revisionist Zionist youth organization) are attacked by workers and residents of Tel Aviv while marching through the city.

19 The United States drops from the gold standard.

20 The Jewish Agency for Palestine, in a manifesto to world Jewry, calls for establishment of a special fund offering constructive aid to German Jewry.

21 Germany enacts a law prohibiting *shechita* (ritual slaughter).

21 Rudolf Hess is named deputy *fuehrer* of the NSDAP.

21 British Prime Minister Ramsey MacDonald meets with President Roosevelt in Washington to discuss the world economic situation.

21/22 Anti-Jewish decrees passed by Nazis hit a record, numbering 400.

22 A law is passed dismissing all non-aryan medical doctors, dentists, and dental technicians from German hospitals, clinics, and public health centers.

22 The Mandatory government announces the immigrant schedule for the upcoming six months; 5,500 certificates out of the Jewish Agency request for 12,500 are made available.

25 *Gesetz gegen der Ueberfuellung von Deutsche Schulen und Hochschulen* (Law for Preventing Overcrowding in German Schools and Colleges) is promulgated, limiting admittance to 1.5 percent for non-aryans seeking higher education.

26 *Va'ad Leumi* establishes a committee to facilitate absorption of German Jewish immigrants, granting exclusive power to coordinate all activities to the Jewish Agency German Department.

26 *Gestapo* begins functioning as a state sanctioned terror organization.

27 Anglo-German trade agreement signed.

28 Cordell Hull assures representatives of American Jewish organizations that the State Department will continue monitoring German Jewry's situation.

29 David Ben-Gurion is attacked by members of BETAR in Riga, Latvia.

MAY

2 *Gleichschaltungsaktion* (Coordinating Action): Nazis close down all independent trade unions, uniting the remains into the *Deutsche Arbeitersfront* [DAF] (German Labor Front).

2 Nazis outlaw the KPD.

3 Opening of the Sachsenburg (Sachsen) concentration camp.

4 Nazis publish second ordinance on the Law for the Restoration of the Civil Service.

5 The Jewish Agency requests 200 emergency certificates from the high commissioner for Palestine to help rescue German Jews.

5 Cologne University students incinerate books concerning Judaism or written by Jewish authors.

6 Teachers dismissed on the basis of the Law for the Restoration, now lose their licenses to teach or lecture.

8 The Tel Aviv City Council unanimously resolves to dedicate LP1,000 per month to benefit German Jews.

8 English Revisionists repudiate Jabotinsky.

10 Dr. Josef Goebbels and his Propaganda Ministry sponsors a book burning session in Berlin; thousands of books by Jewish authors and those that the Nazis consider un-German are fed to the flames. Similar burnings occur throughout Germany.

10 A mass anti-Nazi rally is held at the Trocadero in Paris.

10 The American Jewish Congress stages an anti-Nazi parade through Lower Manhattan.

11 Paraguay declares war on Bolivia.

11 The French Senate discusses the German situation.

12 The U.S. dollar is devaluated fifty percent. Congress passes the Agricultural Adjustment Act.

12 *Jungreformatorische Bewegung* (Young Reform Movement) is founded by the Reverend Martin Niemoeller.

12 Nazis seize the local trade union headquarters in the Free City of Danzig.

14 An Austrian *Heimwehr* (Home Defense) rally is held at Schoenbrunn Palace, Vienna.

15 *Erbhoefe*, a Nazi law regarding hereditary domains is published; no Jew or Negro can be part of these family holdings.

17 Hitler denies intent to subject other nations to German domination in his first major "peace" speech.

17 The Bernheim Petition is submitted to the League of Nations.

17 Strikes and lockouts are banned in Nazi Germany.

17 The Spanish government nationalizes church property and bans church-run schools.

18 The Central British Fund for German Jewry is established in London.

18 The Tennessee Valley Authority [TVA] is established by Congressional act as part of a program for rural development.

23 Dutch church leaders protest Nazi treatment of German Jews.

26 A manifesto protesting Nazi treatment of Jews and others is signed by 1,200 U.S. Protestant clergymen.

26 Australia claims one-third of Antarctican continent.

26 Tensions rise among small nations over the Four-Power Pact.

27 The World's Fair opens in Chicago.

28 Nazis win a majority (50.03 percent with thirty-eight seats out of seventy-two) in the elections to the Danzig *Volkstag* (Senate).

29 A manifesto calling for world-wide action to save German Jewry is published by Lord Cecil, David Lloyd George, General Jan Smuts, Sir Herbert Samuel, Chaim Weizmann, Peter Warburg, M. Rotenburg, and Nahum Sokolow.

29 A temporary concentration camp at Heuberg (Baden) opens; camp closes November 1933 and its inmates are transferred to KL Dachau.

30 The Council of the League of Nations censures Nazi Germany for its anti-Jewish measures in Upper Silesia.

31 A confrontation occurs between members of BETAR and *Hapoel* in Haifa.

JUNE

1 A Sino-Japanese armistice is signed.

2 Chaim Arlosoroff and Selig Brodetsky meet the British colonial minister Philip Cunliffe-Lister regarding aid to German Jewry.

7 *Va'ad Leumi* establishes the Central Fund for German Jewry, with Henrietta Szold as chairwoman.

8 The first plenary session of the Central Fund for German Jewry opens in Jerusalem.

8 The Anglo-Palestine Exhibition opens in London.

12 The World Monetary and Economic Conference opens in London with sixty-four nations attending; Conference ends in failure on July 27.

16 The National Industrial Recovery Act [NRA] takes effect in the United States.

16 Zionist Labor leader, Chaim Arlosoroff, is assassinated in Tel Aviv.

16 Statistics for "believing" Jews in the German *Reich*—the Saar not included—are officially put at 499,682.

19 Leon Trotsky is granted political asylum in France.

21 *Stahlhelm* is absorbed by the Nazis.

21 Austria passes anti-Nazi measures.

22 Nazis order dissolution of the SPD.

22 Goering issues a decree that enjoins all government employees to spy on each other.

24 The *Internationale Bibelforscher Vereinigung* (Jehovah's Witnesses) in Germany state that they have no quarrel with the Nazi regime and its principles, except for swearing an oath of loyalty to Hitler.

26 *Akademie fuer Deutsches Recht* (Academy for German Law) established.

27 An anti-Nazi demonstration at Queen's Hall, London is addressed by the archbishop of Canterbury, Cosmo Gordon Lang.

JULY

1 Jewish student organizations are abolished in Nazi Germany.

1 A conference of German housewives in Berlin expunges all Jewish women from its ranks, in conformity with the aryan principle.

1 Dollfuss threatens that he will implement strong measures against Austrian Nazis if they don't stop their anti-Jewish campaign.

1 Francois Coty, publisher of a newspaper chain in France, is found guilty by a French court for having committed libel against a number of Jewish war veteran organizations.

3 Statutory religious institutions throughout Germany forbidden to employ Jews.

3 Roosevelt rejects the Economic Conference's stabilization plan.

4 Proceedings of the Eighteenth Zionist Congress in Prague will be conducted in Hebrew instead of German.

5 With dissolution of the Catholic Center Party, Nazis remain the only active political group in the *Reichstag*.

5 Neville Laski, president of the Board of Deputies of British Jews, opposes anti-Nazi street demonstrations and boycotts.

5 Kemma (Rheinland) concentration camp opens.

6 A Nazi order dissolves the forty-two year old German non-Jewish Association for Combating Antisemitism.

6 The House of Commons debates treatment of Jews in Nazi Germany; a government statement of sympathy for refugees closes session.

6 German Jewish lawyers are warned to keep away from courts, presumably for their own safety.

6 Jewish students attending German universities limited to 1.5 percent of the total student body.

7 Berlin offices of the *Hilfsverein der deutschen Juden* (Relief Organization of German Jews) are raided by the *Gestapo*.

7 Jewish owned stores are forced to close in Dortmund, as brown-shirted SA prevent aryan customers from entering.

7 A number of universities throughout Germany announce that Jewish students who have matriculated will not receive their degrees.

7 The notoriously antisemitic *Protocols of the Elders of Zion* become official textbooks of Berlin schools.

7 Social Democrat Party members of the *Reichstag* eliminated by decree.

7 Mexican Jewish organizations together establish a fund-raising campaign to help German Jews settle in Palestine.

8 Nazi Germany-Vatican Concordat is signed.

10 A conference on Sabbath observance is held in Tel Aviv under the auspices of the Chief Rabbinate.

10 The *Keren Kayemeth l'Israel* [KKL] (Jewish National Fund) sets aside 1,000 dunams (approx. 220 acres) of land in the Wadi Hawareth to resettle fifty German Jewish families.

10 *Die Bruecke* (The Bridge), a New York based Nazi newspaper, is first published.

10 Intercession service on behalf of German Jewry is held in London's Albert Hall.

10 The London *Daily Mail*, England's largest daily, prints an editorial justifying Hitler's anti-Jewish policy.

11 The German Minister of the Interior, Wilhelm Frick, declares "the German revolution is terminated."

11 The cornerstone for a new *Yeshiva* (Talmudic academy) is laid in Hebron.

11 Itzhak Ben-Zvi, Zionist pioneer and labor leader, is named to the Jewish Agency Executive, replacing the slain labor leader, Chaim Arlosoroff.

12 Germany blocks all German-Jewish relief agencies' bank accounts.

12 The Palestine police detain twelve Revisionists, charging them as members of an illegal revolutionary party.

13 The reorganized German Evangelical Church announces that it will not apply the aryan clause to its membership criteria.

14 All political opposition to Nazism in Germany is outlawed.

14 Nazis pass the Law on the Revocation of Naturalization and Deprivation of German Citizenship of Jews.

14 The *Reich* cabinet issues the Law on the Constitution of the German Evangelical Churches.

14 Nazi Germany institutes a sterilization law for individuals afflicted with hereditary diseases.

14 The *Bund Schweitzer Juden* (Union of Swiss Jews) is established in Saint Gallen in a conference of the Jewish Youth of Switzerland.

14 British Federation of Synagogues contributes L6,000 to the KKL to buy Palestinian land in its name.

14 The British government publishes a French report painting an unfavorable picture of Zionist development in Palestine.

14 Dr. Herman Rauschning, visiting Nazi President of the Danzig Senate, is snubbed by Jewish members of the Warsaw municipality refusing to participate in an official reception for him.

15 The *Yishuv* contributes LP14,600 to help place 1,000 German-Jewish children in the Palestine school system.

15 Britain's Lord Alfred Melchett converts to Judaism.

17 The *Reichsverband* (State Association) is organized; members are non-Aryan Christians, a group of Germans related to Jews.

17 Elections for delegates to the Eighteenth World Zionist Congress are held in Palestine.

17 Arab Executive rejects the French report regarding the development of Palestine, on grounds that it does not completely stop Jewish immigration.

17 The United People's Conference against Fascism holds a protest meeting in Los Angeles.

20 The Jewish Economic Conference opens its preliminary session in Amsterdam; Conference seeks an intensified anti-Nazi boycott.

20 First interrogation of Arlosoroff murder suspects.

20 London streets are jammed with some 30,000 men, women, and children protesting Nazi persecution of German Jewry.

20 The Academic Assistance Council is organized in London to aid expelled German Jewish scholars.

21 The SA arrests 300 Jewish store owners in Nuremberg, parading them for hours through the city's streets.

21 *La Comite National de Secours aux Refugies* (The Central Committee for Aid to the Refugees in France) is established in Paris.

21 The Conference on Land Settlements in Jerusalem proposes settling 2,000 German-Jewish youngsters between 17 and 20 years of age in Palestine.

21 A Conference of the Federation of Polish Jews in Great Britain opens in London.

21 The Pacific Coast Theological Conference in Seattle, Washington deplores Nazi Germany's anti-Jewish policy.

21 A protest meeting in the Portsmouth Guildhall denounces persecution of German Jewry; prominent religious and civic leaders take part.

21 The Board of the Federation of Synagogues in London endorses the anti-Nazi boycott.

22 Opening of the Colditz (Sachsen) concentration camp.

23 German Christians gain a majority in Church elections.

23 The Board of Deputies of British Jews rejects a proposal to join the anti-Nazi boycott.

23 Police raid BETAR headquarters throughout Palestine, in connection with the Arlosoroff murder investigation.

24 The Federation of Polish Jews in America pledges full support in the anti-Nazi boycott.

26 Oliver Locker-Lampson proposes a bill in the House of Commons granting Palestinian citizenship to all stateless Jews.

27 The Dutch Ministry of Justice permits the Committee for Jewish Interests to hold a lottery to benefit German Jewish refugees.

28 Thuringia, one of the German states, expels all Jewish teachers from its schools and orders disbandment of the Jewish Student's Association.

29 Naturalized eastern European Jews have their citizenship revoked in Nazi Germany.

30 The Greek Venizelist press begins a virulent anti-Jewish campaign.

30 The Hungarian government suppresses further publication of the *Nemzet Szava* (Nation's Voice), the official mouthpiece of Hungarian Nazis.

AUGUST

1 Nazi decree prohibits non-Jewish physicians from professional contact with Jewish physicians.

2 Debut of *The National Worker*, a pro-Nazi periodical, published in London by Colonel Graham Seton Hutchinson.

2 A Nazi order closes the *Breslauer Judengemeindeblatt* (Jewish Community News).

2 The Independent Citizens League, a German-American organization, declares its opposition to Nazism.

3 *Gestapo* closes the Osthofen concentration camp.

3 Toronto police investigate the antisemitic Swastika Club.

3 Brazil Socialist Action, an antisemitic organization, alerts the public to the Jews "who are coming to Brazil to rob the poor Brazilians."

4 The International Committee for the Protection of Academic Freedom is established in Paris.

5 Hamburg authorities order the Heinrich Heine monument removed from the city park.

5 Polish agreement with Danzig signed.

5 The Nazi Lawyers' Association threatens to boycott German firms still employing Jewish lawyers.

5 Palestine Exploration Fund archaeologists unearth a sixth century C.E. synagogue near Nahalal.

7 Nuremberg's Jews are forbidden to use municipal baths and swimming pools.

8 A Nazi decree grants *Staatenlose* (stateless) status to approximately 10,000 Jews of eastern European origin who were deprived of their German citizenship.

11 The Palestine government announces it will make 1,000 emergency certificates available to the Jewish Agency to assist German Jewish resettlement.

11 The Supreme Representative Committee of German Jewry establishes a farm, training unemployed Jews for agricultural work.

11 The New York State Senate in Albany unanimously urges President Roosevelt to officially protest German Jewry's persecution.

11 The Sixth International Trade Union Congress in Belgium endorses the continued German boycott.

11 The Hamburg Federation of Grain Merchants, an organization with a large Jewish membership, is aryanized.

11 Jewish shops in Havana are looted.

13 President Machado of Cuba is ousted in violent revolt.

14 Women Against the Persecution of Jews in Germany, a protest committee of non-Jews, announces its establishment in New York.

14 A mob runs wild in Havana during unrest in Cuba.

16 The American Jewish Congress, in an open letter to President von Hindenburg in Germany, urges him to dismiss Hitler from chancellorship.

17 De Valera declares war on Irish Fascists.

18 A border conflict between Syria and Iraq claims 600 lives.

19 Meeting between Dollfuss and Mussolini at the Italian-Austrian border.

19 Hitler's *Mein Kampf* appears in English translation, first published by the Houghton Mifflin Company of Boston.

20 A special presidential decree permits 500 Jewish refugee families from Nazi Germany to enter Uruguay.

20 The American Jewish Congress joins the anti-Nazi boycott.

21 The Eighteenth Zionist Congress opens in Prague where attendants discuss the Nazi takeover in Germany; the growing persecution of German Jews; the assassination of Arlosoroff; the economic situation of the *Yishuv*; the conflict between *Mifleget Poale Eretz Israel* [MAPAI] (the Labour Party) and the Revisionists. The Congress closes September 4.

22 The *Gestapo* suspends *Centralverein Zeitung* publication.

23/29 The World *Maccabee* games are held in Prague: Jewish athletes from fourteen countries participate.

24 Nazis prohibit the German-Jewish *Maccabee* team from participating in the World *Maccabee* games.

25 Nazis publish the first *Ausbuergerungliste* (denaturalization list) of denaturalized East European emigrants.

25 Military authorities in Czernowitz suspend the *Yiddish* daily, *Der Tog*, for criticizing the Rumanian government.

27 Czechoslovak Revisionists establish the Jewish State Party at their first conference in Prague.

29 The Canadian Immigration Department announces that it will not amend its restrictive immigration policy.

29 Rabbi Abba Hillel Silver and Samuel Untermeyer protest against the *Haavara* (Transfer) Agreement.

29 Dr. Chaim Weizmann declines to accept the presidency of the World Zionist Organization but agrees to chair the campaign fund for the settlement of German Jews in Palestine.

30 The Union of German National Jews in a published statement blames the World Zionist Organization for German Jewry's present predicament.

31 The Jewish War Veterans of America disapprove the *Haavara* Agreement.

31 The Council of the Warsaw Jewish Community sends a protest note to the Eighteenth Zionist Congress expressing its opposition to the *Haavara* agreement.

SEPTEMBER

1 The German government approves the Transfer Agreement.

2 The Soviet Union and Italy sign a pact outlining non-aggression, friendship, and neutrality.

2 *Centralverein Zeitung* resumes publication.

4 Fuhlsbuettel (Hamburg) concentration camp opens.

5 The aryan clause is adopted by the old Prussian church Synod.

5 The World Jewish Congress preliminary conference convenes in Geneva, Switzerland.

6 Austria deploys its army along the German border.

8 The Second World Jewish Conference joins the anti-Nazi boycott.

8 Death of Iraq's King Feisal.

11 The Hungarian government prohibits use or display of the Swastika by private citizens or organizations.

14 Greece and Turkey sign a ten-year non-aggression pact.

14 The Dutch education ministry establishes a *numerus clausus* based on race for foreign students attending the country's universities.

15 Rabbi Yisroel Meir Cohen (ha-Chofetz Chaim), Jewish scholar, author, and philosopher, dies at the age of 105 in Radin, Poland.

15 Chancellor Dollfuss, addressing the Austrian Fatherland Front, proposes a "Christian German state on Fascist lines," but one without discrimination against Jews.

17 *Reichsvertretung der deutschen Juden* (State Representation of German Jewry) established by order of the *Gestapo*.

17 The Tel Aviv municipality accepts a LP350,000 development loan from the Palestine government.

18 The Nazi-dominated Danzig Senate agrees to guarantee basic rights to Poles living in the Free City.

20 The Palestine symphony orchestra, The Palestine Philharmonic Society, Ltd., is established in Tel Aviv.

21 *Pfarrernotbund* (Pastor's Emergency League) is founded by Martin Niemoeller.

22 Professor Albert Mendelssohn-Bartholdy, great-grandson of Moses Mendelssohn, is dismissed from his Hamburg University post.

22 *Reichskulturkammergesetz* (State Chamber of Culture Law), reestablishing a *Reich* chamber of culture, is passed in Nazi Germany; Non-aryans are restrained from participation in German culture, the arts, literature, music, and related subjects.

24 Jewish lawyers are banned from German Bar Congress.

24 The Italian government permits a medical and scientific center in Rome to open so that German Jewish refugee scholars can continue their research.

24 Five thousand die in a Mexican earthquake.

25 A League of Nations assembly opens in Geneva amid an atmosphere of unrest.

25 The Relief Conference for German Jews, meeting in Rome under the chairmanship of Chaim Weizmann, adopts a resolution to open special offices in Jerusalem and London dealing with settlement of German Jewish refugees in Palestine.

27 Ludwig Mueller, bishop of Prussia and a confidant of Hitler, is appointed *Reichsbishop.*

27 The Canadian garment industry joins the anti-Nazi boycott.

28 Some 50,000 people are drowned during floods in China.

29 The Dutch government sponsors a resolution urging the League of Nations to formulate plans for an international solution to the German refugee problem.

29 A Communist parade in Havana is routed by Cuban police.

30 One hundred fifty-five Jewish traders are ousted from the Berlin stock exchange.

OCTOBER

1 Theodor Eicke, Dachau concentration camp commandant, publishes "disciplinary camp regulations," later used as a guide for the expanding Nazi concentration camp system.

1 The Arab Higher Committee meeting in Jerusalem deals with responses to German Jewish immigration.

1 A Nazi approved *Juedische Kulturbund* (Jewish Cultural Society) is established.

1 Nine senior *Wehrmacht* generals critical of Hitler are forced to retire.

2 The "University in Exile" is inaugurated by the New School of Social Research.

2 All Jewish military personnel are purged; German army and navy become *Judenrein* (free of Jews).

2 The School of the Jewish Woman, designed to teach Jewish women the background of Jewish culture and history, opens in New York under Dr. Trude Weiss Rosmarin's guidance.

2 The first group of Jewish refugees escaping Germany arrives in Brazil.

3 An assassination attempt is made on Austrian Chancellor Dollfuss.

3 The Quebec municipality adopts a resolution opposing German Jewish refugees seeking asylum in Canada.

3 A British court indicts ten *Brit ha-Biryonim* (Covenant of Terrorists) members in the Arlosoroff murder.

3 A Cuban *coup* attempt fails; over 100 rebels are killed.

3 The Greek government orders closed the EEE, a Greek antisemitic nationalist organization.

3 The Associated Women's Wear Credit Bureau of Montreal and its affiliates join the anti-Nazi boycott.

4 Professor Albert Einstein addresses a crowd of 10,000 at the opening campaign in London's Albert Hall to collect $5,000,000 for exiled German scientists.

5 The British Labour Party endorses the anti-Nazi boycott.

5 Hooligans paint swastikas and antisemitic slogans on New York's Temple Emanuel.

8 The Saint Louis chapter of the Friends of New Germany, an American pro-Nazi organization, begins operating.

8 All Jewish jockeys are barred from German race tracks.

8 Anti-Jewish incidents erupt in the Rumanian countryside.

9 The third all-Polish BETAR conference opens in Warsaw; all delegates wear "brown shirts."

10 A new republican government is installed in Spain.

11 United States Ambassador Christopher Dodd criticizes the Nazi regime in an address to the American Chamber of Commerce in Berlin.

11 The American Federation of Labor [AFL] joins the anti-Nazi boycott.

13 The Arab Executive declares a general strike against the mandatory government's Jewish immigration policy; an Arab anti-immigration rally turns violent.

13 The mandatory government proclaims that it will not allow any procession likely to endanger the peace.

13 Disturbances between Arab rioters and police break out in Jerusalem; subsequent riots occur in Jaffa, Haifa, and Nablus; twenty-four rioters are killed and over 100 wounded.

13 The AFL votes on and approves of the U.S. boycott on German products and services.

14 Ludwig Mueller, bishop of the Nazi Christian Church, states that Christianity started as a war on Jews.

14 The German-Jewish sports organization, *Hagibor,* is liquidated and its property confiscated by the *Gestapo*.

14 Germany withdraws from the Disarmament Commission.

14 Polish government closes down the offices of *Rozwoj*, an antisemitic organization whose main endeavor is waging a boycott campaign against Jewish businesses throughout Poland.

16 The Rumanian pro-Nazi Christian-Fascist Party is established in Bucharest under the leadership of Stepan Tatarescu.

17 *Gestapo* closes the Wittmoor concentration camp.

17 Chaim Weizmann meets King Albert of Belgium: The two leaders address the problems of German-Jewish refugees and the need for a Jewish homeland in Palestine.

19 German assimilationists and Zionists clash over the control of the Berlin *Kehilla* (Jewish community council).

19 Germany pledges to protect all foreigners.

19 The Jewish Refugee Committee in London establishes its first *hachshara* center to train young German-Jewish refugees for agricultural work in Palestine.

20 British Palestine police conduct their first "anti-tourist" sweep. Operation is aimed to weed out illegal immigrants.

21 Germany drops out of the League of Nations.

21 The mandatory government grants only 5,500 immigration certificates to the Jewish Agency.

23 Professor Martin Buber is among fifty-two Jewish educators fired from their university positions in Germany.

23 Jewish *sejm* deputy, Apolinari Maximilian Hartglass, asks Polish Zionists to end their opposition to the Pilsudski government; Hartglass points out that the regime benefits the Polish Jewish community, fighting antisemitism within Poland and supporting Jewish rights before international forums.

25 The French cabinet under Edouard Daladier falls.

27 Arab shopkeepers throughout Palestine begin a strike; Arab riots supporting the strikers are suppressed by British police; Arabic newspapers strike in response to the government's censorship policy.

27 The French government cancels orders issued by local municipal authorities to expel Jewish refugees from Germany.

28 The Nazis boast that their antisemitic propaganda inspired Arab riots in Palestine.

28 Austrian High Court Justice, Gustav Ranzenhoffer, demands a *numerus clausus* for Jews in all professions.

29 Conference for Relief of German Jewry, sponsored by the Joint Foreign Committee of the Board of Jewish Deputies and the Anglo-Jewish Association, the *Alliance Israelite Universelle*, the American Jewish Congress, and the American Jewish Committee, opens in London.

29 The antisemitic Gray-Shirt movement is established in South Africa.

30 James G. McDonald accepts League of Nations appointment as high commissioner for the relief of refugees.

30 The antisemitic White Shirts organization is founded in Ottawa, Canada.

31 The new Haifa Harbor is officially dedicated.

NOVEMBER

1 The Conference for Relief of German Jewry closes after adopting a number of resolutions: Palestine to be the primary locale for resettling refugees; a central allocation committee and a central bureau to be established in order to coordinate the work of the various organizations dealing with German-Jewish problems.

2 Germany aryanizes the well-known *Ullstein Verlag* (House of Ullstein), one of the world's largest publishing houses.

2 Martin Niemoeller speaks out against application of German-enacted anti-Jewish laws within the Church.

5 Leon Motzkin, Zionist leader and president of the Zionist Actions Committee, dies at age sixty-six.

6 The *Va'ad Leumi* and the Jewish Agency Executive hold an emergency meeting to deal with Britain's new immigration policy for Palestine.

6 The Conference of Anglo-Jewish Organizations in London approves the official anti-Nazi boycott.

6 Budapest police raid Hungarian Nazis' annual conference and arrest its leaders.

7 During a large rally in the Berlin *Sportspalast,* the German-Christian movement sets out its basic ideology: Total acceptance of National Socialist totalitarian dogma.

7 Fiorello H. LaGuardia, former member of the United States Congress, elected New York City mayor.

8 King Sardar Mohammed Nadir Khan of Afghanistan is assassinated.

9 Mexican Jews call on their government to stop Nazi antisemitic propaganda.

10 Martial law is declared in Austria.

10 A conference of the World Organization of the *Agudas Yisroel* (Union of Israel) opens in London; urges national Jewish interest groups to help German-Jewish-orthodox institutions, to remember Russian Jewry, and to demand that Britain open Palestine to Jewish refugees.

10 The All-Polish Trade Unions adopt a resolution favoring a boycott of Nazi Germany.

11 The Italian government establishes a chair in Italian language and literature at the Hebrew University in Jerusalem.

11 A local Nazi-sponsored referendum urging the Latvian electorate to deprive Jews of citizenship rights, fails.

12 Ninety-two percent of the German electorate votes for the Nazi party.

12 *Yom Kippur* (Day of Atonement) is proclaimed a legal holiday by the Greek government.

13 Nazi-style mass demonstrations in Berlin's *Sportspalast* are led by the Storm Troopers of Jesus Christ.

15 Revisionist-Zionist leader Vladimir Jabotinsky decries the measures used by the mandatory police in apprehending "illegal" Jewish settlers in Palestine.

16 The United States and the Soviet Union establish diplomatic relations.

16 The United States House of Representatives' Immigration Subcommittee opens an unofficial investigation on the propaganda activities of Nazis in the United States.

16 Brazilian president Getulio Vargas is given dictatorial powers.

17 Italian universities declare readiness to accept students from European countries deprived of attending and/or matriculating at their own universities due to race or religious discrimination.

17 Eastern European Jews living in Amsterdam organize the Congregation *Machzike Hadas* (Strengtheners of Faith).

17 The Zionist Federation of Belgium adopts a resolution to create a Belgo-Palestine chamber of commerce; demands that the Jewish Agency Executive ensure strict Sabbath and *kashrut* observance on KKL land.

19 The *Gestapo* confiscates Einstein's property.

19 The Tel Aviv municipality unanimously approves a resolution protesting British limitations on *aliya* (immigration).

21 *Yishuv* leaders meet with the high commissioner to discuss immigration policy.

21 The Austrian Fatherland Front demands a *numerus clausus* for Jews of every status in the nation.

21 Hungarian student organizations demand *numerus clausus* for all Jewish students in Hungary, threatening strikes and disruption of university classes, unless their demands are met.

22 *Numerus clausus* enacted in Lithuania against Jewish professionals in academic institutions; the use of the Lithuanian language becomes compulsory for lessons taught in all Jewish schools.

22 British tentatively approve the Youth *Aliya* scheme.

23   Rumanian Premier Ion Duca outlaws the antisemitic Cuzist party and the *Garda de Fier* (Iron Guard).

23   Monarchist victory in Spain.

23   Protest meetings are held in all the major Jewish communities in Poland in objection to British restrictions limiting Jewish immigration into Palestine.

24   The Belgian government commissions an inquiry on German-Jewish refugees.

24   A rash of outbreaks against Jewish students occur in a number of Hungarian universities.

25   The fourth annual congress of the League to Combat Antisemitism opens in Paris.

26   Arab Higher Committee calls for general strike to start November 29, 1933.

27   The *Haavara* company, *Paltreu,* begins operations.

27   The German Labor Front establishes *Kraft durch Freude* (Strength through Joy), an agency to provide Nazi controlled recreation.

27   The Polish government forbids street demonstrations against British Palestine immigration policy.

28   A pogrom in Jassy is carried out by the Iron Guard.

28   Hungarian authorities close the University of Budapest until disturbances cease.

29   Jewish stores throughout Germany are warned not to display Christmas symbols.

29   *Mizrachi* (an Orthodox Zionist organization) threatens to quit the World Zionist Organization unless its religious demands are met.

30   Goering's latest decree withdraws the *Gestapo* from the Ministry of Interior control.

DECEMBER

1   The *Gestapo* confiscates Emil Ludwig's property and the writer is classified as "enemy of the state."

1   The German cabinet passes a law "to ensure the unity of Party and State."

1   A bill prohibiting *shechita* in Finland is defeated in the Finnish parliament.

2 The Rumanian Jewish Self-defense Organization repulses Iron Guard attacks in the Jewish quarter of Jassy.

2 British Fascists in Liverpool paint swastikas on the Prince Synagogue.

4 Munich's Michael Cardinal Faulhaber denounces Nazi racial teachings.

5 Prohibition is repealed in the United States.

5 League of Nations High Commissioner for German Refugees, James G. McDonald, estimates the number of refugees from Nazism at 60,000.

6 The Morrison Committee arrives in Palestine to investigate Arab riots during the preceding autumn.

6 More than 20,000 Nazi sympathizers celebrate German Day in Madison Square Garden.

7 Vice-chancellor Franz von Papen exhorts German-Americans to act as Nazi propagandists.

7 Representatives of Britain, France, Holland, Switzerland, and Uruguay are named permanent executive members of the Governing Body for German Refugees; Lord Robert Cecil is elected chairman.

9 The Spanish government crushes an anarchist rebel uprising; hundreds are killed and wounded.

10 The Church in Saxony votes to accept Nazi concept of blood and race in its doctrine.

11 A protest rally by Revisionist Zionists in Tel Aviv results in a clash with the police; a number of Revisionists and police are injured.

12 The archbishops of Canterbury, Wales, and York issue a joint appeal for aid to German refugees.

13 A new German Protestant Church law omits aryan clause.

14 The Synagogue Council of America exhorts American Jewry to observe the Sabbath and Jewish holidays.

15 After a conference of Catholic leaders, Austrians are asked to do their Christmas shopping in non-Jewish stores.

17 Ireland repeals an import tax on *matzoth* to avoid hardship for poor Jews.

18 A Nazi decree bars German Jews from journalism and allied professions.

20 The Aryan Lawyers' Association in Vienna demands that the Austrian Ministry of Justice expel all Jewish lawyers.

21 The Italian Jewish community, with the permission of the Fascist government, launches a fund drive to aid German Jewish refugees.

23 Marinus van der Lubbe, a Dutch Communist, is found guilty of arson at the *Reichstag* and condemned to death.

23 Pope Pius XI condemns the Nazi sterilization program.

24 Henry Ford denies that he ever gave financial aid to the Nazis or that he is an antisemite.

25 *Masada*, a new national Zionist youth movement, is founded in Niagara Falls, NY.

25 At least 200 people are killed in a major train collision in Lagny, France.

26 Members of the Iron Guard burn down the *Kantarschi* synagogue in Jassy.

27 The American-Polish Industrial Bureau is established in New York by the Federation of Polish Jews in America. The bureau's aim is to stimulate trade with Poland, and thereby divert Polish trade with Nazi Germany.

28 Local Fascists destroy the printing machinery of *Die Deutsche Tribuene*, an anti-Nazi German language newspaper, published in Sao Paulo, Brazil.

29 Rumanian Premier Ion Duca is assassinated by members of the Iron Guard.

29 Hohnstein (Sachsen) concentration camp opens.

31 President Roosevelt appoints Henry Morgenthau, Jr. as U.S. Secretary of the Treasury.

31 George Alexander Kohut, Jewish educator and author, dies in New York City at fifty-nine.

1934

JANUARY

1 Jakob Wassermann, well-known author-novelist, dies in Vienna, at sixty.

1 All Jewish holidays are obliterated from official German calendars.

1 The International Telecommunications Union [ITU] is established in Madrid.

4 The Board of Deputies of British Jews reports that some 2,000 native Afghanistani Jews had been uprooted from their homes in recent times.

5 Synagogues throughout Rumania hold memorial services for slain Prime Minister Ion Duca.

6 The National Labor Court in Germany decrees that Jewish employees may be dismissed solely on racial grounds.

6 Fighting between members of BETAR and the *Histadrut* erupts in Rishon le-Zion.

6 The new prime minister of Rumania, George Tatarescu, promises to eliminate antisemitism from the country.

7 Germany bars non-aryan families from adopting aryan children.

9 A student union in Budapest calls for a boycott of university classes until anti-Jewish legislation is passed.

10 Nazis execute van der Lubbe, the Dutchman accused of setting fire to the *Reichstag*, in the Leipzig prison courtyard.

10 James G. McDonald, League of Nations High Commissioner for German Refugees, states that it would cost $50,000,000 to rehabilitate all German refugees.

10 The Dutch government announces that all government employees belonging to the Nazi party will be fired immediately.

10 *Agudas Yisroel's* fourth national conference meets in Warsaw. Its members decide not to participate in the world conference of orthodox Jews that *Mizrachi* proposed.

11 Dissident German clergymen's homes are raided by the *Gestapo*.

11 Berlin Jewish community leaders refuse to permit Zionist representatives speeches at a meeting regarding the condition of German Jewish youth.

12 The Polish *Mizrachi* movement calls for creation of a united orthodox front.

12 The Greek government enacts a strict Sunday rest law.

12 The *Gestapo* permits the *Zionistische Vereinigung fuer Deutschland* [ZVfD] (Zionist Federation of Germany) to hold a Palestine exhibition in Berlin.

12 Police in Kielce {P} close down the KKL bazaar because of fighting between the Palestine Labor League and Revisionists.

14 Due to antisemitic pressure, the Greek government annuls a law making *Yom Kippur* a legal holiday.

14 A vaccine against infantile paralysis is developed by Dr. Maurice Brodie, a 30-year-old doctor from Montreal, Canada.

15 Goering orders the *Gestapo* to arrest all political *emigres* and Jews returning to Germany.

15 Goebbels demands that Jews representing German companies abroad be dismissed from their posts.

15 An antisemitic racial exhibition opens in Munich.

15 Labor strife between *Histadrut* and Revisionist workers in Haifa leads to forty-eight arrests.

16 The League of Nations Governing Commission in the Saar protests German persecution of Jews in the Saar and Upper Silesia.

18 An Indian earthquake kills some 2,000 people.

19 Kemma concentration camp is closed.

19 Portuguese authorities deny reports that they are negotiating with the Nazis about settling German Jewish refugees in Angola.

21 Discussions concerning formation of a united orthodox front begin in Kovno.

21 The Austrian government approves the establishment of a Jewish self-defense corps in Vienna.

22 The American Jewish Congress establishes the Merchandising Council to Strengthen Boycott against German Goods and Services.

22 Street fights between Communists and Royalists erupt in Paris; hundreds are arrested by French police.

24 Alfred Rosenberg is named *Beauftragter des Fuehrers* (Commissioner of the Fuehrer) in order to supervise the total intellectual and philosophical schooling of the NSDAP.

24 The Rumanian government bans government officials from participating in extremist movements.

25 Albert Einstein visits President Roosevelt in the White House.

26 Poland and Germany sign a ten-year non-aggression pact.

26 Zurich Church Council condemns the *Protocols of the Elders of Zion*.

26 Twelfth annual *Juedischer Frauenbund* (Jewish Women's Association) conference in Germany approves a resolution which discourages separating school-aged children from their parents.

27 The American Committee on Religious Rights and Minorities calls on Germany to stop persecuting the Jews.

28 Lithuanian police raid *kehilla* headquarters of Ponivez to squelch anti-Nazi boycott.

28 French government resigns following Stavisky revelations of fraudulent transactions in high places.

28 Norman Thomas urges Socialists to join the anti-Nazi boycott.

29 In an editorial, the Italian newspaper, *Il Popolo Italiano*, ridicules the Nazi racial dogma.

29 Ten thousand people drown in a major Chinese flood.

30 Reorganization strips German states of their sovereignty.

30 The Canadian Jewish Congress is organized.

31 Fritz Haber, exiled German Jewish chemist and Nobel Prize winner, dies in Switzerland.

31 The U.S. dollar is devaluated to sixty cents.

31   A Commission for Settlement of German Jews in Palestine report states that in 1933, 9,000 refugees received assistance when settling in the *Yishuv*.

FEBRUARY

1   Engelbert Dollfuss establishes one-party rule in Austria.

1   Viennese police forbid the sale of anti-Jewish or Nazi periodicals on the streets.

2   Nazis publish an aryanized version of the Psalms of David, eliminating all references to Jews.

3   *Liberation*, an antisemitic publication, publishes the text of a speech that Benjamin Franklin gave during the Constitutional Convention in 1787-88 in which he supposedly remarked that if the immigration of Jews to the United States were not restricted, the Jews would ruin the country; American historians conclude that this document, if it did exist, was a forgery.

4   Quick action by Greek police prevents pogrom against Salonika's Jews; the EEE is credited with organizing the failed massacre.

4   The British government requires a LP60 bond from tourists who visit Palestine.

4   Palestine exhibition opens in Berlin.

6   Fascist agitation leads to street riots in Paris, nearly resulting in a *coup*.

6/14   A debate is taken up by leaders of major Jewish organizations both for and against postponing the proposed World Jewish Congress.

7   Germany begins economic preparations for war.

7   *Avodath Hakodesh* (Sacred Service), a musical score for Reform Temples by composer Ernest Bloch, premiers in Rome.

7   Daladier government resigns; the new French Government of National Concentration is installed.

7   The Soviet *Yiddish* press condemns *Agudas Yisroel* for statements regarding persecution of religious Jews by the Soviet government.

7   An antisemitic Liberal Movement founded in Bucharest.

8   A *Gestapo* order disbands German Bible Circles.

8   U.S. Customs officials impound 300 pounds of Nazi propaganda material.

9 Balkan pact signed in Athens between Turkey, Greece, Rumania, and Yugoslavia.

9 French government bars Communist demonstrations.

9 The Morrison Commission publishes a report on the October 1933 Arab riots.

11 The Austrian *Antisemitenbund* (Antisemitic Association) sets forth its anti-Jewish program.

11 The National Executive of the Zionist Organization of America votes to postpone World Jewish Congress.

12 Austrian *Heimwehr* stages *coup d'etat*: Communists are attacked, and the Socialist *Schutzbund* (Defense Force) is disarmed; over 100 are killed.

12/13 General strike in France.

14 King Albert of Belgium dies in a mountain-climbing accident.

14 Direct flights become available between Egypt and Palestine, with stops in Port Said, Gaza, Jerusalem, Jericho, and Haifa.

16 An Anglo-Soviet trade agreement is signed.

17 Some 5,000 Austrian Jews lose their jobs due to the Dollfuss government's antisemitic policies.

18 Austrian government bans the *Poale Zion* (Zionist Labor) organization.

19 Youth *Aliya* program starts in Germany.

19 Polish Jewish organizations agree to levy a tax on their members to be used for German Jewish relief.

20 The Latvian parliament overwhelmingly rejects proposals to abolish Jewish autonomy.

22 The *Tel Hai* monument dedicated.

22 An Amsterdam court sentences Hans Liepmman to one month imprisonment for defamation of a friendly country, resulting from publication of his book *Murder Made in Germany*; Liepmman is deported to Belgium March 20.

25 *Verband der Juedischer Front Soldaten* (Association of Jewish War Veterans) declares German loyalty in honor of the 12,000 Jews who gave their lives for the fatherland during World War I.

25 Labor Committee for Jewish Affairs formed in New York to combat Nazism, Fascism, and antisemitism.

25 Leopold III is crowned Belgian King.

26 Moscow's *Yiddish* daily, the *Shtern*, proposes that the *Yiddish* language be purged from all Hebrew by-words.

28 The *Wehrmacht* issues orders applying racial criteria to military service.

MARCH

1 Henry Pu-yi, the last of the Manchu emperors, is crowned emperor of Manchukuo.

4 The *Oesterreichischer Beobachter*, Austria's leading Nazi daily, states that Jews should be excluded from all leading positions in Austria.

4 Goebbels renews the war against Jewish actors.

5 The Peruvian Jewish community petitions the government to prohibit antisemitic films from import.

5 *B'nai B'rith* International protests Nazi dissolution of German lodges.

7 A commercial agreement between Germany and Poland is signed.

7 The Spanish government grants automatic citizenship to *Sephardi* Jews returning to Spain.

7 The American Jewish Congress and American Federation of Labor sponsor a mock trial and protest rally against Hitlerism in Madison Square Garden.

8 Nazi incidents take place on the Columbia University campus.

9 The Einstein Institute of Physics opens at the Hebrew University in Jerusalem.

9 A meeting between Benito Mussolini and Weizmann is held in Rome.

10 The Federation of German Jewish Youth Organizations proclaims Youth Day.

10 Twelve Jews elected to new Italian parliament.

10 *Catherine the Great*, a motion picture starring the Jewish actress Elizabeth Bergner, is banned in Germany.

11 The United Jewish Appeal launches its 1934 campaign: goal is to raise $3,000,000.

12 The Nazi Trade and Artisans Union proclaims a new boycott against Jewish business in Germany.

12 The Authoritarian regime of Konstantin Paets seizes power in Estonia.

14 Disturbances at Warsaw University cause class cancellations.

16 Warsaw University is closed due to the *Endek* (Polish National Democratic Party) students' attack on Professor Herceli Handelsmann; six students are arrested two days later.

16 A general strike is held in Tel Aviv protesting high rents.

16/17 Roman protocols are signed between Italy, Austria, and Hungary: The agreement is to be a counterpart against the Little Entente.

20 Nazis lift a ban on Jewish organizations as long as they remain uninvolved in political activities.

20 The Soviet government allows plans for a *matzo* factory to be carried out.

21 The American Jewish Congress and New York Central Labor Council establish the Joint Boycott Enforcement Council against German goods and services.

21 F. W. Woolworth Company announces an end to German goods imported to its American market.

21 Hitler initiates the *arbeitsschlacht* (war on unemployment); emphasizes the necessity to employ 5,000,000 jobless citizens in the coming year.

21 A Jewish *Kolchozi* (collective farms) conference adopts resolution for Jews to continue working during Passover.

22 An Austrian census places 183,000 Jews in some 750 towns and villages.

23 Nazi Germany announces the Law Regarding Expulsion from the *Reich*.

23 NSDAP orders local Nazi leaders to stop all independent actions that might lead to anti-Jewish violence.

26 The *Tarbut* school organization in Poland announces that it will close 200 schools due to financial difficulties.

28 The Zionist Actions Committee convenes in Jerusalem.

28 Dr. Max Naumann, leader of a small group of ultra nationalist/assimilationist Jews in Germany, organizes a Nazi-like party.

29 The German American Bund launches an antisemitic counter-boycott.

29 British Jewry organizes an appeal for Polish Jewry.

30 Warsaw police prohibit meeting of the United Polish Jewish Committee for Combatting German Jewish Persecution, fearing *Endek* violence.

31 An antisemitic bombing campaign begins in Buenos Aires.

APRIL

1 Heinrich Himmler is appointed *Reichsfuehrer-SS*.

2 The Lithuanian government removes all Jewish doctors from government-run medical facilities.

3 *Va'ad ha-Poel ha-Zioni* (the Zionist Inner Actions Committee) meets in Jerusalem for the first time.

4 The German *Gau* (state) of Baden bans *shechita*.

4 The Daniel Sieff Research Institute opens in Rehovoth.

5 New building code begins in Palestine, giving municipalities greater control over sizes and types of buildings to be erected.

5 Dr. Ludwig Marum, former Jewish member of the *Reichstag*, commits suicide while in *Gestapo* "protective custody."

5 Forty-six Iron Guard leaders are freed by a military court in Rumania.

6 The U.S. Congress appoints a seven member committee to investigate Nazi propaganda.

7 After numerous complaints, *Histadrut* agrees to protect *kashrut* observance in its institutions.

9 The Austrian government bans Pan-German Association propaganda activities.

9/10 *Histadrut ha-Ovdim ha-Leumim* (Nationalist Labor Federation) is founded in Jerusalem by members of BETAR and HA-ZOHAR.

12 The German Justice Ministry introduces the *Schutzhaftbefehl* (protective-custody warrant).

12 The British government demands that Polish Jewish capitalists deposit LP1,000 in Palestinian banks before obtaining A-1 visas.

12 Julius Streicher is appointed *Gauleiter* (governor) for Franconia.

13 George Kareski founds the Revisionist oriented *Staatszionistische Organisation* (Zionist State Party) in Berlin.

15 *Oboz Narodowo-Radycalny* [NARA] (National Radical Union) splits off from *Endekcja*.

19 The Czech government prohibits antisemitic books from circulation, including *The Protocols of the Elders of Zion*.

20 Himmler is appointed inspector of the Prussian *Gestapo*.

21 The German Jewish sports club is outlawed in Bavaria.

21 The trial begins in Moscow for three men accused of antisemitic agitation.

22 Reinhard Heydrich becomes *Gestapo* chief.

22 Sir Oswald Mosley, leader of the British Union of Fascists [BUF], in his first public address in London, accuses English Jews of dual loyalty.

23 The Arlosoroff murder trial opens with three defendants: Abba Ahimeir, Abraham Stavsky, and Zvi Rosenblatt.

23 *Gestapo* closes the Brandenburg concentration camp.

26 The Levant Fair opens in Tel Aviv, running until July 5, 1934.

27 The Swiss government informs Nazis that a mutual arrangement between the two countries must take place without prejudice on racial origins of Swiss citizens.

29 Dutch Premier Hendrikus Colijn denies rumors that Holland will permit German Jewish refugees to settle in Surinam.

29 The National Conference of Christians and Jews celebrates Brotherhood Day.

30 The Austrian *Nationalrat* (parliament) approves 471 decrees issued since March 7, 1933.

MAY

1 *Der Stuermer*, ragsheet of Julius Streicher, prints a blood-libel story.

1 German Labor Code published.

2 Twenty-fifth anniversary of Tel Aviv founding.

5 The Palestine government announces a six month (April-September) labor schedule for 5,600 Jewish immigrants.

6 The National Union of Patriotic Israelites is originated in France by a group of World War I Veteran Jewish officers.

7 Birobidjan is officially proclaimed a Jewish Autonomous Region of the Russian Soviet Federated Socialist Republics by the Presidium of the Central Committee of the Soviet Union.

7 Conference of *Yiddish* writers meeting in Kharkov demands that Hebrew loan words be purged from *Yiddish*.

9 Mussolini creates an Italian "Corporate State."

11 The House of Commons passes a resolution protesting London's German embassy's use as an outlet for Nazi antisemitic propaganda.

12 Tel Aviv receives municipal corporation status and is officially recognized as a city by the Palestine government.

12   The Board of Jewish Deputies of Anglo-Jewry delivers an address on behalf of the Jewish community, honoring the British monarch's Silver Jubilee Celebration.

13   Osip Mandelstam, one of Russia's greatest poets, is arrested under Stalin's orders.

13   NARA begins publication of *Sztafieta*, an antisemitic daily newspaper.

14   Flooding in the Sea of Galilee area kills nineteen and causes considerable damage in Tiberias.

15   Latvian *coup* led by Karlis Ulimanis leaves repercussions felt by the 94,000 Jews living in Latvia as Jewish autonomy is abolished.

17   Abba Ahimeir, one of the three suspects accused in the Arlosoroff murder, is released for lack of evidence.

17   An antisemitic terrorist group assassinates the Polish minister of the interior, Colonel Bronislaw Pieracki, in Warsaw.

17   *Deutsch Amerikanische Wirtschafts-Auschuss* (German American Protective Alliance) announces counter-boycott at a rally in New York's Madison Square Garden.

18   Nazis refrain from applying the "aryan clause" to Asians.

19   A Fascist *coup d'etat* in Sofia, Bulgaria leads to military dictatorship.

20   The Polish government bans *Sztafieta*.

21   The American National Christian Committee for German Refugees is organized.

23   *Va'ad Leumi* calls for nationwide protests against immigration limits.

29   Jan Masaryk is reelected president of Czechoslovakia.

29   Lvov's (Lemberg) Zionist headquarters is bombed.

31   *Ifico*, the Palestine Fund for Industrial Development, is founded.

31   All those racially classified as Jews are dismissed from the German army.

31   Colditz concentration camp is closed.

JUNE

3   A conference is held between Hitler and Ernst Roehm, nominal leader of the SA.

3   Anti-Nazi Boycott Committee of the American Federation of Labor and the Non-Sectarian Anti-Nazi League merge.

6   A day-long series of pogroms throughout Poland is sponsored by *Endeks*.

6   Woolworth stores repudiate anti-Nazi boycott pledges as Nazi hoodlums destroy German Woolworth stores in thirteen cities.

6   The British colonial secretary, Sir Philip Cunliffe-Lister, refuses a parliamentary inquiry into Palestine immigration policy.

7   Roehm agrees to furlough the SA for one month, beginning July 1.

8   The Arlosoroff murder trial ends: Stavsky found guilty and sentenced to death, Rosenblatt acquitted.

8   Large-scale Socialist roundups begin in Latvia; many Jewish *Bund* leaders are among those arrested.

9   The *Sicherheitsdienst* [SD] is established as the political counter-espionage arm of the NSDAP.

10   The Afghan government denaturalizes all Jews.

11   The Disarmament Conference ends in failure.

11   *Neudinger* Temple in Vienna is heavily damaged in an antisemitic bombing incident.

14   Marshal Josef Pilsudski refuses to meet with Nazi Propaganda Minister, Josef Goebbels, during the latter's visit to Poland.

14/15   Hitler meets Mussolini for the first time.

15   Dr. Hljamar Schacht decrees a six month moratorium on foreign payments, extending it to a year.

17   In a speech at Marburg, Vice-chancellor Franz von Papen questions the SA's judgment and the policies of the new Germany.

19   The World *Mizrachi* Organization withdraws from the *Va'ad Leumi*.

19   Hitler refuses to accept Vice-chancellor von Papen's resignation.

21   The German state of Franconia cancels citizenship for all Jews naturalized between 1922 and 1929.

23   Italian warships occupy the Durazzo port in Albania.

24   Dr. Leo Pinsker's remains are transferred to Palestine and reinterred in Jerusalem.

27   Hitler halts a move to ban *Stahlhelm*.

30 Night of the Long Knives: Ernest Roehm is murdered, as purges are conducted throughout the SA.

30 On Hitler's orders the SS becomes an independent organization within the NSDAP.

JULY

1 Defense Minister General Werner von Blomberg acknowledges the army's part in the curbing action against the SA and thanks Hitler in the name of the *Wehrmacht*.

2 President von Hindenburg sends Hitler a telegram thanking him for saving the German people from catastrophe.

2 The ZVfD curtails its activities due to constant *Gestapo* interference.

3 The *Reichstag* justifies measures taken against the SA on June 30 and July 1.

4 Chaim Nakhman Bialik, poet of the Jewish national renaissance, dies.

4 Himmler appoints Theodor Eicke, Inspector of the Nazi Concentration Camps, head of the *SS-Totenkopfverbaende* (Death's Heads units).

8 During anti-Communist riots in Amsterdam, some sixty people are killed with the same number wounded.

10/11 Austrian Chancellor Dollfuss reorganizes his cabinet.

12 The Austrian government decrees the death penalty for terrorists.

12 The Soviets dissolve the OGPU (secret service).

12 Belgium outlaws all uniformed political parties.

13 Hitler gives the *Reichstag* a report on the plot of Ernst Roehm to overthrow the German government and puts the number killed during the Night of the Long Knives as seventy-seven.

15 Nazi thugs march the length of the *Kurfurstendam* in Berlin, wrecking Jewish owned stores and attacking all whom they believe to be Jewish.

15 Anti-Jewish riots in Turkish Thrace.

17 James G. McDonald, League of Nations High Commissioner for Refugees from Germany, reports on the difficulties brought on through the flight of over 80,000 refugees from Germany.

19 *Der Stuermer* is to be used as a school textbook in the *Gau* (state) of Franconia.

20 Although the court found him guilty in Arlosoroff's murder, Stavsky is freed for lack of evidence linking him directly to the crime.

24 Max J. Kohler, U.S. author, communal leader, and champion of Jewish rights, dies.

25 A Nazi *coup* is attempted in Vienna: Chancellor Dollfuss is assassinated, but the revolt fails. Italy and Yugoslavia prevent German intervention.

25 High Commissioner Arthur Wauchope agrees to add 1,200 certificates to the new immigrant schedule, previously deemed unacceptable by the Jewish Agency.

28 The Union of Arab Workers established in Jerusalem.

AUGUST

1 The Lithuanian government suppresses all Jewish newspapers.

2 *Reichs* President von Hindenburg dies: Hitler replaces the dead leader adopting the title of *Fuehrer*.

4 The German-American Anti-Nazi Front is established in Cincinnati, Ohio.

4/5 An Arab pogrom in Constantine, Algeria leaves 100 Jews dead and more than 200 injured.

7 Five American citizens are beaten up in Nuremberg after refusing to give the Nazi salute.

7 The Japanese government aborts the Manchukuo scheme to resettle German Jews.

7 The Green Shirts, an antisemitic organization in Belgium, is ordered to disband.

8 Some 2,000 German Jewish refugees form a Jewish community in Barcelona.

8 Arab-Jewish riots in Algeria end with more than two dozen dead.

15 von Hindenburg's testament is published.

15 Hohnstein concentration camp is closed.

19 A German plebiscite approves the dual role of Hitler as chancellor and *fuehrer*.

21 The South African Supreme Court awards a $9,000 judgment to Rabbi Abraham Levy in a defamation case against three South African racists and antisemites.

26/27 The Third World Conference of General Zionists meets in Cracow.

SEPTEMBER

3 The mandatory government appoints special constables to help police prevent "illegal" immigrants from entering Palestine.

12 The *Aliya Bet* ("illegal" immigration) ship Velos lands 350 *ma'apilim* ("illegal" immigrants) near Tel Aviv.

12 Estonia, Latvia, and Lithuania sign nonaggression and mutual cooperation treaty.

15 Poland repudiates National Minority Treaty.

18 The Soviet Union joins the League of Nations and is given a permanent seat on the League's Council.

19 U.S. Secretary of State Cordell Hull denounces all political or racial boycotts in any form.

23 A typhoon in Tokyo kills 1,500.

26 Black nationalists in New York begin boycotting Jewish owned shops.

29 Italy reaffirms a 1928 friendship treaty with Ethiopia.

OCTOBER

1 Nazi Germany starts building its *Luftwaffe* (air force).

1/5 The *he-Halutz* Conference opens in Berlin under the watchful eyes of the *Gestapo*.

3 The *Juedische Rundschau* is warned by Goebbels' Propaganda Ministry to limit its articles to Zionist affairs, or else it will be shut down.

4 An important archaeological discovery in Gezer unearthed by the Palestine Exploration Fund is announced: 2,000 B.C.E. remains of burial ground among other artifacts are uncovered.

5 General strike throughout Spain is called by a coalition of Communists, Socialists, and Syndicalists.

6 The Soviet Union assigns 7,000,000 *rubles* for Jewish settlement in Birobidjan.

7 Armed revolts in Spain are led by both the Socialist-Anarchist-Communists and the Catalonian Separatists.

8 Negotiations begin between the *Histadrut* and Revisionists.

8 The American Jewish Congress reaffirms its plans for a World Jewish Congress.

8 Weizmann demands that Transjordan open to Jewish business and settlement.

9 King Alexander of Yugoslavia is assassinated while visiting France.

9 A new Soviet decree restores full civic rights to religious functionaries.

11 The Turkish government outlaws the Zionist Organization.

11 Peter II, age eleven, is proclaimed Yugoslavian King.

16 A ground-breaking ceremony is held for the University Medical Center (later the Hadassah Hospital) on Mount Scopus, Jerusalem.

16 All Jewish religious institutions in Germany are deprived of their tax free status.

23 The Naval Disarmament Conference is held in London.

23 The House of Bishops of the Protestant Episcopal Church in the United States adopts a sympathetic resolution for persecuted German Jews.

24 The Jewish Agency Executive denounces a MAPAI attack on a Revisionist meeting in Haifa.

27 A plot is uncovered for assassination of *Il Duce* (Mussolini).

27 The Siamese King abdicates; revolution is feared.

28 The Arab Labor Federation calls for a boycott of Jewish enterprises in Palestine.

28 A Revisionist-*mapai* peace pact is signed in Paris by Vladimir Jabotinsky and David Ben-Gurion.

29 The Nazi party in Southwest Africa, the Grey Shirts, is outlawed.

30 The American Legion adopts a resolution condemning Nazism.

NOVEMBER

2 On the seventeenth anniversary of the Balfour Declaration, Arabs throughout Palestine observe a strike protest urged on by the Arab Executive.

2 Baron Edmund de Rothschild, instrumental figure in the formation of some of the earliest settlements in Palestine, dies.

8 The Latvian government deports *Poale Zion* leaders.

8 French Prime Minister M. Doumergue resigns and is succeeded by Pierre Flandin.

11 The National Union for Social Justice established by Father Coughlin.

11 German *olim* found the agricultural settlement of Gan ha-Shomron in the Northern Sharon district.

13 Meeting is held between Mussolini and Nahum Goldmann.

14 *Endek* student gangs attack Jewish students at Cracow University.

14 The British announce a labor schedule coordinating with 7,500 immigration certificates and lasting from October 1934 through March 1935.

16 *Mosad Bialik* (Bialik Institute) opens in Tel Aviv, dedicated to Hebrew literature and culture.

20 The Refugee Economic Corporation is established in New York to finance resettlement and reconstruction activities for German Jews.

26 The World Non-Sectarian Anti-Nazi Boycott Association is founded.

DECEMBER

1 Assassination of S. Mironovich Kirov signals renewed purges in the Soviet Union.

2 KKL acquires the Huleh region for $1,000,000.

3 France and Germany sign agreement prohibiting for a one year period, the discrimination against any inhabitant of the Saar region for racial, linguistic, or religious reasons.

5 British Secretary of State for the Colonies, Sir Philip Cunliffe-Lister, reports to the House of Commons that 627 "illegal" immigrants were deported from Palestine during 1934.

5 Flareups between Italian and Ethiopian Troops at Wal Wal occur along the frontier between Italian Somaliland and Ethiopia.

10 *Palcor*, the Palestine Correspondents' Agency, is founded.

11 The French government refutes reports that it contemplates measures against Jewish immigrants and refugees from Nazism.

14 Women in Turkey are given voting rights.

17 Sir Oswald Mosley, British Fascist leader, is tried on charges of riotous assembly.

19 Polish Jewish business cooperatives form a united front against the fierce competition of non-Jewish cooperatives financed by the Polish government.

19 Japan denounces 1922 and 1930 naval agreements.

21 The *Endek* party gains victory in the municipal elections held in Lodz {P}.

22 An international force to oversee the upcoming plebiscite arrives in the Saar.

27 The French Foreign Office refuses to extend transit visas for thousands of Jews fleeing Germany.

1935

JANUARY

1 The new Palestinian municipal administration system is put into effect.

1 The Soviets discontinue food rationing cards.

2 The Zurich City Council requests that the Swiss government forbid anti-Jewish demonstrations and publication of antisemitic literature.

3 Emanuel Celler introduces a bill in the House of Representatives directing the secretary of state not to enter into any agreement with a state engaged in racial or religious bias; a similar bill is introduced in the Senate by Senator W. Warren Barbour of New Jersey on January 21.

3 Ethiopia appeals to the League of Nations for help in the Italian conflict.

4/5 The National *mapai* conference debates the Ben-Gurion-Jabotinsky agreement; no decision is formed on the substantive issues dealt with in the agreement.

6 The American Jewish Committee reports that since the accession of Kurt von Schuschnigg to the chancellorship of Austria, the Jewish situation in the country has worsened.

7 Franco-Italian agreement signed.

8 Moshe Shertok, head of the Jewish Agency Political Department, meets with Emir Abdullah in Transjordan.

8 The *Gestapo* transforms the Columbia Haus prison in Berlin into a concentration camp under its direct control.

11 Thousands of poor Jews besiege the offices of the Warsaw Jewish *kehilla* asking for coal.

13 The Saar plebescite: majority votes for return to *Reich*.

14 A twelve hundred mile long pipeline, from the Mosul oil fields to Haifa, is inaugurated at Kirkuk, Iraq.

17 The League of Nations formally awards the Saar basin to Germany.

20/21 The National conference on Palestine is held in Washington, DC.

22 The Iraq to Haifa oil pipeline officially begins operation.

30 *SS-Hauptamt* (Main Office) is established.

FEBRUARY

1 The Anglo-German Conference opens in London; Germany's rearmament is the main topic on the agenda.

1 Italy sends troops to East Africa.

1 A Soviet decree writes off loans from the Jewish agricultural collectives in Russia.

8 Max Liebermann, former dean of German artists, dies.

9 The Jewish State Party, meeting in Tel Aviv, decides not to join HA-ZOHAR.

12 One hundred "illegal" immigrants held in the Acre prison begin a hunger strike, protesting their impending deportation from Palestine by the British authorities.

15 A decree is published creating the *Reichsstelle fuer Raumordnung*, a German Agency for Space Arrangement.

17 Workers congress organized by the *Bund, Polska Partia Socjalistyczna* [PPS] (Polish Socialist Party), and the Polish Communist Party [KPP] meets in Warsaw.

22 Demanding higher wages, a joint Jewish-Arab strike is held against the Iraq-Haifa pipeline company.

24 The second annual Brotherhood Day is organized by the National Conference of Christians and Jews.

27 Austrian Chancellor von Schuschnigg denies that the Austrian government intends to expel eastern-European Jews or reduce the number of professional Jews.

28 The Swiss Supreme Court forbids formation of Nazi-like stormtroops.

MARCH

1 The Saar becomes part of Germany and the Nazis apply their anti-Jewish legislation to the area.

3 Street clashes erupt in Tel Aviv between religiously observant and non-observant Jews; ten persons are injured.

4 Britain publishes the Defence White Paper, detailing plans for rearmament.

9 German rearmament begins in secret.

11 Hitler announces the existence of a German air force.

13 Jews are prohibited from reorienting their lives as artisans with the intent to remain in Germany.

15 The Soviet government proclaims the establishment of a fifth Jewish Autonomous region at Larindorf in the Crimea.

15 France extends its military conscription for two more years.

16 Germany re-establishes universal compulsory military service and repudiates the disarmament clauses in the Versailles Treaty.

19 The Society of Friends (Quakers) appeals to the British government for financial assistance to aid its refugee resettlement efforts.

22 The German Ministry of Education reports that not a single Jewish student was admitted to German universities in the academic year 1933-1934.

24 By a three-to-two majority, *Histadrut* members reject the Ben-Gurion-Jabotinsky agreement, after a write-in vote.

24 The Anglo-Jewish Council of Trades and Industries, the World Alliance for Combatting Antisemitism, and the British Anti-War Council proclaim an anti-Nazi boycott.

25/26 Bilateral talks are held between Germany and Britain.

28 The Greek government orders all anti-Jewish organizations disbanded, especially the EEE.

31 An antisemitic manifesto calls for racial restrictions in all branches of Rumanian life.

APRIL

1   Austria reinstitutes military conscription, violating the Treaty of Saint Germain.

8   Adolph S. Ochs, publisher of *The New York Times*, dies.

10   Hebrew University celebrates its tenth anniversary.

11/14   The prime ministers of Britain, France, and Italy meet at Stresa, Italy to discuss Austrian independence, and establish a common front against German encroachment.

17   The League of Nations censures Germany's rearmament policy.

19   *Gazeta Warszawska* publishes an editorial calling for Poland to adopt a policy similar to that of Nazi Germany with forceful mass emigration of Polish Jews.

19   *Agudas Yisroel* announces a rival "Jewish Agency" to deal with the British Mandatory government and the League of Nations.

22   HA-ZOHAR withdraws from the World Zionist Organization.

23   Nazi Race Bureau declares that Jewish children will be excluded from the German public schools.

23   A Polish constitution is adopted; though outwardly democratic, this document severely limits minority rights, especially for Jews.

24   The first meeting of Father Coughlin's organization, the American Union for Social Justice, is held in Detroit.

24   Nazis decree that in order to keep their jobs, publishers and newspaper editors must prove their aryan descent to 1800.

30   A Nazi decree forbids Jews from exhibiting the German flag.

MAY

1   Bucharest university students are required to fill out special forms describing their ethnic origins.

2   Signing of the Franco-Soviet mutual defense pact.

2   The Prussian Administrative Court rules that the *Gestapo* is no longer subject to judicial control.

5   Arab disturbances occur in Palestine.

12   Marshal Jozef Pilsudski, the Polish dictator, dies.

15   A mutual assistance treaty between the Soviet Union and Czechoslovakia is signed.

20 *Sudetendeutsche Partei* (Sudeten German Party), led by Konrad Henlein, an ally of the outlawed Nazi party of Czechoslovakia, receives 250,000 votes and wins 45 of the 300 seats in Czechoslovakia's national parliament.

21 Hitler, in a speech before the *Reichstag*, once again declares himself a man of peace and disavows imperialist designs.

25 The SA stimulates anti-Jewish riots in Munich.

27 The International Congress of Sephardic Jewry is established.

27 The U.S. Supreme Court rules the National Industrial Recovery Act unconstitutional.

29 Austrian Chancellor von Schuschnigg rejects union with Germany.

31 Jews are excluded from conscription in the German army.

JUNE

4 Pierre Laval forms a new French cabinet.

7 Nazis assure the International Olympic Committee that aryans and non-aryans will be treated alike during athletic competitions.

7 Stanley Baldwin becomes British prime minister.

9 Vicious anti-Jewish riots break out in Grodno {P}; at least sixty Jews are injured.

10 The Albanian government announces that only Jews able to invest capital are welcome.

12 The German delegation withdraws from the International League of Nations Society to protest the League's anti-Nazi resolution.

12 The Polish government gives full rights to schools maintained by *Agudas Yisroel*.

15 Mao Tse-tung calls for a united people's front against Japan, but excludes Chiang Kai-shek.

17 The American Federation of Polish Jews launches a fund-raising campaign to relieve Polish Jewry.

18 The Anglo-German Naval Agreement is signed allowing for German naval rearmament.

18 *Towarzystwo Ochrony Zdrowia Ludnosci Zydowskiej* [TOZ] (Society for the Safeguarding of the Health of the Jewish Population), Poland's Jewish health organization, reports that over 40,000 Jewish children are in dire need of sanitary and medical assistance.

19 Ethiopia asks the League of Nations to send neutral observers into disputed areas of East Africa.

19 German consulate in Palestine warns refugees not to return to Germany for even a short visit, as the *Gestapo* will incarcerate them in a concentration camp for "special education."

20 The Soviet Union recognizes the right to own private property in Birobidjan.

21 The German Franconian State cancels citizenship for all Jews naturalized between 1922 and 1929.

23 The Polish government closes down the Anti-Nazi Boycott Committee of Poland claiming that the Committee's funds were mismanaged.

23 Mussolini rejects a British offer of concessions over Abyssinia.

24 Over 10,000 German children, members of the *Hitlerjugend* (Hitler Youth), take a formal oath "to eternally hate the Jews."

26 *Arbeitsdienst* (Labor Service) is established in Nazi Germany; non-aryans are excluded from national labor service.

30 *Obshcheestvo Rasprostraneniya Truda sredi Yevreyev* [ORT] (Society for Manual and Agricultural Work among Jews) in Paris opens workshop for German Jewish refugee students.

30 The Zurich *canton* (state) prohibits the selling of *Der Stuermer*.

JULY

1 The *Gestapo* arrests Martin Niemoeller for the first time.

1 Himmler founds in Berlin the *Studiengesellschaft fuer Geistesurgeschichte Deutsches Ahnenerbe* (Society for Research into the Spiritual Roots of Germany's Ancestral Heritage).

2 A one-day student strike is held at the Hebrew University in Jerusalem.

2 The Swiss government bans *Der Stuermer*, *Reichsdeutsche*, and *Allemane*, three German anti-Jewish publications.

7 The Belgian Catholic daily, *La Libre Belge*, asserts that Catholics in Germany are worse off than the Jews.

12 Alfred Dreyfus dies.

13 The United States and the Soviet Union sign a trade agreement.

15 *Chef der OKW* (Chief of Staff) publishes the order of the day, which bans soldiers from non-aryan shops.

15 The *Integralistas*, a Brazilian Nazi organization, opens convention in Rio de Janeiro.

15 The Hungarian Supreme Court upholds Budapest's Jewish community's autonomy.

16 A violent anti-Jewish outbreak occurs on *Kurfuerstendam* in Berlin.

18 A Report by the League of Nations High Commissioner for Refugees, James G. McDonald, states that 27,000 German Jewish refugees have entered Palestine since 1932.

18 Ecuador agrees to give administrative power over 1,250,000 acres of land to *Emcol*, the Jewish Emigration and Colonization Association.

20 Final edition of the *Jewish Daily Bulletin*, the only *Yiddish* daily in America printed in English.

20 The *Gestapo* closes down Jewish-owned shops along the *Kurfuerstendam* in Berlin.

22 The Refugee Economic Corporation is created in New York.

22 The American Jewish Congress and the Jewish Labor Committee adopt a joint resolution urging the United States government to intercede with Nazis on behalf of German Jewry.

22 Publication is suspended three months for the *Juedische Rundschau*, the official organ of the German Zionist Federation.

23 Lithuanian police suppress Jewish anti-Nazi boycott in Kovno.

24 Elections are held for delegates to the Nineteenth World Zionist Congress.

24 Utah Senator William H. King urges the United States to investigate Nazi persecution of Jews and Catholics in Germany.

25 The Seventh Congress of the Communist International [COMINTERN] opens.

26 The Freeland League for Jewish Territorial Organization is established in London.

27 Nazi leaders forbid individual anti-Jewish actions; all anti-Jewish measures must emanate from the *Fuehrer*'s chancellery.

28 *Hadassah* announces that it intends to transfer all its institutions in Palestine to the authority of the Jewish Agency and *Va'ad Leumi*, except the Hospital on Mount Scopus.

31 The Berlin city council bars provincial Jews from entering city.

AUGUST

6 *Reichsverband juedische Kulturbuende* (Reich Association of Jewish Cultural Unions) established by order of the *Reich* Chamber of Culture, and placed under the Ministry of Propaganda's control.

10 Pennsylvania outlaws restrictions on public places on the basis of race, color, or religious belief.

10/15 *Mizrachi* World Conference opens in Cracow.

12 *Agudas Yisroel* issues a manifesto urging Jewish participation in the upcoming Polish elections.

12 The Massachusetts General Assembly adopts a resolution condemning persecution of minorities by Nazi Germany.

15 A Nazi anti-Jewish rally in Berlin *Sportspalast* is held under the aegis of Julius Streicher.

15 The United States Congress passes Social Security Act.

18 Roosevelt calls on Mussolini to preserve the peace in East Africa.

20 The Nineteenth World Zionist Congress opens in Lucerne, Switzerland; among the key questions reviewed are the *Haavara* agreement and the fate of German Jewry. The Congress closes September 4.

20 The Seventh World Congress of the Communist International calls for a popular front strategy to fight Fascism and support the struggles and wars of national liberation.

22 Government and religious leaders attending a public gathering in Washington, deplore Nazi treatment of Catholics and Jews.

25 Bulgaria plans to enter into a "transfer agreement" with the *Yishuv* in Palestine.

25/30 A seminar on human relations, sponsored by the National Conference of Christians and Jews, convenes at Williams College in Williamstown, Massachusetts.

29 Dr. Judah L. Magnes resigns as Hebrew University chancellor.

31 Italy increases its army to one million men.

SEPTEMBER

1 *Harav* Abraham Isaac Ha-cohen Kook, first *Ashkenazi* Chief Rabbi of Palestine, dies at age 70.

1 The World Zionist Congress selects the Jewish Agency Executive to act as the administrator of the *Haavara* Agreement.

1 Chaim Weizmann accepts the World Zionist Organization presidency at the Nineteenth World Zionist Congress in Lucerne.

4 The League of Nations Council meets to discuss Italy's agression against Ethiopia.

7/12   The New Zionist Organization, *Histadrut ha-Zionit ha-Hadasha* [HA-ZACH], is officially founded at its first congress in Vienna: Jabotinsky presents a ten-year plan to settle 1,500,000 Jews on both sides of the Jordan River. The Congress adopts the Revisionist constitution.

8   The first World Conference of Polish Jews opens in London; conference closes October 4.

10   Hebrew University president, Judah L. Magnes, in collaboration with *Hadassah* announces the creation of a medical school.

11   During the seventh Nazi party congress at Nuremberg, Hitler announces that German scientists have solved the problem of synthetic rubber production.

11   Britain urges that the League of Nations resist aggressive actions.

11   The First International Conference of the Youth *Aliya* Committees opens in Amsterdam.

12   The *Gerer Rebbe* (hassidic rabbi of Gur, Poland), Rabbi Abraham Mordechai Alter, visits Palestine.

13   The World *Maccabee* Congress opens in Brno, Czechoslovakia.

14   Italy rejects a League of Nations compromise on the Ethiopian crisis.

14   Emmanuel Shinwell defeats Ramsey MacDonald in British general elections.

15   The Nuremberg Laws are passed: Under the *Reichsbuergergesetz* (State Citizenship Law), Jews are stripped of citizenship rights, relegating German Jewry to a *staatsangehoerige* (subjects) of the state; the *Gesetz zum Schutze des deutschen Blutes und der deutschen Ehre* (Law for the Protection of German Blood and German Honor) forbids marriages between Jews and German nationals or kindred blood, and defines the racial meaning of Jew, aryan, and *mischlinge* (persons of mixed parentage), an intermediary category.

15   The Swastika becomes part of the official flag of the *Third Reich*.

15   A second wave of Jewish emigration from Nazi Germany begins due to enactment of the Nuremberg Laws.

20   Nazi party ideologists give their official interpretation of Nuremberg Laws.

26   *Va'ad Leumi* withdraws its support from the *Haavara* Agreement.

OCTOBER

1 To avoid offending Arabs, the German Propaganda Ministry explains that Nazism is anti-Jewish rather than antisemitic.

2 German banks are prohibited from giving credit to Jews.

4 Italy invades Ethiopia.

5 The United States embargoes all arms shipments to Italy and Ethiopia.

5 KL Columbia Haus in Berlin is closed.

6 Nazis deploy anti-Jewish terror throughout Germany.

7 The Canadian government postpones national elections for one week for *Yom Kippur* observances.

9 The *Reichsvertretung*, with Nazi permission, announces plans for a separate Jewish winter relief campaign.

10 Monarchy reestablished in Greece.

15 *Kriegsakademie* (War Academy) is reopened in Berlin.

16 The Greek government abolishes the separate electoral college for Salonican Jews.

18 Nazi Germany promulgates its Marriage Protection Law, forbidding persons with hereditary diseases to marry.

18 France offers Britain unlimited military aid in the event that England becomes embroiled in an armed conflict with Italy.

19 *Reichsinstitut fuer Geschichte des neuen Deutschlands* (Institute for the History of the New Germany) opens.

19 The League of Nations imposes sanctions on Italy for its Abyssinian invasion.

21 The Arab Higher Committee declares a one day general strike for October 26.

24 Protestant and Catholic leaders emphatically urge American withdrawal from the Olympic Games.

27 Eighteen thousand attend an anti-Nazi rally in Hyde Park, London.

NOVEMBER

1 The German government announces that the Nuremberg Laws apply to all Jews, German or foreign, without exception.

3 Leon Blum forms the French Popular Front government.

4 The British government declares sanctions against Italy; in Palestine, sanctions are delayed until November 18.

6 Moshe Rosenfeld, a Jewish sergeant serving with the Palestine police, is murdered by Arab terrorists.

11 David Ben-Gurion is named the Jewish Agency Executive's chairman.

14 Nazi Germany implements its definition of who is a Jew.

15 Nazis publish detailed regulations to execute the Nuremberg Laws.

15 The United States grants the Philippines commonwealth status.

18 The League of Nations embargo against Italy goes into effect.

20 The Protestant Federation of France holds a meeting in the Paris Hall of Chopin, protesting the Nazi treatment of German Jews.

20 The Church of England unanimously condemns Nazi persecution of Jews in Germany.

22 *Ha-Oved ha-Ziyyoni* (The Zionist Worker) is founded at Ra'ananah, Palestine.

26 Clement Attlee is chosen leader of British Labour Party.

26 An Arab delegation demands that High Commissioner Wauchope stop Jewish immigration to Palestine.

26 The Nazi racial office rules that the prohibition of racially mixed marriages incorporated in the "Law for the Protection of German Blood and Honor," equally applies to Gypsies.

28 Jewish refugee advocates reject a proposed liquidation bank for German Jewry.

DECEMBER

1 Chiang Kai-shek is elected president of the *Kuo Min Tang,* the Chinese Nationalist government.

2 A number of American colleges urge U.S. athletes not to participate in the Olympics.

4 The Polish Zionist Federation complains to the Jewish Agency about the short allotment of certificates (3,000) for Polish Jews leaving for Palestine.

6 Jewish youth groups protest the Nuremberg Laws during a meeting at the Edison Theater in Tel Aviv.

7 A resolution adopted at the annual National Amateur Athletic Union convention, demands that American teams refuse participation in the Berlin Olympics.

13 More restrictions for German Jews in the medical and legal professions are published.

23 The Italian air force begins using mustard gas against Ethiopia.

24 Congress passes the United States Neutrality Act.

26 Nazis revoke licenses for Jewish traveling salespeople throughout Germany.

27 James G. McDonald, in a widely-circulated letter, publicizes Nazi anti-Jewish excesses in Germany.

30 Lord Reading, Rufus Daniel Isaacs, dies.

31 McDonald resigns as High Commissioner for Refugees.

1936

JANUARY

1 The United Palestine Appeal is founded unifying *Keren Ha-yesod* and KKL fundraising activities.

5 The first Bialik prize is awarded to Zalman Rubashov.

11 Assassination is attempted on Rumanian Chief Rabbi Jacob Isaac Niemirower.

15 Viscount Samuel, Lord Bearsted, and Simon Marks leave England for the United States in order to propose a plan for mass resettlement of German Jews in America.

15 Japan withdraws from the London Naval Conference.

20 Edward VIII is crowned British king.

20 The League of Nations condemns Nazi actions in Danzig.

21 A published ordinance eliminates Jewish accountants from German businesses.

21 Britain's King George V dies.

23 Municipal decree dissolves a branch of *Endekcja* in Lodz.

23 Senator King urges the United States to open its doors as a haven for Jews fleeing Germany.

25 The Catholic Agency of Poland officially condemns antisemitic acts.

27 American Zionists overwhelmingly reject Britain's proposed Palestine Legislative Council.

30 Roosevelt proposes a Pan-American Peace Conference.

FEBRUARY

1/29 A general strike and riots break out in Syria.

4 Swiss Nazi party leader, Wilhelm Gustloff, is assassinated by David Frankfurter.

6/16 The Winter Olympics are held at the German resort town of Garmisch-Partenkirchen.

7 Polish *sejm* deputy, Janina Prystor, introduces a "humane slaughter" bill (if passed, the bill would automatically render all slaughtered meat non-kosher). The Prystor bill is adopted almost unanimously.

14 The governor of the Poznan *Wojewodztwo* (district) unilaterally imposes a ban on *shechita*.

16 General elections are held in Spain and the center-left parties attain power.

17 Second winter *Maccabee* games open in Banska Bystrica, Czechoslovakia.

18 Goebbels issues a decree muzzling church press.

18 Britain's Major General Sir Neill Malcolm is appointed League of Nations High Commissioner for Refugees from Germany, succeeding James G. McDonald after the latter resigns.

18 The Swiss government bans NSDAP propaganda activities in Switzerland.

19 Dr. David Prato is invested as Italy's chief rabbi during a solemn ceremony at Rome's great synagogue.

22/23 The third annual Brotherhood Day is sponsored by the National Conference of Christians and Jews.

23 Hebrew University grants its first doctorate.

26 The first group of German youth *olim* (immigrants) complete *hachshara* at Kibbutz Ein-Harod.

26 A military dictatorship is established in Japan.

27 The Franco-Soviet mutual defense pact is ratified.

27 The United Committee for the Defense of *Shechita* in Poland is organized in London.

27 Mussolini protests the Five-Power Mediterranean Pact.

28 London police are instructed to arrest all antisemitic agitators.

29 August Cardinal Hlond, the Catholic primate of Poland, sends out a pastoral letter urging Poles to boycott Jewish businesses.

MARCH

3 Italy abolishes private banking.

3 The League of Nations calls for peace negotiations between Italy and Ethiopia.

4 *Endek* students at Warsaw University conduct a bloody rampage seriously injuring a number of Jewish students.

4 Twelve hundred Polish rabbis protest the anti-*shechita* bill pending in the *sejm*.

7 Germany reoccupies the Rhineland, violating the Treaty of Versailles and the Locarno agreements.

9 Przytyk {P} pogrom.

11 Anti-Jewish outrage spreads to many parts of Poland in the aftermath of the Przytyk pogrom.

13 Jewish labor groups call for a one day general strike to protest Polish antisemitism; the PPS supports the resolution on March 15.

14 Syndicalists, Socialists, and Communists set fire to the Monarchist newspaper offices of *Nacion* and burn churches in the center of Madrid.

15 *Va'ad Leumi* meets to discuss Jewish suffering in Poland; speakers include Yitzhak Gruenbaum, Itzhak Ben-Zvi, and Shalom Asch. The agency approves a resolution condemning Poland's recent anti-*shechita* law.

15 The Council for German Jewry [CFGJ] is established in London.

17 Jews, Polish workers, and Polish liberals stage a one day strike and mass demonstrations to protest antisemitism in Poland.

18 The German Jewish Relief Fund is created in Australia.

18 Austrian Catholic leaders demand a *numerus clausus* against Jews.

21 The Lithuanian government condemns the spread of anti-Jewish ritual murder accusations in an official publication.

22 Sir Oswald Mosley makes an antisemitic speech that nearly causes riot in London's Albert Hall.

22 The American Jewish Congress adopts a resolution urging the United States government to intervene on behalf of persecuted Polish Jewry.

23 Italy, Austria, and Hungary sign an anti-Nazi mutual defense treaty in Rome.

23 The Latvia-Palestine Transfer Agreement is signed in Riga.

23 Government troops crush civil and political disorders in Mexico.

23 British military forces in Palestine evacuate Jews from Hebron.

24 The House of Commons debates a Palestine Legislative Council proposal; opposes an Arab plan to forbid Arabs from selling all their land to Jews in Palestine.

25 The United States, Britain, and France sign the London Naval Convention.

25 Nazis denationalize and confiscate property belonging to German writers who voluntarily went into exile.

25 Premier Koki Hirota announces that Japan will not go to war.

26 The Union of Jewish War Veterans in Austria protests antisemitic agitation.

29 Forty-four-and-a-half million Germans out of 45,500,000 registered voters vote for Hitler.

29 SS guard formations are renamed *SS-Totenkopfverbande* and their number increases to 3,500.

29 Nazis announce that German Jews will be drafted into the army to perform manual tasks in the event of a war.

29 The third Jewish victim of the Przytyk pogrom dies.

30 The Palestine Broadcasting Company [PBC] in Jerusalem airs its first official broadcast.

30 Thirteen "illegal" immigrants in the Acre prison begin a hunger strike.

30 Britain announces its intention to build thirty-eight new warships.

APRIL

1 Austria introduces conscription.

1 *Hitachdut Olei Polonia*, the organization of Polish Jews in Palestine, earmarks a fundraising appeal for $500,000 to aid Polish Jews.

2   The American Jewish Labor Committee and its affiliated trade unions observe a "hunger day," foregoing one meal and contributing its cost to a special fund for stricken Polish Jews.

4   The Italian air force machine-guns Addis Ababa from the air.

7   Ethiopia appeals to the League of Nations for effective aid against the Italian invaders.

7   A Socialist vote in Spanish *cortes* (parliament) ousts President Alcala Zamora.

9   A Soviet-Japanese skirmish occurs on the Outer-Mongolian border.

15   Armed Arabs fire on Jewish automobiles near Tul-Karm. Two Jews are killed.

16   *Irgun Zvai Leumi* [IZL] (National Military Organization) kills two Arabs near Petah Tikva.

17   The Polish *sejm* passes an anti-*shechita* bill.

17   Leftist unions stage a general strike in Madrid.

19   Armed Arab gangs attack Jews in Tel Aviv and Yaffo, killing nine Jews and injuring forty; police kill two Arabs.

20   An agreement to extend German-Soviet trade is signed in Berlin.

20   The Arab National Committee founded in Shechem.

20   Lord Tweedsmuir, British governor general of Canada, addresses a Zionist Organization of Canada meeting regarding the importance of Palestine as a refuge for German Jews.

20   The Lithuanian-Palestine Transfer Agreement is signed in Kovno.

22   Arab parties in Palestine declare a general strike.

22   The Lithuanian government announces that all Jewish teachers' institutes will be closed.

23   A World Jewish Medical Congress opens in Tel Aviv with 300 doctors from all over of the world. The Congress adopts a resolution to establish a Jewish International Medical Organization.

23   Roosevelt asks Congress for $460,800,000 to set up a security program.

24/27   Anti-Jewish demonstrations in Bratislava {Cz} are connected with the screening of the film *Golem*.

26   *Reichsvertretung* announces that one fifth of Germany's Jews depends on outside relief.

26 A large-scale rally in Paris sponsored by the Palestine Labor Federation protests Arab disturbances in Palestine.

28 Brazilian police close the offices of the pro-Nazi *Integralista* party.

28 A mass meeting of Zionist parties in Vienna protests Arab disturbances in Palestine.

28 King Farouk accedes the Egyptian throne.

29 Arab band attacks a Jewish convoy traveling from Tel Aviv to Haifa near Jenin.

30 The Seventh Levant Fair opens in Tel Aviv.

30 *Ha-Poel ha-Mizrachi* (Religious Labor Movement) breaks relations with the *Histadrut*.

MAY

2 Emperor Haile Selassie flees Ethiopia: Addis Ababa is looted and set afire; mobs rule the capital.

2/3 Special prayers for the persecuted minorities in Nazi Germany are conducted under the sponsorship of the American Christian Committee for German Refugees, the New York Board of Rabbis, and the Committee for the Relief and Liberation of Victims of Persecution in Europe.

3 Italy captures Addis Ababa.

3 An Arab mob burns the Jewish lumber yard in Haifa.

3 A fundraising rally for the Nazi's victims is attended by some 16,000 people in Madison Square Garden.

4 The trial of *Gestapo* agent Hans Wesemann opens in Basle: the accused is charged with kidnapping of Berthold Jacob, a German Jewish journalist.

4 A kickoff campaign for the Palestine Foundation Fund is held at the special convention of the Argentine Zionist Organization in Buenos Aires.

5 Mussolini announces complete victory over Ethiopia.

7 The *Hilfsverein* announces that all its future activities will be geared toward Jewish emigration to Palestine or other overseas countries.

7 Arab leaders at a meeting in Jerusalem demand that Britain stop all Jewish immigration, Jewish land purchase, and establish an Arab majority government. They also inaugurate a civil disobedience campaign.

7 NARA party members are arrested in Warsaw for planning terrorist attacks on Polish Jews.

7 Britain proposes a plan regulating world arms traffic.

8 Haile Selassie arrives in Palestine.

9 Ethiopia is incorporated into the Italian empire. King Victor Emanuel II becomes Emperor of Ethiopia.

10 The Austrian *Freiheitsbund* (Freedom Association) organizes anti-Jewish demonstrations in Vienna.

10 League of Nations vote leaves sanctions against Italy in place.

10 Manuel Azana is elected president of Spanish Republic.

11 The first British troops arrive in Palestine to deal with Arab revolt.

11 A PPS convention condemns antisemitism in Poland.

11 The American Jewish Committee refuses to participate in the World Jewish Congress.

11 The Pope denounces Communism as the "greatest evil to men."

13 Britain accuses Italy of fomenting Arab revolt in Palestine.

16 General Felicjan Skladkowski becomes the new Polish prime minister.

17 Nahum Sokolow, honorary president of the World Zionist organization, dies.

18 The British Colonial Office announces formation of a British Royal Commission (the Peel Commission) to investigate the Palestine disturbances.

18 The Jewish Agency Executive rejects as entirely inadequate the number of immigration certificates granted by the British for the upcoming six months.

18 Emperor Haile Selassie thanks Jews for their support in defending Ethiopia.

19 Italy denies complicity in the Arab disturbances in Palestine.

21 The British League of Nations Union, opens a refugee conference in London.

21 British Prime Minister Stanley Baldwin warns Italy not to meddle in Egypt or Palestine.

21 Kurt von Schuschnigg is elected the Austrian Fatherland Front leader.

22 The London City Corporation announces its decision to boycott the International Union of Local Authorities conference to be held in Munich and Berlin, citing Nazi antisemitism as its reason.

22   The existence of a klan-like society, the Black Legion, is discovered during a Detroit murder investigation.

22   Richard James Horatio Gottheil, American Zionist leader, scholar, professor of semitic languages, and author, dies at age seventy-three.

23   Catholic bishops in Holland demand a ban on the Dutch Nazi party.

24   The British Amateur Athletic Association decides to attend the Berlin Olympics.

24   Arab marauders destroy over one thousand orange trees at *kibbutz* Yavniel.

24   The Belgian Fascist party, the *Rexists*, win twenty-one seats in parliamentary elections.

25   Jewish supernumerary police established in Palestine.

26   Austrian government announces its intention not to participate in the Geneva conference on German refugees.

28   Arabs destroy a few thousand trees planted by the KKL.

30   Directive published by Polish Minister of Religions for elections in all *kehillas* to take place on August 30 (minor *kehillas*) and September 6 (major *kehillas*).

JUNE

1   The English Zionist Federation adopts resolution protesting the Peel Commission.

1   Von Schuschnigg visits Mussolini in Rome. Il Duce persuades the chancellor to agree to a German-Austrian pact.

1   New Soviet Constitution goes into effect.

2   One hundred nineteen Nazis who conspired to overthrow the Polish government are indicted in Warsaw.

4   Polish Premier Felicjan Slawoj-Skladkowski openly favors economic boycott of Jewish businesses.

4   Leon Blum forms popular front government in France.

5   One hundred forty-four stateless *Sephardic* Jewish families are granted Spanish citizenship.

5   Arab bomb injures five Jewish passengers on a Haifa bus.

6   Xavier Vallat, extreme right member of the French Chamber of Deputies, attacks Leon Blum for his Jewish origin.

9   Mussolini appoints Count Galeazzo Ciano Italian foreign minister.

11 An Arab attack on *kibbutz* Tel-Yosef is repulsed.

12 The first Arab attack is made on British troops in Palestine.

13 Britain declares martial law in Palestine.

16 Arabs desecrate the prophet Hosea's tomb in Safed.

17 Himmler is appointed *Reichsfuehrer-SS und Chef der Deutschen Polizei* (Chief of the SS and Head of the German Police), both uniformed and civil.

17 The delegation of Palestinian Arabs travels to London to publicize their case regarding the disturbances.

18 Russian author Maxim Gorky dies at age sixty-eight.

19 France terminates sanctions against Italy.

20 The New Greek constitution includes a clause prohibiting religious conversion by persons under twenty-one years old.

20 The Austrian government prohibits all political meetings and street demonstrations. The order to last until the end of September.

21 Anti-Jewish riots break out in Bucharest.

22 The International Conference on the Right of Asylum, meeting in Paris, urges that political refugees be protected from deportation to their countries of origin.

22 The Italian Jewish community proposes sending a delegation to Ethiopia to organize the Beta Israel (Falasha) community.

25 A British soldier is killed while trying to quell Arab riots in Nablus.

27 The Soviets introduce an anti-abortion law.

27 The German government declares its support for Danzig's independence.

27/30 Five hundred fiftieth anniversary celebrations are held commemorating the Heidelberg University; at least twenty-four American universities participate.

29 A conference on Jewish emigration opens in Paris under the sponsorship of HICEM.

29 Japan repudiates the London Naval Treaty.

30 A Jewish general strike protests Polish antisemitism.

30 France outlaws the French Fascist Party.

30 Dr. Alexander Cuza, the National Christian Party leader, proposes solving the Jewish problem in Rumania in the same manner as Nazis in Germany.

30   Several large anti-Jewish demonstrations break out in Oran, Algeria.

30   Emperor Haile Selassie addresses the League of Nations.

JULY

2   The Intergovernmental Conference opens in Geneva, to deal with the German refugees' legal status.

2   The House of Lords rejects an amendment to the Sunday Closing Bill, which would have permitted Jewish shopkeepers to keep their shops open until 2 PM.

6   The Second World Congress of Jewish War Veterans is held in Vienna where it adopts a resolution calling upon all Jewish parties to form a united front against antisemitism.

8   A one hundred thousand dollar road construction project designed to ease unemployment in Palestine is begun by the Anglo-Palestine Bank, the Jewish Agency, and the *Histadrut*.

8   An Arab memorandum to the British government demands an end to Jewish immigration to Palestine.

8   The Poles declare a Nazi-sponsored movement for Danzig independence a *causa belli* (belligerent act).

8   Hitler guarantees Austria's independence.

9   Goebbels orders anti-Jewish propaganda curtailed during the Berlin Olympics.

10   German Jews begin to transfer part of their capital from Germany, losing 73 percent of the value.

10   House of Commons debates BUF activities.

11   An Austro-German friendship treaty is signed.

12   The Sachsenhausen concentration camp opens.

12   An Anti-Fascist demonstration in London nearly leads to riots.

14   The Union of Rumanian Veteran Army Officers, in a manifesto to the Rumanian government, demands immediate deportation for a few hundred thousand Jews.

14   The American Olympic team sails for Germany.

15   The Western Powers lift Economic sanctions against Italy.

15   All League of Nations member states terminate sanctions against Italy.

17   The Spanish Civil War is triggered by a Fascist military *coup*.

17   France nationalizes its munitions industry.

18   The Nazi controlled Danzig Senate nullifies the Free City's constitution; prohibits *shechita,* prevents Jews from renewing building leases and trading licenses.

18   U.S. Congressman William I. Sirovich suggests to Cuban President Miguel Gomez that Cuba admit 100,000 German Jews.

19   Arab gangs in Palestine derail a British military train.

20   At the Montreux Convention, Turkey is granted sovereignty over the Dardanelles and the Bosphorus.

20   Establishment of *Ahdut ha-Yishuv* (Unity of the Settlement), political association comprised of members of HA-ZACH, *Mizrachi*, General Zionists, and non-affiliated workers in Palestine.

21   Members of the Royal Committee on Palestine (the Peel Committee) are named.

23   Britain, France, and Belgium meet in London to discuss German violation of the Locarno Pact in the Rhineland.

25   Polish authorities in the Cracow district suppress the *Endek* party.

26   Germany and Italy begin to assist Franco's forces in the Spanish civil war.

26   In an address to some 5,000 American farmers, Father Coughlin asserts that under the Roosevelt administration, the coining of U.S. money is benefiting Wall Street's Rothschilds.

26   The Joint Distribution Committee [JDC] announces that during 1935 it contributed $300,000 to Jewish welfare in Germany.

28   The Jewish Agency for Palestine submits a proposal to the Polish government for a $10,000,000 transfer agreement, permitting Polish Jews wishing to emigrate to Palestine to take manufactured goods from Poland with them, in lieu of currency.

31   A resolution adopted by the Rumanian National Peasant Party invites Jewish membership and pledges to fight for equal rights for national minorities and against Nazi propaganda.

AUGUST

1   The Berlin Summer Olympics open. Nazis camouflage all outward signs of antisemitism because of foreign visitors.

1   The French government initiates a non-intervention policy in the Spanish civil war.

2 In order to solve its Jewish problem, Poland asks the League of Nations for colonies in the uninhabited regions of South America and/or South Africa.

3 Jewish and non-Jewish refugee aid organizations petition the League of Nations on behalf of persecuted groups in Germany.

3 The South African Jewish Board of Deputies decides not to send any representatives to the upcoming World Jewish Congress in Geneva.

4 An International convention of *Agudas Yisroel* opens in Marienbad, Czechoslovakia.

6 The United States declares its strict neutrality in the Spanish civil war.

6 An agreement is signed between *Hagana* and IZL-B faction, placing the latter under the discipline of the *Yishuv*'s organization.

8 A meeting to establish a World Jewish Congress [WJC] opens in Geneva.

14 Arthur S. Leese, publisher of the *Fascist*, organ of the Imperial Fascist League, is tried on charges of seditious libel against English Jews.

14 The WJC adopts a resolution requesting that the Soviet Union permit Jewish emigration, lift a ban on Zionism, and permit Jewish religious organizations to form.

15 Arab gangs attack thirty-eight Jewish settlements.

16 Unknown Arab terrorists throw a bomb from a moving train in Tel Aviv. One Jew is killed, ten injured in the incident.

17 *Asefat ha-Nivharim* (legislative assembly) holds an extraordinary session regarding the measures to be taken during the Arab disturbances.

17/18 IZL-B undertakes a series of retaliatory operations against Arabs, including an attack on a train leaving Jaffa.

19/24 The first Stalinist trials of "counterevolutionaries" open: all defendants are sentenced to death.

21 Fawzi Al-Kaukji arrives in Palestine, taking command over Arab rebels.

23 The German Evangelical Church publishes its manifesto.

24 Two-year military service is made compulsory in Germany.

25 The Actions Committee of the World Zionist Organization meets in Zurich, Switzerland to take up British policy regarding Jewish immigration and the continued Arab riots in Palestine.

26 A twenty-year Anglo-Egyptian alliance is signed in Cairo: The treaty ends military occupation of Egypt, except for the Canal Zone.

27 Polish Zionists observe a "Day of Protest" against Arab terrorist attacks in Palestine.

27 The *Hagana* reaffirms its commitment to *havlaga* (self-restraint) and its opposition to retaliatory measures.

SEPTEMBER

3 Al-Kaukji's marauders attack a British Army unit near Tul-Karm, Palestine.

3 The American Christian Conference on Palestine urges that Britain strictly abide by the terms of the Palestine mandate.

4 The Berlin Labor Court decides that German employees who marry a non-aryan may be dismissed from their jobs.

7 Britain announces its intent to increase the number of troops in Palestine.

8 France embargoes all military exports to Spain.

9 Josef Goebbels, the German propaganda minister, accuses Czechoslovakia of harboring Soviet aircraft.

10 Vladimir Jabotinsky states that Poland should call for an international conference of governments desiring the mass emigration of Jews to Palestine.

13 Jabotinsky publicly announces his evacuation scheme.

13 The *Consistoire Central des Israelites de France*, the Central Jewish Consistory, announces the establishment of a bureau to study and combat French antisemitism.

13 The World ORT Federation in Paris adopts a budget of 9,000,000 *francs* to retrain central and eastern European Jews.

18 A group of American philosophers decline an invitation to a conference of the German Philosophical Association in Berlin.

18 The unofficial Congressional Investigating Committee upon returning from Palestine blames the British government for the disturbances in Palestine.

18 David Lloyd George expresses enthusiasm for Hitler after he visits Germany.

20 A number of well-known rabbis and Zionist leaders in Germany are arrested by the *Gestapo*. No reason is given for the arrest.

20 An International Conference against Race Prejudice and Antisemitism opens in Paris.

20   The American Committee for the Settlement of Jews in Birobidjan launches a campaign for settling 1,500 families from eastern Europe.

21   Arthur Leese and two other British Fascists are found guilty of libel and slander.

24   Jewish owned employment offices in Germany are ordered to cease their activities.

24   The League of Nations appoints a subcommittee to work out plans for dealing with refugee problems.

24   Forty-four Arabs are killed in violent clashes with British troops and Palestine police.

27   The Association of Independent Artisans of the Jewish Faith, a German Jewish mutual aid society, is ordered closed by the *Gestapo*.

29   Meir Dizengoff, Tel Aviv's first mayor, dies.

OCTOBER

1   Generalissimo Francisco Franco assumes power and is declared Spanish head of state at Burgos.

1   The Jewish Telegraphic Agency [JTA], is expelled from the Association of News Agencies in Germany.

1   The French *franc* is devaluated.

1   The Soviet Union becomes a party to the Naval Convention of London.

4   Hans Frank draws up a program to remove all Jewish influence from German jurisprudence.

4   The *Reich* Chamber of Culture orders Berlin Jewish art dealers to close their galleries by the end of the year.

4   The first conference on Hebrew culture is held in Jerusalem.

4   Avery Brundage, addressing German Day exercises at Madison Square Garden, praises Germany under the Nazis.

5   Polish representative to the League of Nations proposes an International Emigration Conference.

7   The Polish Foreign Ministry requests that foreign financiers help Jews from Poland emigrate to countries outside Palestine.

10   The League of Nations votes to continue the Office of the High Commissioner for Refugees.

12   An Arab general strike fails, marking the beginning of Arab revolt.

13   The German Ministry of Justice establishes special courts throughout Germany to deal with those who defy the Nuremberg Laws.

14   Belgium ends its military alliance with France.

15   Jewish teachers in Germany are prohibited from tutoring aryan children.

18   The Board of Deputies of British Jews urge the nation's Jews to stay away from BUF disorders.

18   *Hadassah* opens its twenty-second annual convention in Philadelphia: The convention reports that during that year more than $600,000 was raised for projects in Palestine.

19   The Copenhagen Jewish Community receives the Danish government's approval for a new constitution.

19   Founding of the Jewish People's Committee for United Action against Fascism and Antisemitism.

20   Polish authorities close the Warsaw Trade School, following anti-Jewish riots by *Endek* students.

21   Streicher begins a new anti-Jewish crusade with an exhibit titled "World Enemy Number One Jewish Bolshevism."

21   Disorders at the University of Vilna injure a number of Jewish students.

22   Martial law is declared in Belgium to combat the *Rexists*.

22/25   Republicans transfer Spanish gold reserves to the Soviet Union.

23   Palestinian Arabs launch a "buy only Arab" campaign.

24   Germany recognizes Italian King Victor Emanuel II as the Ethiopian emperor.

25   Rome-Berlin Axis established.

25   The high commissioner for Palestine, General Sir Arthur Wauchope, refuses Arab demands that he stop construction of the Tel Aviv harbor.

26   Under pressure from the Royal Army, Al-Kaukji and his remaining rebels flee Palestine.

29   An army *coup* overthrows the Iraqi government.

29   A Diocesan Conference of the Church of England condemns antisemitic disorders in London's East End.

29   Hikmat Suleiman assumes power in Iraq and attacks on Jews subside.

NOVEMBER

4 President Franklin Delano Roosevelt is reelected to a second term with 524 electoral votes over his Republican opponent, Alf M. Landon, who receives only seven electoral votes; FDR carries every state except Vermont and Maine.

5 The Iron Guard denounces members of the Rumanian government as tools of Jews and Freemasons.

6 Hungarian Jewish leaders propose an anti-Communist front.

7 The Arab Higher Committee declares a boycott on the Peel Commission proceedings.

7/8 An International Brigade arrives in Madrid; battle for the city begins.

8 The Polish government protests the limited immigration quota (1,800 labor certificates for the coming six months) granted to Jews by the British Colonial Office for Palestine.

8 The National Christian Party stages the greatest antisemitic demonstration in the history of Rumania.

9 In a conference held in Vienna, Austria, Italy, and Hungary debate the Danube basin.

10 The Public Order Law is introduced in the House of Commons.

11 Members of the Peel Commission arrive in Palestine.

12 Opening session of the Peel Commission.

13 The *Forschungsabteilung judenfrage* (Research Department for the Jewish Question), an arm of the *Reichsinstitut*, opens in Munich.

14 Germany denounces clauses of the Versailles Treaty that enforced internationalization of its waterways.

15 The Rumanian Ministry of Labor announces that German Jewish refugees will not be permitted to establish themselves in Rumania.

15 The German Zionist Federation authorizes Chaim Weizmann to speak before the British Royal (Peel) Commission on behalf of German Jewry.

15 The Friends of the Iron Guards, a rabidly antisemitic party, is established in Rumania.

16 Jewish leaders in New York discuss the ways to promote Polish export to America to help Polish Jews economically.

18 Nazi Germany and Fascist Italy recognize Franco as the legitimate Spanish ruler.

20   The Jewish Agency submits a memorandum outlining its position to the Peel Commission.

21   Anti-Jewish editorials are published in two Italian publications, *Vita Italiana* and *Il Regime Fascista*.

22   At a meeting in London the Jewish Colonization Association [ICA] outlines plans to intensify Jewish colonization work in South America.

22   Yeshiva College in New York celebrates its fiftieth anniversary.

23   The Nazis blacklist some 2,000 works written by Jews.

25   The Anti-Comintern Pact is signed between Germany and Japan; Italy joins later.

25   Chaim Weizmann is first to testify before the Peel Commission on the Jewish situation.

28   The Warsaw Bar Association, voting 1,000 to 400, rejects a proposal barring Jews from the legal profession.

29   The National Council for Palestine, located in New York, urges that the Peel Commission insist on Britain fulfilling its obligation to establish a Jewish homeland in Palestine.

29   Soviet Premier Viacheslav Molotov denounces the Nazi persecution of German Jews.

30   Moshe Shertok, head of the Political Department of the Jewish Agency, testifies before the Peel Commission, blaming the Colonial Office's restrictive immigration policy as the reason for "illegal" Jewish immigration to Palestine.

DECEMBER

1   The Pan-American Peace Conference opens in Buenos Aires.

1   Yitzhak Halevi Herzog and Jacob Meir, respectively, are elected *Ashkenazi* and *Sephardi* Chief Rabbis of Palestine.

1   *Hitlerjugend* becomes a state agency.

1   The Soviet Union adopts a new constitution calling for a Supreme Soviet and a two-chamber parliament.

3   All Jewish charitable institutions in Germany are no longer tax exempt.

6   The Association of Hungarian Jews in America protests a *numerus clausus* in Hungarian higher learning institutions.

6 The start of a new Nazi press campaign aims to totally eliminate Jews from German economic life.

7 British troops clash with Arab terrorists in Palestine.

7 The last remaining German Jewish department store is aryanized.

8 France and Yugoslavia sign a trade agreement.

9 The David Frankfurter trial opens in Grisons *Cantonal* Court, Switzerland.

9 In testimony before the Peel Commission, Dr. Arthur Ruppin urges Britain to encourage Jewish settlement in Palestine.

9 The New York Board of Rabbis adopts a resolution urging people of all faiths to support the American Christian Committee for Refugees campaign.

9 Anti-Jewish riots force the closing of the medical school at the University of Cluj in Rumania.

10 King Edward VIII abdicates; George VI to succeed.

10 Nir David, the *Yishuv*'s first "tower and stockade" settlement, is founded in the Beth-Shean Valley.

12 Chiang Kai-shek declares war on Japan.

13 Arab leaders meet in Jaffa to launch a campaign escalating the anti-Jewish boycott.

14 The Swiss *Cantonal* Court sentences David Frankfurter to eighteen years in prison.

15 A resolution adopted by the Pro-Palestine Federation of America demands that Great Britain stop obstructing Jewish settlement in Palestine immediately.

15 The Jewish Education Association urges that American Jewry undertake greater efforts to improve Jewish education in America.

16 The Jewish Traders' Union asks the Polish government for protection against the anti-Jewish propaganda campaign waged against Polish Jews.

17 The Citizenship Revision Bill is introduced in the Rumanian parliament, aimed mainly at Jews living in annexed provinces.

17 The World Jewish Congress demands that the League of Nations provide greater protection for national minorities.

18 The Nazis declare an anti-Jewish boycott, limited to Breslau.

20 Walter Gross, chief of the Nazi Racial Bureau, announces the start of a nationwide racial propaganda campaign.

25 The United States Treasury Department announces agreements facilitating trade relations with Germany.

26 Arturo Toscanini conducts the first Israel Philharmonic Orchestra concert in Tel Aviv.

27 The Basque autonomous government seizes a German vessel, the *Palos*, in Spanish waters thus precipitating a crisis. The ship is released on December 29.

27 Britain and France agree on a non-intervention policy in the Spanish civil war.

28 The Museum of Jewish Antiquities opens in Paris.

30 *Agudas Yisroel* announces that it will support administrators of the Warsaw Jewish community that the Polish government appointed.

1937

JANUARY

1 The Social Security goes into effect throughout the United States.

1 The Polish anti-*shechita* law is actualized.

1 Most Jewish bakers go out of business because of the Polish Bakeries Mechanization Law.

1 Rumanian police raid the headquarters of the Zionist Organization, the KKL, and the Palestine Foundation Fund and seize all records and collection boxes.

1 All German Jewish-owned employment agencies are ordered closed.

1 The archbishop of Canterbury's New Year message attacks antisemitism.

2 An Anglo-Italian Mediterranean Agreement signed in Rome.

2 The World Executive of the HA-ZACH in London, declares "war" on the Jewish Agency, claiming that the Revisionists are being short-changed of immigration certificates to Palestine.

3 The French High Commissioner in Syria, Comte de Martel, restores the Lebanese constitution.

4 Polish universities reopen amid new *Endek* anti-Jewish riots.

5 Belgium introduces the Foreign Enlistment Law to prevent Belgian recruitment in the Spanish civil war.

5 *Kibbutz* Sedeh Nahum is established in Beth-Shean Valley.

6 The Zionist Organization in Poland votes to support the Polish Socialist parties in future elections.

6 The U.S. Congress passes an arms embargo against Spain.

7 Poland and the Free City of Danzig agree to prolong their 1933 harbor agreement through the end of 1939.

7 The heiress to the Dutch throne, Princess Juliana, is wed to Prince Bernhard.

9 Barracks for German troops in Spanish Morocco will be provided by General Franco, as a reward for Nazi help in the Fascist cause during the civil war.

10 The Polish government dissolves the Warsaw Jewish *kehilla*.

10 *Wehrmacht* detachments arrive at Spanish Tetuan to train and assist General Franco's Fascist forces.

11 Violent outbursts of anti-Jewish speeches mark the opening of the Polish *sejm*.

11 The Jewish Agency and *Haavara* announce the establishment of the Palestine Agricultural Settlement Association, Ltd. with an initial capital of LP50,000.

12 The Grand Mufti of Jerusalem, Haj Amin al Husseini, testifies before the Peel Commission.

12 Dr. Malan, leader of the Nationalist opposition in the South African National Assembly, demands an immediate stop to Jewish immigration.

12/14 Polish *sejm* members verbally attack Jews and Jewish interests.

13 Bavarian Ministry of Education prohibits all courses taught in Hebrew.

13 The American Jewish Congress protests the Polish emigration policy.

13 Goering arrives in Rome on a state visit.

15 The Schuschnigg government proclaims amnesty granted to Austrian Nazis.

15 The Budapest Jewish Community Council votes to expand its community programs. Its main goals are to build new synagogues, hospitals, and religious education centers.

15 The Joint Foreign Committee of the Board of Deputies of British Jews expresses great concern over Polish Jews' economic situation.

16 The *Gestapo* orders all Jewish youth organizations in Germany dissolved.

16 The French government passes over the idea to resettle Jewish refugees in Madagascar and French Guiana.

16 Germany prohibits foreign warships from free passage through the Kiel Canal.

17 *Il Popolo di Roma* lauds Jewish achievements in Palestine and contributions to world civilization.

18 The Polish Supreme Court rules that distributing leaflets calling for an anti-Jewish boycott is legal, since by themselves the leaflets don't threaten public order.

18 Chile passes anti-Communist legislation.

19 The Scandinavian Conference of Rabbis votes to coordinate activities on behalf of Jewish refugees from Germany.

20 Franklin Delano Roosevelt is inaugurated for a second term as President of the United States.

21 Arab terrorists assassinate the Arab mayor of Haifa.

22 All German citizens are asked not to patronize Jewish doctors.

23 The first eight of the sixty-two volumes of the Babylonian *Talmud* translated into English are published under the editorial direction of Rabbi Isidor Epstein.

23 The second Stalinist trial opens in Moscow. Thirteen of the fifteen "counterrevolutionaries" receive death sentence.

24 Goering orders that Heydrich organize emigration of those Jews still remaining in Germany.

24 The Rumanian Ministry of the Interior orders the Zionist Jewish State Party dissolved.

24 Yugoslavia and Bulgaria sign a perpetual peace treaty.

25 Brazilian authorities order eighty German Jews residing in Brazil on tourist visas deported.

25 The Anglo-Egyptian Union is established.

27 Representatives of refugee committees from Austria, Czechoslovakia, England, France, Holland, Italy, Yugoslavia, the JDC, the Jewish Colonization Association, and HICEM meet in Vienna.

27 Austria and Germany sign a new trade agreement.

28 The South African House of Assembly passes a bill regulating the immigration quota for non-British foreigners.

28 A temporary truce is formed between the Nationalist and Communist forces in China, uniting them against a common enemy, the Japanese.

29 An editorial in *Robotnik*, organ of the PPS, accuses the Polish government of encouraging *Endek* students in their anti-Jewish drive.

30 The Peel Commission returns to England.

31 American Jewish organizations in a conference called by the American Jewish Congress, protest Poland's attitude towards its Jewish citizens.

31 The Danzig Senate creates a *Gestapo*-like secret police.

FEBRUARY

1 The Aliens Act restricts Jewish immigration to South Africa more than ever.

1 The Nazis issue a decree prohibiting Germans from accepting any form of Nobel prize.

2 A conference of the Jewish Emigration Aid Society opens in Warsaw, resolving that Jews must ignore all talk of mass emigration.

4 President Roosevelt begins his effort to "pack" the Supreme Court.

5 Turkish Constitution amended by *Kamusay*, the Grand National Assembly.

7 NARA leader Boleslaw Piasecki calls for a Polish totalitarian regime based on the Nazi model.

8 End of Shensi (Communist) revolt in China.

9 Jewish students at the University of Vilna launch a twenty-four hour strike against mistreatment by members of the Polish faculty and student body.

9 Italy assists Franco's forces in the Spanish civil war.

10 The Union of Polish Swimming Clubs rejects a proposal to expel all Jewish clubs from membership.

10 The Nazis close all Catholic schools in Bavaria.

11 The Peel Commission hears testimony from members of the British parliament during its first London session; Jabotinsky testifies before the Commission, demanding "a Jewish state, now!"

14 South Africa passes restrictive immigrant regulations.

14 Malaga falls to Spanish Nationalist forces.

15 A virtual "ghetto" is introduced at the University of Vilna.

15/18 A conference of Balkan states held in Athens.

16/22 Field Marshal Hermann Goering visits Poland.

18   Under the new German conscription law, half and quarter Jews will be eligible for military and labor service.

18   The Czechoslovakian government signs an agreement with Sudeten Germans guaranteeing them broader minority rights.

19   Unrest occurs in Ethiopia: An assassination attempt on Italian Viceroy General Rodolfo Graziani in Addis Ababa leads to widespread arrests and executions.

20/21   The fourth annual observance of Brotherhood Day is held in the United States.

21   Leonard Montefiore, president of the Anglo-Jewish Association, charges that Nazi Germany is spreading antisemitic and racial propaganda throughout Europe.

26   *Hagana* representative Feivel Polkes arrives in Berlin to talk with the *Gestapo* regarding German Jewish emigration to Palestine.

27   An outbreak of anti-Jewish violence, on *Cuzist* instigation, occurs in Rumanian Moldavia.

27   The French government establishes a defense ministry.

MARCH

1   *Oboz Zjednoczenia Narodowego* [OZN], the Camp of National Unity, a paramilitary, antisemitic organization, is created by Colonel Adam Koc in Poland. The OZN is under the official tutelage of Polish President Ignaci Moscicki and Minister of Defense, Marshal Eduard Rydz-Smigly.

1   The Central Committee for the Relief and Reconstruction of the Jews in Germany publishes a special report on the conditions and developments in the Jewish communities during 1936.

2   The Association of Polish Electricians adopts a resolution barring Jews and persons of Jewish descent from membership.

3   A bill to regulate the legal profession is introduced by the Polish government; if adopted, the bill would affect thousands of Polish Jews.

4   Pogrom in Sokolow-Podliaski {P}: Jewish communal institutions are vandalized and windows in hundreds of Jewish homes smashed.

5   Nazis announce that the German film industry is now completely cleansed of Jews.

5   Ferenc Szalasi, leader of the pro-Nazi Fascist party in Hungary, is arrested and charged with conspiracy.

8 The *Va'ad Leumi* calls upon Jews to reject provocations and anti-Arab acts of revenge.

14 A papal encyclical, *Mit Brennender Sorge* (With Burning Sorrow), is published, dealing with the condition of the Catholic Church in Germany, and condemning Nazi racism.

15 A mass anti-Nazi rally sponsored by the American Jewish Congress and the Jewish Labor Committee is held in New York's Madison Square Garden. Mayor Fiorello LaGuardia brands Nazism "the gravest menace to peace, civilization, and democracy."

17 The *Va'ad Leumi* blames the Mandatory administration for the worsening security in Palestine because it has not pursued Arab terrorist bands with sufficient vigor.

19 In a radio address, President Mosciczki makes it clear that the Polish government fully supports the OZN.

20 British officials enact additional emergency measures in Palestine.

21 The Polish *sejm* passes a law prohibiting Jews from manufacturing, distributing, or selling Catholic religious paraphernalia.

21 The Nansen Assistance Organization is established in Oslo. Its aim is to aid victims of Nazism and Fascism and protect the rights of stateless individuals.

22 The Jewish community of Plock {P}, celebrates its 700th anniversary.

22 Jews in Germany who have converted to Christianity are expelled from the League of Saint Paul, an organization originally established for and by baptized Jews.

25 Italy and Yugoslavia sign a five-year agreement for mutual assistance.

APRIL

1 The Jewish community in Zurich celebrates its seventy-fifth anniversary.

2 The tiny, newly established Jewish community in Tirana, Albania is officially recognized by the Albanian government.

2 The South African government bans foreigners from participating in political activities.

9 The *Gestapo* seizes all *B'nai B'rith* lodges in Germany.

9 Bet Yosef, a *moshav* in the Beth Shean Valley, is built under Kurdistani Jewish direction as a "tower and stockade" settlement.

11 A new order from the Ministry of the Interior deprives all German Jews from municipal citizenship.

13 The *Gestapo* bans all Jewish public meetings for sixty days, with the exception of synagogue service.

13 Fifteen "illegal" immigrants reach Palestine, arriving in a small motor-boat.

13 Dr. E. Moses, member of the *Bene Israel* Jewish community, is elected mayor of Bombay.

15 The Jewish Writers Club, the *Yiddish* Culture Society, and the Workmen's Circle, jointly establish a *Yiddish Buch Gezelschaft* (Yiddish Book Company).

16 Swiss authorities state that they refuse to grant permanent residential permits to German Jewish refugees to avoid flooding the labor market.

16 An Argentine section is created in the Jewish Agency for Palestine.

20 Franco declares Spain a totalitarian state and assumes dictatorial powers.

20 Colonel Jan Kowalewski, official spokesman for OZN, declares that the camp is not antisemitic, but will strive for an organic solution of the Jewish problem.

20 The International Order of *B'nai B'rith* is banned throughout Germany.

22 Von Schuschnigg-Mussolini meeting in Venice: Mussolini suggests that the Austrian government make friendly overtures to the Nazis, and not enter into a mutual treaty with Czechoslovakia.

24 Belgium is released from Locarno Treaty obligations.

25 Hebrew Sheltering and Immigrant Aid Society [HIAS] holds its annual conference in New York.

26 New York's *Yiddish* newspaper, the *Jewish Daily Forward*, celebrates its fortieth anniversary.

27 *Irgun-B* splits: part of the organization returns to the *Hagana*, the remainder establishes the *Irgun Zvai Leumi* [IZL].

27 Guernica, a small village in the Spanish province of Basque, is bombed by the *Legion Kondor*, a special German *Luftwaffe* unit helping Franco's forces during the civil war; 1,654 civilians are machine-gunned to death and 889 are wounded. The town is obliterated during the three-and-a-half hour attack.

28   The Bakers union of Vilna rejects the "aryan paragraph" resolution proposed by some of its Christian members.

MAY

1   President Roosevelt signs the third U.S. Neutrality Act.

2   New York's mayor, Fiorello LaGuardia, receives the American Hebrew Medal.

3   The Union of Orthodox Rabbis, at its annual convention in Atlantic City, New Jersey, makes a strong appeal to allow more Jewish refugees into the United States.

4   A group of Belgian pro-Nazi diamond dealers demand that the Belgian government remove all Jews from the diamond industry.

5   The British Colonial Office announces the Peel Commission hearings concluded.

6   Hindenburg disaster: The German dirigible explodes during landing at Lakehurst, New Jersey, killing thirty-six people.

9   A Nazi decree excludes German Jews from acquiring university degrees.

9   The Union of Polish Physicians adopts the aryan paragraph; no Jew is to be admitted to medical school. The Union of Polish Lawyers demands a *numerus clausus*.

9   Great Britain's *Agudas Yisroel* urges that all relief efforts in England for Polish Jews should be coordinated in England.

9   *Hadassah*, the women's Zionist organization, implores Great Britain to do nothing to infringe upon Jewish rights in Palestine.

10   Roberto Farinacci, member of the Fascist Grand Council and editor of *Il Regime Fascista*, viciously attacks world Jewry in an address before the Cremona Fascist Cultural Institution.

12   Former Hungarian prime minister Count Stephen Bethlen warns the House of Deputies that Hungary will suffer economic chaos if it initiates Nazi-like methods for treating Jews.

13   Anti-Jewish riots, assuming pogrom proportions, erupt in Brest-Litovsk (Brescz), Poland.

14   German Jews are forbidden to play music by Beethoven or Mozart during Jewish cultural concerts.

15   The Union of Rumanian Lawyers votes to bar from membership all persons with "impure" Rumanian blood.

15   The Danish Jewish community marks the twenty-fifth anniversary of King Christian X.

15   A Moslem uprising erupts in Albania.

17   The Federation of Rumanian Free Professional Associations adopts a resolution demanding removal of Jews from Rumanian professional life.

18   The Catholic archbishop of Chicago, George Cardinal Mundelein, launches a drive against the Nazi treatment of German Catholics.

19   The Association of Polish Merchants in Warsaw, resolves to introduce the aryan paragraph.

25   The second mass demonstration against anti-Jewish excesses is organized by Polish Jewry.

27   Argentinian police raid eleven Jewish schools, claiming that they were teaching communism.

28   Stanley Baldwin retires as British prime minister; Chancellor of the Exchequer Neville Chamberlain is elected leader of the Conservative Party of Britain and forms a new British cabinet.

30   Spanish government forces bomb the German battleship *Deutschland* off Ibiza: The Germans report twenty-six killed and seventy-one injured.

31   In retaliation to Spain's attack on the *Deutschland*, the German fleet bombards Almeira.

JUNE

1   *College de France* (French College) rejects a German invitation to participate in the Goettingen University bicentenary celebrations.

3   The Duke of Windsor marries Mrs. Wallis Warfield in Tours, France.

3   The International Labor Conference opens in Geneva with fifty-one countries represented.

4   Italian Chief Rabbi David Prato protests Italy's antisemitic press campaign when he meets Foreign Minister Galeazzo Ciano.

4   The Council of Polish Trade Unions protests the Brest-Litovsk pogrom.

4   The Bratislava Chamber of Commerce establishes a branch of the Prague League against Antisemitism.

5   A pro-Arab radio broadcast on WNYC nearly causes a riot in New York City.

6   The conference of the United Rumanian Jews of America condemns the Rumanian government for its anti-Jewish actions.

6   The Twenty-eighth Convention of the International Rotary opens in Nice, France.

7   Hitler bestows upon Mussolini the Grand Cross of the Order of Merit of the German Eagle.

8/9   Air raids on Madrid, Barcelona, Bilbao, and Valencia cause heavy loss of life and property.

9   The Central Committee of the Trade Unions in Poland and the Socialist press issue a manifesto against antisemitism.

10   The British Federation of Polish Relief Organizations appeals to the Polish government, demanding that it immediately restore full rights to Polish Jewry.

11   "Generals' trials," the third Stalinist purge trial, opens in Moscow. Soviet Marshall Mikhail Tukhachevsky and seven generals are found guilty of treason and condemned to death. The sentence is carried out on June 12.

12   Heydrich issues a secret directive committing Jewish "race-violators" to protective custody after they have served their prison sentences.

13   Japan announces an economic five-year plan.

13   The Swiss *Canton* of Geneva bans the Communist party.

14   A Conference of Italian Jewish leaders in Florence renounces Zionism as a political faith and pledges allegiance to Fascism.

14   The Federation of Polish Jews in America urges the federal government to fill the quota for Polish immigration.

14   The Irish constitution passed by the *Dak* (parliament).

15   The Pro-Palestine Federation of America petitions President Roosevelt to ensure that Britain does not modify the Palestine Mandate.

16   In a speech before the *sejm*, General Lucjan Zieligowski declares that "there is no place in Poland for the Jews."

16   The *Asefat ha-Nivharim* votes to increase the number of representatives by thirty.

16   The *Deutsche Volkskirche* (the German People's Church) is accredited the official Nazi church.

16   A Kurdish insurrection breaks out in Turkey.

16 New Stalinist purges are carried out in Belorussia.

16 The Polish press reports harassment and arrest of Jews in German controlled Upper Silesia.

17 Holland removes its ban on gold exports.

17 Three Soviet aviators begin a 6,000 mile arctic flight from Moscow to San Francisco, falling short of their objective after sixty-three hours because of bad weather.

19 A pogrom in Czestochowa {P} causes material damage exceeding half a million *zlotys*.

20 The Czech government institutes compulsory military training for all citizens from ages six to sixty; actual military call-up is from ages seventeen to thirty.

21 Leon Blum resigns as French prime minister. Camille Chautemps forms a Radical-Socialist government, with Blum as vice-premier.

21 The International Labor Conference opens in London.

22 The Peel Commission report is completed.

23 The Fifteenth International Congress of Pen Clubs, meeting in Paris, condemns antisemitic persecutions in central and eastern Europe.

24 A royal decree prohibits marriages, or any other conjugal relations between Italians and East-Africans (Abyssinians) in order to preserve the "racial purity" of the Italian people.

25 Most American universities and institutions of higher learning are absent from the 250th anniversary celebrations at the University of Goettingen as they protest against official German racial practices.

28 The Ninth Congress of the International Chamber of Commerce opens in Berlin.

30 *Kibbutz* Tirat Zvi is established.

30 The French legislature votes emergency powers for the Chautemps government.

JULY

1 The *Gestapo* arrest Pastor Dr. Martin Niemoeller, leader of the German Confessional (Evangelical) Church in Berlin.

2 The South-West African government prohibits political activities of non-naturalized Germans. Naturalized Germans create new party, the *Deutscher Suedwest-Bund* (the German Southwest Association), to replace the former *Deutscher Bund*.

2 American aviatrix Amelia Earhart and her copilot Frederick Noonan, on a round-the-world flight, disappear over the Pacific Ocean after suddenly losing radio contact.

4 There is an assassination attempt on the Portuguese premier, Dr. Antonio de Oliviera Salazar, in Lisbon.

5 *Kibbutz* Ein Hashofet established in the Manasseh Hills.

6 A decree is issued which forbids German Jews from studying medicine.

7 Japan invades China.

7 The Peel Commission report is published. Partition of Palestine to create separate Arab and Jewish states is proposed.

8 The Treaty of Saadabad, a non-aggression pact, is signed by Iran, Iraq, Turkey, and Afghanistan.

9 *Ha-Shomer ha-Zair* (Young Watchman) votes to reject the Peel partition plan.

9 One hundred thirty Ohio clergymen appeal to the United States government to help Polish Jewry.

10 A Franco-German trade agreement is signed in Paris.

11 The Federation of Lithuanian Jews is established in New York; Sidney Hillman is elected president.

12 The United States, Britain, and France agree to establish a permanent refugee body.

14 An army *coup* in Bolivia deposes the government of President (Colonel) David Toro.

14 The Congress of National Minorities, representing eleven different nationalities from thirteen European countries, opens in London.

15 The German-Polish Convention of May 15, 1922, which upheld the minority rights of Jews and others living in Upper Silesia, expires. The Nazis apply all anti-Jewish laws with a vengeance.

15 The Rumanian Palestine trade agreement is signed in Bucharest.

15 The American *Mizrachi* Organization adopts a resolution opposing the Peel partition plan for Palestine.

16 The Union of Polish Restauranteurs petition the government to restrict Jewish restaurant licenses.

16 The German Ministry of Education publishes new regulations regarding Jewish education in the Third *Reich*.

16 Germany announces the reconstruction of the Prussian Academy of Arts on purely National Socialist principles.

17 Britain signs bilateral naval treaties with Germany and the Soviet Union.

19 The Ettersberg concentration camp opens: its name is changed to Buchenwald on July 28.

19 An anti-Zionist demonstration takes place in Baghdad. Two Jews are killed and scores injured.

19 Germany signs a trade agreement with Nationalist Spain.

20 The British House of Lords debates the Peel Plan.

23 The Arab Higher Committee rejects the Peel Plan.

24 An order segregating Jews from aryans in German health resorts and public baths is published.

27 English refugee advocates urge the League of Nations to create a permanent body to give constructive aid to Jewish refugees.

27 U.S. Congressman Leon Sacks (D-Pennsylvania) introduces a resolution condemning the Peel partition plan.

27 Violence aimed at Jewish-owned commercial establishments breaks out in a number of localities in Upper Silesia.

27 The ritual murder trial of five Jews begins in Bamberg, Germany. Nazis resurrect the case of an alleged murder that took place in 1929.

28 Japanese forces occupy Peking.

29 Violent anti-Jewish disorders break out in Czernowitz, Siret, and other parts of Rumania.

30 The League of Nations Permanent Mandates Commission debates the Peel partition plan for Palestine.

AUGUST

3 Italy bars foreign Jews from admittance to Italian universities and institutions of higher learning.

3 The Prague municipality installs a bronze statue of Moses in front of the world-famous *Altneu* Synagogue.

3/16 The Twentieth World Zionist Congress in Zurich addresses the question of partitioning Palestine as proposed by the Peel Commission.

4 Most Jewish teachers are barred from teaching in Italian schools.

4 Anti-Jewish disorders break out in Hindenburg and Ratibor, two small towns in German Upper Silesia.

5 Rumanian antisemites declare an anti-Jewish boycott.

7 Clashes between Blackshirts and anti-Fascists break out in front of the Johannesburg Town Hall.

8 The World Zionist Congress debates Palestinian partition: Weizmann and Ben-Gurion defend the plan.

8 The Rumanian government prohibits the singing of the Zionist national anthem, *Hatikvah*, in Jewish schools.

10 Forty-one U.S. Congressmen sign a resolution requesting that Britain reconsider partitioning Palestine.

11 Iraqi strongman Bakr Sidqi is assassinated.

12 Swiss Nazis attack delegates to the Twentieth World Zionist Congress as they walk along Zurich streets leading to the *Stadttheater*, where the Zionist convention is held.

13 The *Reich* Ministry of Education orders all Germans knowing foreign languages to register.

13 A military *coup d'etat* replaces the Don Rafael Franco government in Asuncion, Paraguay.

18 The Rumanian Orthodox Church exhorts the Rumanian people to fight the "Jewish parasite."

18/24 The world congress of *Agudas Yisroel* opens in Marienbad, Czechoslovakia. A resolution unanimously rejects a Jewish state in Palestine.

19 Jews in Germany may only patronize Jewish owned bookstores, while owners are forbidden to sell works by aryan authors.

22 The Jewish Agency for Palestine adopts a resolution accepting the Peel Plan, while also providing for negotiations with Arabs for a peaceful solution short of partition.

23 The League of Nations Permanent Mandates Committee votes to neither accept nor reject the Peel Plan, pending further clarification of national boundaries in the event of Palestine's partition.

23 The Radical Peasant Party criticizes Rumanian Orthodox Church antisemitism.

23/25 The second annual conference of the World Federation of Polish Jews Abroad opens in Antwerp, dealing with antisemitism in Poland, and the Polish government's failure to address the problem.

25 The Dublin *Standard*, a leading Irish Catholic journal, condemns Jewish persecution in Germany.

26 Jan Ignaz Paderewski, the Polish Republic's first president, issues a manifesto attacking the new Polish government's fascist tendencies; Polish police seize the manifesto and it is banned by press censors.

27 The annual congress of the World ORT Union is held in Paris.

29 China and the Soviet Union sign a nonaggression treaty.

SEPTEMBER

3 Arab gangs attack Jewish worshipers returning from the Western Wall in Jerusalem.

3 The Revisionist sponsored ship *Af-al-Pi* lands with fifty-one "illegal" immigrants aboard.

4 Nazis order all Rotary Club chapters in Germany to dissolve.

4/10 The Mediterranean Anti-piracy Conference is held in Nyon {F}, where its attendees set up a system of international anti-piracy patrols.

7 The Second World Conference of the Society of Friends condemns Nazi antisemitism.

8 Attendees of the Pan-Arab Conference held at Bludan, Syria reject the Peel Plan, but endorse Palestinian Arabs' accelerated effort to boycott Jewish goods and enterprises.

8 Rumania announces revision of naturalization and citizenship laws.

9 Sachsenburg concentration camp is closed.

12 The Rumanian National Soldiers Front calls on Rumanians to deal with the "Jewish plot."

12 General Gonzalo Quiepo De Llano delivers an antisemitic speech over the Nationalist radio station in Seville.

13 Polish antisemitic groups declare an anti-Jewish month.

14 Thomas G. Masaryk, the founder of the Czechoslovak Republic, dies at age eighty-seven.

15 The Union of German Jewish War Veterans holds a memorial service for the 12,000 Jewish soldiers killed in World War I.

16 A decree against broadcast of abusive remarks against any race, religion, or creed is promulgated in Canada.

20 An Argentinian court sentences Nazi agent Wilhelm Wilke to prison for attacking Jews.

21 Poland declares its support for the Palestine partition proposal, provided that the Jewish state would be large enough to absorb a mass Jewish immigration.

24 The Dutch government begins extending compulsory military service from five to eleven months, in order to increase its war preparedness.

25/28 Mussolini and Hitler meet in Berlin.

26 British commissioner for the Galilee, Louis Andrews, is murdered by Arab terrorists.

27 The Rumanian government prohibits Zionist fundraising collections.

OCTOBER

1 The Arab Higher Committee is banned by the British administration in Palestine.

4 The Mufti of Jerusalem, Amin al-Huseini, flees Palestine for Lebanon.

5 The rector at the Polytechnic Institute of Warsaw orders "ghetto benches" instituted for Jewish students.

5 English Jewry proclaim a "day of mourning," sympathizing with suffering Jews in Poland.

5 Roosevelt delivers a major speech in Chicago, warning that isolationism will not protect America if aggression continues to go unchecked.

8 Jewish philanthropic organizations in Berlin begin a fundraising campaign for winter relief.

13 Germany guarantees Belgian independence.

14 A train carrying British troops is wrecked by Arab terrorist gangs in Palestine. Nine Arabs are killed during the ensuing battle.

15 The Jewish Economic Council declares that "Polish Jews belong on Polish soil" and strongly protests government proposals for mass emigration of Polish Jewry.

16 *A Magyar Nemzeti Szocialista Part* (The Hungarian National Socialist Party) forms in Hungary.

16 Czech police suppress a Sudeten German party rally at Teplitz: Party leader Konrad Henlein demands ethnic German autonomy within Czechoslovakian borders.

17 The Council of Federations and Welfare Fund meets in Pittsburgh to define the aims of the JDC.

20 Ground-breaking ceremonies are held for the *Hadassah* Hospital and Medical Center on Mount Scopus, Jerusalem.

20 Jewish market stalls and shops in Danzig are picketed by black-shirted Nazi police.

20 Two outstanding American Jewish leaders pass away: Rabbi Henry Pereira Mendes, dean of the American rabbinate, and Felix M. Warburg, philanthropist, and communal leader.

20/27 Polish Jewry, angry about anti-Jewish outbursts in the Polish universities, proclaim "A Week for Jewish Students."

21 The Danzig Catholic Center Party is eliminated and Nazis take absolute control over the Free City.

21 The Universalist General Convention condemns Nazi antisemitism.

22 TOZ describes the appalling condition of Polish Jewry.

23 Nazis and Nazi sympathizers stage a massive pogrom in Danzig.

23 The Humanities faculty at the University of Warsaw objects to "ghetto benches."

27 The Balfour Forest in the Nazareth Hills with some 50,000 trees planted by the KKL, is destroyed by Arabs: *Va'ad Leumi*, even in light of the numerous Arab attacks on various parts of the *Yishuv*, is against retaliatory attacks.

27 Jews are barred from public bathhouses in Danzig, except for specified hours, one day a week.

27 *Hadassah* holds a convention in Atlantic City, New Jersey to celebrate its 25th anniversary. Some 2,500 delegates from across the United States and Canada attend, demanding that Britain strictly follow its mandate over an undivided Palestine.

28 The Spanish Loyalist government escapes to Barcelona.

29 The League of Nations High Commissioner in Danzig declares that he is powerless to act in the Free City's internal affairs.

NOVEMBER

3 The Danzig Senate isolates Jewish merchants and confiscates their bank deposits, valued at some 2,000,000 *gulden*. The seizure is justified under alleged charges of tax evasion.

3 Signatories to the 1922 Nine Power Treaty meet in Brussels to work out a plan to end hostilities between China and Japan.

5 Hitler outlines secret plans for European domination during the *Hosbach* Conference, and tells OKW that he intends to destroy Czechoslovakia.

5 Germany and Poland sign an agreement regarding treatment of each other's minorities.

6 Italy joins the German-Japanese Anti-Comintern Pact.

8 *Der Ewige Jude* (The Eternal Jew), an anti-Jewish exposition sponsored by Goebbels' Propaganda Ministry, opens in Munich under the direction of Julius Streicher. The exhibit closes on February 4, 1938.

9 Japanese forces occupy Shanghai.

9 Five settlers are killed in an Arab terrorist attack on Kiryat Anavim, a village in the Jerusalem hills.

10 A British court martial is established to deal with acts of terrorism in Palestine.

10 President Vargas dissolves the Brazilian government; the new constitution calls for a corporate (Fascist) state.

12 The All-Polish Congress of Christian Merchants adopts a resolution on the "Polonization" of commerce.

13 *Bund*, the Jewish Socialist Party, celebrates the 40th anniversary of its founding in Poland.

14 First official anti-Arab operation of the "independent" IZL.

15 Jewish Agency for Palestine donates 2,000 Syrian pounds to aid flood victims in Syria.

16 The Migration Committee of the International Labor Office convenes in Geneva, Switzerland. A proposal by the Polish government for the emigration of 80,000 Polish Jews annually is on its agenda.

17 The Night of Stars benefit at Madison Square Garden raises $100,000 for the United Palestine Appeal.

17 Antisemitic parties join in a short-lived coalition to reelect Stepan Tatarescu prime minister of Rumania. The coalition's failure leads to new national elections on December 20.

17/21 A meeting between Lord Halifax and Hitler attempting peaceful settlement of the Sudeten problem marks the beginning of Britain's appeasement policy.

19 Syrian Premier Jamil Bey Mardam denies allegations that Syrians are helping Palestinian rebels.

21 The Palestine Conference of Polish Jews opens in Warsaw with some 2,000 delegates attending from all of Poland, excepting Galicia.

22 The Jewish Union Society and the Christian Students Organization at London University, protest "ghetto benches" in Polish universities during a joint rally.

24 Hljamar Schacht is ousted as German minister of the economy and is replaced by Walther Funk.

25 The American Federation of Teachers assails the "ghetto benches" at Polish universities.

26 Aryanization of Jewish business begins in Danzig.

28 The Bar Association of Lublin {P} restricts the total number of Jewish lawyers to a percentage corresponding to the ratio of Jews to the total population.

29 In an attempt to counteract the widespread Polish antisemitic boycott campaign, the Jewish Merchants Union proclaims December an anti-boycott month in Poland.

29 Pro-Nazi Sudeten German deputies resign *en masse* from Czech parliament, precipitating a national crisis.

DECEMBER

1 *Maccabi* House is dedicated as the new London headquarters of the international Jewish sports organization.

1 A *Yiddish* translation of the Bible, by the late Solomom Bloomgarden (Yehoash), is published.

2 French General Brissaud Desmaillet proposes agricultural settlements for Jewish refugees in French colonies.

5 The Arab National Youth Organization threatens violence against Arab merchants who buy goods from Zionists.

5 Spanish Loyalists begin a last-ditch counteroffensive in the civil war.

6 A second antisemitic party, the Dutch People's Party, is established in Holland.

6 The American Youth Congress sends a strongly worded complaint to the Polish Ministry of Education about segregation of Jewish students in Polish academic institutions.

7 Turkey breaks its 1926 friendship treaty with Syria, perpetrating a crisis.

8 The Iron Guard announces the opening of a chain of cooperatives aiming to undersell Jewish-owned stores and force them out of business.

8 Dr. Louis Finkelstein, provost of the Jewish Theological Seminary of America, urges convocation of an international conclave of Jewish leaders to adopt and modernize *halacha* (Jewish religious law).

9 Sir Charles Teggart arrives in Palestine as assistant to the High Commissioner for security affairs.

11 Italy withdraws from the League of Nations.

12 *Yeshiva* University celebrates its 50th anniversary.

12 *Panay* incident: Japanese forces sink a U.S. gunboat in China's Yangtze River. Japan apologizes and agrees to pay indemnity.

12 In the first elections to the Supreme Soviet of the USSR, Communists receive 98 percent of the votes.

13 Nanking, the Chinese Nationalist capital, falls to the Japanese.

14 Himmler orders all those defined as "asocials" incarcerated in concentration camps.

14 Violent anti-Jewish riots break out in Radauti, Bukovina.

15 Polish bishops call for segregation of Jewish students in Polish elementary schools.

15 A verbal attack against Jews is made by Nazi members of the Dutch parliament.

16 The Jewish Artisans School in Warsaw marks its fiftieth anniversary.

19 The American Committee on Religious Rights and Minorities, outraged by the way Polish Jews are treated, asks that the Polish government take immediate steps to alleviate existing conditions.

19 The rector of Yugoslavia's Zagreb University rejects students' demands for "ghetto benches."

20 The Jewish Party in Rumania fails to win a single seat during elections for the country's new parliament.

21 Britain officially repudiates the Peel Partition Plan.

28 Octavian Goga and Alexander Cuza are appointed by King Carol to head a National Christian Party government. During its forty-four days in power, and under the slogan "Rumania for the Rumanians," the government issues numerous anti-Jewish decrees.

29 A Zionist Revisionist Organization in Dublin is organized under the leadership of Robert Briscoe.

1938

JANUARY

6 U.S. Secretary of State Cordell Hull announces that America cannot intervene in Rumania's internal affairs.

8 The British government indefinitely postpones the Palestine partition plan. The Woodhead Commission sent to Palestine to examine the situation.

9 A Report of the Polish Madagascar Committee is published in *Gazeta Polska*.

10 Professor Otto Warburg, scientist, communal and Zionist leader, dies.

10 The American Jewish Committee rejects Palestinian partition.

12 The *SS Poseidon* arrives in Palestine with sixty-five "illegal" immigrants.

12 The Brazilian government suspends deportation orders for 1,000 German Jewish refugees living illegally in Brazil.

13 The Rockefeller Museum for Archaeology opens in East Jerusalem.

13 A mass rally in Madison Square Garden, sponsored by the Joint Boycott Council of the American Jewish Congress and the Jewish Labor Committee, protests the Nazi rise to power in Germany five years ago.

13 The Committee for the Defense of Jews in Eastern Europe, asks the French government to ensure that the Rumanian government immediately takes steps to stop anti-Jewish excesses.

14   A Rumanian decree prohibits Jews from employing Christian female servants under forty years old.

14   Rumanian police order all Jewish libraries and Jewish-owned bookstores closed in Bessarabia.

14   The Rumanian press publishes instructions for dismissing all Jewish doctors from social insurance institutions.

16   The American Jewish Committee calls attention to the fact that Rumania has violated the Minorities Treaty.

16   The Winnipeg City Council denounces antisemitic and Fascist activities.

17   The Yugoslavian Interior Ministry announces new regulations restricting residence of foreign Jews.

17   Forty-eight American book publishers refuse to participate in the forthcoming International Congress of Book Publishers, to be held in Leipzig, Germany.

19   Ecuador's government orders the expulsion of several hundred Jewish immigrants who entered the country illegally.

19   American and European Jewish organizations submit a protest petition to the League of Nations regarding the treatment of Jews in Rumania.

21   The Goga government in Rumania passes the Citizenship Revision Law on the lines of the Nuremberg Laws: its purpose is to review and eliminate Jewish citizenship.

21   ORT transfers a majority of its activities in Russia to the government-run OZET.

25   The *Gestapo* is given the power to decide and place prisoners in "protective custody" at its own discretion.

27   Certain Jewish properties in Czernowitz are to be confiscated and transferred to public use, according to a Goga government announcement.

28   Roosevelt asks Congress for increased appropriations to strengthen the U.S. armed forces.

30   The American Jewish Congress appeals to the League of Nations to protect the rights of the Jews in Rumania.

31   A new bill totally abolishing *shechita* is introduced in Poland's *sejm*.

FEBRUARY

2 Jewish stores in Czernowitz are ordered to remain open on the Sabbath and Jewish holidays.

3 The Rumanian-Orthodox clergy is forbidden to baptize Jews who are not Rumanian citizens.

4 Joachim von Ribbentrop replaces Constantin von Neurath as German foreign minister.

4 Austrian Nazis vandalize numerous Jewish stores in the Viennese suburbs.

4 Hitler assumes complete control of the *Wehrmacht* and announces complete reorganization of the OKW.

6 Prime Minister Goga warns that Rumania will not tolerate any foreign interference in its domestic antisemitic policy.

6 The second annual Conference on Jewish Affairs is held at the Jewish Theological Seminary of America in New York.

10 The Goga government in Rumania is dissolved: The new government nullifies some anti-Jewish legislation.

12 The new Rumanian premier, Dr. Miron Christea, who is also head of the Rumanian Church, promises equal rights to all citizens.

12 The Berchtesgaden conference between von Schuschnigg and Hitler paves the way for a greater Nazi role in Austrian government and public life.

15 Polish *sejm* deputy Stanislaw Wojciechowski outlines a plan for the "polonization" of Polish industry.

16 *Informazione Diplomatica*, the organ of the Italian Foreign Ministry, suggests that the only solution to the Jewish problem is to create a Jewish state, but not in Palestine.

16 Lithuania adopts a new constitution with a clause guaranteeing equal rights to all citizens regardless of race or creed.

16 Von Schuschnigg names the virulent Nazi, Arthur Seyss-Inquart, Austrian minister of the interior.

17 The Rumanian Ministry of the Interior suspends publication of all *Yiddish* and Hebrew newspapers.

20 Anthony Eden resigns as British foreign secretary and is replaced by Edward F. L. Wood, Lord Halifax.

21 General Stanislaw Skwarczynski, one of the leaders of OZN, calls for mass Jewish emigration from Poland.

23 *Volksruf*, a violently antisemitic Austrian newspaper, begins publication.

23 Tel Aviv Port officially opens.

24 The Rumanian government ratifies a new constitution.

24 Von Schuschnigg calls for a plebiscite on Austrian independence. Nazi-instigated disturbances erupt throughout the country.

27 The first World Congress of International Youth Against Antisemitism opens in Prague.

28 *Kibbutz* Tirat Zvi beats back a major Arab attack.

28 The American Legion undertakes a nationwide campaign against the spread of the German-American Bund.

MARCH

1 High Commissioner General Sir Arthur Wauchope is replaced by Harold MacMichael.

1 *B'nai B'rith* establishes its Vocational Service Bureau.

1 Thousands of Jews are deprived of their livelihood when the Polish government revokes Jewish tobacco dealers' licenses.

2/15 A purge trial is held for veteran Bolshevik Nikolai Bukharin on trumped-up charges of espionage: Bukharin is found guilty on all counts and is executed by firing squad.

4 Hitler rejects a British offer giving Germany certain concessions in Africa.

7 The J. Dreyfus and Company investment bank, a large financial institution in Germany, is aryanized by the Nazis.

8 A two thousand-strong Nazi demonstration marches in the center of Vienna shouting anti-Jewish slogans.

11 Hitler issues an ultimatum to Austria, demanding that von Schuschnigg resign; Seyss-Inquart becomes chancellor, paving the way for a complete Nazi takeover.

12 *Anschluss (*Annexation): the *Wehrmacht* rolls into Austria unopposed.

13 The Reichstag "legalizes" *Anschluss* by passing the Law Concerning the Reunion of Austria with the Third *Reich*. Hitler, with OKW Chief General Wilhelm Keitel by his side, enters Vienna in triumph, where thousands of Austrians greet him with enthusiasm.

13 The *Gestapo* launches a reign of terror against Jews in Vienna; looting of Jewish shops and apartments is carried out on a grand scale.

13 Leon Blum begins his second term as French premier; his *Front Populaire* government lasts only to April 15.

14/30 Polish Jewry, protesting the pending anti-*shechita* bill, refrain from eating all meat except poultry, which remains unaffected by the bill.

15 Austria enacts its first anti-Jewish laws since the *Anschluss*.

15 Hitler places Hermann Goering in charge of the Austrian economy.

16 Sir Samuel Hoare, British home secretary, raises the Austrian refugee question during a cabinet meeting.

16/19 Poland sends Lithuania an ultimatum calling for an end to hostilities and restoration of diplomatic relations. Lithuania acquiesces.

18 Himmler's *Gestapo* and SD are empowered to act in Austria outside those powers enacted by law.

18 The *Gestapo* closes Jewish community offices and institutions in Vienna, arresting its officers and leaders. In addition, all Jewish organizational offices throughout Austria are ordered to close.

19 Mexico announces all American and British oil companies nationalized.

20 A transportation fund to help Jewish refugees from Europe is established by the United Hebrew Sheltering and Immigrant Aid Society [HIAS].

20 Brazilian police arrest six hundred *Integralistas* because of their involvement in an alleged plot to assassinate President Vargas.

20/21 The Polish Association of High School Teachers in Cracow, proposes a ban on Jewish teachers.

21 *Kibbutz* Hanitah is established in the Western Upper Galilee.

21 Lichtenburg concentration camp, near Prettin (Torgau), reopens.

22 On the first full night of the settlement's existence, Arab bands attack Hanitah.

22 Britain launches a concerted drive against Jewish "illegal" immigrants to Palestine.

23 The French government announces a plan to permit legalized residence for illegal Jewish refugees who become farmers.

24 The Rumanian Agriculture Ministry bans *shechita*.

24 The U.S. State Department proposes to create a committee to help resettle German and Austrian refugees.

25 Belgium's *Rexist* party calls for an anti-Jewish boycott.

25 *Sejm* adopts a bill amending the 1936 *shechita* law and thus completely outlaws the practice of Jewish ritual slaughter. *Sejm* also adopts a bill allowing Polish-Jewish citizens from Austria to reenter Poland.

26 Jewish professors and instructors are dismissed from Austrian universities.

26 Jews of Frauenkirchen are forced to "contribute" RM80,000 to the local Austrian Nazi treasury.

28 Law Regarding the Legal Status of Jewish Communities, places German Jewry outside the law.

28 Berlin Jewish community loses its incorporated status.

28 Hitler gives conduct lessons to leaders of the Sudeten German Party in Czechoslovakia.

29 The Spanish civil war ends.

31 Austria adopts the Law for the Exclusion of Jews from the Professions.

31 *Sejm* passes the Expatriots Law which cancels citizenship for Polish nationals living abroad, unless their passports are checked and stamped by Polish consular officials before the end of October.

31 The Danzig Senate orders segregation in the Free City's resorts.

APRIL

1 A number of Austrian Jews are sent to Dachau.

1 Jewish patients in Danzig are barred from public hospitals and welfare institutions; all Jewish physicians and nurses are dismissed.

5/6 A conference of Scandinavian foreign ministers on the development of a common defense policy ends in utter failure.

7 A Hungarian law to become effective June 28 reduces the number of Jews in business to twenty percent over five years.

8 Eduard Daladier forms a new French government.

8 The Rothschild Bank is aryanized and control is taken over by the Austrian Credit Institute.

9 All Jewish professors are summarily dismissed from Austrian universities.

10 Nazis hold a referendum in Austria to legalize the *Anschluss*; Austrian Jews are excluded from voting in a plebiscite on the basis of the Nuremberg Laws.

10 After an eighteen year lapse, Poland resumes diplomatic and economic relations with Lithuania.

11 Bulgaria outlaws the *Ratnizi*, the Bulgarian Nazi party.

15 All Jewish doctors are dismissed by the Danzig Senate from hospitals, clinics, health, and welfare institutions.

16 An Anglo-Italian pact is signed: Britain is to recognize Italian sovereignty over Ethiopia; Italy is to stop meddling and spreading propaganda in the Near East, and withdraw its troops from Spain at the conclusion of the civil war.

17 The Freeland League for Jewish Territorial Organization proposes a Jewish settlement in the Kimberleys, Australia.

17 An IZL activist throws a bomb into an Arab coffee house in Haifa: one Arab is killed and six are injured.

17 A Fascist and Iron Guard *coup* attempt is smashed by the Rumanian government and many instigators are arrested.

19 The *Gestapo* confiscates the lodges of the Independent Order of *B'nai B'rith* in Germany.

19 All remaining Austrian Jewish banks are aryanized.

21 Jewish organizations protest a newly enacted Hungarian *numerus clausus*.

22 Nazis publish a law making it illegal for non-Jews to help conceal Jewish holdings.

24 Polish Vice-Premier and Minister of Finance Eugene Kwiatkowski demands that all non-Polish elements be eliminated from the country economically and physically.

24 The Sudeten German Party Congress at Karlsbad demands full autonomy for the Sudeten Germans.

25 An Anglo-Irish agreement is signed in London.

25 Anti-Jewish riots in Theusing are perpetrated by Nazis.

26 Nazis publish a law requiring the registration of all assets over 5,000 *Reichsmark* belonging to German Jews, whether held in banks in Germany or abroad. Only American and British Jews residing in Germany are exempted.

27 The Woodhead Commission arrives in Palestine to study the possibility of partition.

28 Anti-Jewish demonstrations take place in Cairo and Alexandria.

MAY

1 The Syrian parliament adopts a resolution protesting resurrection of the Peel partition plan for Palestine.

2 Jewish community offices in Vienna are allowed to reopen under *Gestapo* order.

2 The rights of refugees living in France are severely restricted by the latest French decree.

3 Flossenburg concentration camp opens.

3/9 Hitler pays a state visit to Mussolini in Rome.

4 A government law goes into effect for the Regulation of the Structure of the Legal Profession in Poland.

4 The Council of Jewish Organizations in Belgium announces that a central Jewish representative body will coordinate defenses against economic and social discrimination.

5 In line with the Nuremberg doctrine, German firms in Denmark begin discharging their Jewish employees.

6 Brazil allows illegal immigrants, mostly refugees from Germany, to legalize their status.

7 Octavian Goga, former premier of Rumania, dies from a stroke.

10 *Kibbutz* Hanitah repels an Arab attack.

10 Argentina, Brazil, and Chile agree on a common policy to combat Nazi and Fascist influences.

11 A *coup* against the Vargas government in Brazil fails. A government decree places all schools operated by foreign organizations under close supervision.

12 The South American Pro-Palestine Congress urges Britain to increase Jewish immigration to Palestine.

13 A major anti-partition demonstration takes place in Beirut, Lebanon.

13 Egyptian police prevent an attack by Moslem students of *Al-Azhar* University on *Haret El-Yahud*, the Jewish quarter of Cairo.

15 The League of Nations approves a special report on aid to refugees from Germany and Austria.

16 The Woodhead Commission begins collecting Jewish testimony.

16 The second *Sephardic* World Conference in Amsterdam decides to establish a *Sephardic* Rabbinical Seminary in Jerusalem.

17 Finland and Sweden recognize Italian sovereignty over Italian East Africa.

17 The Czech government confiscates the two Nazi-run newspapers, *Die Rundschau* and *F.S.*, published by the Henlein Sudeten German parties.

17 The United States Congress passes the Naval Expansion Act, appropriating funds for a two-ocean navy.

18 Arabs destroy a large citrus grove at Hadera.

19 Belgian *Katholik Bureau voor Israel* (Catholic Bureau for Israel), an organization devoted to fighting antisemitism, discontinues its activities.

19 Britain and France reject Hitler's demands from Czechoslovakia.

20 Operation *Fall Gruen:* Hitler instructs his generals to draft plans for a swift attack on Czechoslovakia.

20 In response to Nazi belligerent acts the Czechoslovakian government orders partial mobilization.

20 PPS adopts a platform plank regarding Jewish emigration from Poland.

21 Austrian Nazis plunder three synagogues in the Viennese Jewish quarter.

22 OZN adopts a thirteen-point plan to increase Jewish emigration from Poland.

22 JDC reports that it is spending $1,000 a day for emergency aid to Jews in Austria.

24 Nuremberg Laws are officially introduced in Austria: Jewish books, anti-Nazi, and those not favoring Nazi ideology are purged from library and bookstore shelves in Vienna.

24 The Hungarian Senate adopts an anti-Jewish bill.

25/29 The thirty-fourth World Eucharistic Congress opens in Budapest, attended by some 200,000 Catholics from all over the world.

26 The House Un-American Activities Committee [HUAC], to investigate activities of the right and left, is established.

26 The General Assembly of the Church of Scotland adopts a resolution condemning Jewish persecution in central and eastern Europe.

29 The first Hungarian anti-Jewish law is published, limiting number of Jews in the professions and economy to twenty percent.

29 A decree is published by the Swiss Federal Council against subversive propaganda.

29 The Union of Physicians of the Polish Republic demands that the government pass a law assuring Polish doctors exclusive rights in the medical profession.

29 *Histadrut's* construction firm, *Solel Boneh,* wins a contract to build the Tegart Fence along the Palestine-Lebanon border.

30 Mass arrest of Communists in Japan: some 1,300 are incarcerated.

30 Hitler signs a revised OKW *Fall Gruen* plan of attack on Czechoslovakia.

30 Many members of Egypt's parliament urge Egyptian Jews to repudiate Zionism.

30 The *Gestapo* conducts a series of raids on Jewish cafes in Berlin and Vienna, arresting close to 2,000 Jews; some 1,000 Austrian Jews are sent to Dachau.

JUNE

1 All German Jews with previous criminal records are interned in Buchenwald, including Jews who have committed minor infractions, such as traffic violations.

1 All Jewish schools in Germany are excluded from tax exemptions.

1 Yugoslavia grants temporary refuge to forty Jewish refugees from Austria.

2 Italian Fascist leader Roberto Farinacci, arch Jew-hater, is appointed minister of state.

2/22 The International Labor Conference meets at Geneva.

3 The Sunday Rest Law, designed to eliminate Jewish bakeries in Poland goes into effect.

3 Shlomo Ben-Yosef receives the death sentence from a British court for firing on an Arab bus in Rosh-Pina.

5 Captain Orde Charles Wingate suggests establishment of a joint British-Jewish special unit to fight Arab marauders.

7 Estonia and Latvia sign non-aggression treaties with Germany.

9 Munich's synagogue is vandalized and destroyed.

9 The Australian government agrees to establish a quota of 300 landing permits per month for German and Austrian Jews.

12 Mutual Aid Association of Polish universities calls for a *numerus nullus*.

13 The General Jewish Council is formed by the American Jewish Committee, *B'nai B'rith*, and the Jewish Labor Committee; its main agenda is to safeguard Jewish rights worldwide.

13 The State Council on Health proposes a bill that would restrict medical practice to Poles.

14 Jewish or partially Jewish-owned factories within the *Reich* must be identified and registered according to a published German ministry of the interior decree.

15 *Juni Aktion* (June Operation), sends some 1,500 German Jews to concentration camps.

17 British army Captain Orde Wingate leads Special Night Squads made up of *Hagana* members in Palestine.

19 A memorial monument commemorating 8,000 American, British, and French Jews killed during World War I is unveiled near Verdun by General Andre Weiller.

20 German Jews are no longer permitted to work in the stock and commodity exchanges.

20 An International Red Cross Conference opens in London with 600 delegates from fifty-eight states of the sixty-four signatories of the Geneva Convention attending.

20 The Woodhead Commission holds its first public hearing; Professor Benjamin Akzin, acting president of the New Zionist Organization, is the first to testify.

21 A U.S. Federal Grand Jury indicts sixteen men and two women for conspiracy and espionage.

21 The Jewish Manual Training School in Berlin is vandalized by Nazi hooligans.

21/22 The Scandinavian Intergovernmental Conference discusses collaborative actions to solve the refugee problem during the Evian conference.

22 American boxer Joe Louis beats German boxer Max Schmeling during a match in New York City.

22   In testimony before the Woodhead Commission, the World State Volunteers urge the establishment of an Arab state in both Palestine and Trans-Jordan, with the Jews given a minority status.

22   The International Labor Conference in Geneva condemns discrimination against workers because of religion or race.

23   Three Jewish youngsters from Givat Ada, in the Plain of Sharon, are kidnapped by an Arab band: their fate is unknown.

23   The Anti-Jewish boycott is renewed in Tangier, Spanish Morocco.

25   Terrorist outrages continue in Palestine. Sir Charles Tegart, completing his six-month Palestinian mission, will evaluate and report on the outcome of his review of Palestine's security needs.

26   Nazis in Austria order all non-aryans dismissed from all Jewish-owned firms and close all Viennese parks to Jews. Jewish school children are completely segregated from non-Jews in all Austrian schools.

27   Congress passes the U.S. Fair Labor Standards Act.

27/28   The second completion of the *Shas* (Talmud study), via an international *Daf Yomi* (daily page), is celebrated at the world-famous Lublin, Poland *Yeshiva*.

28   Germany and Italy recognize Swiss neutrality.

29   The British hang Shlomo Ben-Yosef in Palestine.

29   Some 40,000 Austrian Jews are dismissed from their jobs.

JULY

2   The antisemitic campaign intensifies in Austria; close to 4,000 Jews are taken into "protective custody."

3/4   Both a Franco-Turkish agreement for military cooperation and a treaty of friendship are signed in Ankara, Turkey.

4   A judicial committee is appointed to investigate denationalization of Rumanian Jews.

5   Viennese trade unions are dissolved and all property and funds seized by the German Labor Front.

5   The League of Nations indicts Japan for propagating opium traffic in China.

5 A barter agreement between Italy and Japan-Manchukuo is signed in Tokyo.

6   The Law for the Alteration of Regulations of Industrial Enterprises in the Third *Reich* prohibits German Jews from operating real estate, information, loan, private security, marriage, brokerage, or administration offices; all German Jews must declare their assets and "sell" their businesses.

6/12   The Evian Conference attempts to find a solution for the refugee crisis: unwilling to specifically deal with the needs of Jewish refugees, even though Jews comprised the vast majority of those unable to find refuge, the conference ends in almost complete failure.

7   The Kenyan government agrees to admit a small group of German and Austrian Jews.

7   *Va'ad Leumi* issues a manifesto condemning violent Jewish reprisals against Arabs.

8   The Polish National Defense Council creates a new department to control raw materials.

8   On Hitler's express orders, the main synagogue in Munich is demolished.

8   Nazi ideologue, Alfred Rosenberg, proposes a plan for a Madagascar reservation for fifteen million Jews.

9   U.S. Supreme Court Justice Benjamin Cardozo dies.

10   *Va'ad Leumi* deals with the question of *havlaga,* calls for self-discipline, and rejects blind revenge.

10   Alexander Zayid, one of the founders of *Hashomer* (Watchman's) association, is murdered near *kibbutz* Alonim.

10   A Franco-German trade agreement is signed.

11   Border fighting begins between Japanese and Russian ground forces at Calchim Gol in Manchuria. The clash ends August 10.

11   Three hundred Arab marauders attack Givat Ada: four Jewish settlers are killed and one seriously injured, but the Jews manage to repulse their attackers after heavy fighting.

11   The French chamber passes a law empowering the prime minister to govern by decree in the event of war.

12   Sheikh Nuriel-Katib, an opponent of the Grand Mufti of Jerusalem, is shot dead by Arab assailants.

13   Colonial Secretary, Malcolm MacDonald, states that Britain believes that partition of Palestine would offer the best solution in solving the territorial controversy between Jews and Arabs.

14   The third regulation under the *Reich* Citizenship Law is published: all Jewish-owned businesses are advised they must register themselves.

14 *Manifesto degli scienziati razzisti* (Manifesto of the Racial Scientists) is published in Italy under the auspices of the Ministry of Popular Culture.

17 Intercession Day is observed in all synagogues and churches throughout England.

17 Five Revisionists are arrested for the alleged murders of three Arabs in Tel Aviv.

18 The Fifteenth International Geographic Congress opens in Amsterdam; 1,200 delegates from twenty-nine countries attend.

19 The New Zionist Organization in Poland launches a campaign against the *havlaga* policy in Palestine.

19/22 King George VI of Great Britain pays a state visit to France.

20 All members of the *Wehrmacht* are forbidden to live in Jewish-owned homes or apartments.

20 The Anglo-French entente is reaffirmed.

21 The Estonian government announces that it will not admit any more refugees from Germany and Austria.

23 All German Jews are ordered to apply for special identity cards obtained from the police before the year's end.

23/24 The International Peace Campaign meets in Paris and issues a resolution against the bombing of open towns.

24 A bomb thrown at Tel Aviv beach injures twenty-two Jews, while several Jews are killed and injured in other Arab attacks all over the country.

25 The fourth ordinance under the *Reich* Citizenship Act bars all Jewish doctors from medical practice beginning September 30, although they may treat Jews as only "medical orderlies."

25 Austrians celebrate the fourth anniversary of Dollfuss' assassination as a "day of national pride."

25 Antisemitic graffiti is smeared all over London.

25 Father Coughlin calls for creation of a Christian Front.

26 The House of Commons debates Czechoslovakia and the prospects of Anglo-German understanding.

26 Prime Minister Chamberlain announces that the Runciman Commission will investigate conditions in Czechoslovakia.

27 The Bishop of Chichester strongly condemns the Nazi treatment of German Jews in his first speech in the House of Lords.

28 Poland renews its claim to Czechoslovak Teschen.

28 IZL attack on the Haifa melon market kills thirty-nine Arabs.

28 Argentina announces a stricter immigration policy.

29 The Greek government suppresses an attempted revolt in Crete.

30 Germany sets up a number of *Sperrgebiete* (prohibited areas); preparations are made for the new fortifications on the western frontier.

30 Dr. Kleinlehrer, Rome correspondent for the JTA, is expelled from Italy.

31 The Bulgarian government signs a nonaggression pact with the Little Entente.

AUGUST

2 A major clash occurs between Socialists and Nazis in Zurich.

2 *Der Ewige Jude* (The Eternal Jew), an antisemitic exhibition, opens in Vienna.

3 Anti-Jewish legislation is introduced in Italy; foreign and resident Jewish students are refused admittance to all Italian schools and universities.

4 Rumania publishes the text of its new Nationalities Statute which affects close to one million Rumanian Jews.

4 The Zionist Federation of Brazil is dissolved by order of the Ministry of Justice.

5 A new Polish law regulating the cattle and meat industry virtually eliminates Jews.

6 *Difesa della Razza* (Defense of the Race), an official Italian journal on the racial question, is published.

6 British Colonial Secretary Malcolm MacDonald arrives in Palestine for meeting with Sir Harold MacMichael, High Commissioner for Palestine, to discuss the present situation.

7 The Beirut synagogue is bombed by Arab terrorists.

8 Mauthausen, the first concentration camp in Austria, starts functioning.

10 The great synagogue and Jewish community center in Nuremberg is destroyed and torn down on Nazi orders.

11 Poland withdraws its permanent delegate from the League of Nations.

12   The South African government announces that 1,059 Jews entered the Union in 1935; 3,330 in 1936; 954 in 1937; and 281 in the first half of 1938.

12   Italy defines its basis for racial policy.

13   The *Wehrmacht* undertakes large-scale army maneuvers.

14   The Lithuanian government organ, *Lietuvos Aidas*, proposes segregated bathing beaches for Jews.

16   The *Gestapo* further increases its powers in Austria by order of the Ministry of Justice.

17   Hitler orders that all *SS-Verfuegungstruppen* (field troops) be placed under the command of OKW.

17   A Nazi law is published requiring that all German Jews add the name *Israel* or *Sarah* to their given names.

19   Swiss authorities take measures to check Jewish refugees trying to enter Switzerland.

20   The Italian Fascist Party and the Catholic Action Movement reaffirm their 1931 agreement.

21   A special court is established in Vienna for the trial of former Austrian government officials, members of the "old regime."

23   The Central Jewish Relief Committee of Czechoslovakia announces completion of a camp in Moravia to house 1,800 refugees.

26   *Zentralestelle fuer Judische Auswanderung* (the Central Office for Jewish Emigration) under the direction of Adolf Eichmann is founded in Vienna.

27   The Jewish Agency's Inner Actions Committee in Jerusalem unanimously condemns violence.

27   *Generaloberst* (Colonel General) Ludwig Beck, one of the top *Wehrmacht* generals, resigns in disagreement over Hitler's Czechoslovakian policy, which he believes would lead to war.

28   Negotiations between *Hagana* and *Irgun Zvai Leumi* begin, but break off without success October 26.

SEPTEMBER

1   Jewish residents who settled in Italy after 1919 are ordered to leave the country within six months or be deported.

2   Jews are forbidden to teach in Italian schools.

3 *Keren Hayesod* holds a special conference in Antwerp. Chaim Weizmann warns that Jews will reject any solution limiting Jewish immigration to Palestine.

5 All Jews in Italy are excluded from attending public educational institutions from kindergarten through university levels.

5 Nazi-staged riots and disorders break out in the Sudetenland.

6 Congress passes the Alien Registration Act.

6/12 Hitler uses Nuremberg Nazi party rallies for vicious attacks on Benes and Czechoslovakia; demands self-determination for the Sudeten Germans.

7 All Jews naturalized in Italy after January 1, 1919 lose their citizenship.

7 France declares partial mobilization in response to Hitler's demands from Czechoslovakia.

8 An Arab band attacks Tel Aviv.

8 The British Inner Cabinet meets on the Munich crisis.

10 *Va'ad Leumi* protests the British refusal to increase Jewish defense forces in light of the present situation in Palestine.

10/13 Large-scale riots occur in Jaffa, Jerusalem, and Bethlehem.

12 Expulsion from Italy is decreed for foreign Jews.

12 British reinforcements arrive in Palestine. All police forces are placed under emergency military control.

13 Benes declares martial law in the Sudetenland.

13 A decree issued by Polish President Ignacy Moscicki dissolves *sejm* and *Senat*.

14 *Der Emes* (The Truth), a Soviet Communist *Yiddish* newspaper, ceases publication.

15 Chamberlain and Hitler meet at Berchtesgaden over the Czechoslovakian crisis.

16 Lord Runciman recommends that Czechoslovakia relinquish all border territories with a majority of ethnic Germans to Germany.

17 The Swedish Congress of Free Churches adopts a resolution calling on the government to ease entry for Jewish refugees fleeing to Sweden.

18 British and French cabinet members in London finalize an Anglo-French "appeasement" plan.

18 Sir Charles Tegart returns to Palestine to review his work as police advisor.

18 Horn, a small village in Austria, becomes *Judenrein* as all Jews are forced to leave "voluntarily."

20/21 Czech government is forced to accept the Anglo-French Plan, when bluntly told that France and Britain will not come to the country's aid if Germany attacks it.

21 A killer hurricane strikes the New England coast, killing some 700 people; property damage runs into millions of dollars.

22 A second meeting between Chamberlain and Hitler takes place in Bad Godesberg, Germany. Czech premier Milan Hodza resigns, and a new government is formed by General Jan Sirovy.

22 International Brigades withdraw from Spain.

23 Sudeten deutsche Nazis burn down the synagogue at Marienbad.

23 The Rumanian government invites the League of Nations to an inter-governmental conference especially to deal with the question of Jewish emigration.

23 The new Czech government mobilizes its army.

23 Mussolini offers to mediate the Czechoslovakian crisis; a Munich conference is called for, setting the stage for a sellout of Czechoslovakia.

24 Anti-Jewish riots break out in Strasbourg.

25 A Quebec City Council resolution asks the Canadian government to immediately take steps to prevent all Jewish immigration to Canada; *L'Action Catholique* of Quebec supports the resolution.

25/26 The French government, changing its position on the Anglo-French plan, commits itself to defend Czechoslovakia if Germany attacks it.

26 Hitler violently attacks Czechoslovakia during a speech in the Berlin *Sportspalast*.

27 The fifth ordinance under the *Reich* Citizenship Act closes legal professions to Jewish lawyers in German lands.

27 Hitler warns that he will crush Czechoslovakia if his demands are not met.

27 Danish police adopt strict measures to prevent illegal Jewish immigrants from entering the country.

27 The British Home Fleet mobilizes.

29 Munich Conference: Czechoslovakia is surrendered by Britain and France for "Peace in Our Time." An agreement dismantling sovereign

Czechoslovakia is signed by Chamberlain, Hitler, Daladier, and Mussolini the next day.

30   An Argentinian law bans schools operated by foreign organizations from teaching foreign ideologies.

30   The Alsatian Federation of Labor denounces antisemitic attacks on Jews from Alsace-Loraine.

30   A new wave of anti-Jewish riots breaks out in Poland.

30   The Nansen Office for Refugees merges with the Office of the High Commissioner for Refugees from Germany.

OCTOBER

1   German troops occupy the Sudetenland.

1   German police issue identity cards (*Kenkarte*) for all persons fifteen years old and over, including German Jews.

1   Gelnhausen, a small town in western Germany, reports it is *Judenrein*.

2   Polish troops occupy Czech Teschen.

4   On Swiss advice, the letter "J" is imprinted on the front page of German Jews' passports.

5   German Jews have their passports revoked.

6   The Fascist Grand Council passes a resolution permitting European Jews limited immigration into parts of Ethiopia.

6   Dr. Eduard Benes, President of Czechoslovakia, resigns.

6   Thousands of Jews with Polish passports who live in Germany and Austria have their passports recalled for "inspection and validation."

7   Slovakia, under Josef Tiso, and Transcarpathian Ruthenia are granted autonomy from what is left of Czechoslovakia.

7   Anti-Jewish legislation is enacted by the Fascist Grand Council in Italy; *shechita* is forbidden, though in other measures, Jewish religious freedom is guaranteed.

7   U.S. Secretary of State Cordell Hull protests Italian antisemitic legislation.

7   The first meeting of the World Interparliamentary Congress of Arab States for the Defense of Palestine opens in Cairo.

8   Hitler issues a decree establishing *Sicherheitspolizei Sonderkommandos* for use in the Czech Sudetenland.

9 The British Colonial Office announces additional troops to be despatched to Palestine. Three infantry battalions land from India.

10 The Zionist Organization of America founds the National Emergency Committee on Palestine.

10 The Argentinian government bans anti-Jewish public rallies and censors antisemitic radio broadcasts.

13 The Italian government announces that no new business licenses of any kind will be granted to Jews.

18 Martial law is instituted in Palestine.

19/20 Polish Foreign Minister Colonel Joseph Beck and King Carol of Rumania hold talks in Bucharest.

20 Persecution of Jews and anti-Nazis, especially Communists, begin in Czechoslovakia.

20 The National Fascist Party of Cuba obtains legal standing.

23 Protest meetings against British policy in Palestine are held throughout the United States.

25 German Foreign Minister von Ribbentrop raises the question of Danzig with Jozef Lipski, Polish ambassador to Nazi Germany.

26 The Rumanian government repudiates clauses from the National Minorities Treaty which relate to Jews.

28 Nazis order Jews with Polish citizenship expelled from Germany.

29 Zbaszyn incident: approximately 18,000 Polish Jews are deported from Germany and dumped on the Polish border.

29 French Premier Edouard Daladier warns that France will disintegrate if the individual rights of Christians or Jews are not defended.

30 The sixth ordinance under the *Reich* Citizenship Act bars Jews from working as patent agents.

30 Polish-Jewish organizations convene in a pro-Palestine congress.

30 The "Invasion from Mars" radio play, narrated by Orson Welles, drives thousands of American listeners into panic; many people think that Martians have landed on Earth.

31 The *Yishuv* declares "Jewish Defense Day"; a show of unity is observed throughout Jewish Palestine.

NOVEMBER

2 Hungary occupies and annexes southern Slovakia.

3 *Der Israelit*, organ of the *Agudas Yisroel* in Germany, ceases publication.

5 Arabs call off a general strike. Due to strong British military measures, the Palestine situation is improving.

6 Herschel Grynszpan assassinates Ernst von Rath, secretary of the German embassy in Paris, to protest his parents' deportation to Zbaszyn as well as Nazi persecution of Jews.

6 Poland holds general elections: OZN is declared the victor.

6 Two Jewish senators and five Jewish *sejm* deputies are elected to the Polish legislature.

7 Nazis order all German Jewish publications, publishing houses, and bookstores to close.

9 The Woodhead Commission scuttles the Palestine partition plan, suggesting three-way negotiations in London in its stead.

9 Hitler authorizes Goering to deal with all Jewish political affairs.

9 Britain announces its intent to invite neighboring Arab states (Egypt, Iraq, Jordan, and Saudi Arabia) to the London Conference; the Jewish Agency is unhappy with the idea.

9/10 *Kristallnacht*, the Goebbels-sponsored, SS-organized, anti-Jewish pogrom throughout Germany and Austria: 267 synagogues, 815 shops, 29 department stores, and a large number of Jewish homes are burned down and are partially or completely destroyed; at least 100 Jews lose their lives and perhaps as many as 30,000 young male German Jews are rounded up and held for transportation to the concentration camps.

10 The *Gestapo* closes the *Centralverein Deutscher Staatsbuerger Juedischen Glaubens* (Central Organization of German Citizens of the Jewish faith).

10 Mustafa Kemal Ataturk, first president of the Turkish Republic, dies.

11 *Va'ad Leumi* accepts its invitation to the London Conference.

11 A special conference of the Zionist Actions Committee meets in London to draft a united program for the forthcoming London Conference.

12 The aftermath of *Kristallnacht* is discussed under Goering's guidance; German Jews are fined one billion *Reichsmark* and Jewish property owners are ordered to pay the cost of repairing the damage done to their properties; decision is taken to completely eliminate all Jews from the economic and cultural life within the *Reich*, with the *Verordnung zur Ausschaltung der Juden aus dem Deutschen Wirtschaftsleben* (Decree for the Removal of the Jews From German Economic Life); between 26,000 and 30,000 male Jews are taken to Dachau, Buchenwald, and Sachsenhausen concentration camps.

12 The Swiss national police stage raids against local Nazis.

12/14 Danzig Nazis burn down two synagogues, while two others are badly desecrated.

13 Nazis toy with the Madagascar Plan for the first time.

15 *Numerus nullus* is decreed: Jews are forbidden to attend all German schools.

15 The United States, outraged by the *Kristallnacht* pogrom, recalls its ambassador to Germany, Hugh Wilson.

16 Neville Chamberlain suggests that Jewish refugees come to Britain as a temporary measure.

16 The Uruguay Chamber of Deputies condemns the Nazi pogroms (*Kristallnacht*) in Germany.

17 Italian racial laws previously enacted become official; Italian-born Jews, however, are not deprived of their citizenship, but become a new anomalous category of "Italian Citizens of the Jewish Race."

17 Socialist members of the French Chamber of Deputies blast the government for not speaking officially out on behalf of persecuted German Jewry, and attack Germany for the *Kristallnacht* pogroms.

18 U.S. State Department announces extension of visitors' visas to some 15,000 refugees already in America, on account of the German situation.

18 The Legislative Assembly of the American Virgin Islands adopts a resolution offering the islands as a haven for refugees.

18 Iron Guard members blow up the synagogue in Ereschitza, Rumania.

20 The Canadian Jewish Congress sponsors a "Day of Mourning."

20 The *Va'ad Leumi* requests 10,000 emergency certificates for German and Austrian Jews in need of rescue after *Kristallnacht* from the high commissioner for Palestine; the British grant 500 certificates.

20 Argentinian Jewry, joining many other Jewish communities through-out the world, declare a week of mourning over the *Kristallnacht* pogrom.

21   All Jews with assets over 5,000 *Reichsmark* must pay 20 percent of their registered assets in the form of a special tax to the German treasury.

21   The Danzig Senate passes a law to aryanize industrial and commercial enterprises.

21   The British House of Commons passes a resolution objecting to Nazi Germany's persecution of racial and political minorities.

22   Canadian Jewish leaders meet with Prime Minister McKenzie King and urge that he intercede on behalf of Jewish refugees.

22   Belgium announces its willingness to admit more refugees into the country on a temporary basis, provided that the United States and Britain would guarantee permanent homes for them.

23   All Jewish retail businesses in Germany must terminate under an administrative order; Jews are completely eliminated from German economic life.

23   Ministry of the Interior decree dissolves the Finnish Fascist Party, the Patriotic National Movement.

24   The Danzig Senate introduces Nuremberg Laws for Jews living in the Free City.

24   Nazis publish second decree regarding the registration of Jewish property.

24   *Zidovska Ustredna Uradovna pre Krajinu Slovenska* [ZUU], the Jewish Central Office for the Land of Slovakia, is established.

24   Anti-Jewish riots break out in Johannesburg.

24   The Institute Against Fascism, Racism and Antisemitism holds protest rallies throughout Uruguay in light of *Kristallnacht*.

25   Kefar Ruppin established in the Beth Shean Valley.

25   The National Labor Committee for Palestine asks Britain to open Palestine's doors to Jewish refugees.

26   Russo-Polish non-aggression and trade pacts are signed.

26   The Czech Party of National Unity announces that Jews are excluded from membership.

27   In the wake of *Kristallnacht*, Soviet Jews hold protest meetings in Moscow, Leningrad, Odessa, and Kiev.

27   The Polish government threatens to copy Nazi methods for dealing with the Jewish problem "if other means fail."

28   Nazis introduce residential restrictions for German Jewry; movements of Jews from locality to locality are prohibited.

28 A survey by the British Institute of Public Opinion shows that 77 percent of the country's population believe that the Nazi persecution of the Jews constitutes a major obstacle to Anglo-German understanding.

29 Special schools for Jewish students open in Italy; textbooks by Jewish authors are prohibited from use in Italian schools.

29 Jewish community leaders discuss the dire situation of Polish Jewry at a Warsaw conference.

29 General Jan Smuts invokes the Riotous Assembly Act of 1914 to ban Fascist meetings and antisemitic agitation in South Africa.

29 The Council of the Protestant Federation of France condemns the *Kristallnacht* pogrom.

29 Kefar Masaryk is established in the Zebulun Valley.

30 All Jewish lawyers within the *Reich* are ordered to cease practicing their professions.

30 The Central Fund for German Jewry requests that 10,000 German Jewish youngsters be transferred to Palestine.

30 Italy demands that the French surrender control of the island of Corsica and the colony of Tunisia.

DECEMBER

1 Britain initiates accelerated rearmament measures.

1 The Australian government announces that it will admit 15,000 refugees over the next three years.

2 Danzig Jews are ordered to contribute to the "atonement" fine of one billion *Reichsmark* that Goering had imposed on German Jewry in the aftermath of *Kristallnacht*.

2 Jewish schools in the Rumanian town of Cernauti are ordered closed down.

3 An *arisierung* decree legalizes aryanization of Jewish industrial firms, securities, and real estate in Germany.

3 The Dutch Reformed Church organizes a special collection of funds on behalf of Nazi Jewish victims.

3 An annual tax from 500 to 10,000 *lei* is imposed on all foreigners living in Rumania; all disenfranchised Jews fall within this category and are therefore taxed.

3 The Polish government announces its intent to sponsor a wide range of antisemitic laws, in order to reduce the number of Jews in Poland and eliminate their social, political, and economic influence.

4 Father Charles Coughlin attacks the "Jewish international banking houses" during a radio address.

4 The International Jewish Colonization Society is established in London.

5 The seventh ordinance under the *Reich* Citizenship Act orders reduced pensions for compulsorily retired Jewish officials.

5 The blockade runner, *Gepo 1*, departs Vienna with 734 *ma'apilim* ("illegal" immigrants), lands at Netanyah December 18.

6 Jews are forbidden to enter certain Berlin streets, squares, parks, and buildings and those still living in restricted areas must secure special residence permits from the police.

6 Germany and France sign a non-aggression pact.

6 The Canadian League of Nations Society opens a national refugee conference in Ottawa.

7 The U.S. State Department asks Germany to assure that American Jewish citizens living in Germany would be exempt from the Nazi decree calling for confiscation of 25 percent of Jewish property in Germany.

8 All Jews are banned from conducting research at German universities and other institutions.

8 The Lord Baldwin Fund is launched in Britain on behalf of the victims of Nazi persecution.

8 The archbishop of Canterbury, during the Palestine debate in the House of Lords, pleads that Britain approve a plan to help German-Jewish children immigrate to Palestine.

8 Himmler signs an order concerning the need to regulate the Gypsy question in Germany.

9 The Estonian Minister of Economics announces the beginning of an economic "Estonialization" campaign.

10 Goering demands that a percentage of profits derived from *arisierung* should go to the state.

11 Twenty thousand Libyan Jews lose their Italian citizenship.

11 The Nazi Party wins in Memel elections; Jewish situation is in a very precarious position.

12 At a meeting of the *Va'ad Leumi* David Ben-Gurion speaks of *Kristallnacht* as a "warning of the coming destruction of European Jewry."

13 KL Neuengamme is established as part of the Sachsenhausen concentration camp, but eventually becomes independent with many satellite camps of its own.

13 Aryanization of Jewish property is speeded up through compulsory means.

13 The Canadian cabinet debates the refugee problem.

13 An anti-Jewish campaign in Slovakia leads to pillage of Jewish property and synagogues burned down.

14 Goering announces that he has taken charge of all Jewish affairs.

14 *Betriebsfuehrer Erlass* (general manager decree): all Jewish-owned business are replaced by an aryan general manager.

14 *La Scala* Opera House in Milan cancels ticket subscriptions for all Jews.

15 The governor of Bukovina orders Jewish stores to remain open on the Sabbath and Jewish holidays.

15 King Carol of Rumania orders establishment of the Front of National Renascence, to act as the only legal political organization in the country.

16 The Mexican Population Congress debates the Jewish question in Mexico.

16 Jews in Italy are ordered to register their real estate and industrial properties.

17 Italy annuls its 1935 treaty with France.

18 Coughlin supporters picket the WMCA radio station in New York.

18 The first elections to the Slovak *Diet* (parliament) fall along Nazi lines. Jews are not permitted to vote.

20 Orthodox Jewish leaders meet with Hungarian Premier Bela Imredy regarding the pace of Jewish emigration.

21 The Camp of National Unity demands that the Polish government immediately take steps to drastically reduce the number of Jews living in Poland.

21 The Jewish Agency Cultural Department calls upon Jews throughout the world to read one page from the Bible every day, at which rate a complete reading of the twenty-four volumes of the Old Testament would take one year.

22 All Jews are retired from Italian military service.

23 New racially-defined antisemitic laws are introduced by the Hungarian parliament.

24 The Declaration of Lima is adopted by the twenty-one Western Hemisphere nations at the Eighth International American Conference in Peru.

28 Jews are forbidden to use sleeping compartments or dining cars on German railways.

31 One hundred sixteen out of 208 Polish *sejm* deputies demand that the government immediately take steps to greatly increase Jewish emigration from Poland.

31 The exclusion of Jews in Danzig from the professions and economy is almost complete.

1939

JANUARY

1 A decree is published eliminating Jews from the German economy.

1 The Office of the High Commissioner for Refugees is established. Its first commissioner, Sir Herbert Emerson, is appointed for a five year period.

1 The Chief Rabbinate of Palestine declares a one day fast on behalf of German Jewry, to coincide with the Tenth of *Teveth* fast.

1 The high commissioner for Palestine institutes a Jewish settlement police.

5 The Polish foreign minister, Joseph Beck, meets with Hitler at Berchtesgaden.

5 The Committee for Jewish Emigration, organized by Polish Chief Rabbi Moses Schorr, calls for international aid to resettle Jews.

5 The American Committee for Relief and Resettlement of Yemenite Jews is founded in New York as a fundraising arm of the American Federation of Yemenite Jews.

6 Yugoslavia's government cancels orders to deport foreign Jews who have lived in Yugoslavia for over four years, provided that their residential permits are in order.

6 Rumanian Foreign Minister Gregoire Gafencu announces that all minorities, except Jews, are invited to join the Front.

9 The *Reich* Office of Racial Research exempts *Karaites* from anti-semitic legislation.

9 Protestant and Catholic clergymen petition President Roosevelt on behalf of German refugee children.

10 Neville Chamberlain and Lord Halifax (Edward F. L. Wood) arrive in Rome for talks with Mussolini.

11 The Danzig Senate orders 1,000 of the 4,000 Jews still remaining in the Free City area to leave before the end of the month.

11 Rumanian Jews request that the government allow them to set up their own representative body, since they were excluded from the Front.

13 The Jewish Agency for Palestine and the Czechoslovak government sign the *Haavara* agreement.

14 An increasing number of Uruguayan newspapers take on an anti-semitic and racist tone.

14 Pope Pius XI urges foreign diplomats at the Vatican to grant as many visas as possible to victims of German and Italian racial persecution.

15 The National Conference for Palestine urges a greater number of needy Jewish refugees admitted into Palestine. The United States, too, is urged to drastically increase the number of Jewish refugees it will admit.

15 The National Federation of Temple Youth is founded by the Union of American Hebrew Congregations.

16 Gafencu proposes a cooperative solution for Rumanian and Polish Jewish problems.

17 Slovakian Premier Tiso declares that his foremost task is to solve the Jewish problem.

17 The eighth ordinance under the *Reich* Citizenship Act is passed. Jewish dentists, veterinarians, and chemists are barred from practicing their professions. Jewish dentists, now called "dental orderlies," may only treat Jewish patients.

17 Denmark, Estonia, and Latvia sign a nonaggression pact with Nazi Germany; Finland, Norway, and Sweden refuse to enter into any agreement, insisting on strict neutrality.

19 The Italian Chamber of Deputies is disbanded and replaced by the Assembly of Corporations.

19 The *Va'ad Leumi* and the Jewish Agency decide to attend the London (Saint James) Conference.

19 The Slovakian government agrees to continue a $2,000,000 "clearing" agreement negotiated between the former Czech government and the Jewish Agency for Palestine.

21 Hitler tells Czechoslovakian Foreign Minister Jan Masaryk that "we are going to destroy the Jews."

21 Hitler dismisses Hjalmar Schacht as president of the *Reichsbank* and replaces him with Walter Funk.

23 Some 25,000 Jews in Italy depend on Jewish communal institutions to survive because of government restrictions.

24 Germany and Poland reach an agreement on Jewish deportees. One thousand Jews at a time may return to Germany to settle their accounts: for this purpose a special proprietary account would open in Germany for deposits only.

24 *Endek* student disturbances occur at the University of Warsaw Law School.

24 Goering orders Reinhard Heydrich to establish the *Reichszentralstelle fuer Juedische Auswanderung* (State Central Office for Jewish Emigration). Heydrich names chief of the *Gestapo*, Heinrich Mueller, head of the department.

25 Antisemitic leaflets in Sofia {Bu} call for "death to all Jews."

25 A list of candidates for election to the Slovak *Diet* excludes Jews.

26 Barcelona falls to Franco's Nationalist forces.

26 Anti-Jewish riots erupt in Mexico City.

28 An anti-Jewish graffiti campaign arises in Kovno {Lit}.

29 Lithuanian Premier Mironas calls for an end to the anti-Jewish boycott.

30 In a speech before the *Reichstag* Hitler warns that in the event of war, European Jews will be exterminated; Hitler also notes the lack of offers by the so-called democratic states to accept Jewish refugees.

30 The entire *Asefat ha-Nivharim*, meeting in a special session, approves the *Va'ad Leumi*'s decision to attend the London Conference.

31 An antisemitic Slovak-German society is founded in Bratislava with Vojtech Tuka as its president.

31 The Mexican government promises to guarantee life and property for Jews throughout Mexico.

31 *Va'ad Leumi* elects delegates to the London Conference.

31 Bulgaria orders Jewish refugees to leave the country within a week. The order affects a large number of German, Italian, Spanish, and Greek Jews.

FEBRUARY

1 General Jan Christian Smuts, deputy prime minister of South Africa, urges against nazification of the Nationalist Party.

1 A law is passed promulgating the revision of Czech citizenship for persons nationalized after November 1, 1918. Refugees living in areas of Czechoslovakia that were occupied by Germany, Poland, and Hungary are ordered to leave Czech territory within six months.

2 Pope Pius XI dies.

2 The Thuringian Evangelical Church passes a law that forbids Jews to join the Church.

3 Members of the Arrow Cross perpetrate a terrorist attack on the worshipers in the Great Synagogue in Budapest.

3 The Finns start a nationwide collection of funds for German refugees.

5 The French president attacks the racist policies of Nazi Germany.

5 Republican leaders flee Spain for France.

6 *Einsatz des Juedischen Vermoegens* is published, decreeing complete aryanization of Jewish property within the *Reich*.

6 Home Secretary Sir Samuel Hoare states publicly that refugee enterprises in Britain provide employment for nearly 15,000 Englishmen.

6 Seventeen "illegal" immigrants are seized by British police as they land near Herzliya.

6 *Va'ad Leumi* announces the *Pidyon Shevuim* (redemption of captives) fund, to aid German and Austrian Jewish refugees.

7 At a press conference in Berlin, Alfred Rosenberg discusses a plan to settle all the world's fifteen million Jews on the island of Madagascar.

7 The Saint James Palace Conference on the future of Palestine, opens in London.

9 Restrictions for Italian Jews are placed on real estate ownership and industrial and commercial activities.

11 Italy establishes the Institute for the Administration and Liquidation of Immovable Property, to which Jews are ordered to surrender their possessions.

13 *Yishuv* leaders warn Britain that without Jewish consent an Arab state in Palestine would need to rely on British guns.

13 United States Supreme Court Justice Louis D. Brandeis resigns.

15 Count Pal Teleki becomes prime minister of Hungary.

20 Some 20,000 American Nazis, Nazi sympathizers, and supporters of Father Coughlin attend a large-scale rally in Madison Square Garden.

20 *Gepo II* departs for Palestine from Vienna with 750 refugees. The ship sinks near Crete, but the *ma'apilim* are rescued and reach Palestine.

21 German Jews are ordered to surrender all the gold and silver they possess, with the exception of wedding rings.

21 The Slovak *Diet* decrees compulsory transfer of Jewish pupils from public schools to Jewish schools.

21 The Breslau *Juedisch-Theologisches Seminar*, a Jewish Reform seminary, ordains its last two students before it is ordered shut down by the *Gestapo*.

22 The Bulgarian government announces that the country's Jews enjoy the same equal rights as other Bulgarian citizens.

24 The Hungarian government outlaws the Arrow Cross.

24 Hungary joins the Anti-Comintern Pact.

26 IZL bombs explode in the Haifa *shuk* (marketplace). Twenty-seven Arabs are killed and thirty-nine injured.

26 The British government submits a proposal calling for an independent Palestinian state allied to Britain.

27 Britain and France recognize the Franco regime in Spain.

MARCH

1 The Rumanian government announces that 43,000 Jews have been officially denationalized. The government also declares that it is willing to negotiate a "clearing" agreement with the Jewish Agency for Palestine.

2 Pius XII is elected Pope.

4 Nazis introduce a compulsory labor law for Jews in Germany, but this forced labor law for German Jews is not a part of the German *Arbeitsdienst*.

4/20 Sixteen meatless days observed by all factions of the Jewish population of Poland in protest of the anti-*shechita* bill.

8 The *SS Astir*, with 850 "illegal" Jewish immigrants aboard, leaves the Rumanian port of Galatz bound for Palestine.

9 The *Mossad Le-aliya Bet* ship *Atrato* with 378 German and Austrian Jews departs for Palestine from Bari, Italy.

10 The Eighteenth Congress of the Communist Party opens in Moscow.

10 The central government in Prague dismisses Slovak Prime Minister Josef Tiso.

10 Violent disorders break out in Rypin {P}.

11 The Hungarian government passes a law introducing the Hungarian Labor Service System for Jews of military age.

12 Tiso meets Hitler in Berlin.

14 Slovakia is established as an independent Nazi axis state under the leadership of the Fascist Hlinka Party, headed by Monseigneur Josef Tiso. Slovak Nazis celebrate their proclamation of independence by unleashing a wave of terror against Slovakian Jews.

14 Anti-Jewish violence occurs at the University of Lvov.

15 Nazis occupy Prague, trapping some 56,000 Jews. Hitler orders establishment of the Protectorate of Bohemia and Moravia. The Zionist leadership decides to remain in the country so as not abandon the Jewish people at this time of crisis.

15 Britain proposes an independent Palestinian state: Arabs and Jews would govern together under British protection; proposal is not accepted by Arabs and Jews.

16 Czechs and Jews become *Staatsangehoerige* or Bohemia and Moravia Protectorate subjects.

16 Hungarians occupy Czechoslovakian Carpatho-Ruthenia. Hitler declares that Czechoslovakia no longer exists.

16 The Jewish delegation at the London Conference threatens to leave.

17 The London Conference on Palestine fails to reach an acceptable settlement between Jews and Arabs.

17 A French assembly gives liberal power to Edouard Daladier to speed rearmament.

17 A disappointed Chamberlain accuses Hitler of breaking his promise.

18 British warships intercept the "illegal" immigrant ship *Artemis* and force it to return to Europe.

19 The Conference of National Jewish Youth Organizations is founded in Washington, DC.

20 The *Yishuv* proclaims a twenty-four hour strike in outrage over British Palestine policies.

20   *Reichsprotector* of Bohemia-Moravia, Konstantin von Neurath, bans all "unofficial" aryanization of Jewish property in former Czech territories. The last group of Jewish municipal employees in the Protectorate are dismissed from their jobs.

20   The United States ambassador to Germany is recalled in protest over Czechoslovakia.

21   Nazis seize the Free City of Memel.

22   American-Jewish philosopher, Dr. Isaac Husik, dies.

23   Nazis in Memel initiate anti-Jewish terror; thousands flee to Lithuania.

23   Germany endorses obligatory labor service.

23   Poland rejects German proposals on Danzig.

23   A German-Rumanian economic agreement gives Nazis access to Rumanian oil.

23   Anti-Jewish riots break out in Kovno. The Jewish hospital, synagogues, and many Jewish homes are stoned.

25   The Vatican recognizes newly created Slovakia.

25   The Polish *sejm* adopts bill outlawing *shechita*.

26   The Polish Merchants Union petitions the government to reduce Jewish commercial licensing to ten percent of the total.

27   Spain joins the Anti-Comintern Pact.

27   Unrest in Egypt leads to a government ban of the German antisemitic news service, *Weltdienst*.

27   The London Conference ends in failure.

27   The last three Jewish organizations still functioning in Danzig, the *Zentralverein* (Central Association), the Frontfighters Union, and the Union for Progressive Judaism, are ordered dissolved by Danzig Senate.

27   Germany launches a vicious anti-Polish press campaign, accusing the Poles of atrocious conduct toward the German minority in Poland.

28   Madrid falls to Franco forces.

28   The Central Committee of the Zionist Organization of Poland declares Polish Jewry's readiness to fight for the preserved integrity of the Polish borders.

29   In a public address, Lithuanian Premier Mironas, declares that the government will respect the rights of all minorities, including the Jews.

31 Anglo-French guarantees to Poland are announced. Hitler denounces the nonaggression pact with Poland.

31 Germany and Spain conclude Friendship Treaty.

31 British warships fire on the "illegal" immigrant ship *Aegius Nikolaius*, killing one passenger.

APRIL

1 Spain's civil war ends: the total cost of the war is staggering, with some 750,000 dead on both sides.

2 Belgian Nazis fail to win seats in the House of Deputies.

4 The Godesberg Declaration accepts the Nazi *Weltanschauung* (world perception).

4 Violent anti-Fascist incidents break out in Mexico City.

4 Uruguay announces its readiness to admit a limited number of Jewish refugees from Europe, in line with the Evian conference.

5 The Colonial Office passes measure curbing Jewish immigration to Palestine.

5 The National Air Defense Loan fund is launched in Poland; with 35 percent of the total, Jews are the loan's largest group of bond purchasers.

7 Italy invades Albania.

10 Chaim Weizmann meets with Egypt's Prime Minister Mohammed Mahmud in Cairo.

10 A Bulgarian decree is published denouncing the instigation of antisemitic and racist propaganda in public schools.

11 Hitler issues a directive, Operation White, which forms a possible plan to attack Poland.

11 Hungary withdraws from the League of Nations.

13 Britain and France guarantee Rumanian and Greek sovereignty.

13 The French Canadian Saint Jean Baptiste Society adopts a resolution to oppose any further admission of refugees into Canada, especially Jews.

15 Alfred Rosenberg opens the *Institut der NSDAP zur Erforschung der Judenfrage* (Institute of the Nazi Party for Research into the Jewish Question).

15 President Roosevelt appeals to Hitler and Mussolini to respect the independence of European nations.

16 The Jewish National Fund in Chicago meets in an emergency conference to accelerate its fundraising activities to alleviate the crisis in Palestine.

17 Britain and France reject a Soviet offer to form an anti-Nazi alliance.

18 Antisemitic legislation introduced in Slovakia defines Jews primarily by religion.

18 Hungarian army officers protest new antisemitic laws applied to war veterans.

20 Joint U.S. Senate-House hearings are held concerning the admission of 20,000 German refugee children over a two-year period on a non-quota basis.

20 *Aghia Nicholaus II* sails from Rumania to Palestine with 600 *ma'apilim*; most are interned by the British when they arrive on May 19.

22 An "illegal" immigrant ship, *SS Assimi*, is expelled from Haifa with 240 Jews aboard.

22 *Aghia Zioni*, a Revisionist blockade runner, lands near Rehovot where most of the 400 *ma'apilim* are captured by the British.

24 A Slovak decree dismisses Jews from the civil service and corporation staffs.

24 Ben-Gurion declares that Jews would rather be killed than surrender to British Palestinian policies.

26 The British Colonial Office announces that future immigration quotas will be deducted from the number of "illegal" immigrants to Palestine.

27 Britain enacts the Conscription Law.

27 Hitler denounces the 1935 Anglo-German naval agreement.

27 The Seventh Congress of the Jewish Communities of Yugoslavia opens in Belgrade.

27 Danzig Jewish art treasures are transferred to New York for safe keeping.

28 Hitler, speaking before the *Reichstag*, annuls the German-Polish non-aggression pact, denounces the British-Polish pact, and rejects the Roosevelt peace proposals.

28 Britain enacts legislation punishing passengers and crews of "illegal" immigrant ships.

28 Sudeten-German Nazis incite anti-Jewish riots in Jihlava (Iglau), Czechoslovakia; many Jewish shops are demolished.

30   German landlords are sanctioned by decree to evict Jews because German tenancy laws are not applicable to Jews.

MAY

2   A congress of the *Werslinkai* Traders' and Artisans' Association, Lithuania's main antisemitic body, opens in Kovno.

2   *Kibbutz* Daliyyah is established in the Manasseh Hills.

3   Two new Jewish settlements, Dan and Dafna, are founded in the Huleh Valley.

3   Vyaczeslav Molotov replaces Maxim Litvinov as the people's commissar of public affairs.

4   Hungary institutes severe antisemitic laws similar to the German Nuremberg Laws; at its core is restriction (on a grand scale) of a Jewish presence in public and economic life. The law exempts those who converted to Christianity before 1919, and Jewish war veterans.

4   A Rumanian ordinance creates stiff penalties for those assisting "illegal" Jewish immigration to Palestine.

4   The Housing Segregation Law is enacted in Germany.

4   Hungary's second anti-Jewish law deprives citizenship to Jews naturalized after July 1, 1914.

5   Chile suspends all immigration for a year.

5   Legislation introduced in the Dutch parliament bans racial defamation.

7   *Kibbutz* Sedeh Eliyahu is founded in the Beth Shean Valley.

7   The American Association for Jewish Education is organized.

8   The National Fascist Party, in a broadcast over Cuba's national radio station, incites Cubans to drive Jews out of the country.

8   Spain withdraws from the League of Nations.

8   The Belgian Medical Association proposes to ban all foreigners from practicing medicine.

9   The British Cabinet Committee on Refugees discusses a petition to settle 500 German Jewish refugee families in British Guiana.

13   The London Jewish Agency Executive outlines a six-point resistance program against British Palestinian policies.

13   Due to the massive surge in conversions to Christianity, the Union of Jewish Communities in Hungary issues a proclamation begging Jews not to abandon the faith of their fathers and the Jewish people.

15 The *SS St. Louis* leaves Hamburg for Cuba with approximately 1,000 German Jews aboard.

15 KL Ravensbrueck, a concentration camp for women, opens.

15 An Argentinian government decree dissolves the Nazi party, including Italian and Spanish Fascist groups.

15 Brazil issues a decree providing for greater government regulations and calling for foreign associations to register with the local police.

16 The Warsaw Municipal Council votes to dismiss a large number of Jewish municipal employees.

17 The White Paper announces the slowing growth of the *Yishuv* through limitations on immigration and Jewish land purchase.

17 A population census in Greater Germany lists 330,539 "racial" Jews, 138,819 male and 191,720 female. This figure includes 94,530 Jews in Austria and 2,363 in the Sudetenland. Among them are 52,005 *mischlinge* of the first degree, and 32,669 *mischlinge* of the second degree.

17 In a joint venture between *Maccabi* and the Revisionists, *Liesel* sets sail with 921 *ma'apilim*. The ship is intercepted and captured by the British on June 2.

18 *Der Stuermer* proposes the extermination of all Jews within the Soviet Union.

18 Britain reinstates conscription.

18 The *Yishuv* declares a one day general strike to protest the White Paper.

18 Jewish veterans of the Royal British Army demonstrate against the Palestine White Paper.

19 Spanish Nationalists conduct a tremendous victory parade in Madrid.

20 A *Mossad* ship, *Atrato IV*, sails from Constanta, Rumania and is captured on May 28 by HMS *Sutton*. After a brief detention, the 430 *ma'apilim* are released.

20 Pan American Airways inaugurates the first commercial trans-Atlantic crossing, with a flight of the Yankee Clipper from New York to Portugal.

21 Palestine police arrests David Raziel, commander of the *Irgun Zvai Leumi*.

21 *Keren Hayesod* calls on world Jewry to accelerate its drive to upbuild the Jewish national home in answer to the White Paper.

21 *Va'ad Leumi* declares an "emergency situation" in response to the White Paper, taking a stance of "non-cooperation."

22 The Pact of Steel signed by Germany and Italy.

22 The House of Commons stormily debates the White Paper.

22 Britain outlines its White Paper position before the Council of the League of Nations.

23 Hitler decides on war with Poland.

23 The British parliament approves the White Paper by a vote of 268 to 179. The House of Commons approves a plan for an independent Palestinian state by 1949, but the plan is denounced by Jews and Arabs.

23 The Christian Republican Movement, an antisemitic party, is established in South Africa; "Jews to Palestine" is its motto.

25 Jews of Argentina are prohibited from displaying the Blue-and-White Zionist flag on the grounds that it represents no state.

26 Rabbi Jacob Meir, *Sephardi* Chief Rabbi of Palestine, dies.

27 Cuba refuses to admit the 930 Jewish refugees aboard the *SS St. Louis*.

28 *Va'ad Leumi* sends a memorandum to the League of Nations Permanent Mandates Committee protesting the White Paper.

28 The Jewish Palestine Pavilion at the New York World's Fair opens.

28 The British Royal Navy intercepts the *Aliya Bet* ship *Atrato VII*, carrying 390 *ma'apilim*, in Palestinian territorial waters.

28 The *Nyilaskeresztes Part* (Arrow Cross) party elects forty-five representatives to the Hungarian parliament.

29 Count Julius Karolyi resigns as president of the Hungarian Senate because he opposes the anti-Jewish laws.

29 The *SS Frossoula*, sailing from Varna {Bu} with 658 *ma'apilim* is stranded in Beirut when an epidemic breaks out on board.

30 IZL assassinates officer Arye Polonski, a Jewish member of the Palestine police, after accusing him of aiding the British.

31 The Hungarian Ministry of Commerce applies strict *numerus clausus* to Jewish businesses, canceling hundreds of commercial licenses held by Jews.

JUNE

1 Oswald Pohl is named chief administrator of the SS.

1 Italian Jews are ordered to assume "Jewish" surnames. Collaboration between Jewish and non-Jewish professionals is strictly prohibited.

1 *SS-Gericht*, or the SS Legal *Hauptamt*, is established upon Himmler's orders.

2 The *SS St. Louis* is forced to leave Havana harbor.

3 The U.S. government refuses to admit even those Jewish refugees from the *SS St. Louis* who possess American quota numbers.

4 While the *SS St. Louis* sails along Florida's coast, all efforts go unheeded to gain permission for refugees to land on American soil.

4 Telephone cables are cut in the first IZL attack on British installations in Palestine.

5 The Jewish Agency orders a special operations unit, *Palmah* (assault companies), as an integral arm of the *Hagana* to deal with Arab terrorists.

6 President Roosevelt ignores telegram sent to him on behalf of the *SS St. Louis* refugees. Argentina, Colombia, Chile, and Paraguay also refuse to shelter the refugees. The ship, with all of its refugees aboard, is forced to return to Europe.

6 The chief rabbi of Rumania, Dr. Niemirower, is appointed to the Rumanian Senate.

6 Anti-Jewish violence erupts in Uswentis, Lithuania; two synagogues and a number of Jewish homes are burned down.

7 King George VI and Queen Elizabeth arrive in the United States for a state visit.

9 Anti-Jewish outbursts staged by the Nazis break out throughout the Czech Protectorate.

12 A congress of all Jewish financial institutions in Argentina opens in Buenos Aires to plan a united colonization fund.

12 The Rumanian government passes a law imposing a special tax on denationalized Jews. The tax ranges from 2,000 to 10,000 *lei* annually.

13 Belgium, the Netherlands, France, and Britain agree to take in the *SS St. Louis'* refugees.

13 *Palmah* begins operations.

14 The Japanese blockade British and French concessions at Tientsin, China.

16 *Gazeta Polska* denounces the violent disturbances at the Polish universities and urges that the government immediately take steps to restore order.

17 The *SS St. Louis* refugees land at Antwerp; within a year most of them come again under German rule and are murdered eventually by the Nazis.

18 A bomb explosion in a Jewish cafe in Prague injures thirty-nine people.

20 *Generaloberst* Walther von Brauchitsch publishes a directive regarding *Wehrmacht* cooperation with *SS-Verfuegungstruppen*.

21 A Nuremberg style anti-Jewish law enacted in the Protectorate of Bohemia and Moravia, orders Jews to register their business and personal property before July 31.

21 *Irgun Zvai Leumi* blows up the Haifa telephone exchange.

22 Slovak Minister of Propaganda Aleksander Mach declares that within a year's time Slovakia will be *Judenrein*.

26 The blockade runner *Rim* sinks near Rhodes on July 4, but the 450 refugees are picked up by the *Aghia Nicholaus*, landing near Netanyah on August 20.

27 The Zionist Organization of America unanimously declares its opposition to British policy in Palestine.

27 Israel Davidson, Jewish scholar, dies.

29 Italian Jews are either prohibited from working in a number of professions or are allowed to practice their professions only among other Jews.

29 Numbering 440, the first group of Gypsy women from Austria are deported to the Ravensbrueck concentration camp.

30 A suspicious fire destroys part of the Jewish district in Silal, Lithuania.

JULY

3 The British government requests the cooperation of European governments in uprooting "illegal" Jewish immigration.

3 A bill before the Cuban House of Representatives provides for a special census of all Jews who entered the country since January 1, 1937.

4 The tenth ordinance of the *Reich* Citizenship Act establishes the *Reichsvereinigung der Juden in Deutschland* (State Association of Jews in Germany), replacing all other Jewish organizations, including the *Hilfsverein*.

5 David Ben-Gurion once again proposes a binational state for Palestine.

6 Eichmann arrives in Prague to take charge of Jewish emigration from Czechoslovakia.

6 The Mexican government closes the antisemitic Party of National Salvation headquarters as a "public nuisance."

7 An editorial in *Voelkischer Beobachter* proclaims that the Jewish problem in Germany will only be solved when Germany is *Judenrein*.

8 Italian companies dealing with the government are prohibited from employing Jews.

8 The *SS Patria* sails from Constanta, Rumania with 850 Polish *ma'apilim*; the ship is impounded by the British after debarkation.

9 The Slovakian government orders all Jewish-owned land registered.

9 Churchill urges a military alliance with the Soviet Union.

10 Jews in the Protectorate are ordered to pay their non-Jewish employees wages until year's end, even though their businesses were aryanized.

10 The American branch of *Agudas Yisroel* is established in New York City with Rabbi Eliezer Silver as its first president.

12 *Kibbutz* Negbah is established in the Southern Coastal Plain (Malakhi Region).

12 British Colonial Secretary Malcolm MacDonald announces that Jewish immigration to Palestine will be suspended for six months, beginning October 1.

13 Italy introduces aryanization program.

14 Luxembourg police confiscate the Nazi newspaper, *Luxemburger Freiheit*, on the grounds that it endangers public order.

15 Under Adolf Eichmann, an office for Jewish emigration, the *Zentralstelle fuer Juedische Auswanderung*, opens in Prague with a branch office in Brno. Jews wishing to emigrate from the Czech Protectorate must get permission from the *Zentralstelle*.

16 Mosley declares that one million British Fascists would refuse to fight in a "Jewish war."

16 Jewish university students in Italy are segregated from their Gentile classmates during examinations.

19 The permanent Intergovernmental Committee meets in London.

20   The Coordinating Foundation, an international interdenominational refugee organization, is instituted.

21   The Bolivian government reports that a number of Jewish refugees entered the country illegally.

23   *Gazeta Polska* accuses Polish Jewry of false sympathies to Poland in time of national crisis.

24   A *numerus clausus* introduced in Slovakia restricts Jews in the professions to four percent.

24   Arab terrorists in Beirut bomb French government installations.

24   Slovak decree dismisses all Jews from the army.

25   A number of Yemenite Jews are arrested in Aden while attending *Tisha b'Av* services in a makeshift synagogue.

26   The United States rescinds its 1911 trade agreement with Japan.

29   Slovakian Jews are forbidden to live in rural areas.

30   Elections are held for the Twenty-first Zionist Congress.

AUGUST

1   The United States Congress passes a bill outlawing the use of uniforms and firearms by any organization conflicting against the American government.

1   The Austrian province of Steiermark (Styria) is reported *Judenrein*.

2   Professor Albert Einstein informs President Roosevelt on the possibility of the development of an atom bomb.

3   The French government drafts plans outlining ways to curb anti-French and anti-Jewish propaganda.

3   Memel Jews are permitted to liquidate their property without Nazi interference.

4   The Polish government sends an ultimatum to the Danzig Senate, demanding that the Senate stop interfering with the activities of Polish customs inspectors.

4   The antisemitic Malanite Nationalist Republican Party demands a total stop to Jewish immigration to South Africa.

9   *Hagana* units sink the British police boat, *Sinbad II*.

9   The Bolivian government allows the Jewish community to practice *shechita*.

11   Jews begin to be expelled from the Protectorate.

11 British military mission arrives in Moscow.

12 Negotiations on a military alliance between the Soviet Union, Britain, and France start in Moscow.

14 All Jews in the Protectorate are barred from public parks, beaches, hotels, and restaurants; all Jews in old-age homes, hospitals, and welfare shelters must be segregated.

14 The South African Jewish Board of Deputies sets up a special public relations committee to deal with anti-Jewish propaganda.

15 Jews in Italy are prohibited from employing non-Jewish servants, or else face severe penalties.

16 The Palestinian government announces that "illegal" immigrants will be imprisoned for an unlimited period.

16/26 The Twenty-first World Zionist Congress is held in Geneva, Switzerland. The Congress strongly opposes the British White Paper, and expresses great concern for German and eastern European Jewry, particularly for Polish Jews.

17 The Permanent Mandates Commission of the League of Nations rules that the British White Paper is inconsistent with the Mandate's provisions.

19 A Nazi-Soviet economic agreement is signed as part of the upcoming Ribbentrop-Molotov nonaggression pact.

19 Weizmann and Churchill meet in London.

20 German U-boats take up positions in the North Atlantic Ocean.

20 The Soviets gain a major victory over Japan in the conflict along the Outer Mongolia-Manchukuo border; Japan sues for peace.

22 British Prime Minister Neville Chamberlain warns Hitler that Britain's commitment to Poland is ironclad.

22 Compulsory aryanization of Jewish-owned enterprises is accelerated in the *Grossreich* (Greater Germany).

22 The *SS Parita*, with 850 "illegal" immigrants, beaches on the Tel Aviv shore; all refugees successfully disperse.

22 The Emek Hefer settlement near Netanyah is established.

23 Belgium proclaims neutrality, but mobilizes its army as a precaution.

24 The Molotov-Ribbentrop Nonaggression Pact is signed: this secret agreement provides for Poland's partition.

24 The House of Commons approves the Emergency Powers Bill. Britain begins general mobilization.

24 Croat-Serbian agreement grants Croatia a degree of limited autonomy.

24 Local Nazi *Gauleiter,* Dr. Albrecht Foerster, is declared Danzig's *fuehrer.*

25 The Anglo-Polish Mutual Assistance Pact is signed.

25 Hitler demands a free hand in dealing with Poland.

26 IZL assassinates two British detectives accused of torturing suspects.

26/27 Mobilization increases in Poland.

28 For defensive reasons the Polish army orders certain areas in its western territories evacuated.

28 British-French negotiations with Hitler over Poland fail.

28 Hitler resolves to destroy Poland even at the risk of all-out war. Closes the entire German-Polish frontier in preparation for *Fall Weiss* (Case White), a code name for an attack on Poland.

28 Slovak Premier, Josef Tiso, invites the German army to occupy Slovakia.

28 Holland orders general mobilization.

29 The Swiss Federal Council orders full mobilization of the nation's frontier forces. Colonel Henri Guisan is appointed commander-in-chief of the Swiss army.

29 *Noemi Julia* sails from Constanta with 1,130 *ma'apilim*, landing in Haifa September 19.

30 The Polish army is ordered to fully mobilize.

30 The German embassy in London advises German nationals to leave Britain immediately.

30 Hitler issues a decree that sets up the permanent Council of Ministers for the Defense of the State.

30 Poland takes drastic measures to stop large-scale sabotage by the pro-German "fifth column."

31 Hitler signs Directive Number 1 outlining Germany's war plans, and issues a sixteen-point plan to forge a settlement with Poland. The latter plan never reaches the Polish government, since Hitler orders communication cables with Poland cut. Hitler also stages the Gleiwitz affair, blaming Poland for starting war, and giving the Nazis a pretext to invade Poland.

31 Mussolini calls for a five-power conference to arbitrate the German-Polish crisis.

31 The Supreme Soviet ratifies the non-aggression pact with Germany.

SEPTEMBER

1 At 0445 hours Nazi Germany invades Poland with fifty-three divisions. Hundreds of *stuka* dive bombers and other warplanes blacken the skies, destroying much of the Polish air force on the ground.

1 Britain and France send Hitler an ultimatum demanding that he immediately withdraw his forces from Poland.

1 The Euthanasia program, known as operation T-4, begins in Germany.

1 Eight thousand Czech intellectuals are arrested by the *Gestapo*.

1 Italy declares its neutrality concerning Germany's war with Poland.

1 An 8 PM curfew applies to all Jews in Germany.

1 *Aktion Tannenberg*: while Germany conquers Poland, *Einsatzgruppen*, or special SS task forces, violently attack Jews, burning down synagogues filled with hundreds of worshipers, and conducting a terror-murder campaign against members of the Polish intelligentsia. The operation officially ends October 25.

1 Nazi *Gauleiter* for Danzig, Dr. Albrecht Foerster, proclaims an *anschluss* of the Free City with Germany.

2 An SS civilian prison camp opens in Stutthof, outside Danzig, with hundreds of Jews from the area forming the first group interned.

2 A British coastal patrol vessel fires on the *SS Tiger Hill*, an "illegal" refugee ship, while 1,400 passengers embark. Two refugees are killed.

2 The *Gestapo* orders all Jews in Germany between sixteen and fifty-five to report for compulsory labor.

2 Sweden, Denmark, Norway, Finland, and Iceland simultaneously declare their absolute neutrality.

2 The Lichtenburg concentration camp is closed and its inmates are transferred to KL Ravensbrueck.

2 Portugal announces its intention to remain neutral.

3 World War II begins: Britain, France, Australia, and New Zealand declare war on Germany; Chamberlain forms a war cabinet, with Winston Churchill as first Lord of the Admiralty.

3 Fifteen hundred Polish civilians are killed during indiscriminate German *Luftwaffe* air raids.

3 The German army occupies Bochnia {P}.

3 The Jewish Agency publishes a declaration offering unlimited support for the anti-Nazi war.

4   Bloody Monday, a Nazi organized pogrom, takes place barely twenty-four hours after *Wehrmacht* occupation of Czestochowa. A few hundred Jews are murdered.

4   Germany promulgates its War Economy decree.

4   The British Royal Air Force [RAF] raids German warships in Heligoland Bight.

4   Argentina and Chile declare their neutrality in the European war.

4   Japan declares a policy of non-intervention in the European war.

5   Hitler visits the Polish front.

5   The United States announces its strict neutrality in war.

5   Jan Christian Smuts becomes premier of South Africa.

5   *Brennkommandos* (arson squads) destroy the main synagogue and *bet ha-midrash* (house of learning) immediately upon German occupation of Ozorkow {P}. Dozens of Jews caught on the streets are shot to death.

6   The Nazis occupy Cracow, the third largest Polish city, trapping nearly 60,000 Jews.

6   While occupying Zdunska Wola (the district capital of the Lodz province), Nazis burn down the town's well-known wooden synagogue along with all its liturgical objects.

6   Nazis unleash anti-Jewish terror upon their occupation of Dzialoszyce, a small town in central Poland.

6   South Africa declares war on Germany.

6   The *Hagana* appoints its general staff. Yaakov Dori becomes the first Chief of Staff.

7   Slovakian Jews are barred from military draft.

7   Stockholm's daily *Social-Demokraten* urges the Swedish government to adopt tough measures to combat Nazi hate propaganda in Sweden.

7   Upon German occupation, *Brennkommandos* immediately burn down all the synagogues in Ropczyce {P}.

8   *Wehrmacht* units reach and surround Warsaw, the Polish capital; other units occupy Lodz, Radom, and Tarnow. Anti-Jewish terror activities begin.

8   The German army burns down the main synagogue in Aleksandrow Lodzki {P}, immediately after occupation.

8   The *Wehrmacht* occupies Gora Kalwaria, the famous seat of the *Gur Hasidic* dynasty.

8 *Volksdeutsche* (Ethnic Germans) and Poles initiate a pogrom as soon as the Germans occupy Sierpc {P}.

8 Chamberlain gives the House of Commons the final report on Germany regarding its invasion of Poland.

8 President Roosevelt declares limited state of emergency.

8 Egypt's government announces that Jewish refugees from Nazism are free from the precautionary measures adopted against German citizens residing in Egypt.

9 All male Jews of Gelsenkirchen (Ruhr) are deported to Sachsenhausen.

9 The Main Bedzin synagogue is burned down by an *Brennkommando*.

9 One hundred thousand Jews are drafted into Polish army.

9 *Wehrmacht* occupies Rymanow after a twenty-four hour battle; the army drives all inhabitants into the town's center, threatening to immediately execute Jews and Gentiles alike.

10 Canada declares war on Germany.

10 The first British Expeditionary Force units land in France.

11 The *Luftwaffe* firebombs and destroys the Jewish quarter of Bilgoraj {P}.

11 Nazis initiate a pogrom when they occupy Wyszkow {P}.

11 *Wehrmacht* crosses the San River.

12 The Germans seize large number of young Jews from occupied areas of Poland for forced labor.

12 All male Jews of Grojec {P} between fifteen and fifty-five are marched to Rawa Mazowiecka {P} for slave labor. Stragglers on the 60 km. march are shot to death.

12 A Czech army in exile is formed in France.

13 *Brennkommandos* burn down the synagogues in Bielsko {P}.

13 The French government creates the Ministry of Armaments.

13/15 *Brennkommandos* in Poland burn down the two major synagogues in Mielec: many Jews are burned alive or shot to death during this *aktion* (operation).

14/16 Warsaw's Jewish quarter is heavily bombed by the *Luftwaffe*, causing many casualties.

14/28 Nazis massacre hundreds of Jews in Przemysl {P}.

15 *Brennkommandos* burn down the synagogue at Kutno {P}. Jewish property is plundered by German troops, while scores of Jews are rounded up, beaten, and otherwise intimidated.

16 The Polish garrison rejects a German ultimatum to surrender Warsaw.

16 The *Gestapo* orders a *Judenrat* (Jewish Council) established in Czestochowa {P}.

17 The Red Army invades and occupies eastern Poland.

17 Immediately after the German army occupies Tarnobrzeg {P} it instigates a pogrom.

18 The Polish government flees to Rumania.

18 The World Federation of Polish Jews Abroad opens its biennial convention in New York City.

18 The *Wehrmacht* occupies Lublin {P}, trapping some 45,000 Jews.

18/20 A large-scale pogrom is committed by roving Polish antisemitic bands during the interval between the Polish army's withdrawal and Soviet occupation of Grodno.

19 In a triumphant procession Hitler visits Danzig under German occupation.

19 The Red Army occupies Vilna.

19/20 All German Jews must hand in their radios.

20 *Va'ad Leumi* establishes an emergency tax to help Palestine Jews in dire need.

20 Anti-Jewish violence breaks out in Sofia.

21 Reinhard Heydrich, head of the *Reichssicherheitshauptamt* [RSHA] (State Security Main Office), outlines plans to remove Polish Jewry from Poland's occupied areas; issues orders to all the *Einsatzgruppen* leaders on the importance of keeping secret the ultimate solution to the Jewish question; pens orders to establish ghettos and *Judenraete* (Jewish Councils) in occupied Poland.

21 Polish Jews living in communities with fewer than 500 people are ordered to move to the larger towns.

21 The Iron Guard assassinates Rumanian prime minister Armand Galinescu.

22 Orders are published for confiscation of Jewish property in Nazi-occupied Poland.

22 The Red Army occupies Lvov.

22   *Wehrmacht* commanders order Jews living in the vicinity of the San River expelled into Soviet-occupied territory. Many small Jewish communities are affected, including Dukla, Iwonicz, Lancut, and Rymanow.

23   Polish Mayor Stefan Starzynski appoints Adam Czerniakow the overseer responsible for Warsaw Jewry.

23   Sigmund Freud dies at age eighty-three.

24   The *Luftwaffe* firebombs Warsaw.

24   Many synagogues in Poland are burned down by *Brenn-kommandos*, the German arson squads, but the Nazis accuse Jews of setting the fires, and impose huge fines on the Jewish communities.

26   German local military commanders in the vicinity of the German-Soviet demarcation lines, issue a second order for Jews to leave their villages and cross over to the Russian side of the San River. Thousands of Jews are uprooted, robbed, and locked out of their apartments, while hundreds are killed in the process.

27   RSHA begins to function, eventually becoming responsible for carrying out the Final Solution.

27   Warsaw surrenders after a thirty-six hour *Luftwaffe* bombing and strafing barrage which kills thousands of civilians.

27   The Bulgarian government suppresses antisemitic violence.

28   The German-Soviet Friendship Treaty is signed in order to regulate the Polish border.

28   Polish army surrenders. Thousands of Polish soldiers were killed and wounded during the four-week war, with close to 750,000 Poles taken prisoners-of-war by the Nazis and Soviets.

28   General Wladyslaw Sikorski is entrusted to command the new Polish army forming in France.

28   Some 10,000 Polish Jews from Jaroslaw {P} are driven across the San River to Soviet-occupied Poland.

29   Germany and the Soviet Union partition Poland as per previous agreements.

29   Food rationing is enforced in Czechoslovakia.

29   The Nazis initiate their euthanasia program in occupied Poland: thousands of mental patients, the chronically ill, and the feeble are murdered.

OCTOBER

1 Hungarian anti-Jewish laws take effect.

2 The Polish government-in-exile becomes established in Paris under the premiership of General Wladyslaw Sikorski, and is recognized by the United States.

2 The SD takes over the Pawiak prison, located on Pawia Street in the Jewish quarter of Warsaw, transforming it into an interrogation center and horror place for political prisoners and Jews.

3 The last Polish units on the Westplatte surrender near Luck.

3 The Mandatory administration bans Jews from "enemy countries" from entering Palestine.

4 *SS-Obergruppenfuehrer* (General) Friedrich Wilhelm Krueger is named *Hoeherer SS undPolizeifuehrer* [HSSPF] (Higher SS and Police Leader) in occupied Poland.

4 The Nazis appoint Adam Czerniakow *Judenaelteste* (Elder of the Jews) of the Warsaw *Judenrat*.

4 A few thousand Jewish refugees in England volunteer their services to the British Auxiliary Pioneer Corps.

5 Forty-three *Hagana* members are arrested near *kibbutz* Yavniel.

6 Hitler calls on the western powers to accept Germany's conquest of Poland as a *fait accompli*.

7 Hitler names Himmler *Reichskommissar fuer die Festigung des deutschen Volkstums* [RKFVD] (State Commissioner for the Strengthening of Germandom). The office is set up to deal with repatriation of *Volksdeutsche* and settlement of German colonies in eastern occupied territories.

8 Propaganda Minister Josef Goebbels visits Lodz: Nazis stage a pogrom in his honor.

8 Polish elementary schools are permitted to open while Jewish schools are ordered closed under the pretext of epidemics.

8 Polish Silesia and Pomerania are incorporated into the *Grossreich*.

8 Nazi order creates Poland's first ghetto, in Piotrkow Trybunalski.

8 The Swiss chief of police orders deportation for all refugees in Switzerland who entered the country after September 6, 1939.

9 Hitler issues a secret directive in preparation for an early offensive in the west.

9 The Dutch government, opens a central camp for German Jewish refugees at Westerbork that is controlled by the Ministry of the Interior.

9 Kefar Warburg is established in the Malakhi Region.

10 The *Generalgouvernement* (General Government), an administrative unit of those parts of occupied Poland not incorporated into the *Reich*, is established.

10 The Soviet Union and Lithuania ratify a mutual assistance pact. The Soviets transfer the city and province of Vilna (formerly part of Poland) to Lithuanian jurisdiction, where thousands of Polish Jewish refugees find temporary refuge.

10 The Chilean government prohibits any more European political refugees into the country.

12 Hans Frank is appointed governor general of Poland.

12 First deported Jews from Austria and Czechoslovakia are sent to the Nisko-Lublin region of Poland.

12 Malcolm MacDonald stops legal immigration of Jews to Palestine for the next six months.

12 The Soviet Union presses territorial demands from Finland.

12 Chamberlain rejects Hitler's peace plan.

12 Conference of the Relief Committee for Jewish Masses in Poland opens in New York City.

13 Jewish *kehilla* of Lodz is disbanded by German order. An *Aeltestenrat* (Council of Elders), with Mordechai Chaim Rumkowski at its head, serves in its place.

15 Over one thousand patients are murdered in Owinska near Posen (Poznan), as part of the euthanasia program carried out in Nazi-occupied Poland.

15 Jews in Slovakia are to be recruited for compulsory labor service.

16 Cracow is named capital of the *Generalgouvernement*. Jews are urged to leave the city on a "voluntary basis."

17 Hitler issues a decree exempting SS and police from military service.

17 *Gestapo* arrests thousands of Austrian Gypsies and issues a decree prohibiting Gypsies from changing their place of residence within the *Grossreich*.

17 Twelve hundred Jews from Ostrava {Cz} are deported to the Nisko Nad Lanem {P} labor camp.

17   The Intergovernmental Committee on Political Refugees meets with President Roosevelt at the White House.

17   A Swiss federal decree authorizes the police to immediately deport all foreigners who entered the country illegally.

19   Warthegau is incorporated into the *Reich*. The Lublin ghetto is established.

19   The first Congress of Jewish Farm Youths opens in Moisesville, Argentina.

19   Signing of British-French-Turkish treaty.

20   Some 1,000 Jews from Vienna are deported to Nisko.

20   Papal encyclical, *Summi pontificatus,* attacks the war as anti-Christian, but does not mention Nazi atrocities against Jews or Poles.

23   The German civil administration established in the *Generalgouvernement* replaces the military occupation government.

24   The *Gestapo* in Wloclawek {P} orders Jews to wear a yellow triangle. Eight hundred Jews are arrested, many of whom are shot to death, while "trying to escape."

25   The American Christian Emergency Council for Palestine urges President Roosevelt and the Intergovernmental Refugee Committee to intercede with Britain to admit 100,000 Jewish refugees into Palestine annually.

26   *Zwangsarbeit*, a forced labor decree for Polish Jews, and *Arbeitspflicht*, a decree for Polish labor duty, are both promulgated in occupied Poland. The first decree affects all Jews between fourteen and sixty years old, while thousands of young Polish nationals are deported to Germany for labor duty under the second degree.

26   A second contingent of Austrian and Czech Jews is deported to the Lublin-Nisko area.

26   Nazis prohibit *shechita* in the General Government.

26   The Rumanian section of the YMCA announces that it is contributing one million *lei* for the relief of Polish-Jewish refugees in Rumania.

27   Moravska-Ostrava {Cz} is rendered *Judenrein.*

27   Congress passes the U.S. Neutrality Act.

28   The German administration in Warsaw orders a Jewish census.

28   Cracow's *Judenrat*, with Dr. Marek Bieberstein as *Judenaelteste,* is established by Nazi order.

28   Clashes between Czech student demonstrators and police erupt in Prague.

30   Himmler orders all Jews deported from the annexed Polish western provinces within four months.

31   The Brazilian Ministry of Justice rejects an appeal to revoke the ban on the Zionist Federation of Brazil.

31   Social Justice, the Father Coughlin antisemitic organization, is banned in Canada.

NOVEMBER

1   Egypt and Iraq demand amnesty for all interned Arabs in Palestine.

1/2   The Soviet Union annexes the western Ukraine and western Belorussia, formerly part of Poland.

2   Germany and Lithuania reach an agreement regarding Jewish refugees.

4   A "Cash and Carry" amendment to the Neutrality Act is passed by the U.S. Congress allowing for European democracies to buy American arms.

5   The Berlin Jewish Community Library is seized by the *Institut der NSDAP zur Erforschung der Judenfrage*, the Nazi Institute for Racial Research.

5   The National Labor Committee for Palestine launches a one million dollar campaign to upbuild the *Yishuv*.

6   The *Gestapo* arrests Polish professors and lecturers from the Jagellonian University in Cracow.

7   First expulsion of Jews from Warthegau.

8   An attempt is made on Hitler's life in the Munich *Buergerbrau Keller*, the top Nazis' favorite tavern.

9   Nazis annex Lodz, now Litzmanstadt, to the Third *Reich*. A campaign of terror accelerates against the city's 200,000 Jews.

9   Nazis close down Lublin University and arrest a number of its professors.

10   The Jewish Labor Committee begins a fundraising campaign to help Polish war victims.

11   The *Gestapo* unseats the thirty-one member Lodz *Judenrat* and appoints a new council in its stead, deporting the former members to a nearby slave labor camp at Radegast.

11   Some 600 Jews in Ostrow Mazowiecka {P} who did not escape to the Soviet side, are driven to a forest outside the town and murdered by German police.

11/15   *Brennkommandos* burn down ten synagogues in Lodz.

12   Hitler and the OKW plan for *Fall Gelb* (Case Yellow), the invasion of Holland.

12   The Belgian government bans the antisemitic and racist Rexist party journal *Le Pays Reel* and *Der Stuermer*.

12   Hundreds of Slovakian Jews are arrested on drummed-up charges of complicity in an anti-Nazi plot.

12   The majority of Gniesno's {P} Jews are deported to the *Generalgouvernent* on orders of Wilhelm Koppe, HSSPF of Warthegau. Koppe also orders that Poznan {P} be *Judenrein* within three months.

14   Nazis report that Bydgoszcz {P} is *Judenrein*.

14   Lodz Jews are forced to wear a yellow armband ten centimeters wide on their right arms.

14   Theodor Eicke is appointed commander of the SS-*Totenkopf* Division.

14   The Ministry of Justice reports that over one-third of Rumanian Jewry, or close to 250,000 people, have lost their citizenship.

14   *Umsiedlungsaktion* (resettlement action) in Inowroclaw {P}: all Jews are deported to two other Polish towns, Gniezno and Kruszwica, and Inowroclaw is declared *Judenrein*.

15   Nazi order blocks all Jewish bank and credit accounts in Poland.

17   The SS takes over all universities in Czechoslovakia. Many Czech student leaders are murdered.

17   Rumanian chief rabbi and senator, Dr. Jacob Isaac Niemirower, dies and is given military funeral.

17   A Czechoslovak National Committee is set up in Paris.

18   All Jews in the Cracow district over twelve years old are ordered to wear a white armband with a blue Star of David.

18   Britain signs an agreement with the Polish government-in-exile to integrate the Polish navy within the structure of the Royal Navy.

18   Palestine police arrest thirty-eight IZL members.

20   Thousands of Czech university students, Communists, and trade unionists are deported to the Sachsenhausen concentration camp.

20 Himmler orders all Gypsy women astrologers and fortune tellers arrested and incarcerated in concentration camps.

20 By order of Berlin, *Einsatzgruppen* operations in Poland are terminated.

20 In accordance with general British policy, South Africa bans all refugees from Nazi-occupied territories.

20 *Hadassah* announces arrangements for the *aliya* of 1,200 children.

21 The Council of the Evangelical Pastors' Union protests the treatment of Jews in Slovakia.

23 Hans Frank decides that all Polish Jews must wear a blue Star of David embossed on a white armband.

24 *Juedisches Nachrichtenblatt/Zidovske Listy* (Jewish News Bulletin), a weekly newspaper in German and Czech, is published in Prague with *Gestapo* approval.

28 Nazis order *Judenrats* to replace the Jewish *kehillahs* in Poland.

30 The Soviet Union invades Finland after the latter rejects demands for a Russo-Finnish border alteration.

DECEMBER

1 Jews living in areas under Nazi occupation face loss of special food allocations.

1 As of this date, all Jews in the *Generalgouvernement* over twelve years old must wear the Star of David as formerly announced; *Judenrats* are held responsible for implementing this order.

1 The Greek government announces a subsidy grant of 550,000 *drachmas* for Jewish philanthropic institutions in Greece.

1 A death march begins in Poland for 1,800 Jews from Chelm to the Soviet-held town of Sokal {P}. The Nazis murder seventy-five percent of the victims *en route*.

1 Lithuanian Writers Association honors the 100th anniversary of Mendele Mocher Seforim (Shalom Jacob Abramovitch).

1 The Soviet Union forms a Finnish puppet government.

2 Finland appeals to the League of Nations for help.

3 *Umsiedlungsaktion* in Nasielsk {P} renders the town *Judenrein*.

3 Sir Harold MacMichael, High Commissioner for Palestine, refuses to grant clemency to Arab terrorists.

5 For a third time, thousands of Jews are expelled across the border into Soviet-occupied Poland.

5/6 Terror *aktion* occurs in the Jewish quarter of Cracow. Similar incidents, such as the burning of synagogues and looting of Jewish properties, are magnified throughout the General Government.

7 Jews in Germany are denied clothing ration cards and their food rations are reduced.

7 The *Fuehrer* of the Nazi party of Schleswig-Hollstein is convicted of subversion by Danish court.

9 The *Mossad* ship *Hilda* departs from Balchik {Ru} with 728 *ma'apilim*. On January 24, 1940 the British capture the ship and detain its refugees.

11 A second order concerning forced labor for the Jews of the *Generalgouvernement* is published. Severe restrictions on Jewish movement are also imposed.

11 The Mandatory government begins recruiting Palestine Pioneer Battalions.

11/12 The majority of Jews in Poznan {P} are deported to Ostrow Lubelski {P} and other towns in the General Government.

12 Slave labor camps for Jews, *Judenlagern*, are set up throughout the *Generalgouvernement*.

12/14 Over 10,000 Jews are deported from Lodz to the General Government.

13 A mass protest rally in Madison Square Garden is held in response to Nazi and Soviet aggression in Poland.

14 The Soviet Union is expelled from the League of Nations for attacking Finland.

14 Another mass rally at Madison Square Garden protests the treatment of Polish Jews under Nazi occupation.

17 Battle of River Plate: *SMS Graf Spee* is scuttled to avoid capture.

19 The Polish government-in-exile announces its intention to grant equal rights to all minorities in a reconstituted new Poland.

20 The Radomsko {P} ghetto is established.

24 *Brennkommandos* in Poland burn down the Siedlce synagogue.

25 *Brennkommandos* set fire to the Great Synagogue of Czestochowa during the second Nazi-instigated pogrom.

25 A conference representing all major Jewish organizations in Latin America opens in Buenos Aires: 260 delegates attend and launch a five million *peso* campaign for overseas aid.

27 All Jews are driven out from Aleksandrow Lodzki {P} and the town is declared *Judenrein*.

28 The Peruvian Chamber of Deputies defeats a bill aimed against the Jewish community, entailing registration and control of all Jewish residents as a precautionary measure against war profiteering.

29 *Umsiedlungsaktion* in Pulawy {P}: some 4,000 Jews are expelled to the Polish city Opole Lubelske.

1940

4 Hitler names Goering plenipotentiary for all German war industries.

5 All ritual baths in Warsaw are closed by German order.

5 The British government announces that holders of German and Austrian passports will not be allowed into Palestine, because they are "enemy aliens."

6/7 The First National Conference of the United Palestine Appeal [UPA] elects Abba Hillel Silver chairman, and calls upon Great Britain to open Palestine as a refuge for Poland's 3,500,000 Jews.

7 Negotiations between Hindu and Moslem nationalists in India break down.

8 Britain institutes food rationing.

10 Twentieth anniversary of the League of Nations.

13 Hans Frank issues strict orders implementing the October 26, 1939 compulsory labor law. All Jews in the *Generalgouvernement*, both male and female, from fourteen to sixty years old are affected.

13 Belgian and Dutch governments order a state of war readiness.

14 A British search of the *kibbutz* Mishmar-Hashelosha yields hidden *Hagana* arms.

15 Due to violence between supporters and opponents of presidential candidate Fulgencio Batista, Cuban elections are postponed until January 28.

15 The Belgian government refuses to allow French and British forces to pass through its territory.

16 Hitler cancels plans for attacking the Low Countries and France on January 17.

17 The British Royal Navy intercepts the *SS Hilda*, a chartered Greek vessel on its way to Palestine with 728 refugees.

17 Costa Rica requests United States naval protection for its coastal waters.

18 Slovakia and the Protectorate of Bohemia and Moravia institute compulsory labor for Jews and Gypsies.

18 British Catholic newspaper, *The Tablet*, agitates against admitting Jewish refugees into England.

18 All Jewish judges in Hungary are forced to retire.

20 *Einsatzstab Reichsleiter Rosenberg* [ERR] is established under the direction of Alfred Rosenberg, to confiscate Jewish libraries, archives, art collections, and museums.

21 Istanbul's *Ashkenazic* community dissolves and merges with the larger, officially recognized, *Sephardic* community.

21 The Lithuanian commissioner for refugees announces broad restrictions against letting refugees into the country.

24 A decree is published announcing that all Jewish property in the *Generalgouvernement* must be registered.

25 *Reichsprotector* Konstantin von Neurath's decree eliminates all Jews from the Czech Protectorate's economy.

25 Goering orders ruthless exploitation of all available manpower and material resources in occupied Poland, including Polish state-owned property.

25 Lublin's {P} *Judenrat* is created under *Gestapo* order.

26 The *Gestapo* orders the Jews of Warsaw to pay 100,000 *zlotys* as ransom, or else 100 Jews would be executed.

26 Polish Jews are forbidden to travel by train or change residence without specific authorization.

26 Public worship in the synagogues of Warsaw is prohibited under the pretext of danger from epidemics.

27 Chaim Weizmann addresses the General Assembly of the Council of Jewish Federations and Welfare Funds meeting in Detroit, asking for undivided support for the *Yishuv*.

30 Dominican Republic Sosua refugee settlement agreement signed.

30 In a speech at the Berlin *Sportspalast* Hitler demands still more *lebensraum* (living space).

31 A special Jewish Labor Exchange established by the *Gestapo* in Berlin.

31 The Lithuanian government officially recognizes Vilna's Jewish community.

FEBRUARY

1 Jews in Italy are prohibited from acting as notaries or from employment as journalists.

1 The Blockade runner *Sakarya* departs from Constanta with 2,228 *ma'apilim* under the command of Eri Jabotinsky. The ship is captured by the British on February 13 and its refugees detained.

5 The United States establishes diplomatic relations with Saudi Arabia.

5 Britain and France decide to intervene against German designs on Norway.

6 Some 8,000 Jewish refugees in Belgium volunteer to join the Belgian army, but their offer is temporarily rejected by the government for safety reasons. Instead, many are interned.

7/8 The debate over Jewish immigration in Chile leads to government reorganization.

8 The Nazis designate an area for a Jewish ghetto in Lodz: over 160,000 Jews are crowded into an area measuring about 4 km. in circumference, with only slightly more than half of the area occupied by buildings.

8 Chaim Weizmann meets with President Roosevelt regarding Palestine negotiations between Jews and Arabs.

9 Hungary prohibits kosher meat imports.

10 The Soviet Union deports approximately 200,000 Poles from Russian-occupied eastern Poland.

10/12 Jews from Stettin and other parts of Upper Silesia are deported to the Lublin-Nisko district of Poland.

11 The Soviet Union and Germany sign a trade agreement.

12 The American Jewish Congress urges during its Washington convention that American Jewish leaders adopt a uniform approach to worldwide Jewish problems to present before an international peace conference.

13 The *SS Zechariah* is intercepted by the British Royal Navy. The 2,300 *ma'apilim* are interned in Athlit.

13 The *Hachnasat Orechim* (Hospitality) society in Salonika reports that it is maintaining seventy-five refugees from central Europe.

14 Governor Lehman of New York signs legislation banning labor union discrimination on racial or religious grounds.

14 Britain decides to arm all of its merchant ships in the North Sea.

15 A ghetto is established in Staszow {P}.

17 The Free Speech Forum in New York City holds a mass meeting to protest the antisemitic activities of the Christian Front.

21 *SS Oberfuehrer* (Brigadier-General) Richard Gluecks, the head of the Concentration Camp Inspectorate, suggests to Himmler a perfect site for a new camp—the grounds of a pre-World War I Austrian cavalry barracks located outside Auschwitz (Oswiecim), an out-of-way marshy little town.

21 Former President Herbert Hoover urges that the U.S. Congress appropriate $20,000,000 for Polish relief.

23 In Yugoslavia, Croat authorities decree severe limitations on refugees.

24 Hitler adopts *Fall Manstein*, a plan for an attack on the West, to be put into action in the spring.

26 Doctors at the National Jewish Hospital in Denver announce the discovery of a tuberculosis vaccine.

27 The land transfer regulation in the White Paper comes into force: Jewish land acquisition is restricted in Palestine.

27 The Rumanian Supreme Court upholds denaturalization for Rumanian Jews.

27 Churchill declares that the British Royal Navy and RAF have destroyed half of the German U-boat fleet.

28 The first Palestine Pioneer Battalion becomes operational: of the 1,050 officers and men, 750 are Jews.

29 The League of Nations condemns British Land Regulations for Palestine (Command #1040) as a repudiation of the Mandate.

29   Demonstrations and strikes break out all over Palestine in reaction to the British "Land Law."

MARCH

1   Bloody Thursday: thousands of Jews are attacked by Nazi-instigated gangs throughout the *Generalgouvernement*.

1   The Sieradz {P} ghetto is established.

3   Yugoslavia's government orders a census of all refugees living in the country.

6   Chile orders all persons with tourist visas to leave the country.

8   An antisemitic book, *The Mystery of Freemasonry*, is published by the Catholic prelate of Chile, Archbishop Jose M. Caro.

9   The first transport with Polish prisoners arrives in Mauthausen.

9   Gusen, is established as a subcamp of KL Mauthausen.

10   British Fascist leader, Sir Oswald Mosley, advocates expulsion of Jews from England.

11   Britain repudiates the authority of the International Court of Justice in The Hague.

11   The New York World's Fair opens: closes October 27.

13   Finland signs an armistice with the Soviet Union.

14   Vladimir (Zeev) Jabotinsky arrives in America.

15   A ghetto established in Bochnia {P}.

17   HIAS opens its fifty-fifth annual convention with a campaign for $1,000,000 to aid refugees and immigrants.

18   Hitler and Mussolini meet at the Brenner Pass.

18   Netherlands Jewish Society founded.

20   The Belgian government bans two antisemitic publications, *Volksverwering* and *National Socialiste Volken en Vaderland*.

21   French government under Edouard Daladier resigns. Paul Reynaud forms a new cabinet.

23   By Goering's order, deportations from the *Grossreich* to the Lublin-Nisko reservation cease.

24   Lublin's {P} 40,000 Jews are ordered into a ghetto.

29   The Italian government revokes commercial licenses for Jewish-owned tobacco shops and coffee stands.

31 *Ausserordentliche Befriedungsaktion* [ABA], or Special Tranquilizing Operation against Polish Intelligentsia, begins, to continue through July 12.

31 Mohammed Ali Jinnah demands that India be partitioned into Hindu and Moslem states.

31 The Conference of Jewish Youth Organizations in New York denounces the British land restriction law in Palestine.

APRIL

1 The Shanghai Refugee Aid Committee reports that some 14,000 of the close to 20,000 refugees receive aid in the form of food and shelter.

2 The Greek government promulgates a law forbidding intermarriage.

2 Hans Frank declares that his city, Cracow, must become *Judenfrei* (free of Jews).

2 Hitler orders occupation of Denmark and Norway.

3 Mosley accuses Jews of causing the war.

7 Cyrus Adler, American Jewish scholar, communal leader, editor of the *Jewish Quarterly Review*, and a founder of the Jewish Publication Society of America and the American Jewish Committee, dies at age seventy-seven.

7 The Chilean Jewish Congress votes to affiliate with the World Jewish Congress, and supports the Pan American Jewish Congress movement.

7 The United Galician Jews in America opens its campaign to aid Polish Jews.

8/11 Katyn massacre of Polish prisoners of war.

9 Germany invades Denmark and Norway.

9 Vidkun Quisling, head of the *Hirdmen*, the Norwegian storm troopers, establishes a collaborationist government in Norway.

11 The Chilean Foreign Ministry announces that under no circumstances will Jews be given immigration visas.

11 The Palestine government bans all forms of military and paramilitary training by private groups.

13 The second deportation is effected, with the dispatch of over 250,000 Poles from Soviet-occupied Poland to Siberia.

14 British naval forces land in Norway. Their attempt to take Trondheim fails.

14 Bet Yizhak, a rural settlement in the Central Sharon, is established.

15   Anglo-French forces land in Norway.

15   Nazis remove the Star of David from the last synagogue in Poznan {P} and declare the city *Judenrein*.

19   The *Institut fuer deutsches Ostarbeit* (Institute for German Work in the East) opens in Cracow.

20   The Danish army is demobilized.

22   *SS-Gruppenfuehrer* (Lieutenant-General) Odilo Globocnik proposes plans for an elaborate slave labor camp system for Jews.

24   The *Reichskommissariat* for Norway is established.

24   High Commissioner Harold MacMichael permits non-Arabs to transfer out of Arab villages in Palestine.

25   David Ben-Gurion leaves for the United States.

25   Britain announces that the Palestine certificate allotment for the next six months will be 9,000, from which the number of "illegal" immigrants in the country will be deducted.

25   King Carol frees some 1,000 Rumanian political prisoners, many of them members of the notoriously antisemitic Iron Guard.

26   An Anglo-Swiss trade agreement is signed.

27   Heinrich Himmler orders a large concentration camp built at Auschwitz.

28   A ghetto is established in Loewenstadt, formerly Brzeziny {P} in the German annexed province of Wartheland.

29   *SS-Sturmbannfuehrer* (Major) Rudolf Hoess, the first camp commandant, arrives in Auschwitz.

29   The Australian government announces that it will bar entry to all refugees coming from Nazi-occupied countries.

30   The Lodz ghetto is sealed off.

30   Italian Fascist leader Roberto Farinacci denounces the Vatican journal *Osservatore Romano* (Roman Observer) as the mouthpiece of the Jews.

MAY

1   The Norwegian government-in-exile is established in London by King Haakon.

1   Jews in Cracow are prohibited from using the city's main streets, boulevards and thoroughfares.

2 *Kibbutz* Sedot Yam is established in the Northern Sharon, the first settlement after the new "land laws."

2 A slave-labor camp is established in Bortatycze {P}.

3 Bolivia suspends issuing immigration visas to Jewish refugees.

9 Belgian and Dutch forces are placed on war alert.

9 President Roosevelt names Professor Louis Finkelstein, chancellor of the Jewish Theological Seminary, as the Jewish religious representative to the president's advisory council on peace efforts.

10 Germany invades the Low Countries and France.

10 Chamberlain resigns: Winston S. Churchill becomes the new prime minister of Great Britain and forms new cabinet.

10 Switzerland orders general mobilization of its reserves.

10 British troops land in Iceland to prevent a possible German invasion.

10 The Belgian government releases all refugees previously interned in special camps.

11 Allied units occupy Dutch Caribbean islands to defend oil fields in Curacao.

12 The *Gerer rebbe,* Abraham Mordechai Alter, arrives in Palestine.

13 The Dutch government-in-exile is established in London.

13 Britain orders internment of 3,000 German and Austrian nationals on the Isle of Man, which affects a large number of Jewish refugees.

13 Churchill delivers his "blood and toil" speech to the British commonwealth and the English-speaking world.

14 Intense *Luftwaffe* attacks on Rotterdam kill close to 1,000 people.

14 Germany occupies Luxembourg.

15 Holland capitulates to Germany.

15 Chaim Weizmann and David Ben-Gurion meet with British Colonial Secretary Lord George A. Lloyd in London.

16 President Roosevelt asks Congress for sharp increases in defense spending in view of the rapidly deteriorating condition in Europe.

16 All so-called "B" category male aliens between ages sixteen and sixty are detained by the British government. On May 27 the order is amended to include all "B" category females within the same age group.

18 The Organization of American States [OAS] adopts the Panamanian resolution condemning German invasion of the Low Countries.

18 A decree is promulgated ordering Cracow's Jews to leave the city on a "voluntary" basis.

19 Arthur Seyss-Inquart is appointed *Reichskommissar* for Nazi-occupied Holland.

19/21 At its twenty-third annual convention in Baltimore, the *Mizrachi* Organization of America votes to establish a settlement in Palestine, in honor of the late Chief *Ashkenazi* Rabbi, *Rav* Abraham I. Kook.

20 KL Auschwitz begins functioning.

20 The German army reaches the English Channel.

20 German occupation authorities in Holland order roundup and internment of all refugees.

20 Hitler approves Himmler's memorandum on the treatment of non-Germans in the East.

20 American airplane designer Igor Sikorsky achieves the first successful helicopter flight.

21 An aborted British counter-attack takes place near Arras {F}.

22 The Emergency Powers Act provides for martial law in England.

22 French police order thousands of Jewish refugees in France interned.

22 President Roosevelt proposes transfer of the Immigration and Naturalization Service from the Labor Department to the Justice Department.

23 German aircraft bomb Dover.

23 BUF leader Sir Oswald Mosley is arrested under the Emergency Powers Act.

24 The Canadian war cabinet debates the refugee problem.

25 The Nazi Lodz *Gettoverwaltung* (ghetto administration), under Hans Biebow, orders factories set up to manufacture goods for the German war machine.

25 The Canadian government agrees to admit 10,000 non-Jewish refugee children of British, Belgian, Dutch, or French origin.

26 Operation Dynamo, the evacuation of British and French forces from Dunkirk, begins, and is completed by June 3.

27 Members of the *SS-Totenkopfverbande* commanded by *SS-Obersturmfuehrer* (First Lieutenant) Fritz Knoechlein machine-gun to death some 100 British POWs from the Royal Norfolk Regiment in the village of Le Paradis in France's Pas-de-Calais.

28   Belgium surrenders to Germany.

28   A Women's Zionist Organization is announced in Mexico City.

29   Belzec opens as a slave labor camp, later becoming one of the six most notorious extermination camps humanity ever knew.

29   Rumania announces internment for all Polish refugees who could not prove they had an opportunity to emigrate.

30   The majority of the Jewish communal organizations in Holland are taken over by the *Gestapo.*

30   The Canadian government closes the antisemitic National Unity Party and arrests its leaders.

31   President Roosevelt announces a "million dollar defense" program.

JUNE

2   The National Conference of *Poale Agudas Yisroel* [PAY] and *Aguda* are strongly criticized for their former attitudes. The Conference calls on *Aguda* to cooperate fully in the build-up of Israel.

3   Nightly blackouts between 9 PM and 4 AM are ordered for all of Palestine.

4   The first Interfaith Conference on Unemployment opens in Washington, DC.

4   Ferramonti di Tarsia, an internment camp for Italian and foreign Jews is established in southern Italy.

5   Children's homes and refugee shelters in Holland are taken over by the *Gestapo*.

9/10   Norway surrenders to Germany.

10   Italy enters the war on Germany's side.

10   Governor General Hans Frank announces plans to deport Jews from the *Generalgouvernement*.

11   The Argentinian government outlaws the publishing of "opinionated articles."

11   The Nationwide Conference on Religious liberty, with 600 educators and clergymen attending, opens in Washington, DC.

11/12   The first clashes between British and Italian air and sea forces occur in the Mediterranean.

13   Mexico suspends its immigrant quotas.

13 The Uruguay chamber of deputies passes a bill to dissolve all organizations instructed from abroad.

14 Nazis occupy Paris after it is declared an open city.

14 The first transport of 700 Polish political prisoners arrives at Auschwitz.

14 Spain occupies Tangier.

15 The first Jewish aid committee under Nazi occupation is set up in Paris.

15 The United States ignores France's appeal for help.

15/17 Soviet forces occupy Lithuania.

16 Paul Reynaud resigns as French premier. Marshal Henri Philippe Petain becomes the new prime minister.

16 Britain offers political union with France.

16 A ghetto is created in Kutno {P}.

17 Petain proposes a ceasefire.

17/18 A Palestinian-Jewish unit covers British and French withdrawal to Dunkirk.

18 General Charles de Gaulle creates Free France on British soil and appeals to young Frenchmen to bear arms against Nazi oppressors.

18 The Uruguayan government issues a decree prohibiting the dissemination of anti-democratic propaganda.

19 Polish troops evacuate from western France to England.

19 In a radio address, Polish General Wladyslaw Sikorski declares that Poland will continue to fight on Great Britain's side.

20 The United States Committee for the Care of European Children is created.

20 Soviet forces occupy Latvia and Estonia is occupied the next day.

21 The 52,000 Jewish refugees in Britain are exempted from the restrictive orders applied to "enemy aliens."

21 Technocracy, a semi-Fascist Canadian organization, is closed by police order.

21 The British Colonial Defense Act is officially amended.

21 Rumania becomes a totalitarian state, with the new totalitarian Party of the Nation replacing the Front of National Renascence. The Iron Guard joins the Party.

22 France signs an armistice agreement with Germany and a collaborationist government is established at Vichy under Marshal Petain.

24 A Franco-Italian armistice signed.

24 Yugoslavia and Russia resume diplomatic relations.

24 A Rumanian royal decree bars Jews from joining the Party of the Nation.

24 Hungarian Fascist and pro-Nazi parties amalgamate into one organization.

25 The Bilgoraj {P} ghetto is established.

25 The American Jewish Press Club is founded.

26 The Soviet Union gives a twenty-four hour ultimatum to Rumania to surrender the Bessarabia and Bukovina provinces.

26 Polish air, land, and naval forces escaping to Great Britain unite to form the Polish army in exile.

27 Soviet forces occupy Northern Bukovina and Bessarabia.

27 Initial contact is made for an anti-Japan alliance between U.S. Secretary of State Cordell Hull and representatives of Australia and Britain.

30 In the wake of the Soviet occupation of Bessarabia and Northern Bukovina, Rumanian soldiers stage a bloody pogrom, killing hundreds of Jews. The towns of Dorohoi and Galati bear the brunt of the massacres.

30 Nazis occupy the English Channel islands.

30 The forty-third annual convention of the Zionist Organization of America opens in Pittsburgh where it urges Britain to give *Yishuv* the right to arm itself in view of the general situation.

JULY

1 Rumania repudiates the trilateral defense treaty with England and France.

1 The Bedzin {P} ghetto is established.

3 The British Royal Navy attacks the French naval base at Mers el-Kebir to prevent Vichy from handing vessels over to the Nazis.

4 Berlin Jews are permitted to go food shopping only between the hours of four and five in the afternoon.

4 A Fascist government gains power in Rumania under Ion Gigurtu.

5 President Roosevelt delivers his "four freedoms" speech.

5   Vichy France breaks off diplomatic relations with Britain.

7   Vichy orders the roundup and internment of all German and Austrian Jews.

9   A sea battle between British and Italian fleets takes place near Malta.

9   Rumania places itself under German protection.

10   Marshal Petain becomes president of Vichy and the French Third Republic is considered finished.

10   The Battle of Britain begins, as seventy *Luftwaffe* aircraft attack targets in southern Wales.

13   New regulations affect admittance of refugee children to the United States, particularly those from Britain.

13   Soviet NKVD begin arresting Bessarabian Zionists.

15   The Italian air force bombs Haifa.

16   Jews of Alsace-Lorraine are deported to the Vichy zone.

17   Hitler orders Operation Sea Lion (directive #16), the invasion of England.

18   Under Japanese pressure the British temporarily close the Burma Road.

19   Hitler attempts another peace proposal, which Great Britain rejects.

19   The *Gestapo* confiscates all telephones in Jewish possession in Germany.

21   Russia annexes Lithuania, Latvia, and Estonia.

22   The latest Vichy law strips immigrant Jews of their French citizenship.

22   The Special Operations Executive [SOE] is created by British War Cabinet to assist resistance movements throughout Europe.

23   Hans Frank orders all independent Jewish institutions in Poland liquidated.

23   The House of Commons approves the highest income tax in British history.

28   Slovakian government leaders Josef Tiso, Voitech Tuka, and Sano Mach meet in Salzburg with representatives of the Third *Reich* to exchange ideological views. They decide to attach German racial advisors to the various Slovak governmental departments, especially those dealing with the Jewish question.

AUGUST

1   Church leaders in Sydney make a public appeal to help refugees from Nazism settle in Australia.

2   *Straflager* (punishment camp) Gross-Rosen {G} opens as a subcamp of KL Sachsenhausen-Oranienburg.

3   Italy invades British and French Somaliland.

4   Vladimir (Zeev) Jabotinsky, leader of HA-ZACH, dies.

5   Signing of a British-Polish military agreement.

5   German occupation authorities in Holland prohibit *shechita*.

6   Britain evacuates its forces in China.

7   Alsace-Lorraine is incorporated into the *Grossreich*.

7   Britain recognizes the French Committee of National Liberation. General de Gaulle becomes the "Free French" leader.

7   Jews in a number of streets in the Warsaw Jewish quarter are ordered to build a wall (*aussperrmauer*) as a preliminary to formation of a ghetto.

8   Germany begins concerted attacks on British shipping and naval bases.

8   Rabbi Chaim Ozer Grodzinski, talmudic scholar and spiritual leader of Lithuanian Orthodox Jewry, dies in Vilna.

10   A series of racial laws are enacted in Rumania.

10   Gypsy males in the Protectorate of Bohemia and Moravia are incarcerated in special labor camps *en masse*.

13   Vichy promulgates law excluding Freemasons from holding public office.

13   *Adler Tag* (the Day of the Eagle): official start of the German *Luftwaffe* campaign to destroy the British RAF.

13   Italy begins invading Egypt: the unsuccessful Italian offensive ends September 18.

14   The *Irgun Zvai Leumi* is divided over a proposal for a truce with the British.

14   *Hazit Dor Bnei Midbar* [HDBM], a Zionist youth movement, is founded in the Lodz ghetto.

15   The *Luftwaffe* renews its large-scale air attacks in the Battle of Britain.

17   A mass demonstration is held in the Lodz ghetto.

17   *Forteresse Juive* is established in France.

17 Germany declares a total blockade of Great Britain.

17 The United States and Canada agree on joint defense measures.

18 Hans Frank declares that Cracow, capital of the *Generalgouverne-ment*, must become *Judenrein*, and that international Jewry must vanish from the face of the earth.

18 The *Luftwaffe* launches its biggest air raid in the Battle of Britain on RAF installations in southern England.

21 Leon Trotsky is murdered in Mexico City by Stalinist agents.

23 Cabinet crisis in Argentina.

24/25 The *Luftwaffe* blitz London.

27 Vichy repeals the Marchandeau Law that had effectively suppressed antisemitic newspaper articles.

27 The U.S. Congress votes for peacetime compulsory military service.

27 Presidential candidate Wendell Wilkie repudiates his support for Father Coughlin and others because of their antisemitic and racial bigotry.

29 The Jewish Agency Executive proposes to the British the establish-ment a Jewish military unit for Palestine.

30 The Soviet Union demands the territory of North Transylvania from Rumania.

30 A military junta under General Ion Antonescu forces Carol II, King of Rumania, to abdicate in favor of his son Michael.

31 Roosevelt announces a limited call-up of the National Guard.

SEPTEMBER

3 The "Destroyer for Bases" deal is arranged between the United States and Britain.

4 Ion Antonescu is appointed prime minister of Rumania and assumes dictatorial powers.

4 During a Nazi rally in the Berlin *Sportspalast*, Hitler threatens to "exterminate British cities."

5 Nuremberg Laws are extended to the small Jewish community in Luxembourg.

6 Antonescu proclaims himself *Conducator* of Rumania.

6 The Mlawa {P} ghetto is established.

9 Tel Aviv is bombed by Italian air force: 112 people are killed, 150 wounded.

13 A decree is published restricting Jewish residence to within the *Generalgouvernement*.

14 The Italian army invades Egypt from Libya.

14 Vichy arrests former French Premier Leon Blum.

14 Palestine's government announces its intent to recruit Jews and Arabs for separate, but equal, infantry battalions as part of the "Buffs" regiment (First Royal Fuisileers).

14 Ion Antonescu declares Rumania a National-Legionnaire state.

15 London is blitzed in another *Luftwaffe* air raid.

16 The United States institutes peacetime draft.

17 Hitler cancels Operation Sea Lion, the invasion of Britain.

19 Fifty thousand Jews from the Warsaw district are ordered into Warsaw's Jewish quarter.

20 Nazis establish a *Polizeihaftlager*, a police internment camp, in the Breendonck Fortress near Antwerp.

25 Germany begins Nazification of Norway.

26 The Slovakian government orders formation of the *Ustredna Zidov* (Jewish Center), a Jewish Council.

27 The Tripartite Pact is signed by Germany, Italy, and Japan.

27 Antisemitic legislation is enacted in the German-occupied zone of France: Jewish shops must be marked with the Star of David; Jews who fled from the occupied zone are forbidden to return to their homes.

27 Germany orders a census of the Jewish population in all of France.

27 The Rumanian government expropriates all Jewish-owned land.

27 The U.S. Senate ratifies the Havana Convention.

OCTOBER

2 Hitler declares that the area of the *Generalgouvernement* will be transformed into a big Polish labor camp.

2 German U-boats sink the *Empress of Britain*, which carried evacuee children bound for Canada.

3 *Statut des Juifs* (Statute on the Jews) is enacted by Vichy.

4 Hitler confers with Mussolini.

4 A new Vichy law allows French police to arbitrarily arrest any foreign Jew.

4   In its first edition *De Geus onder Studenten*, a Dutch college students' underground paper, informs its readers of Nazi antisemitism.

5   Rumania enacts a law allowing for confiscation of Jewish property in rural areas of the country.

7   German troops occupy the Rumanian oilfields.

7   The Polish *Judenraete* must pay for the cost of equipment and food for Jewish forced labor gangs.

7   Hans Frank, Governor General of Poland, declares that, unfortunately, he "could not eliminate all lice (vermin) and Jews" in one year's time.

7   Vichy annuls the Cremieux Decree of October 1870, which granted Algerian Jews French citizenship.

10   The Japanese mayor of Shanghai murdered.

14   All Jewish students are banned from attending Rumanian educational institutions.

15   A ghetto is established in Falenica {P}.

16   The Warsaw ghetto is officially established, comprising 4.6 percent of the city's residential area.

18   The Vichy government introduces antisemitic legislation.

18   The second published German ordinance in occupied France concerns the registration and transfer of Jewish property.

20/22   Operation Buerckel: the Nazis deport 7,500 Jews from Baden, the Palatinate, and the Saar to Gurs in the south of Vichy France.

22   Liquidation of the Speyer {G} Jewish community: all Jews are deported to Gurs {F}. Some 2,000 Jews from Mannheim {G} and at least one-third (350) of the Jewish population in Heidelberg {G} are also deported to Gurs.

22   The Women's Council of *B'nai B'rith* is formed.

23   Hitler and Franco meet at the Spanish-French border; Hitler attempts to persuade Spain to join the war.

23   The German administration in Belgium prohibits ritual slaughter.

23   The United States declares its intention to defend the Philippines.

24   Hitler and Petain meet at Montoire: French collaboration with Germany is settled.

27   The entire Jewish population of Albania (150 families) is ordered to leave the country within two months.

28 Nuremberg Laws are introduced in Belgium: A Jewish census is ordered; Jews of Antwerp are forced to register their businesses with Nazi officials; Jewish shops are marked with trilingual signboards; all Jews are ordered eliminated from public administration.

28 A meeting is held in Florence, Italy, between Hitler and Mussolini along with their foreign ministers.

28 Italy invades Greece.

30/31 The *Commission Centrale des Organisations Juives d'Assistance* [CCOJA] (Central Commission of Jewish Organizations for Assistance), a Jewish umbrella organization of various welfare societies, is set up in Marseilles through the efforts of the chief rabbi of Strasbourg, Rene Hirschler.

31 The Belgian government-in-exile established in London.

NOVEMBER

1 American civilians are evacuated from Shanghai.

1/3 The British forcefully transfer 1,771 *ma'apilim* from the *SS Pacific* and *SS Milos* to the *SS Patria*.

5 Roosevelt is reelected to an unprecedented third term.

6 Michael Cardinal Faulhaber, a leader of the German Catholic Church, speaks out against euthanasia.

8 Pustkow {P} *Judenarbeitslager*, one of the earliest and most vicious camps for Jews, is established.

9 The British Colonial Office announces that "illegal" Jewish immigrants will be deported to the Mauritius Islands.

10 Neville Chamberlain dies.

11 The British Royal Navy attacks and destroys most of the Italian fleet anchored in the Bay of Taranto.

11 An emergency meeting of *Asefat ha-Nivharim* deals with immigration and especially with the passengers of the *Pacific* and *Milos*.

12/14 Molotov-Hitler negotiations are held in Berlin.

14 Greek forces launch an all-out counterattack, pushing the Italians into Albania by November 21.

14/15 Coventry, England is bombed.

15 The Holy Synod of the Bulgarian Church protests that the wording of the Law for the Protection of the Nation is anti-Jewish.

15 The prison on 24 Gesia Street within the Warsaw ghetto begins operation. The prison is officially under *Judenrat* authority, but in reality under the *Gestapo*.

15 The Wlochy {P} ghetto is established.

16 The Warsaw ghetto is ordered closed off.

17 The Lodz "ghetto archive" is instituted by *Juden-aelteste* Mordechai Chaim Rumkowski.

17 *Lietuviu Aktyvistu Frontas* (Lithuanian Activist Front), a pro-Fascist nationalist organization, is set up in Berlin.

20 Hungary joins the Axis.

20 The Palestine government announces that it intends to deport the *Patria*'s passengers to an unnamed British colony; in response *Yishuv* declares one day hunger strike.

23 Rumania joins the Axis.

24 Pope Pius XII prays for peace during a radio broadcast.

24 Slovakia joins the Axis.

24 The *SS Atlantic*, with 1,770 "illegal" passengers, arrives in Haifa.

27 The *SS Patria* sinks in Haifa Bay after *Hagana* sappers try to scuttle the ship to prevent the British from deporting the Jewish refugees aboard. Two hundred Jews are killed in the explosion that follows. The survivors as well as the refugees aboard the *SS Atlantic* are transferred to Athlit prison.

27 The Dies Committee publishes its "Red Paper" on illegal Communist activities in the United States.

30 Some 250 Jewish refugees in Luxembourg are deported to Vichy.

DECEMBER

1 Death of Rabbi Dr. Bernard Revel, founder and first president of *Yeshiva* University.

2 Hungarian Jewish labor servicemen are segregated from non-Jews and organized into separate units.

9 Operation Compass, a British counteroffensive under General Archibald Wavell, defeats the Italian army in North Africa.

9 A twenty-four hour *Luftwaffe* attack marks the high-point of the London blitz.

12 The *SS Salvador*, an "illegal" ship on its way to Palestine, sinks in the Sea of Marmara. Out of 326 Bulgarian Jews aboard, over 200 drowned, including seventy children.

13 Armed gangs of Macedonian refugees, assisted by members of the Iron Guard, attack, rob, and destroy Jewish-owned shops in Constanta, Rumania.

14 Petain ousts Pierre Laval from Vichy cabinet.

15 The Skierniewice {P} ghetto is established.

16 The Nobel Committee announces cancellation of the 1940 Peace Prize.

16 British troops in North Africa surround the Italian garrison at Bardia.

18 Hitler secretly orders OKW to prepare plans for a quick campaign against the Soviet Union (directive #21/Barbarossa), to be ready by May 15, 1941.

19 Refugees from the *SS Atlantic* are deported from Palestine to the British Island of Mauritius.

19 Italian high command requests German military assistance in North Africa.

20 *Mapai* and HA-ZACH agree to cooperate for the duration of the national emergency.

24 Bulgaria enacts an antisemitic bill, to create the Law for the Protection of the Nation.

29 London is firebombed.

29 In a "fireside chat" broadcast from the White House, President Roosevelt tells the American people that the United States must become an "arsenal of democracy."

1941

JANUARY

4 Henri Bergson, French-Jewish philosopher, dies.

6 President Roosevelt asks Congress to support a lend-lease program for the Allies.

10 The Belgian government-in-exile broadcasts its intention to annul all Nazi-imposed laws at the war's end.

10 All Dutch Jews are ordered to register.

10 Jewish merchants in Craiova {Ru} are forced to sign over ownership of their shops to members of the Iron Guard.

10 Charles A. Lindbergh, testifying before Congress, opposes the Lend-Lease Bill.

12 The first edition of the *Biuletyn Kroniki Codziennej* (Daily Chronicle Bulletin) in the Polish language, appears in the Lodz ghetto.

14 Ion Antonescu meets with Hitler in Berlin.

16 Japanese forces demand administration of Indo-China.

16 *Luftwaffe* Stuka dive-bombers appear over Malta for the first time.

20 Franklin Delano Roosevelt is inaugurated to his third presidential term.

21 The Rumanian government decrees that Jews must pay a special "military tax" in lieu of military service.

21/24 Iron Guard attempts a *coup d'etat* in Bucharest which leads to anti-Jewish pogroms.

22 Darquier de Pellepoix is appointed Commissar for Jewish Affairs by the Vichy government.

22/27 The Jewish community in Piaseczno {P} is liquidated; all Jews are transferred to the Warsaw ghetto.

23 Bulgaria adopts the Law for the Protection of the Nation; Jews married to non-Jews, converts to Christianity, and war veterans are exempted.

29 *Va'ad Leumi* and Jewish Agency representatives publish emergency policy guidelines.

30 The British Eighth Army captures Tobruk.

30 Hitler repeats the threat he made to the *Reichstag* on January 30, 1939 to wipe out European Jews.

30 A pro-British uprising breaks out in Abyssinia.

30 *Comisia Autonoma de Ajutorare*, a Refugee Aid Committee for Jews in Rumania, is established in Bucharest.

FEBRUARY

2 The Warsaw ghetto is divided into twenty-eight rabbinical districts under the jurisdiction of sixteen rabbis.

2 German Nazis, with the help of local Dutch Nazis of the *Nationaal Socialistisch Beweging* [NSB] (National Socialist Movement), try to burn down the great synagogue in The Hague, but the local fire department interferes and puts out the flames.

3 Britain completes occupation of Cyrenaica.

3 NKGB is founded as a section of the Soviet NKVD.

4 The United Service Organization [USO] is created to provide for the social and emotional needs of American service personnel.

5 The Law for the Protection of the State is enacted by Rumanian legislature.

6 British forces capture Benghazi, Cyrenaica.

6 Hitler orders Rommel to rescue the Italians in North Africa.

8 Lord Moyne (Eric Arthur Guiness) succeeds Lord Lloyd as British Colonial Secretary and scuttles plans to form a Palestinian-Jewish fighting division.

9 A general protest-strike paralyzes Amsterdam.

9 The *Gestapo* conducts first raid on the Jewish quarter of Amsterdam.

9 The British war cabinet decides to transfer troops from North Africa in order to reinforce the Greek military.

11 Most Gypsies are prohibited from serving in the *Wehrmacht*.

12 The *Afrika Korps* lands in Tripoli.

12 *Joodse Raad* (Jewish Council) is established in Amsterdam on Nazi orders, with Abraham Asscher appointed chairman. The Jewish quarter of Amsterdam is sealed off.

16 The British free forty-three *Hagana* and ten IZL members.

17 Gideon Force, a guerrilla unit to harass the Italians in Ethiopia, is organized under General Orde Wingate.

20 Polish Jews are barred from using all forms of public transportation.

20/28 Liquidation of the Plock {P} Jewish community: most Jews are sent to the Dzialdowo {P} *zwangsarbeitslager*.

22/23 Amsterdam *aktion*; 400 Jews taken hostage are deported to Mauthausen.

23 A recruitment order is published calling for Palestinian Jewish engineer and pioneer companies.

23/24 Nazis halve the Jewish population of Poland's Grojec ghetto, sending close to 3,000 Jews to the Warsaw ghetto.

25 General strikes are held in all the larger Dutch cities to protest mistreatment of Jews.

25 British forces occupy Italian Somaliland.

25/26 Gur becomes *Judenrein* when all Jews are transferred to the Warsaw ghetto.

27 The Board of Rabbis in the Lodz ghetto permits non-*kosher* meats for the sick and the weak.

27 Britain and Hungary sign a friendship pact.

MARCH

1 *SS-Reichsfuehrer* Heinrich Himmler visits Auschwitz.

1 Bulgaria joins the Axis.

1 A "House of Culture," under the tutelage of Rumkowski, opens in the Lodz ghetto.

1 The Belchatow {P} ghetto is established.

2 German army units enter Bulgaria in force.

3 The German district governor, Otto Wachter, publishes a decree ordering the remaining Jews of Cracow into a ghetto in Podgorze by March 20.

4 British commandos raid the Lofoten Islands, destroying German installations in Norway's coastal islands.

7 German Jews are drafted as forced laborers.

7 British troops invade Abyssinia.

11 President Roosevelt signs the Lend-Lease Act (Bill 1776) into law.

11 Belgian Jews are ordered to enlist for slave labor.

13 The first of a series of mass Jewish arrests in occupied France begin.

13 Hitler orders OKW to begin planning for an invasion of the Soviet Union.

17 Hans Frank discusses with Hitler the fate of Polish Jewry in the *Generalgouvernement*.

18 The *Darien II*, with 800 refugees aboard, successfully evades a British blockade and reaches Haifa. The passengers are interned in Athlit by the British.

20 The Cracow {P} ghetto is sealed off by a wall and barbed-wire fence; some 20,000 Jews are squeezed together within its narrow confines.

20 The *Gestapo* in Amsterdam raids the Refugee Committee offices and orders the Committee for Special Jewish Affairs and all its subcommittees to dissolve. All committee funds are blocked.

24 The last Jews of Juelich {G} are deported.

26 The Institute for the Study of the Jewish Question begins operation in Frankfort.

27 Yugoslavia refuses to join the Axis.

29 The *Commissariat-General aux Questions Juives* [CGQJ], an office for Jewish Affairs is established in Vichy with jurisdiction over all of France. Vichy Premier Admiral Francois Darlan names Xavier Vallat commissioner.

30 Hitler briefs OKW generals on the upcoming ideological warfare with the Soviet Union.

30 The 34,000 Jews in Lublin {P} are ordered into a ghetto.

31 Field Marshal Edwin Rommel begins his counter-offensive in Cyrenaica.

APRIL

1/3 Rashid Ali leads an anti-British *coup* in Iraq. Pro-Nazi activists attack Jews in Baghdad.

2 Hungarian Premier Count Pal Teleki commits suicide rather than collaborate with Nazi Germany.

3 Arab anti-Jewish riots break out in Benghazi, Libya.

5 Yugoslavia and the Soviet Union conclude their friendship treaty.

5 British forces liberate Addis Ababa.

6 British units, including the Gideon Force, complete Ethiopian liberation.

6 German forces invade Greece and Yugoslavia. A heavy *Luftwaffe* air attack destroys large parts of Belgrade.

7 Himmler establishes a special murder task force, the *Einsatzstab*, independent from the *Einsatzgruppen*.

7 Two separate ghettos are created for the 35,000 Jews in Radom {P}.

9 *Juedischer Wohnbezirk*, a Jewish living district in reality an open ghetto is ordered for Czestochowa {P} Jews. The ghetto is sealed off August 23.

10 Jews in Amsterdam are prohibited from moving to other parts of Holland.

11 Hungarian forces invade Yugoslavia and occupy the Delvidek region.

11 Nazis forbid the *Messagero*, a Judeo-Spanish daily newspaper published in Salonika, Greece.

11 The *Joodse Weekblad* (Jewish Weekly), an officially German-approved paper, appears for the first time.

12/13 The *Wehrmacht* occupies Belgrade, Yugoslavia surrenders, and King Peter and his government flee to Egypt. Most of the country is divided between German and Italian occupation zones.

13 A Japanese-Soviet nonaggression pact is signed in Moscow.

14 Belgian Nazis rampage through Antwerp.

14 German soldiers helped by *Volksdeutsche* (who point out Jewish shops) rob and ransack Jewish businesses in Belgrade.

15 The Warsaw ghetto *Judenrat*, with German permission, declares the Sabbath, *Rosh Hashana, Yom Kippur, Sukkoth*, Passover (the first two and last two days), and *Shavuot* designated rest days.

15   The *Gestapo* raids Jewish communal offices in Salonika and arrests the Jewish community leaders.

16   The Croat Republic is declared, led by Ante Pavelic.

17   The newly established Croatian state promulgates the Protection of the People and the State Act: Yugoslavian Jews are its first victims.

18   The United States declares a zone of influence out to 30 degrees west longitude (the mid-Atlantic), including Greenland and Iceland.

20   Hitler appoints Alfred Rosenberg Minister for the Eastern Territories.

22   British forces begin withdrawing from Greece. The evacuation ends May 2.

22   American Friends of Hebrew University is founded.

26   A new German ordinance limits French Jews to less than a handful of occupations and professions that they may pursue.

27   German troops occupy Athens; Greece capitulates.

28   OKW gives the *Einsatzgruppen* the responsibility of carrying out special security police tasks.

29   The *Histadrut* Executive Committee demands a maximum number of Palestinian Jews enlisted in the army.

30   The Croatian government enacts Nuremberg-like anti-Jewish laws: its first such act is to deprive Yugoslav Jews of their citizenship.

MAY

1   Rashid Ali, Iraqi prime minister, sends troops to attack the British-controlled airfield at Habbaniya.

1   Gross-Rosen becomes an independent concentration camp under camp commandant *SS-Obersturmbannfuehrer* Arthur Roedi.

1   Jews are forbidden to trade on the Dutch stock exchange.

2   The Jewish Agency and *Va'ad Leumi* publish a recruitment order for all Jewish bachelors 20-30 years old.

2   Evacuation of British troops from Greece is completed.

5   The Skarzysko Kamienna {P} ghetto is established.

5   Emperor Haile Selassie returns to Ethiopia.

6   Stalin assumes the post of Chairman of the Council of People's Commissars of the Soviet Union.

9 Nazis in Holland promulgate a decree for the registration of all Jewish-owned businesses, or those who have even one Jewish partner or Jewish director on its board.

9 The British capture a German *Enigma* code machine intact.

10 Deputy *Fuehrer* Rudolf Hess leaves Augsburg, Germany on a solo flight and lands by parachute near Glasgow, Scotland.

10 The British House of Commons is destroyed during London's heaviest air raid.

11 *Institut d'Etudes des Questions Juives* (the French Institute for the Study of Jewish Questions) opens in Paris.

11 Colonel Draza Mihailovic organizes the *Centrici*, a guerrilla unit, on the plateau of Ravna Gora {Y} in the western Serbian mountains.

12 A second transport of Jews from Holland arrives in Mauthausen.

13 French police order 5,000 immigrant Jews to report to designated police stations within twenty-four hours.

14 Close to 4,000 "foreign" Jews who reported to French police stations as ordered, are taken to Pithivers; 3,600 additional Polish Jews living in Paris are rounded up and arrested by French police.

14/15 *Palmah*, the assault companies of the *Hagana*, are created.

15 Jewish forced labor enacted in Rumania.

15 The National Command publishes the principles of the *Hagana*.

15 President Roosevelt orders the government to take into "protective custody" all French flag ships in U.S. ports.

17 David Raziel, with British Army Intelligence cooperation, leads a group of IZL members to Habbaniyya, Iraq on a sabotage mission to blow up the oil depots that service the German *Luftwaffe*.

18 During the mission of the *"23 Yorde ha'Sira"* to Tripoli, all twenty-three members of the *Palmah* unit, along with their British officers and noncommissioned officers, are killed.

19 Italian troops surrender in East Africa.

20 Nazi airborne invasion of Crete.

20 David Raziel and a British officer are killed in a *Luftwaffe* bombing attack on their car, preventing Raziel from completing his mission in Iraq.

21 A German U-boat torpedoes and sinks the *SS Robin Moore*, an American freighter.

23   A German decree bars Jews from participating in the Dutch Labor Service.

25   Chaim Weizmann meets with American Jewish leaders at the St. Regis Hotel in New York.

27   Yellow Star instituted in Belgium.

27   *SMS Bismark* sunk.

27   President Roosevelt declares a state of unlimited national emergency.

28   Himmler orders establishment of *Arbeitserziehungslager(n)* (work education camps), to be controlled by the *Gestapo*.

30   Jewish badges are introduced in Serbia.

JUNE

1/2   Anti-Jewish pogroms in Baghdad leave more than 150 dead and thousands injured.

2   Vichy publishes the second *Statut des Juifs* which defines who is a Jew, including baptized Jews with three Jewish grandparents.

2   All Jews are ordered to register in both zones of France.

2   The National conference of *Agudas Yisroel* demands reevaluation of the party's stand toward Zionism and cooperation with the institutions of the *Yishuv*.

2   An administrative internment law is aimed against Jews in France.

5   U.S. consular offices are ordered not to issue visas to applicants who have close relatives in territories under German, Italian, or Soviet control.

6   *Kommissarbefehl* (Commissar Order), Nazi order for the liquidation of all Soviet political commissars.

8   British and Free-French forces invade Syria and Lebanon with *Palmah* participation.

8   The Iraqi government appoints a commission of inquiry to look into the causes of Baghdad's massive pogrom.

10   The *Gestapo* closes all Christian Science Churches in Berlin.

12   Hitler briefs Ion Antonescu at a Munich meeting.

12   The first conference of Allies opens in London with a pledge of mutual assistance.

13   Vichy France tightens its anti-Jewish program, arresting 12,000 Jews and expropriating Jewish property.

13 The Soviets carry out large-scale anti-Jewish purges in Bukovina and Bessarabia. Thousands deemed disloyal to the Soviet regime are deported to Siberia, perhaps inadvertently saving their lives.

14 The United States freezes German and Italian assets.

15 Odilo Globocnik announces a reversal in Nazi policy over to the Lublin Reservation: henceforth the Lublin territory will be cleared of Poles and Jews and populated with *Volksdeutsche* from Bulgaria, Rumania, Yugoslavia and other areas.

16 Germany and Turkey sign a nonaggression treaty.

17 *Umsiedlungsaktion* in Lowicz {P}. All Jews are deported to the Warsaw ghetto.

17 Heydrich, in his Berlin office, briefs all *Einsatzgruppen* commanders, *Einsatzkommandos,* and *Sonderkommandos* on implementation of the Final Solution.

18 Four thousand Jews from Soviet-occupied Bukovina are deported to Siberia.

19 Antonescu orders 40,000 Jews expelled from the Rumanian countryside to urban Jewish centers.

19 Otto Hirsch, German-Jewish community leader and chairman of the Nazi imposed *Reichsvereinigung*, is murdered by the *Gestapo* in Mauthausen.

21 Tobruk besieged by Rommel's *Africa Korps*.

22 Operation Barbarosa: Nazis begin their invasion of the Soviet Union; *SS-Einsatzgruppen* operating near the front start exterminating Russian and Polish Jewry.

22 Rumania joins the Nazi attack on the Soviet Union.

22 Italy declares war on the Soviet Union.

22 Nazis occupy Grodno and anti-Jewish terror begins.

22 Finland invades Soviet-held Karelia.

23 Approximately 10,000 Jews from Vilna are among the evacuees to the Soviet hinterland.

23 *Einsatzkommando 4a* sets out from Bad Schmiedeberg, Saxony, destined for Lvov.

23 Vichy France yields Indochina to Japan.

24 German army occupies Vilna.

24 President Roosevelt announces that America is ready to aid Russia in its war against Nazi Germany.

25 *Unzer Wort*, a *Yiddish* paper in the Soviet Union, appears for the first time.

25 Sweden permits German troops limited passage through its territory, from Norway to Finland.

25/26 On the heels of the German occupation, Lithuanian Fascists helped by *Einsatzgruppe A* institute a massive pogrom in Kovno {Lit SSR}.

26 As in other areas of Nazi-occupied Europe, Jews in Croatia are charged with collective responsibility for any infraction of Nazi-imposed rules.

27 Hungary declares war on the Soviet Union.

27 Iron Cross legionnaires, with the help of Rumanian and German soldiers, stage a pogrom in Jassy killing thousands of Jews.

27 Red Friday: Bialystok is occupied by Nazis. During the first anti-Jewish *aktion*, hundreds of Jews are burned alive in the city's synagogue.

27 British military and economic missions arrive in Moscow.

27 The Soviet government orders large segments of the population plus important industrial machinery and materials evacuated so that they will not fall into Nazi hands.

28 Lithuanian police grab Jews off the streets of Vilna for slave labor.

28 Minsk {B/R SSR} is captured by Nazis, trapping close to 100,000 Jews.

28 Jewish prisoners-of-war and Soviet Communist officials are segregated and executed.

28 Urged on by Nazis, freed convicts in Kovno {Lit SSR} beat thousands of Jews to death with iron bars.

28/29 First *aktion* in Brest-Litowsk {B/R SSR}: *Sonderkommando 7b* of *Einsatzgruppe B* murders 5,000 young male Jews outside of the town.

29 Nazis capture Lvov {Uk SSR}, in its wake plundering and murdering hundreds of the city's Jews.

29 Black Sunday: thousands of Jews are rounded up and shot dead in the courtyard of the Jassy police headquarters.

29 Polish statesman, composer and pianist, Ignaz Jan Paderewski, dies at age eighty.

30 *Einsatzkommando 6* of *Einsatzgruppe C* conducts its first murder *aktion*, killing 90 Jews in Dobromil.

30 Rumanian troops perpetrate new massacres on Jassy's Jews.

30 *Orhanizatsyia Ukrainskych Natsionalistiv* [OUN] (Organization of Ukrainian Nationalists) declares itself the provisional Ukrainian government.

30 The State Committee of Defense established in the USSR.

JULY

1 New United States visa regulations initiated by the State Department. All applicants who have relatives living in Greater Germany are denied immigration visas.

1 An eight member *Hagana* National Command is appointed by the Jewish Agency Executive.

1 Nazis occupy Riga, the Latvian capital.

1 A Nazi instigated pogrom in Lyakhovichi {B/R SSR} claims the lives of close to one hundred Jews.

1 All Jews in Plunge {Lit SSR} are massacred by an *Einsatzkommando* with local help.

1 The first transport of German Jews from Stuttgart {G} leaves for Riga.

2 Heydrich distributes secret written instructions to the *Einsatzgruppen* commanders and HSSPF on the Russian front.

2 Some 7,000 Jews are murdered during a Ukrainian sponsored pogrom in Lvov.

2 Vichy enacts a third Jewish statute.

2 Ukrainians, with German help, carry out a pogrom in Kamenka-Bugskaya {Uk SSR}, murdering hundreds of Jews.

2 Rumanian troops go on a murder rampage upon entering Novoselista {Uk SSR}. Eight hundred Jews are slaughtered on the pretext that they had sniped at the soldiers.

2 Ukrainians stage pogrom upon German occupation of Stryj {Uk SSR}. Hundreds of Jews are killed.

3 The *Gestapo* murder thirty-six Jewish and Polish intellectuals on Cadet Hill, Lvov.

3 An *aktion* in Bialystok kills 100 Jews on the spot; many others are buried alive.

3 Nazis sanction a massacre by Ukrainians in Zloczow {Uk SSR} which claims 3,500 Jewish lives.

3 Stalin appeals to the Russian people to defend the Soviet Union by creating a partisan force behind the front lines.

3 When Germany occupies Drohobycz {Uk SSR}, local Ukrainians stage a pogrom. Hundreds of Jews are driven to the Jewish cemetery and slaughtered.

4 German military occupation authorities order a *Judenrat* for Vilna. Important Jews are incarcerated in the Lukishka prison and their property is confiscated.

4 First *aktion* in Lutsk {Uk SSR}: approximately 7,000 Jews are massacred nearby in the Lubart fortress ruins.

4 Over four hundred Jews from Kovno are executed by *Einsatzkommando 3* in Fort VII during the first of many executions carried out in the Lithuanian Forts.

4/11 *Einsatzgruppen* units institute a number of violent *aktionen* in Tarnopol {Uk SSR}: at least 5,000 Jews are murdered and the Jewish community is fined 1,500,000 *rubles*.

5 Ukrainians carry out a pogrom when German troops occupy Buczacz {Uk SSR}.

5 The German and Rumanian armies occupy Chernovtsy {Uk SSR}: *Einsatzgruppe D*, and *Einsatzkommando 10b* trap nearly 50,000 Jews.

5 Jews of Kovno {Lit SSR} are ordered to wear a yellow Star of David.

6 Soviet forces withdraw from occupied eastern Poland, retreating to the "Stalin Line," the pre-1939 Soviet-Polish frontier.

6 Ukrainian nationalists perpetrate a massacre of close to 600 Jews in Skalat {Uk SSR}.

6/8 At least 3,000 Jews are murdered during a bloodbath in Chernovtsy and hundreds of Jewish homes are looted and vandalized.

7 Jews in occupied Lithuania are ordered to wear a distinctive badge consisting of a white square with a yellow circle and the letter J in the center.

7 Nazis occupy Berdichev {Uk SSR}, trapping nearly 20,000 Jews.

7 The Ukrainian National Movement [OUN] joins with the Nazis.

7 German army units organize a pogrom after they occupy the city of Balti {Uk SSR}.

7 United States Marines land on Iceland.

7 German and Rumanian troops occupy Khotin {Uk SSR} and massacre 2,000 Jews.

8 Jews in the Nazi-overrun Baltic Republics are ordered to wear a yellow Star of David.

8 Upon entering the city of Noua Sulita, Bessarabia, the Rumanian army herds 3,000 Jews into an abandoned spirits factory. After they are robbed of all their possessions, many Jews are murdered there.

9 Six *Einsatzkommandos* of *Einsatzgruppe B* start murder operations in a large area of Soviet-occupied Poland and Ukraine.

9 The *Gestapo* executes Jewish leaders and a number of other Jews in Beltsy {Mold SSR}, after forcing them to dig their own graves.

10 Using the excuse that Jews shot at the German army, Nazis perpetrate a large scale pogrom in Vilna, killing 123 male Jews to start with.

10 Ukrainians with German help stage a bloody pogrom in Chortkov {Uk SSR}. More than 300 Jews are murdered.

11 First mass extermination of Jews from Vilna takes place at Ponary {Lit SSR}.

11 The Palestinian government proposes to ban all strikes and protests for the war's duration.

11 Four thousand Jews from Bialystok are slaughtered outside of the town.

11 A Nazi decree creates a ghetto in Slobodka {Lit SSR}. All Jews from Kovno and its suburbs (approximately 30,000) must move into the ghetto by August 15.

11 The Office of Strategic Services [OSS] is established by President Roosevelt.

12 A British-Soviet mutual assistance pact is signed.

12 Nazis arrest Provisional Ukrainian Government officials.

12 The first transport of Jews from the Yugoslavian countryside who were arrested by the *Ustase* (insurgents; the Croatian *SS*) arrives at a temporary camp in Zagreb.

13 German occupation authorities in the occupied zone of France issue a decree calling for aryanization of Jewish-owned apartment buildings.

15 Jews in Lvov are ordered to wear the yellow star.

15 Lithuanian police start systematic roundup of Jews: by day, Jews are taken from off the streets; nighttime, from their homes.

15 An attempt by LEHI members to rob an Arab bank in Jerusalem fails.

16   The German 11th Army occupies Kishinev.

16   Luxembourg is incorporated into the *Reich*.

16   The Bulgarian government prohibits *shechita*.

16   Hitler and his top advisers secretly discuss what is to become of Russia, especially the Crimea.

17   During the first *aktion* in Slonim {B/R SSR}, 1,200 Jews are murdered on the outskirts of town. In addition, Nazis exact a two million *ruble* fine from the Jewish community.

18   Stalin asks Churchill to open a front in Northern France.

18   Britain recognizes the Czech government-in-exile.

20   The Minsk {B/R SSR} ghetto is established.

21   *Aussiedlungsaktion* in Rozwadow {P} wipes out most of the Jewish community. A number of young men are deported to the Pustkow {P} *Judenzwangsarbeitslager* (Jewish forced labor camp).

21   The *Histadrut* officially protests Palestine's government proposal to ban strikes.

22   Vichy passes the third *Statut des juifs* relating to the aryanization of Jewish property in France and orders dissolution of 320 associations, federations, fraternities, and sports clubs suspected of Jewish or Communist connections.

22   *Ordnungsdienst:* Czestochowa ghetto's Jewish police are put under official control of the Polish (Blue) police.

23   The United States and Britain freeze Japanese assets.

23   All Jewish safe-deposit boxes in French banks are blocked by German authorities.

24   During the Liepaja {Lat SSR} massacre 3,000 Jews are murdered at the Schkeden lighthouse.

24   The Kishinev {Ru} ghetto is established for some 11,000 Jews.

24   Vichy permits Japanese troop bases in Indochina.

25   The De Gaulle-Lyttelton agreement leaves Syria and Lebanon within the French sphere of influence.

25   The Latvian *Perkonkrust* (Fascist Party) orders a ghetto at Griva for Dvinsk's Jews.

25/27   Ukrainians with German help initiate *Aktion Petlura* against Jews of Lvov. A few thousand Jews perish as a result.

26   A *Judenrat* is set up in Bialystok.

26 The Natzweiler-Struthof camp opens.

26 In response to Japanese threats in Indochina, Japanese assets in the United States and Britain are frozen. The Philippine army is incorporated into the U.S. Far Eastern Forces under the command of General Douglas MacArthur.

27 Japanese forces occupy Indochina.

27 With German blessings, Ukrainians stage a pogrom in Gliniani {P}, killing and wounding scores of Jews, and destroying and pillaging a large number of Jewish homes.

28 Himmler gives a general directive ordering total annihilation of Jews in Nazi-occupied areas of the Soviet Union.

28 Some 900 men are murdered during the first *aktion* against the Jews in Vilkaviskis {Lit SSR}.

29 Jassy {Ru} pogrom ends with 4,000 Jews murdered.

29 The Fulda Conference of German Bishops adopts a pastoral letter condemning Nazi massacres without specific reference to Jews.

29 The first mass execution of hostages, primarily Jews, takes place in Serbia.

30 Erich von dem Bach-Zelewski is commanded to carry out the *Sauberungsaktion* (purification) of the Pripet marshes by killing all partisans and Jews found in that precinct of occupied Russia.

30 Bialystok's Jews are ordered into a ghetto. Within three days 60,000 Jews are crowded into a tiny area.

30 A Soviet-Polish reconciliation agreement is signed, formally repudiating the Molotov-Ribbentrop agreement of 1939. The Soviet Union resumes diplomatic relations with the Polish government-in-exile.

30 Anti-Jewish measures introduced by the Antonescu government in Rumania go into effect.

30 Roosevelt's special representative, Harry Hopkins, arrives in Moscow for consultations. The United States recognizes the Czechoslovakian government-in-exile in London.

30 Vichy orders a census of Jews and Jewish-owned property in Algeria.

31 Goering authorizes Heydrich to prepare a *Gesamtloesung* (total solution) to the Jewish question.

AUGUST

1 Nazis annex eastern Galicia to the *Generalgouvernement* as the Galicia district.

1 First *Einsatzkommandoaktion* in Kishinev {Ru} leaves more than 400 Jews dead.

1 Siemiatycze {P} ghetto is established.

1 Antonescu orders formation of Jewish forced-labor battalions.

2 Hungarian racial laws go into effect.

2 *Gestapo* orders a "voluntary contribution" of 100,000 *rubles* from Jews of Braslav {B/R SSR}.

4 *Einsatzkommandoaktion* in Ostrog {Uk SSR}: at least 3,000 Jews are murdered.

4 The Jewish Committee for the Transfer to the Ghetto, elects Dr. Elchanan Elkes as *Oberjude* (elder of the Jews) of the Kovno ghetto at Slobodka.

5 The United States and Great Britain impose embargoes on sales of raw materials to Japan.

5/8 At least 11,000 Jews in Pinsk {B/R SSR} are killed over four days.

6 Rumanian troops murder 200 Jews in Orgeyev {Mold SSR} and throw their bodies into the Dniester River.

6 A detention camp for Jews is established in Kruscica {Y}.

6 The Japanese propose concessions in China but these fall short of U.S. demands.

7 During a Kovno manhunt Lithuanians with German police help seize 1,200 Jews off the streets, promptly murdering them.

7 Nazis set official racial classifications of "pure Gypsies and part Gypsies."

7/8 A second *aktion* takes place against Jews in Kishinev, with both an *Einsatzkommando* and Rumanian police taking part in the slaughter.

8 The Race Protection Law is the third major anti-Jewish law adopted by the Hungarian parliament. The major clause of law concerns prohibition of marriages between Jews and aryans.

8 The Federation of Jewish Relief Organizations in London establishes a 25,000 pound trust fund to maintain Jewish refugee children from eastern Europe.

8 Nazis publish an order for all Dutch Jews to deposit their money in the Lippmann-Rosenthal Bank.

8/9 In a number of *aktionen* in the Dvinsk {Lat SSR} ghetto, thousands of Jews are taken to the Pogulanka Forest and murdered.

9 Members of the Rumanian Legion stage a massacre at the Tataresti camp.

10 Vichy anti-Jewish laws are extended to Jews in Morocco.

11 The Japanese declare general mobilization.

12 Russia grants amnesty to all Polish prisoners of war in the Soviet Union.

12 In Lomza {P} a ghetto is established for over 10,000 Jews.

12 In a radio address, Henri Petain announces his support for the German invasion of the Soviet Union and also announces a tightening of the Vichy regime.

14 Churchill and Roosevelt sign the Atlantic Charter.

14 A military agreement between the Soviet Union and Polish high commands is signed in Moscow. Recruitment for the new Polish army in Russia starts.

14 *Aussiedlungsaktion* in Lesko {P}: the entire Jewish community is deported to Zaslaw {P} where they are murdered together with the Jews of that city.

17 Fall of Kiev.

17/18 The Rumanian government agrees to the return of some 20,000 Jews from Transnistria to Rumanian Bessarabia. However, many are murdered by Rumanian or German soldiers on their way back.

18 The *Gestapo* raids the Antwerp diamond bourse.

18 The Hungarian governor of Kolomyya {Uk SSR} prevents Ukrainian locals from slaughtering some 2,000 Jews.

18 The *Gestapo* establishes a *Polizeiliches Durchgangslager* (police transit camp) in Amersfoort {Ho}, where prominent Dutch Jews are imprisoned.

18 Brazil permits extension of tourist visas for the duration of war.

19 General Wladyslaw Anders heads the Polish army which is established in the Soviet Union.

19 In Chruslice {P} a labor camp is created for Jews and Soviet prisoners of war.

19 *Aktion* in the Mogilev {B/R SSR} ghetto: close to 4,000 Jews are murdered by units of *Einsatzgruppe B,* helped by German military field police.

20 The Banat region of Yugoslavia is declared *Judenrein.*

20 Drancy *Sammellager* (assembly camp) opens as an internment camp for Jews in France, who would be deported at a later stage to perish in eastern Europe. The camp is run by the Vichy French and guarded by armed French police under direct control of the *Sicherheitsdienst* [SD] and *Gestapo*, until July 1, 1943.

20 Jews in Minsk {B/R SSR} are ordered to wear the yellow badge and to move into a ghetto to be established in a suburb.

20 *Reichskommisariat* Ukraine established.

20 A transit camp is set up in Edineti {Ru}.

20/21 German and French police round up 4,300 Jews in Paris. The victims, who include 1,300 French citizens, are all sent to Drancy.

21 Hitler issues directive #34: the capture of the Crimea before the onset of winter.

21 Spain's "Blue Division" departs for the Soviet front.

21/24 *Agudas Yisroel* holds a convention in Baltimore and declares its readiness to join other Jewish organizations in a unified Palestine front.

24 The *Yidisher Antifashistisher Komitet* (Jewish Anti-Fascist Committee) within the *Sovinformbureau* established under the chairmanship of Ilya Ehrenburg.

24 Vichy promulgates a law to create special tribunals to deal with "antinational uprisings."

24 Under pressure, Hitler terminates the euthanasia program in Germany.

25 A ghetto is created at Berdichev {Uk SSR}.

25 Joint Anglo-Soviet invasion of Iran begins.

25 The Topovske Supe massacres begin; 8,000 male Jews aged sixteen and older, previously rounded up in Belgrade and taken to a slave-labor camp in Topovske Supe, a suburb of Belgrade, are all murdered by the middle of October.

25 Polish government-in-exile repeals 1938 law which deprived Polish citizenship to thousands of Jews living aboard for more than five years.

25 During liquidation of the Tykocin {P} Jewish community 1,500 Jews are driven outside of town to prepared pits and killed.

27 A decree is published calling for the expropriation of all Jewish-owned real estate in Croatia.

27/28 Kamenets-Podolski {Uk SSR} massacre: nearly 18,000 stateless Jews previously deported from the Carpatho-Hungarian region together with some 5,000 Jews from Kamenets-Podolski and vicinity are killed by *Einsatzkommandos* with local Ukrainian help.

28 Thousands of Jews in Czyzewo Szlacheckie {P} are slaughtered by German police and Ukrainian collaborators.

28 All Jews in Kedainiai {Lit SSR}, are killed by the locals with Ukrainian cooperation.

29 Five hundred male Jews, 1,700 Jewish females, and 1,500 Jewish children are slaughtered by *Einsatzgruppe A* in Utena and Moletai {Lit SSR}.

29 Jews in Belgium have their freedom of movement restricted.

31 Germany bans the Christian Science movement and the *Gestapo* confiscates all properties and funds of the Church.

31 The Shavli {Lit SSR} ghetto is established.

SEPTEMBER

1 All Jews in Germany over six years old are ordered to wear the *Judenstern* (Jewish Star) as of September 19. The order also applies to Jews in Slovakia and the Protectorate of Bohemia and Moravia.

1 All Jewish children are expelled from Rotterdam {Ho} public schools.

1 The Slovakian government levies a series of special taxes ranging from 25 percent to 40 percent on Jews to finance their deportations.

1 The Marculesti {Ru} labor camp is established.

2 The *Gestapo* executes all ten members of the Vilna *Judenrat*.

3 Nazis perform their first human experiment with *Zyklon B*, gassing 600 Soviet prisoners of war in the Auschwitz extermination camp.

3 *SS* units helped by German military police and the *Ustase* begin roundups and deportations of Yugoslavian Jews to the East.

4 An *aktion* takes place in the Berdichev {Uk SSR} ghetto. Fifteen hundred young Jews are rounded up, presumably for a labor detail, marched out of town and shot to death.

5 Hitler issues directive #35: capture of Moscow.

6 The Vilna ghetto is established. Forty-six thousand Jews are incarcerated in two sub-ghettos.

6 Seventy Jewish intellectuals from Zbaraz {Uk SSR} are murdered in the Lubienicki forest.

7 The Lvov ghetto is established. While it existed, over 130,000 Jews were killed within its confines.

7 The Forty-fourth Annual Convention of the Zionist Organization of America adopts a resolution urging the British government to open the gates to Palestine for Jewish refugees.

8 Siege of Leningrad begins.

9 The Legal Status, closely resembling the Nuremberg Laws, is adopted by the Slovak government for Slovakian Jews.

9 The Spanish Blue Division reports for service on the Soviet front.

12 Field Marshal Wilhelm Keitel's directive concerning "Jews in the Occupied Eastern Territories" calls for speedy action (elimination) against the Bolshevik menace, the Jew.

13 Close to 2,000 Jews from Arnhem {Ho} are forced to move to Amsterdam, in one of the first Nazi steps toward liquidating Dutch Jewry.

13 At an "America First" rally in Des Moines, Iowa, Charles A. Lindberg accuses American Jews of steering the Roosevelt administration towards the war.

15 The Nazis provide the Kovno *Judenrat* with 5,000 *Lebenshaynen* ("Life Certificates").

15 A major Nazi *aktion* almost liquidates the Berdichev {Uk SSR} ghetto. Over 18,000 Jews are killed in prepared pits outside of town, leaving behind just a few hundred skilled craftsmen and their immediate families—some 2,000 Jews in all.

15 Those Jews of Bukovina and Bessarabia who were not killed by the *Einsatzgruppen* are ordered expelled to Transnistria.

15 All Jews in eastern Galicia are ordered to wear the yellow star.

15 The *Gestapo* arrest OUN leader Stefan Bandera and sends him to the Sachsenhausen concentration camp.

16 Keitel issues an order stipulating that 100 civilian hostages will be executed for every German soldier killed in occupied Europe.

16 Liquidation of the short-lived Yedintsy {Mold SSR} concentration camp: all Jews are deported to Transnistria.

17 During the first *aktion* in the Lomza {P} ghetto, 3,000 Jews are massacred in the Galczyn forest outside of town.

17 Slovakia introduces a series of new anti-Jewish laws to completely bar Jews from any participation in the political, social, economic, or cultural life of the country.

17/18 Himmler orders complete *Judenreinigung* (clearing of Jews) from the *Altreich* and the Protectorate. *Gesamtaussiedlung*, the total deportation of German Jews to the east, begins.

19 Fall of Kiev: 60,000 out of 160,000 Jews in the city are trapped, but approximately 100,000 manage to escape before Nazi occupation.

19 Nazis liquidate the short-lived Zhitomir {Uk SSR} ghetto and thousands of Jews perish.

20 Free Denmark is organized.

21 Vandals destroy an *Ashkenazi* synagogue in Ferrara {I}. Local Fascists distribute vicious antisemitic propaganda.

22 The Jewish community of Vinnitsa {Uk SSR} is liquidated. Close to 30,000 Jews are slaughtered during the *aktion* held on the first day of *Rosh Hashana*.

22 All Jews in the Litin {Uk SSR} ghetto are murdered when the ghetto is liquidated.

22 A ghetto is established in Pruzhany {B/R SSR}.

23 The second gassing experiments in Auschwitz are conducted.

24 The Free French National Council established in London.

24 All Jews remaining in Vilkaviskis {Lit SSR} are murdered.

25 German Jews are removed from court jurisdiction and become wards of the *Gestapo*.

25 The Kovno *Judenrat* is ordered to hand out 5,000 protective "white certificates" (dubbed *Jordan-shaynen*) to workers and their families.

25 An antisemitic exhibition entitled, "Jews and France," opens in Paris.

25 Reinhard Heydrich becomes new *Reichsprotektor* of Bohemia-Moravia.

25 Charles de Gaulle, leader of the Free French Forces in London, declares the Vichy anti-Jewish decrees are null and void.

26 An Anglo-American-Soviet military conference opens in Moscow. The conference closes October 2.

27 Heydrich proclaims martial law in the Protectorate of Bohemia-Moravia.

27 *Yishuv* leaders broadcast encouragement to the Jews in the Soviet Union.

28 The first Arctic convoy to the Soviet Union leaves Iceland.

28 All males fourteen years old and above in the Kruscica {Y} detention camp are transferred to the Jasenovac {Y} concentration camp. Women with children are transferred to the newly established detention camp at Lobor {Y}.

28 Liquidation of the Kremenchug {Uk SSR} Jewish community begins. Thousands of Jews are taken in small groups to pits prepared near the village of Peschanoye, forced to undress, and murdered. Most Jews who try to escape are killed by local Ukrainians.

28/30 Nazis begin to massacre Kiev Jews at Babi Yar: 33,771 Jews are machine-gunned to death by *Sonderkommando 4a*, with the help of *Waffen-SS* units, German police, detachments of the Sixth Army, and Ukrainian auxiliary police.

30 The German army begins its Moscow offensive.

30 Liquidation of the Troki {Lit SSR} Jewish community ends with all Jews murdered and only the *Karaite* community, who are classified as non-Jews, remaining.

30 During the Berezhany {Uk SSR} massacre, approximately 700 young male Jews are driven to a nearby forest outside of town and executed.

OCTOBER

1 Private schools for Jewish children open in Algeria because of a Vichy order to exclude Jewish children from public schools.

1 The *Reichskommissariat Ostland* rules that *Karaites* should not be considered Jews racially.

2 The Jasenovac concentration camp is established.

2 Germany launches Operation *Taifun*, the assault on Moscow.

2 Menachem Ussiskin, president of the Jewish National Fund, dies.

2/3 Several Paris synagogues are burned down by French Fascists.

4 In the Kovno ghetto's first *aktion*, 1,500 Jews are murdered at Fort Nine. The little ghetto is eliminated.

4 Sixteen hundred Jews form the first group from Kishinev deported to Transnistria.

5 The Berdichev {Uk SSR} ghetto is liquidated, with all remaining Jews murdered.

5 United States Supreme Court Justice Louis D. Brandeis dies.

5 President Eduard Benes, in an address before the Czechoslovak State Council in London, promises that a future Czechoslovakia would be free of antisemitism.

5 In the Przemyslany {Uk SSR} massacre, 500 Jewish men are marched off to the Brzezina forest to be murdered.

6 The Lobor {Y} detention camp opens for mostly Jewish women and children.

7 Construction of the Birkenau (Auschwitz II) camp, begins: located approximately 3 km. from the main camp (Auschwitz I), Birkenau will house four gas chambers and crematoria, becoming the major extermination site in Nazi Europe.

7 The first national conference of Jewish army volunteers in Palestine opens.

8 First *aktion* against Jews in Vitebsk {B/R SSR}.

8 Nazis impose a collective fine of thirty million *rubles* on the Dnepropetrovsk {Uk SSR} Jewish community.

9 All Jews from Burdujeni {Moldavian Rumania} are deported to Transnistria.

9 The Pro-Nazi government in Panama is overthrown.

9 The Slovak government orders that Jewish personal income may not exceed 1,500 *kronen* ($50.00) a month.

10 Some 3,000 Jews from Gura-Humorului {Ru} are deported to Transnistria.

10 Terezin (Theresienstadt), the model ghetto in Czechoslovakia, opens.

10 Soviet General Georgi Zhukov takes command of the western front.

10 Heydrich orders 30,000 German Gypsies deported to the Riga ghetto.

10 The Reichenau Order on the Conduct of Troops in the Eastern Territories is distributed to all *Wehrmacht* members on the Russian front. Severe but "just" revenge on "subhuman" Jewry is called for.

11 The Rumanian government orders mass deportation of Jews from Bukovina to Transnistria.

11 A ghetto is established in Chernotsy, Rumanian Bukovina for approximately 75,000 Jews. The majority of them are later deported to Transnistria.

11 The Edineti {R} transit camp is liquidated. Thousands of Jews die or are killed on their way to Transnistria.

12 *Grossaktion* takes place in Stanislawow {Uk SSR}. Over 10,000 Jews are slaughtered in the Jewish cemetery.

12 Six thousand Jews from the newly established Chernovtsy ghetto leave in the first transport to Transnistria.

12/13 Jews and Gypsies in the Sabac {Y} concentration camp are mass executed.

13 Broniewo {P} *Judenlager* is established.

13 Jews in Vichy are barred from breeding horses and cattle or trading in grain.

13 During the Dnepropetrovsk {Uk SSR} massacre, close to 15,000 Jews are murdered by *Einsatzgruppe C* in a ravine outside town.

14 Nazis begin deporting German Jews from *Altreich* to Lodz ghetto.

15 Hans Frank, governor-general of Poland, orders the death penalty for all Jews found outside ghettos or assigned Jewish living quarters.

15 The Australia-First political party is launched. Its slogan is "Aryanism against Semitism."

15/17 Antisemitic posters appear on the main streets of Torino {I} calling for death to Jews.

16 Odessa is occupied by Rumanian-German troops.

16 Thousands flee Moscow, as the fall of the Soviet capital seems imminent. Government offices are transferred to Kuibishev, but Stalin remains in Moscow.

16 In a second sweep through Dnepropetrovsk {Uk SSR} the remainder of the Jewish population—some 5,000—are murdered by the fast-moving *Einsatzkommandos*.

17 Hideki Tojo becomes prime minister of Japan.

17 The last twenty-one German Jews holding Dominican Republic visas are allowed to leave Germany.

17 The Jewish population in Odessa is ordered to register.

17 Rumania sets up the province of Transnistria on captured Soviet land.

18   The first transport from Berlin leaves for Lodz ghetto with 1,000 Jews. Nine more transports with 1,000 Jews each leave for different parts of eastern Europe before the year's end.

19   Field Marshal von Reichenau, commander of the German Sixth Army, warns his men against mistaken feelings of compassion for the civilian population.

19   A *Histadrut* general conference deals with *Yishuv's* defense policy.

19   The first deportation of Jews from Frankfort-am-Main are sent to Lodz ghetto.

19   The *Gestapo* imposes a 500,000 *ruble* fine on Jews of Nesvizh {B/R SSR}.

19   The Lutsk {Uk SSR} *Judenlager*, a camp for some 500 Jewish prisoners, is established.

20   Moscow is declared under a state of siege.

21   All Jews in Koidanovo {B/R SSR} are murdered by an *Einsatzkommando aktion*.

21/23   Thousands of Serbian Jews and non-Jews are massacred by Nazis at Kraljevo {Y} and Kragujevac {Y} extermination sites.

22   Partisans blow up the Rumanian military command headquarters in Odessa. Mass retaliation is planned.

22   The Greek government-in-exile invalidates antisemitic legislation enacted by the German occupation regime.

23   *Reichsfuehrer-SS* Heinrich Himmler bars all additional Jewish emigration from Nazi Europe.

23/25   The Odessa massacre is carried out: thousands of Jews are shot, hung, and burned alive.

24   Mass slaughter in the Vilna ghetto is preceded by the Night of the Yellow Certificates.

24   Kharkov {Uk SSR} falls to the *Wehrmacht*.

24   Hundreds of Jews are shot to death during the first *aktion* in the Romarno {Uk SSR} ghetto.

25   A rebellion breaks out in the Tatarsk {RFSSR} ghetto: all Jews are massacred.

25   Riga's ghetto is established.

26   *Aktion* in Kleck {B/R SSR}: Germans and Lithuanians murder 4,000 Jews near the Catholic cemetery, while another 2,000 are kept alive in a makeshift ghetto.

28   Vilna's "small ghetto" is liquidated.

28   About 10,000 Jews from the Kovno ghetto are driven to the Ninth Fort and machine-gunned: thousands among them are buried alive in the three meter wide by 120 meter long prepared pit.

30   Nesvizh {B/R SSR} massacre: some 4,000 Jews are murdered in an *Einsatzkommandoaktion* outside of town; the remainder, approximately 500 Jews, are ordered into a closed ghetto.

30   The United States extends its Lend-Lease Act to the Soviet Union.

30   *Wehrmacht* assault on Moscow peters out as German units are halted due to inclement weather.

NOVEMBER

1   Jews in Grodno {B/R SSR} are ordered into a two-part ghetto, one for skilled workers, the other for "unproductive elements."

1   Construction of the Belzec extermination camp begins as part of *Aktion Reinhard*.

2   The Krynki {P} ghetto is established and liquidated one year later.

2   *Kibbutz* Ramat ha-shofet is established in the Manasseh Hills.

5   Natzweiler-Struthof becomes a special *SS* camp.

5/6   The Rovno {Uk SSR} massacre wipes out two-thirds of the town's Jewish population with the murder of some 17,000 out of 25,000 Jews in the Sosenki forest.

5/9   Five thousand Gypsies from Austria are deported to the Lodz ghetto.

6   Jews from Germany arrive in Riga, Kovno, and Minsk and are promptly murdered.

6   Twenty-five hundred Jews are murdered during an *aktion* in Nadvornaya {Uk SSR}.

7   Some 20,000 Jews from Bobruisk {B/R SSR} are murdered.

7   Jews from Radauti {Ru} and Darabani {Ru} are deported to Transnistria.

7   *Grossaktion* takes place in Minsk ghetto. Approximately 13,000 Jews are taken outside town to pits prepared in the Tuchinka forest. There they are machine-gunned to death or buried alive; *aktionen* continue throughout November.

7/9   During a major *aktion* in the Dvinsk {Lat SSR} ghetto, close to 5,000 Jews are murdered in prepared pits in the Pogulanka forest. Only workers with special pink *arbeits-scheine* (work permits), not their families, are spared.

9 In Mir's first *aktion* two-thirds, or approximately 1,500 Jews, are massacred on the outskirts of town. Surviving Jews are ordered into a ghetto.

9 Chaim Weizmann officially declares the failure of negotiations with Britain to establish a Jewish army.

10 Dr. Ludwig Fischer, German Governor of Warsaw, warns that any Jew, including children, found outside or caught leaving the Warsaw ghetto, will be shot.

10 Nazis ban Jewish emigration from Austria.

11 Rumania sets up Transnistria as a penal colony for Jews.

12 Over 1,000 German Jews from the Rhine-Westphalia district are deported to Riga.

12 The Quisling government orders registration of all Jewish-owned property in Norway.

12 Jews of Dorohoi {Ru} are deported to Transnistria.

14 The United States amends the Neutrality Act.

14 General Wladyslaw Anders, under pressure from the American embassy, issues an order stressing equal rights for all Polish citizens—including Jews—in the newly formed Polish army in the Soviet Union.

14 In the first *aktion* in Zaleszczyki {Uk SSR} nearly 800 Jews are murdered and most of the Jewish youth are taken to the Kamionka {Uk SSR} *zwangsarbeitslager*.

14 A second *aktion* takes place in the Slonim {B/R SSR} ghetto. *Einsatzkommandos* with Belorussian and Lithuanian volunteers murder 9,000 Jews in prepared pits near the village of Czepielow.

15 Jews of Lvov are ordered to move into the new ghetto between November 16 and December 15. Ukrainians and *SS* troops rob thousands of Jews of the few possessions they manage to take along.

15 Antonescu orders a stop to deportation of Rumanian Jews from Chernovtsy to Transnistria: however, until cease of deportation order is confirmed, an additional 28,000 Jews are in the meantime deported.

15/16 Three thousand Jews in Sarajevo {Y} are deported to the Jasenovac concentration camp.

16   The first *aktion* against *Krimchaks*, a small group of Tatar-speaking Jews, takes place in the Crimea. By year's end 18,000 to 20,000 *Krimchaks* are murdered by the *Einsatzgruppen*.

17   Eight Jews caught on the aryan side of the Warsaw ghetto are executed.

17   Twelve hundred Czech students are sent to the Sachsenhausen concentration camp.

17   The Swiss Protestant Relief Society adopts a resolution condemning German treatment of European Jewry.

17   Japanese representatives arrive in Washington to begin negotiations regarding Japan's frozen economic assets. These negotiations are later discovered to be a cover for Japan's naval assault on Pearl Harbor.

18   The British Eighth Army launches Operation Crusader to relieve Tobruk.

20   In a follow-up *aktion* in the Minsk ghetto, another 5,000 Jews are removed to the Tuchinka forest and murdered in prepared pits.

21   Gypsy children are prohibited from attending German schools.

23   Nearly 30,000 Jews are killed as Rumanian army troops, ordered by Antonescu, go on an antisemitic rampage in occupied Odessa.

23   Poltava {Uk SSR} massacre: some 1,500 Jews are machine-gunned to death in an anti-tank ditch by members of *Einsatzgruppe C*.

23   *Toten Sonntag* (Sunday of Death) takes place in North Africa. Heavy German combat losses force Rommel to abandon siege of Tobruk.

23/25   The Inter-American Conference is organized by the American Jewish Congress and the World Jewish Congress.

24   The first transport of Jews from the Protectorate is sent to Terezin.

25   Deported German Jews in Kovno are massacred.

25   A Nazi published ordinance creates the *Association des Juifs en Belgique* [AJB] (Association of Belgian Jews). The main function of the association is registration of Jews for forced labor and deportation.

25   The first transport of Jews from Breslau leaves for Terezin.

25   The House of Lords debates the Palestinian Jewish army issue.

25   The eleventh ordinance of the *Reich* Citizenship Act totally deprives German Jews of even elemental civil rights and legalizes their deportation.

26   Two hundred fifty Jews from Essen {G} deported to the Lodz Ghetto.

26   Lebanon unilaterally declares independence.

26 The Japanese task force for Operation Tor-to-to, the attack on Pearl Harbor, sets sail.

27 A majority of the Jews in Bayreuth {G} are deported to Riga.

27 The *Gestapo* informs the *Judenrat* of its intent to start liquidating the Riga ghetto beginning November 29.

27 The Soviet Union, under Marshal Semion K. Timoshenko, launches a counter-offensive.

27 Vichy withdraws the parliamentary mandates of twelve Jewish former members of the French Senate and Chamber of Deputies, Leon Blum among them.

28 A resolution in the U.S. House of Representatives, introduced by Congressman Andrew L. Somers of New York, petitions Britain to permit an all-Jewish military unit in Palestine.

28 A meeting in Berlin opens between Hitler and the Grand Mufti of Jerusalem, Haj Amin al Husaini.

29 *Union Generale des Israelites de France* [UGIF] (General Union of Jews in France) is established by Vichy on Nazi initiative; all other Jewish organizations are ordered to dissolve.

29 The first deportation of Jews from Nuremberg brings over 500 Jews to Riga.

29/30 An *aktion* in Borislaw {P} claims 1,500 Jewish lives.

30 A major *aktion* is carried out in the Riga ghetto by *Einsatzgruppe A* under *SS-Brigadefuehrer* Friedrich Jeckeln. Over 10,000 Jews are murdered in the Rumbula Forest.

DECEMBER

1 The Soviet army launches a limited counter-attack on the Moscow front.

2 The Dakovo {Y} camp for Jews opens.

2 The Central Conference of American Rabbis issues a five-point plan for postwar world reconstruction.

3 Polish Generals Sikorski and Anders meet with Stalin in Moscow.

4 During the first *aktion* in the Gorodenka {Uk SSR} ghetto, some 2,500 Jews are driven to a forest a few miles outside of town, murdered, and buried in mass graves.

4 Liquidation of the Jewish community of Feodosiya, Crimea.

4 The Committee for a Jewish Army of Stateless and Palestinian Jews is officially inaugurated in Washington, DC.

5 Britain declares war on Finland, Hungary, and Rumania because they refuse to withdraw from the war against the Soviet Union.

6 The last 1,000 Jews from Cologne {G} are deported to Riga.

7 The Japanese launch their surprise attack on the American fleet in Pearl Harbor.

7 Sajmiste (Semlin) officially opens as a holding camp on the Sava River across from Belgrade for Jews, Gypsies and some Yugoslavs. Five thousand Jewish women and children are transferred there from Belgrade to await deportation.

7 *Nacht und Nebel Erlass*, Hitler's Night and Fog decree, creates a new category of prisoners; it deals with the methods to be used in suppressing resistance movements in German-occupied western Europe.

7 *Aktion Jeckeln,* under *HSSPF* Friedrich Jeckeln, is the second *grossaktion* within a week in the Riga ghetto; close to 15,000 Jews are then murdered in the Rumbula Forest.

8 President Roosevelt asks Congress to declare war on Japan.

8 Japanese forces occupy Thailand and invade the Philippines.

8 The Chelmno (Kulmhof) {P} extermination camp opens; its victims are murdered in specially erected gas vans.

8 The Semlin {Y} transit camp is converted into a concentration camp.

8 Nazis and their Latvian helpers, the *Perkonkrust,* stage a massacre in Riga, murdering thousands of Jews.

8 *Aktion* in the Novogrudok {B/R SSR} ghetto: 4,000 Jews or close to 50 percent of the Jewish community, are murdered by *Einsatzkommando* units with the help of *Wehrmacht* units.

9 China officially declares war on Japan and Germany.

10 Jewish-owned pharmacies are confiscated in Sofia.

10. The siege of Tobruk is raised when units of Rommel's *Afrika Korps* retreat westward.

11 Germany and Italy declare war on the United States.

11 *Umsiedlungsaktion* in the Ciechanow {P} ghetto eliminates the town's Jewish community.

12 Close to a thousand French Jewish leaders are rounded up and arrested by German police units and *Gestapo* in occupied and unoccupied (Vichy) France.

12 Jews of Baranowicze {B/R SSR} are ordered into a ghetto.

12 Panama declares war on Germany.

12 The *SS Struma* leaves Constanta {Ru} with 769 refugees aboard.

12 Seven hundred French Jews are sent to the Vichy holding camp at Compiegne. Camp conditions are extremely poor and unsanitary.

12 Japanese forces capture Guam.

12 The Ecuadorian government orders closed the German news agency, Transocean, for spreading Nazi propaganda.

13 Four hundred twenty German Jews are deported from Bielefeld to Riga and the city becomes *Judenrein*.

13 The Wolkowysk {B/R SSR} ghetto is established.

14 Himmler's directive for "Operation 14 F 13," sent to all concentration camp commanders, is a cover to exterminate Jews.

14 Special identification cards are introduced for Jews in Bulgaria.

15 Nazis execute ninety-five hostages, among them fifty-three Jews, in retaliation for partisan activity against the German army in Yugoslavia.

15 Parisian Jews are fined one billion *francs*.

15 The Irish Republic declares its strict neutrality.

15/16 A second *aktion* is held in Liepaja {Lat SSR}. About 3,000 Jews are taken to the fishing village of Skeden, where they are ordered to undress in the freezing cold and are murdered in a deep trench by German and Latvian police. Hundreds of naked victims freeze to death while waiting to be shot.

16 Antonescu orders dissolution of the *Federatia Uniunilor de Counitati Evreesti* (the Union of Jewish Communities) in Rumania, to be replaced by a central Jewish office, the *Centrala Evreilor*. All Jews, regardless of affiliation, are ordered to register with the *Centrala* or face ten years in jail.

16 Liquidation of the Marculesti {Ru} camp.

16 The Tel Aviv municipality establishes an "emergency court" to deal with black-marketeering.

16 A Cuban presidential decree prohibits visas to belligerent nationals.

19 Hitler takes over supreme command of the *Wehrmacht,* dismisses Field Marshal Walther von Brauchitsch, and assumes supreme command of the Russian front.

20 The American Volunteer Group [AVG], the "Flying Tigers," goes into action for the first time to protect Kunming, China.

20 "Seabees," U.S. Navy construction battalions, are established.

21/30 On German orders, Rumanian troops and *gendarmerie* helped by Ukrainian police and local civilians murder about 50,000 Jews at a ravine near the Bug River, outside the Bogdanovka (Transnistria) camp. Thousands freeze to death while waiting naked for their turn to be shot. To obliterate any traces of this crime, bodies are burned on giant pyres.

22 An *aktion* against Jews in Zablotov {Uk SSR} claims 1,000 lives.

22 The Arcadia Conference between Britain and the United States establishes an Allied strategy of "beat Hitler first." As part of the conference, the United Nations is established on January 1, 1942. The Conference closes January 7, 1942.

22 The first U.S. forces arrive in Australia.

23/24 Japan occupies Wake Island.

25 Hong Kong surrenders to Japan.

26 British Prime Minister Winston Churchill addresses a joint session of Congress.

1942

JANUARY

1 Abba Kovner calls for Jewish resistance in the Vilna ghetto.

1 Twenty-six nations sign a declaration of solidarity and unity of purpose in Washington, DC, which serves as a foundation for the United Nations.

1 Bulgarian Jews are barred from the mining industry and their mines are aryanized.

1 Anti-Jewish legislation, drafted by pro-Nazi *Clausenist* members of the Danish government, is rejected by the Danish parliament.

1 A law banning strikes and work stoppages takes effect in Palestine.

2 Japanese forces capture Manila.

2 The Allies pledge not to conclude separate peace treaties with the Nazi and Fascist enemies.

5 *Polska Partia Robotnicza* [PPR], the Polish Workers Party, an illegal organization, is established in Nazi-occupied Poland.

9 A United Nations declaration on war criminals is signed.

9 Two civilians are killed during an abortive LEHI-sponsored robbery at *the Bank Ha-poalim* branch in Tel Aviv.

9/12 Klodawa {P} Jews are deported to Chelmno.

10 German Jews are ordered to hand over all of their fur and woolen articles.

10 Odessa Jews are ordered to relinquish all of their remaining valuables to the Rumanian authorities.

10/11 Japanese forces invade the Dutch East Indies.

12 The Argentinian Polish Jewish Federation reaches an agreement with the International Red Cross to transport medicine to the Polish ghettos.

13 The Saint James Palace Declaration: the Inter-Allied Conference on German War-Crimes is established. The dire situation of European Jewry is not mentioned as such.

13 The status of Stutthof is changed from a special *SS*-camp to a concentration camp.

13 The Joint Distribution Committee [JDC] inaugurates a program to aid some 500,000 needy Polish Jews in the Soviet Union.

15 Rumania reports that up until this date 120,000 Jews have been deported to Transnistria.

15 Palestine announces rationing of sugar, rice, wheat, corn, flour, and bread.

15/28 The Pan-American Conference is held in Rio de Janeiro. All Latin American countries, except Argentina and Chile, break diplomatic relations with the Axis.

16 Lodz ghetto deportations to the Chelmno extermination camp begin.

17 Jews in Belgium are forbidden to leave the country.

17 *Generalfeldmarschall* Walter von Reichenau, commander of the German Sixth Army and Southern Army Group, dies of a mysterious infection.

18 The National Conference of the United Palestine appeal urges President Roosevelt to intercede with Britain to permit creation of a Jewish army in Palestine.

18 Nazis launch second phase in the liquidation of the Warsaw ghetto.

20 The *Wannsee* Conference (held at a villa in Wannsee, a Berlin suburb), is attended by fifteen bureaucrats representing a cross-section of the German government. Under the direction of *SS-Obergruppenfuehrer* Reinhard Heydrich, they discuss, approve, and prepare for the measures to be taken to implement the *Endloesung der Judenfrage*, the "Final Solution of the Jewish Problem": total liquidation of the 11,000,000 Jews in Europe.

20 Japanese forces invade Burma.

21 *Fareinikte Partizaner Organizatsye* [FPO], the United Partisan Organization, is founded in the Vilna ghetto.

21 The German North African offensive begins.

21/23 Hungarian troops massacre 1,500 Jews and 500 Serbs on the banks of the Danube River in the town of Novi Sad, Yugoslavia.

22 Karl Otto Koch, *SS* camp commandant of Buchenwald, is transferred to Majdanek to become the camp commander of that death camp.

23 Nazis use the Jewish religious ban on eating pork as a pretext to invalidate ration books held by Jews in the Protectorate of Bohemia-Moravia.

24 Hitler's decree gives Martin Bormann control over all NSDAP directives, laws, and undertakings.

25 Thailand declares war on the United States.

26 The First American troops land in Northern Ireland.

27 Two LEHI militants are killed by the British police during a raid on their hideout in Tel Aviv.

27 A pogrom in the Jewish quarter of Benghazi, Libya takes place with Italian-German recapture of the city.

31 *Centralei Evreilor din Romania*, the Center of the Jews in Rumania, is established by government order.

31 The *Gestapo* sets up a special *Arbeitsamt fuer Judenarbeiter* (Labor Exchange for Jew-Workers) in Berlin.

FEBRUARY

1 *Wirtschaftsund Verwaltungshauptamt* [WVHA] (SS Economic and Administrative Office) is established.

1 U.S. naval forces attack Japanese held bases in the Gilbert and Marshall Islands.

1 The two *Yiddish* language newspapers published in Uruguay, are ordered closed by the government, but they are allowed to resume publication on April 12.

3 The Croatian government orders confiscation of all Jewish movable property.

4 The *Afrika Korps* [DAK] temporarily halts its North African offensive at the Gazala-Bir Hacheim line.

4 The Brazilian government closes down a number of newspapers controlled by Axis interests.

5 Vidkun Quisling abrogates all citizenship rights for Norwegian Jews. *Hirdmen*, the Norwegian storm troopers, unleash anti-Jewish terror.

5 The pro-Nazi German-Brazilian Chamber of Commerce is ordered to dissolve.

8 Hitler names Albert Speer minister of armaments after Fritz Todt dies in an aerial accident.

10 Nazi planners officially give up on the Madagascar Plan.

11 The majority of non-Dutch Jews in Utrecht are deported to Westerbork *durchgangslager* (transit camp).

12 Avraham (Yair) Stern, founder of *Lohamei Herut Israel* [LEHI] (Fighters for the Freedom of Israel), is murdered by agents of the British CID in his apartment in Tel Aviv.

15 Singapore surrenders to Japanese forces.

19 Former French premiers Leon Blum and Paul Reynaud are put on trial by Vichy authorities charged with responsibility for the French defeat in 1940.

20 America grants a one billion dollar war loan to the Soviet Union.

23 Odessa is declared *Judenrein*.

23 Turkish police board the *Struma* preparing to tow it into the Black Sea.

24 In Berlin a conference between Germany, Rumania, and Hungary opens. The Jewish question is discussed.

24 The *Struma* sinks in the Black Sea. Out of 750 passengers, only one survives.

24 Vichy bans distribution of news bulletins received by the Jewish Telegraphic Agency.

24 Premier Wladislaw Sikorski, in his opening speech to the newly appointed National Council of the Polish government-in-exile, praises Polish Jewry for the loyalty they have shown in Poland's hour of need, promising that the Polish people will never forget this.

25 Liquidation of the Tomaszow Lubelski {P} ghetto: some 1,500 Jews are deported to the Cieszanow {P} *zwangsarbeitslager*.

25 The *Pracovna Skupina* (Working Group), a semi-underground Jewish organization, is established in Slovakia.

27 The Central Conference of American Rabbis adopts a resolution favoring establishment of a Jewish army in Palestine.

27. The Jewish Agency and *Va'ad Leumi* declare a one day strike in memory of the *Struma* martyrs. The annual *Purim* celebrations for 1942 are cancelled in their memory.

MARCH

1 Construction begins on the Sobibor extermination camp, one of the three *Aktion Reinhard* death camps in the eastern part of the Lublin district in Poland.

1 All passports and identity cards issued to Jews in Norway must be marked with the word "Jew."

1 One thousandth anniversary of the death of *Rav* Saadia Gaon.

1/2 During the Ratomskaya Street massacre, thousands of Jews are butchered by *Einsatzkommandos* and Ukrainians in a pit dug inside the Minsk {B/R SSR} ghetto on Ratomskaya Street. Thousands of others are driven to Koidanovo {B/R SSR} and slaughtered there.

2 "Unemployed" Belgian Jews are forced to work for the Nazi *Organisation Todt*.

3 Fifteen hundred Jews are murdered in an *aktion* in Dolginovo {B/R SSR}.

3 Twenty-three hundred Jews are murdered in an *aktion* in Baranowicze {B/R SSR}.

5 The British War Cabinet debates the question of "illegal" immigration into Palestine.

5 Jewish leaders in Slovakia launch an appeal to the Slovak government to halt deportations to the East, as deportation amounts to a death sentence.

6 In Berlin a conference opens on the fate of *mischlinge*.

7/9 *Umsiedlungsaktion* in Mielec {P} is staged by German police. A group of young male Jews are sent to the Pustkow {P} *Judenzwangsarbeitslager*, the old and the sick are murdered during *aktion*, while the rest of the Jewish community is deported to a number of towns in the Lublin {P} district.

8 The German military administration in Belgium issues a forced labor decree. Jews not drafted by the *Todt* organization, are affected.

9 *Asefat ha-Nivharim* demands a worldwide program to rescue European Jewry.

9 Heydrich initiates a *"Peitsche und Zucker"* (whip and sugar) policy in the Protectorate of Bohemia and Moravia.

9 Miklos Kallay becomes Hungary's prime minister.

9 German police execute over 700 Jews in the Cihrin-Berezovca slave labor camp in Transnistria.

9 Java surrenders to Japan.

11 Two thousand Jews are deported to their deaths in Mielec {P}.

11 General Douglas MacArthur leaves the Philippines declaring "I shall return."

13 The *SS* execute 650 Jews from the Hulievca-Berezovca slave labor camp in Transnistria.

14 The Vatican sends an official note protesting the deportation of Slovakian Jews.

15 The second *Aktion Reinhard* extermination camp at Belzec is opened.

16 All concentration camps are transferred to the *Wirtschaftsund Verwaltungshauptamt* [WVHA] under *SS-Obergruppenfuehrer* Oswald Pohl.

16/17 *Grossaktion* in the Lublin ghetto almost completely depletes the Jewish population as the rate of deportation is fixed at 1,500 per day. By April 21 between 35,000 and 40,000 Jews are murdered in the Belzec extermination camp.

17 An abridged version of a message sent to the *Reichsprotektor* Seyss-Inquart protesting the Nazi treatment of Jews, is read from the pulpits of the Dutch Reformed Church.

19 Two thousand Jews of Rava-Ruska deported to Belzec.

19 *Intelligenzaktion* in the Cracow ghetto: a number of prominent Jews from the Cracow ghetto are deported to Auschwitz and exterminated.

19/20 Five hundred patients and the Jewish medical staff of the Belgrade Jewish hospital are murdered in gas vans.

20 During the *aktion* in the Rohatyn {Uk SSR} ghetto, 2,000 Jews are driven outside of town and murdered.

21 Fritz Sauckel, *Gauleiter* of Thuringia, is appointed by Hitler as *Generalgevollmaechtigte fuer den Arbeitseinsatz* (plenipotentiary for labor recruitment) with full power to draft foreign civilian laborers into the war economy of the *Reich*.

22 Mass gassing begins at Auschwitz.

24 Three separate closed ghettos are established in Kolomyya {Uk SSR}.

24 *Aussiedlungsaktion* (deportation operation) takes place in Izbica Lubelska {P}; 2,200 Jews are deported to Belzec.

25 The American government seizes the vested interest of I.G. Farben in the United States.

25 One hundred Jews are killed in a Nazi *aktion* in Glebokie {B/R SSR}.

25 Five hundred Jews are sent to Izbica Lubelska {P} in the second Jewish deportation from Nuremberg.

25 One thousand Jews are murdered during the second *aktion* in the Tarnopol {Uk SSR} ghetto.

26 The First transport from Slovakia consisting of approximately 1,000 Jewish women arrives in Auschwitz.

27 Succeeding transports of Jews from Slovakia leave for the various Polish death camps.

27 In the second recruitment order published by *Yishuv*, all married men 20-30 years old are to be drafted except those with children.

27 The first transport of Jews from France leaves for Auschwitz.

27 A joint training program for *Hagana* and *Palmah* is initiated.

27 *Asefat ha-Nivharim* publishes a call to the British people to assure that their government open Palestine for the rescue of European Jewry.

27 Jews in Vichy are prohibited from changing their family names.

31 Five thousand Jews from the Stanislawow {Uk SSR} ghetto, among them many Jewish refugees from Hungary, are deported to Belzec.

31 Giuseppe Burzio, the Vatican *charge d'affaires* in Slovakia, sends a report to the Holy See in Rome stating that some 80,000 Slovakian Jews deported to Poland will face certain destruction. The Vatican, however, remains silent.

APRIL

1 *SS* takes over direct administration of the Blechhammer *Judenz-wangzarbeitslager*.

1 The Lachva {B/R SSR} ghetto is established.

2 In the first *aussiedlungsaktion* in Kolomyya {Uk SSR} ghetto, 1,000 Jews are deported to Belzec.

3 Deportation of Augsburg (Bavaria) Jews.

3 *Umsiedlungsaktion* in Tlumacz {Uk SSR}: some 1,200 Jews are deported to Stanislav {Uk SSR} and murdered.

4 Fifteen hundred Jews are executed during the second *aktion* in the Gorodenka {Uk SSR} ghetto.

4/9 Japanese fleet sorties enter the Indian Ocean. Carrier groups launch air attacks against British installations on Ceylon.

6/7 The Jewish Anti-Fascist Committee is established in Moscow and publishes its first appeal to Jews throughout the world.

9 U.S. forces on Bataan surrender.

9 A two-part ghetto in Radziwillow {Uk SSR} is created for the "fit" and "unfit" for work.

10 *Einsatzkommandoaktion* in Kuty {Uk SSR} leaves 950 Jews murdered and their homes burned down.

10/11 With final liquidation of the Leczyca {P} ghetto, all its remaining Jews are transported to Chelmno.

11 First deportation of Zamosc {P} Jews to Belzec.

11 First deployment of Hungarian Jewish labor servicemen on the Russian front.

13 Some 22,000 Jews of Vladimir Volynski {Uk SSR} are ordered into a two-part ghetto: the "*geto fun leben*" (the ghetto of life) for young skilled craftsmen, and the "*geto fun toyit*" (the ghetto of death) for older and non-productive Jews.

14 Pierre Laval becomes premier of Vichy.

15 American and British Commonwealth citizens living in Poland are ordered to register with the German police.

15 Jews in Germany are ordered to paint the Star of David on their homes.

15 The U.S. State Department asks all American residents in unoccupied France (Vichy) to leave for home because it would be difficult to guarantee their safety.

16 A new ghetto at Majdan Tatarski {P} is set up for the 4,000 Jewish survivors of the Lublin ghetto.

16 Nazis declare Crimea *Judenrein*.

18 Cuba denies admission to any new refugees born in Axis-controlled areas.

18 Close to 1,000 Jews from Ceske Budejovice {Cz} are deported to their death.

18 Doolittle Raid: taking off from the aircraft carrier *USS Hornet*, sixteen American B-25 bombers attack Tokyo and three other Japanese cities.

18/28 A series of small *aktionen* is undertaken by the *Gestapo* in both the small and large ghettos of Radom {P}. Hundreds of Jews are murdered.

19 President Roosevelt names General Douglas MacArthur Commander-in-Chief of the United Nations forces in the southwest Pacific.

19 The Bulgarian government orders confiscation of properties owned by Bulgarian Jews living abroad.

20 Fritz Sauckel, Plenipotentiary-General for the Mobilization of Labor, orders massive conscription of able-bodied men and women from German-occupied territories.

20 Laval announces a program of reconciliation with Nazi Germany.

20 The last issue of the antisemitic *Social Justice* is circulated in the United States.

21 Mexico passes a law that denies entry to anyone not born in the American hemisphere.

22 A Hitler decree establishes a Central Planning Board within the Four-Year Plan.

22 Decree is published calling for confiscation of all property owned by German Jews in Belgium.

23 Jewish doctors in Hungary are barred from practicing at public hospitals and health clinics.

24 LEHI fails in its attempts to assassinate the Palestinian High Commissioner, Sir Harold MacMichael.

24 The *Gestapo* bans Jews in Germany from using any form of public transport.

26 Hitler demands from and is given extraordinary powers by the *Reichstag*.

27 The Jewish badge is introduced in Holland.

27 The Wloclawek {P} ghetto is liquidated and all its Jews are deported to Chelmno.

28 Franz Stangl becomes the second commandant of the Sobibor extermination camp.

28 *Kibbutz* Gat is established in the Southern Coastal Plain.

29   A second group of Jews from the Lodz ghetto is deported to the Chelmno extermination camp.

29   Japanese cut Burma Road.

30   An *aktion* in the Diatlovo {B/R SSR} ghetto leaves some 1,200 Jews murdered.

MAY

1   The Pinsk {B/R SSR} ghetto is created for close to 20,000 Jews.

1   Except for about 450 young people left behind in a camp, all remaining Jews in the Dvinsk {Lat SSR} ghetto are killed when the ghetto is liquidated.

1   The *Histadrut* cancels all May Day celebrations in light of the emergency. Workers are asked to donate half that day's earnings to the *Yishuv*'s war effort fund.

1/2   Hitler and Mussolini meet near Salzburg, Austria.

4   A *Va'ad Leumi* meeting deals with the rapidly deteriorating military situation in the Middle East.

4/8   The Battle of Coral Sea is the first naval battle fought exclusively by carrier based aircraft.

5   British troops land on Madagascar.

6   U.S. forces surrender the Corregidor fortress in Manila Bay, after twenty-seven days of bitter fighting.

6   Petain names Darquier de Pellepoix Commissioner-General for Jewish Affairs.

6   Italian Jews between the ages of eighteen and fifty-five are ordered to register with the civilian mobilization office for labor service.

7   *Sekretariat fuer das Sicherheitswesen* (State Security Secretariat), is created in the Government General under Hitler's orders.

8   The German army starts its spring offensive on the Russian Kerch Peninsula.

8   The last U.S. forces in the Philippines surrender.

8   Five thousand Jews are killed during a massacre in Lida {B/R SSR}.

9   The Markuszow {P} ghetto is liquidated.

9   In the first of three *aussiedlungsaktionen* in Konskowola {P}, victims are dispatched for extermination in Sobibor.

9   The Japanese cancel plans to invade Port Morseby, New Guinea.

9/11 A conference sponsored by the Zionist Organization of America, attended by Chaim Weizmann, David Ben-Gurion, Abba Hillel Silver, Stephen S. Wise and Nahum Goldmann, among others, convenes at the Biltmore Hotel in New York City. The Biltmore Resolution calls for Palestine to be established as a Jewish Commonwealth.

10 Churchill threatens to use poison gas on Germany, if the Nazis use it on the Soviet Union.

10 The last group of Jews from the Semlin {Y} concentration camp are exterminated in gas-vans.

10 One thousand Jews are murdered in the Wolozyn {B/R SSR} *aktion*.

12 The first mass gassing of Jews at Auschwitz begins when a transport of 1,500 men, women, and children from Sosnowiec {P} are sent straight to the gas chamber.

12 *Aussiedlungsaktion* in Gabin {P}; the town becomes *Judenrein* as Jews are transported to the Chelmno extermination camp.

12 The *aktion* in the Ivye {B/R SSR} ghetto wipes out 2,500 Jews—over two-thirds of the Jewish community.

12 *SS-Brigadefuehrer* Karl Albrecht Oberg, is appointed HSSPF in occupied France.

13 The Ministry of Propaganda stages an antisemitic exhibition in Berlin, *Das Sowjetparadies* ("Soviet Paradise").

13 The United States assumes responsibility for defending the Fiji islands.

15 The Slovak parliament passes a bill authorizing expatriation and deportation of all Jews still in Slovakia.

15 A small group of young Jewish fighters break out from the Stolpce {B/R SSR} ghetto and join other partisans in the nearby forests.

15 *Wehrmacht* captures the Kerch Peninsula.

16 The Pabianice {P} ghetto is liquidated. Thirty-five hundred able-bodied Jews out of some 8,000 are sent to the Lodz ghetto, the other 4,500 to Chelmno.

18 The Herbert Baum group sets fire to the *Das Sowjetparadies* exhibit.

18 The Slovakian government announces the impending deportation of 45,000 Slovak Jews to Poland.

19/21   Liquidation of the Brzeziny {P} ghetto: *selektion* sends 3,000 Jews to be exterminated in Chelmno, while approximately the same number of younger people and craftsmen are sent to the Lodz ghetto.

20   The Convent of Lutheran Bishops in Slovakia issues a pastoral letter on the Jewish question.

21/23   Over 4,000 Jews are deported to Sobibor from Chelm, a little Polish town in the Lublin district famous in Jewish folklore as the *Chelmner Naroonim* (the fools of Chelm).

21/23   A large scale *aktion* takes place in the Ozorkow {P} ghetto. Some 2,000 Jews are deported to Chelmno, while 800 craftsmen are sent to the Lodz ghetto.

22/23   An *Aktion* in Dolginovo {B/R SSR} wipes out the entire Jewish community.

23   The First Wlodawa {P} ghetto *aktion* is carried out, but a number of Jews manage to escape to the forests and join partisan units.

26   The Anglo-Soviet treaty of mutual assistance is signed.

26   Beginning of Rommel's second offensive.

26   *Histadrut* proposes a general conscription for all males ages 17-50.

27   The yellow badge is introduced in Belgium.

27   Reinhard Heydrich, *Reichsprotektor* of Bohemia and Moravia, is mortally wounded in an assassination attempt by SOE agents in Czechoslovakia.

27   Some 2,000 Jews from Czechoslovakia and Germany, first deported between the first and third of May to Zamosc {P}, are now transported to Belzec.

28   The first large scale *aktion* in the Cracow ghetto begins, lasting until June 8. About 6,000 Jews are deported to Belzec while hundreds of other Jews are killed on the spot.

28   The *Yishuv* Security Committee appoints a new presidium for the *Kofer Ha-yishuv* (defense fund).

28   Mexico declares war on the Axis.

29   An *aktion* in Radziwillow {Uk SSR} liquidates the "unfit"-for-work part of the ghetto by murdering some 1,500 Jews outside town.

30   One thousand Allied bombers blacken the skies over Cologne during a massive air raid.

30   A British convoy reaches the Soviet Union despite heavy *Luftwaffe* air attacks.

JUNE

1 The Star of David is instituted in occupied France. All Jews six years old and up are ordered to wear a yellow star with the word *Juif* or *Juive* inscribed on it.

1 *Judenaelteste* Chaim Rumkowski orders that all bearded Jews in the Lodz ghetto must shave or face severe penalty.

1 The third *Aktion Reinhard* extermination camp, Treblinka, opens.

1 A decree in Nazi-occupied Belgium forbids Jewish doctors, dentists, and nurses from practicing their profession.

1/8 In the second *aktion* in the Cracow ghetto, some 7,000 Jews are deported to Belzec.

2 *Aktion* takes place in the Kobrin {B/R SSR} ghetto B. Approximately 3,000 Jews, or about fifty percent of Jewish community, are driven to Bronna Gora—a hilly area outside town—where they are murdered.

3 Governor-General Hans Frank transfers all matters pertaining to Jews to HSSPF *Obergruppenfuehrer* Friedrich Wilhelm Krueger, thus officially removing all Polish Jews from the control of the German civil administration in Poland and placing them under the sole authority of the *SS*.

3 The Baranow Sandomiersky {P} ghetto is established.

3/5 Three thousand Jews are murdered with the active help of local farmers during the first *aktion* in the Braslav {P} ghetto.

3/7 Battle of Midway Island.

4 The United States declares war on Rumania, Hungary, and Bulgaria.

4 Heydrich dies of his wounds.

4 Rumania resumes deportation of Jews from Chernovtsy to Transnitria.

5 Belgian municipal authorities refuse to cooperate with the Nazis in the distribution of the yellow badges.

6 The first *aktion* in Biala Podlaska {P} sends 3,000 Jews to Sobibor.

6 The first transport of Jews from Berlin leaves for Terezin.

7 Franco-Jewish war veterans parade in Paris in defiance of the Nazis and the French police.

7 Axis forces launch the final attack on Sevastopol.

9 During a speech in the House of Lords, Lord Moyne declares that Jews are not descendants of the ancient Hebrews, but are a mongrel race with no legitimate claims to the Holy Land.

9/11 The Germans obliterate the Czech town of Lidice in retaliation for the attack on Heydrich.

10 The Free French evacuate Bir Hacheim.

11 Nazi plans call for the roundup and deportation of 100,000 Jews from France.

11 Eichmann orders the *Gestapo* heads of the Jewish sections of Paris, Amsterdam, and Brussels to start deporting Jews from those countries.

11 A twenty year mutual assistance treaty is signed between Britain and the Soviet Union.

11/12 The first *grossaktion* in the Tarnow {P} ghetto takes place. Thousands of Jews are driven to the Jewish cemetery grounds and machine-gunned to death, while close to 10,000 others are deported to Belzec.

12/16 *Operation Pastorius*: German *Abwehr* agents land from U-boats in Amagansett, Long Island and at Ponte Verde near Jacksonville, Florida for espionage and sabotage; all are caught by Federal agents within a short time.

13 The first transport of Jews from Belgium leaves for forced labor in northern France.

13 In the battle of the Knightsbridge Box, British armored forces are decisively defeated by Rommel's *Afrika Korps*.

14/15 The Disna {B/R SSR} ghetto is liquidated. All Jews are taken to Piaskowe Gorki and murdered. An attempt to escape the Nazi trap is foiled.

15 Japanese forces occupy Attu and Kiska, two of the Aleutian Islands.

15 Eighteen hundred Jews are murdered in the village of Borki {P} by the *SS-Sonderbataillon Dirlewanger*, a band of marauding criminals under the command of Oskar Dirlewanger.

17 Some sixty survivors manage to flee the Druya {B/R SSR} ghetto during an *aktion* and join partisans operating in the region.

18 Churchill visits Washington for the second time in six months.

19 Twenty-five hundred Jews from Glebokie {B/R SSR} are machine-gunned to death in the Borek forest.

19   Jews in Germany are ordered to hand over all optical and electrical apparatus, typewriters, bicycles and musical items.

20   All Jewish schools in Germany are ordered closed.

21   German forces under Rommel capture Tobruk.

21   *Yishuv* declares conscription of males ages 17-45.

22   *Joodse Raad* succumbs to *Gestapo* threats and agrees to help with Nazi deportation orders.

22   The Swedish *Riksdag* (parliament) passes a law that any propaganda aimed at provoking hatred against groups or individuals on account of their race or religion will be a punishable offense.

22   The Ropczyce {P} ghetto is established.

22   The first transport from Drancy {F} transit camp consisting of 1,000 Jews leaves for Auschwitz.

23   A large-scale *aktion* is held in Paris by order of Theo Dannecker, chief of the SD in France.

23   Palestine's chief rabbinate declares an emergency prayer rite in response to Germany's Libyan offensive.

24   A bloody *aktion* takes place in the Lvov ghetto. Thousands are taken to the Janowska Camp and butchered at the *Piaski* (sands).

24   Nazis murder all adult inhabitants of Lezaky {Cz} to avenge Heydrich's assassination.

25   Dwight David Eisenhower is appointed commander-in-chief of Allied forces in Europe.

25   The majority of Jews from Duisburg {G} are deported to Terezin.

25   One thousand RAF bombers raid Bremen {G}.

26   Reports of the extermination of Polish Jewry are broadcast by the BBC.

26   The *Gestapo* advises the *Joodse Raad* that Dutch Jews will be deported to the east to perform light work duties.

27   The Axis penetrate 115 miles inside Egypt.

27   Eight German spies who landed in the United States are captured by the FBI.

28   The German offensive in the Don River basin begins.

28/29   The Rabbinical Council of America holds a convention and takes up the problem of *agunot* (married women who cannot remarry because of uncertainty [due to conditions of war] whether their husbands are still alive).

29 The Office for Studying the Jewish Question opens in Trieste.

30 Adolf Eichmann arrives in Paris to coordinate the German-French roundup of Jews in France.

30 A second gas chamber is put into operation at Auschwitz-Birkenau.

30 During liquidation of the Slonim {B/R SSR} ghetto, Jews fiercely resist as Nazis set the ghetto on fire. Most of its 15,000 Jews are killed or burned alive in the giant fires which continued to burn into the middle of July.

30 Nazis impose an 8 PM to 6 AM curfew upon all Jews in Holland.

JULY

1 Nazis take over the Central Camp for Refugees at Westerbork {Ho}. The *Gestapo* enlarges and reclassifies the camp to serve as a *Polizeiliches durchgangslager*—an assembly point for Dutch Jews on their way to the Polish extermination camps.

1/3 At the first battle of El Alamein, the *Afrika Korps* advance is halted.

2 Vichy France agrees to round up and deliver foreign Jews to the Germans for deportation.

2 With liquidation of the short-lived Ropczyce {P} ghetto, all of its Jews are deported to Belzec.

3 One hundred ten Jews from the Warsaw ghetto are taken as hostages and executed as a reprisal for "civil disobedience" against the German authorities.

3 Sevastopol {Uk SSR} falls to *Wehrmacht*.

3 All available *Palmah* units are redeployed in the south in anticipation of a possible German-Italian invasion of Palestine.

4 The U.S. 8th air force strikes Germany in its first air raid.

5 A mass protest meeting in Sydney, Australia, holds Britain responsible for the *Struma* tragedy.

5 The Dakovo {Y} camp for Jews is liquidated.

6 First edition of *Einikeit*, the *Yiddish* journal of the Jewish Anti-Fascist Committee, is published.

6 Anne Frank and her family move into the "annex" in Amsterdam, their hiding-place from the Nazis.

6 Argentina declares its strict neutrality in World War II.

7/13 During a *grossaktion* in the Rzeszow {P} ghetto, some 22,000 Jews from Rzeszow and vicinity are deported to Belzec, with another 1,000 Jews murdered in the nearby Rudna Forest.

8 The first transport of over one thousand Frenchmen arrives at Auschwitz.

10 Deportations of Jews from Groningen {Ho}, begin.

10 A Vichy decree bars Jews from all public places in France.

11 All Jews between eighteen and forty-five living in Salonika, {Gr} are ordered to register prior to deportation to forced labor camps in Macedonia and Bulgaria.

11 Jacob Gens is appointed *Judenaelteste* in the Vilna ghetto.

11 The first transport of Berlin Jews leaves for Auschwitz.

12 The Liepaja {Lat SSR} ghetto is established.

13 A *grossaktion* takes place in Rovno {Uk SSR} ghetto. More than 5,000 Jews are exterminated at Janowa Dolina.

13 All non-Jewish refugees in Westerbork are ordered out from the camp.

15 Eichmann becomes furious when a deportation train from Paris misses its schedule.

15 The first transport of Dutch Jews from Westerbork leaves for Auschwitz. Twelve additional transports leave within the next six weeks (two transports per week), totaling more than 10,000 victims.

15 Jews in Antwerp are forbidden to frequent public places.

15 A large-scale *aktion* in Sasov {Uk SSR} almost depletes the Jewish community; at least 1,000 Jews are deported to Belzec.

15 The *Gestapo* orders the AJB to set up a special *Arbeitseinsatz* (work command) to oversee deportation of Belgian Jews to "labor camps."

16/17 French collaborationist police begin roundups of Parisian Jews. Over 13,000 persons, including 4,000 children, are held at the Velodrome d'hiver prior to being deported to Auschwitz.

17 Germany declares Frankfort-am-Main *Judenrein*.

17 The first transport of Dutch Jews arrives in Auschwitz.

17 Hundreds of Jews in Poland with American and British Commonwealth passports are taken to the Pawiak *Gestapo* prison in Warsaw.

17/18 Himmler visits Auschwitz for the second time.

18 The Szarkowszczyzna {B/R SSR} ghetto is liquidated.

18 Fascist thugs vandalize the Trieste synagogue. Some school-age children participate in the destruction.

19 The All-India Congress votes for independence, and petitions for withdrawal of British rule over India.

19 Himmler orders liquidation of all remaining ghettos and labor camps in the *Generalgouvernement* by quickly dispatching their inhabitants to the extermination centers. All Jews still alive are to be transferred to five specially established *zwangsarbeitslagern* before year's end.

19 The *Hochschule fuer die Wissenschaft des Judentums*, a center for the scientific study of Judaism and a rabbinical seminary in Berlin, is closed by order of the *Gestapo*.

21 The Nesvizh {B/R SSR} ghetto is liquidated. Jews from the town use arms to resist the Nazis, leading to combat in the first ghetto revolt.

21 The *Gestapo* raids six UGIF-sponsored children's homes and seizes close to 300 children.

21 A huge rally to protest the slaughter of European Jewry is organized by the American Jewish Congress in New York.

21 Twenty-eight persons are indicted by Federal Grand Jury in Washington on conspiracy charges.

21 *Einsatzkommandos* liquidate the Kleck {B/R SSR} ghetto by setting it afire and murdering most of its Jews. Only a few dozen succeed in escaping to the nearby forests from where they take up the fight against Nazis.

22 *Zydowska Organizacja Bojowa* [ZOB], the Jewish Fighting Organization, is established in the Warsaw ghetto.

22 A Nazi *Aktion* destroys the Children's Hospital in the Warsaw ghetto.

22 The *Judenrat* is informed that all Jews living in Warsaw, regardless of age and sex, will be deported to the East. Daily transport of 5,000 Jews to Treblinka begins.

22 *Aussiedlungsaktionen* begin in Galicia.

23 The Treblinka extermination camp becomes operational.

23 Mass roundups and deportation of Dutch Jews begin.

23 Adam Czerniakow, chairman of the Jewish Council of the Warsaw ghetto, commits suicide.

23   The Synagogue Council of America proclaims *Tisha b'Av* (the ninth of Av, a Jewish religious fast day) to be a day of mourning for the Jewish victims of Nazism.

24   Rostov falls to German forces.

24   Liquidation of the Derechin {P} ghetto: Dr. Yehezkel Atlas succeeds in escaping and organizes a partisan unit in the nearby forests.

25   The U.S. Congress opens its summer session with a special prayer for European Jewry.

26   Most Dutch Roman Catholics of Jewish origin are deported to Auschwitz to be gassed.

26   The Dutch clergy protest from their pulpits Nazi deportations of Dutch Jews.

27   Germany begins a campaign of mass murder in the Warsaw ghetto.

28   News of the mass deportations of the Jews from the Warsaw ghetto to Treblinka reaches London and Jerusalem.

28/31   *Grossaktion* takes place in the Minsk {B/R SSR} ghetto: more than 30,000 Jews are murdered by *Einsatzkommandos*, German military police, and their Belorussian and Lithuanian collaborators in prepared pits or in roving gas-vans. Among those murdered are thousands of children and thousands of Jews previously deported from Germany, Austria, and Czechoslovakia.

30   The Axis air force bombs Cairo for the first time.

30   *Histadrut* rejects the recruitment agreement between the Jewish Agency and the Revisionists.

AUGUST

1   Jews in the Warsaw ghetto are urged to report voluntarily to the *umschlagplatz* (assembly point). Volunteers are promised 3 kg. of bread and 1 kg. of jam, an unbelievable luxury to a starving people.

1   Gerhard Riegner, the representative of the World Jewish Congress in Switzerland, is notified by an anonymous German industrialist of Nazi implementation of the Final Solution.

1   All Jews remaining in Lancut {P} are deported. The sick, elderly, and children are murdered in the Nechezioli forest.

3   *Aussiedlungsaktion* in Przemysl {P} sends more than 12,000 Jews to Belzec.

4 First of twenty-six transports from Malines *durchgangslager* leaves for Auschwitz; 25,000 Jews are deported from here to their death through July 1944.

4 In Sambor's first *aktion* {Uk SSR}, 4,000 Jews are deported to Belzec.

5 Dr. Janusz Korczak and the children from his orphanage, are marched to the *umschlagplatz* in the Warsaw ghetto. The world-famous pediatrician perishes together with "his children" in Treblinka.

5 First Belgian transport leaves for Auschwitz.

5 Pilica {P} ghetto is liquidated.

5 The "smaller" ghetto in Radom {P} is liquidated and all 10,000 Jews are deported to Treblinka.

5 The British government repudiates the Munich Agreement.

5 All foreign Jews residing in Vichy who entered France after January 1, 1936 are ordered deported to the occupied zone of France.

6 The approximately 15,000 Jews from the "small ghetto" of Warsaw are sent to their death at Treblinka.

6 The Diatlovo {B/R SSR} ghetto is liquidated, but a large number of Jews manage to escape to the nearby forest where they form a partisan group.

6 The second mass roundup of Amsterdam Jewry nets about 2,000 Jews.

6 The first transport of Jews leaves Gurs {F} for Auschwitz.

6/17 A *grossaktion*, claiming the lives of over 20,000 Jews (after they are deported to Treblinka), reduces the "larger" Radom {P} ghetto to barely 4,000 Jews, who are then transferred to a small part of the former "small" ghetto, which is reclassified as a *Judenlager*.

7 In the Novogrudok {B/R SSR} ghetto's second *aktion*, some 2,000 Jews are killed and the ghetto is liquidated. Only a few hundred Jews are left in two camps, one for artisans and the other for construction workers.

7 The Atlas' partisan group is established near Puszcza-Lipiczanska {B/R SSR}.

7 United States Marines land in Guadalcanal.

7 All Gypsies in Alsace are deported to occupied France.

7 The British establish a Palestine regiment, to consist of separate Jewish and Arab battalions.

7 Mahatma Ghandi calls for civil disobedience against British rule in India. The British arrest Ghandi the following day.

9 Armed uprisings break out in the Mir {B/R SSR} and Kremenets {Uk SSR} ghettos.

9 Liquidation of the Radun {B/R SSR} Jewish community: with the exception of a few who manage to escape, all Jews are killed.

10 Liquidation of the Brzozow {P} ghetto: during *aktion* some 800 women, children, and the elderly are murdered in prepared pits in a nearby forest.

10/30 A three week long *grossaktion* in the Lvov ghetto is carried out by *SS Einsatzkommandos* aided by Ukrainian volunteers. Approximately 50,000 Jews are deported to Belzec.

11 The *Ihud* (Unity) movement, calling for a binational Palestinian state, established by Dr. Judah L. Magnes and Professor Martin Buber.

11 Riots break out in Bombay and New Delhi.

11 Leaders of the Copperheads, an American Nazi group, are convicted of sedition.

11/13 Liquidation of the Belchatow {P} ghetto: some 850 Jews deemed labor-worthy are transferred to the Lodz ghetto, the bulk—some 5,000— are deported to Chelmno for extermination.

12 Five thousand Jews are deported to Auschwitz in a major *aktion* in Bedzin {P}.

12 The *Gestapo* imposes a 250,000 *zloty* fine on Jews of Gorlice {P}.

12 Orthodox American Jews observe a one-day fast on behalf of European Jewry.

12/15 Churchill-Stalin conference in Moscow.

13 Au*ssiedlungsaktion* takes place in Rymanow {P}. The town's entire Jewish population, close to 3,000 people, is deported to Belzec. About 100 to 150 of the very old and sick are shot outside of town in a prepared pit. Only ninety-seven young male Jews who are in the middle of a road-building project are left behind in a former school building on the outskirts of town, in Posada Dolna.

13 By an official Hitler order, all partisans in eastern Europe are to be called "bandits."

13 The Mir {B/R SSR} ghetto is liquidated. All of its remaining Jews are taken to Yablonovshchina and murdered.

13 Switzerland seals its borders to Jewish refugees.

13 The first Yugoslavian transport to Auschwitz leaves from Lobor *durchgangslager*, via Zagreb {Y}.

13 Nazis seize all radio sets belonging to French Jews.

13 A *grossaktion* takes place in the Grodek Jagiellonski {Uk SSR} ghetto. Those not murdered outright are deported to Belzec.

13 General Bernard Montgomery is appointed commander of the British Eighth Army at El Alamein.

13/14 During an *aussiedlungsaktion* in the Gorlice {P} ghetto, some 700 old and infirm Jews are shot in a prepared pit and about the same number of young people are left behind, while the remainder are transported to Belzec and their deaths.

13/15 Two separate camps are established in Dukla {P} for some 400 male Jews, the *arbeitslagers* Artur Walde-Breslau (for Jews working on construction of a new highway) and Emil Ludwig-Muenchen (for Jews employed in a stone-quarry).

14 A transport of 1,000 Jews, for the first time including many children, leaves Drancy for Auschwitz.

15 A one-building temporary labor camp is established in Bukowsko {P} for 100 Jews who work on road construction for the *Firma Kirchhof*. The camp is liquidated on October 15.

15 The Falenica {P} *Judenlager* is established.

15 Himmler visits Treblinka.

16 *Organizacja Bojowa Zydowskiej Mlodziecy Chalucowej*, a pioneer Jewish underground fighting organization, is established in Cracow ghetto by young Zionists from different orientations.

16 The Auschwitz *Frauenabteilung* (women's section) is relocated to Birkenau (Auschwitz II).

17 Stalin, Churchill, and U.S. Ambassador Averell Harriman confer in Moscow.

17/18 An *aktion* in the Drohobycz {Uk SSR} ghetto sends 2,500 Jews to the Belzec extermination camp. Over 500 Jews are murdered by German and Ukrainian police during *selektionen*.

17/18 The U.S. Marine Corps raid Makin Island.

18 Fort-Paillet and Venissieux near Lyon become assembly points for foreign Jews arrested by the French police.

18 Hitler issues War Directive Number 46 on the treatment of partisans ("bandits") in the East.

18 Nazis begin deporting Jews from the Dutch capital, The Hague, to Westerbork.

19 Two transports of 12,000 Jews from a number of Galician towns are gassed at Belzec.

19 Operation Jubilee: combined Allied forces raid Dieppe, France.

19/23 *Grossaktion* takes place in the Lutsk {Uk SSR} ghetto. Approximately 17,000 Jews are driven to the Polanka hill on the outskirts of town and machine-gunned to death. Only 500 artisans are left in a temporary labor camp which is liquidated on December 12, 1942.

20 The first transport of Jews from the Rivesaltes {F} camp leaves for the East.

20 Thousands of Jews in Paris are rounded up by German and French police and taken to Drancy.

20 ZOB member Israel Kanal assassinates the head of the Warsaw ghetto, *Juedischer Ordnungsdienst* Joseph Szerynski.

20 . The Falenica {P} ghetto is liquidated. All of its remaining Jews, except for some 100 workers in a town saw mill, are deported to Treblinka.

21 *Grossaktion* in the Minsk Mazowiecki {P} ghetto: at least 1,000 Jews are murdered during proceedings, while all other Jews—with the exception of about 650 men left behind in a makeshift camp in the former *Kopernik* school building—are deported to their deaths in Treblinka.

21 Liquidation of the Ozorkow {P} ghetto.

21/24 An *Agudas Yisroel* conference in Belmar, New Jersey, establishes a *Keren ha-Torah* fund to foster religious education among American Jews.

22 Jews in Stolin {B/R SSR} are ordered to pay a one million *ruble* fine.

22 With liquidation of the Jewish community in Wielun {P}, 10,000 Jews of Wielun and vicinity are deported to Chelmno with only a small number of the "physically fit" sent to the Lodz ghetto.

22 The Jewish community in Losice {P} is liquidated and all of its Jews are deported to Treblinka.

22 Liquidation of the Siedlce {P} ghetto: 10,000 Jews are deported to Treblinka; a "small" ghetto is established for the 2,000 remaining Jews which is liquidated on November 25.

22 Brazil declares war on Nazi Germany.

23 Over 50,000 Jews are murdered in a *grossaktion* defying description in the Lvov ghetto.

23/24 Final *aktion* and liquidation of the Zdunska Wola {P} ghetto: hundreds of Jews are murdered on the spot and about 8,000 Jews are sent to their death at Chelmno.

24 The Swiss Central Office for Refugee Aid, a conglomorate of all the aid organizations operating in Switzerland, meets with Swiss authorities on behalf of refugees to discuss their status.

24/28 *Aussiedlungsaktion* in the Nowy Sacz {P} ghetto: the entire Jewish community, consisting of over 10,000 people, is deported to Belzec.

25 *Membres du Service d'Orde*, an internal police force made up of Jewish internees at Drancy, is established on orders of Alois Brunner, German camp commandant.

25/26 During the first large-scale *aktion* in Miedzyrzec Podlaski {P}, thousands of Jews are deported to Treblinka.

26 V-League, an organization to aid the Soviet Union, is established in Palestine.

26/28 French police in Vichy conduct a massive roundup of Jews and hand them over to the *SS*.

27 The majority of Jews from Frankfort-am-Oder {G} are deported to Terezin.

27 The Wieliczka {P} Jewish community is liquidated. During *selektion*, 500 of the young and strong are sent to the Stalowa-Wola {P} *zwangsarbeitslager*, 200 to Plaszow {P}, and the overwhelming majority, 8,000, are sent to Belzec.

27 American Jewish organizations protest deportation of Jewish refugees by Vichy France.

27/28 Liquidation of the Sarny {Uk SSR} Jewish community ends with some 14,000 Jews from Sarny and vicinity murdered.

28 Dr. Gerhart Riegner, Swiss representative of the World Jewish Congress, cables Rabbi Stephen S. Wise about the extermination of European Jewry.

28 Jews of Antwerp are deported to extermination sites in Poland.

28 The first *aktion* in Zloczow {Uk SSR} ghetto sends close to 3,000 Jews to the Belzec extermination camp.

28   A sizable *aktion* takes place in Chortkov {Uk SSR}. Two thousand Jews are dispatched to their deaths at Belzec, while hundreds of Jews are murdered on the streets.

28   Miedzyrzec {P} *grossaktion*: 10,000 Jews are deported for slaughter.

28   Members of the Jewish underground in Belgium assassinate Robert Holcinger, a member of the AJB, for his close collaboration with the Nazis in the deportation *aktionen*.

29   The Jewish population of Olesko {Uk SSR} is deported to Belzec.

29/31   The third *aktion* in the Tarnopol {Uk SSR} ghetto sends 4,000 Jews to Belzec.

30   A pastoral letter by the French bishop of Montauban, Monseigneur Pierre-Marie Theas, protests the roundup of Jews by French police.

30   The Rabka {P} ghetto is liquidated.

30   Luxembourg's citizens are drafted into the German army.

SEPTEMBER

1   The German army reaches the Volga River.

1   Under the caption "A Day for Polish Jewry," the *Reprezentacja* (representatives of the Polish government-in-exile) in Palestine sponsors a one-day protest against the Nazi extermination program.

1   *Aktion* in Stryj {Uk SSR}: thousands of Jews are deported to their deaths in Belzec.

1   Documents received in London from the Polish and Jewish underground on the extermination of Polish Jewry, are met with shock and disbelief.

1   The Rozwadow {P} *Zwangsarbeitslager* is established.

1   The Czarny Dunajec {Y} *Judenlager* is established.

1/15   A series of *aktionen* starts in the Vladimir Volynski {Uk SSR} ghetto. Eighteen thousand Jews are murdered by Germans and Ukrainians in the course of two weeks, some in the prison courtyard and others in prepared pits outside of town.

2   During a massacre at Majdan Tatarski {P}, 2,000 out of the 4,000 Jews transferred from the Lublin {P} ghetto during its liquidation are killed.

2   *Judenlager* HASAG-Apparatenbau in Czestochowa {P} is established.

2   A transport with 1,000 Jews from Belgium leaves for Auschwitz.

2 The Zionist Emergency Committee adopts a resolution opposing incorporation of Palestine into any Middle Eastern federation.

2/3 The Lachva {B/R SSR} ghetto is the scene of a Jewish revolt. A fierce struggle erupts as Jews resist the Nazi's attempt to liquidate the ghetto. Seven hundred Jews die as they fight with axes, knives, bare hands and set their homes afire. Their heroic efforts make it possible for some 1,000 Jews to escape, but only about half of them reach the Pripet marshes—all other Jews are taken to prepared pits and massacred.

3 The Belgian Commissariat for Jewish Affairs is established.

3 One thousand Jews are murdered during roundup in the Dzialoszyci {P} ghetto's first *aktion*. Thousands more are deported to Plaszow or Belzec.

3 German police start the hunt for Belgian Jews in the vicinity of the central Brussels railway station.

4 Vichy institutes labor conscription.

5 A second *grossaktion* takes place in the Lodz ghetto and some 20,000 Jews are deported to their death.

5/10 *Aussiedlungsaktion* is carried out in Sanok {P}: close to 8,000 Jews from Sanok and vicinity are deported to the *Judenlager* at Zaslaw {P} and from there they are dispatched to Belzec.

6 The battle of Stalingrad begins.

6 Approximately 15,000 Jews are deported from the French camps of Gurs, Rivesaltes, and Les Milles to their death.

6 The American Jewish Congress appeals to President Roosevelt to publicly denounce the Nazi atrocities against the Jews in Europe.

6 The Gorodenka {P} ghetto is liquidated.

6/7 Liquidation of the Wolbrom {P} ghetto: close to 8,000 Jews are driven to the railway station, where—after a *selektion*—2,000 of the sick, feeble, and elderly are murdered in prepared pits. The other 6,000 Jews—except for some 200 selected for slave labor—are transported to the Belzec death camp.

7 The Lvov ghetto is sealed. Jews found outside the ghetto will be summarily executed.

7 The Sniatyn {Uk SSR} ghetto is liquidated. All Jews are deported to Belzec.

9 Bamberg {G} is made *Judenrein*, when its entire Jewish community consisting of some 300 people is deported to the East.

10   In the third deportation of Jews from Nuremberg, the last 533 Jews are sent to Terezin.

10   Mass roundup of Jews in Antwerp.

10   During the second *aktion* in the Tarnow {P} ghetto 8,000 Jews are deported to Belzec.

13   The Checiny {P} ghetto is liquidated.

13   The Argentinian government orders the Federation of German Welfare and Cultural Clubs, a Nazi front organization, to disband.

15   Canada conveys its concern to the Vichy government over the latter's Jewish policy.

15   The *Comite de Defense des Juifs* (Jewish Defense Committee), an underground organization, is established in Belgium.

15/17   Liquidation of the Kalush {P} ghetto: all Jews are deported to Belzec.

15/21   Ghettos in the vicinity of Kamenka-Bugskaya {Uk SSR} are liquidated. Jews not working for the German army are either killed on the spot or deported to Belzec.

16   *Aussiedlungsaktion* in Jedrzejow {P}: the entire Jewish community consisting of some 6,000 people is deported to Treblinka, except for 200 male Jews left behind in a small labor camp.

17   The Polish Directorate of Civil Resistance [KWC] issues a statement condemning the Nazi extermination of Polish Jewry.

17   An *aktion* in Sokal {Uk SSR} sends 2,000 Jews to Belzec.

18   There is a drastic reduction of food rations for Jews still residing in Greater Germany.

18   "Asocials" imprisoned in Germany who have served their sentences are to be turned over to the *Gestapo* for further incarceration in concentration camps.

19   Liquidation of the Parczew {P} Jewish community begins.

19/21   The first *aktion* in the Brody {Uk SSR} ghetto sends some 2,000 Jews to Belzec.

20   The Broniewo {P} *Judenlager* is liquidated.

22   Liquidation of the Jewish community of Wegrow {P}: A large number of Jews, acting on a tip of the approaching disaster, manage to escape to the forests just before the start of the *aktion*.

22   The second large-scale *aktion* in the Baranowicze {B/R SSR} ghetto, kills 3,000.

22 The National Council of the French Reformed Church condemns persecution of Jews.

22 The First *aktion* in the Czestochowa {P} ghetto begins; *aktionen* continue until October 5, and a total of 40,000 Jews are deported to Treblinka.

22 The Bolivian government bans additional immigration of Jews, Negroes, and Mongols.

23 *Aussiedlungsaktion* takes place in Szydlowiec {P}. Ten thousand Jews from Szydlowiec and vicinity are deported to Treblinka.

23/25 Jews in the Tuczyn {Uk SSR} ghetto stage a nearly successful revolt when they learn of Nazi liquidation plans. Under cover of fire and smoke, as many as two-thirds (2,000 Jews) of the ghetto population are able to flee the *aussiedlungsaktion* to the nearby forests; however, most of the fighters fall in battle with the German and Ukrainian forces.

24 In an act of defiance the Jews of Korzec {Uk SSR} set their homes—and in some cases themselves—ablaze to avoid a Nazi *Aussiedlungsaktion*.

25 Without exception, all Germans aged sixteen to sixty are drafted into the *Volksstrum* (peoples' army) to bear arms for the fatherland.

25 During a *grossaktion* in the Kaluszyn {P} ghetto the Jewish population is nearly wiped out. A forced labor camp is established for the few remaining Jews.

26 A Swiss decree specifies five categories of refugees that may be admitted: (1) sick persons and pregnant women; (2) those over sixty-five years old; (3) children under sixteen without parents or escorts; (4) parents with children under sixteen; (5) those with close relatives in Switzerland.

26 Jews of Biala Podlaska {P} are deported to the Miedzyrzecz {P} ghetto. One month later all are deported to Treblinka.

29 The Serniki {P} ghetto is liquidated. A few hundred Jews escape to the forest during the *aktion*.

29 The Free French Government under Charles de Gaulle repudiates the Munich Agreement.

30 Hitler declares (for a second time) that World War II will destroy European Jewry.

30 The Zelechow {P} ghetto is liquidated and all Jews sent to Treblinka.

30 The Assembly of the Swiss Pastors' Union condemns antisemitism.

OCTOBER

1 The Bodzechow {P} *Judenlager* is established.

1/2 Ten thousand Jews from Luboml {Uk SSR} and vicinity are murdered when the Jewish community is liquidated.

2 Jewish partisans led by Dr. Yehezkiel Atlas capture a German aircraft.

2 *Grossaktion* liquidates the remaining Jews in Belzyce {P}. Three thousand Jews are sent to Majdanek for extermination, including many Jews previously deported from Germany.

2 The Swiss Federal Department of Justice and Police appoints a special commissioner in charge of refugee questions.

3 A final *aktion* is carried out in the Kolomyya {Uk SSR} ghetto: 5,000 Jews deported to Belzec and the ghetto is liquidated.

3 The Jewish community of Wislica {P} is liquidated and some 3,000 Jews are deported to Treblinka.

3 Liquidation of the Radzymin {P} Jewish community: all Jews are deported to Treblinka.

4/6 Jewish community of Wolomin {P} is liquidated during a three-day *aktion*. About 600 Jews are murdered outright, while the rest—2,400— are deported to Treblinka.

5 A second *aktion* liquidates the Radziwillow {Uk SSR} ghetto; some youths attempt to escape, but most Jews are murdered.

5 During the first *aktion* in Tolstoye {Uk SSR} 1,000 Jews are deported to Belzec.

5 All Jewish prisoners in labor or concentration camps within the *Grossreich* are ordered transferred to Auschwitz or Majdanek for extermination.

6 Nazis request that the Kallay government extend the Final Solution to Hungary.

6/27 Second and third *aktionen* (October 27) are held in Miedzyrzec Podlaski {P}. Close to 10,000 Jews are deported to Treblinka; a few hundred Jews succeed in escaping to the forests.

7 The OKW orders the chaining of all British prisoners of war taken captive at Dieppe.

7 The Allies establish a commission to investigate Axis war crimes; President Roosevelt pledges U.S. cooperation.

9 The Soviet army abolishes political commissars.

9 The Zionist Federation of South Africa officially repudiates the *Ihud* program advocated by Dr. Judah L. Magnes.

9/12 An exceptionally large number of Jews escape to the forests during *aussiedlungsaktionen* in the Radomsko {P} ghetto. All remaining Jews, except for 500 left behind in a greatly reduced ghetto area, are deported to Treblinka. Most escaped Jews return to the ghetto due to the terrible hardship of forest life and the approaching winter—relying on German promises that no harm will come to them.

9/12 Liquidation of the Jewish community in Przedborz {P}: all 4,500 Jews are deported to Treblinka.

10 The last transport of 1,300 Jews deported from Vienna leaves for Terezin.

10 A published decree issued by *SS* General Krueger calls for the establishment of fifty-five ghettos in the *Generalgouvernement*. This decree is a sham, however, since most of Polish Jewry are dead by then or in the process of being exterminated.

10 The Dabrowa Tarnowska {P} ghetto is established.

11 Liquidation of the Bychawa {P} ghetto.

11 *Aussiedlungsaktion* in Lubatrow {P}: the entire Jewish community is deported to Sobibor, including 1,000 Jews previously deported from Slovakia to Lubatrow.

11/12 A *grossaktion* is carried out in Ostrowiec {P}: 11,000 Jews, or 80 percent of the Jewish population, are deported to Treblinka. A slave-labor camp is established for the approximately 2,000 Jews who remain.

12 Deportations from Upper Silesia commence. Fifteen thousand Jews are transported to various murder sites.

12 HASAG establishes six new *zwangsarbeitslagern* in the area around Radom {P}. During the camp's existence a total of some 40,000 Polish, Czech, German, Austrian, and Hungarian Jews are forced to do hard work for the German armament industry under terrible conditions.

13 Final *aktion* against the Jews in Zdolbunow {P}.

14 *Aussiedlungsaktion* in Mizocz {Uk SSR}: all victims, mostly women and children, are shot at close range in a ravine, and the village is declared *Judenrein*.

14 A second *grossaktion* liquidates the Kobrin {P} ghetto; a number of resisters manage to escape to forests and join partisans.

14 *Generalleutnant* (Lieutenant-General) Hermann von Hanneken, a close Nazi sympathizer, is appointed the new German military commander of Denmark.

15 The Ostrog {Uk SSR} ghetto is liquidated. All of the town's Jews are driven into the woods and murdered and the town is declared *Judenrein*.

15 The Berezhany {Uk SSR} ghetto is established.

15 A ghetto is created in Sokal {Uk SSR}. Some 5,000 Jews from Sokal and neighboring villages are crowded into a very small area with very little drinking water.

15 The Bishop of Chichester, in a convocation speech before the House of Lords, attacks the Nazi and Vichy treatment of Jews.

15 Jews in Bereza Kartuska {B/R SSR} set the ghetto afire during a Nazi *aktion* to liquidate the ghetto. Those Jews not killed outright in Bereza are driven to Brona Gora, a rail spur and extermination site, and slaughtered.

15 Liquidation of the Brest-Litovsk {B/R SSR} ghetto: a number of Jews succeed in escaping to join Soviet partisans in the forests, while most Jews are murdered upon their arrival in Brona Gora.

15/22 A *grossaktion* takes place in the Piotrkow Trybunalski {P} ghetto and some 22,000 Jews are deported to Treblinka.

17 Jewish inmates from KL Buchenwald are transferred to Auschwitz.

17 A *grossaktion* sends thousands of Jews from Buczacz {P} to the Belzec extermination camp.

18 *Kommandobefehl* (commando order): Hitler secretly orders all captured Allied commandos immediately executed.

19 Food rations for Jews in the *Reich* are severely curtailed.

20 Liquidation of the Bar (Transnistria) forced labor camp results in the murder of some 12,000 Jews.

20/22 The Opatow {P} ghetto is liquidated and 6,000 Jews are deported to Treblinka.

21 The Szczebrzeszyn {P} Jewish community is eliminated when all Jews are deported to Belzec.

21 A rally on behalf of European Jewry under Nazism is held at the Royal Albert Hall, London under the auspices of the Jewish Board of Deputies.

21 A large *aktion* in Skalat {Uk SSR} sends 3,000 Jews to Belzec.

21   U.S. Congress passes the largest tax bill in American history.

23   Himmler appoints *SS Obergruppenfuehrer und General der Polizei* Erich von dem Bach-Zelewski to the post of *Bevollmaechtigte fuer die Bandenbekampfung in Osten* (Plenipotentiary for the Combating of Partisans in the East).

23   Oszmiana {Lit SSR} massacre: 500 Jews are murdered by Nazis with the help of *Juedischer Ordnungsdienst* of Vilna.

23   Battle of El Alamein.

24   The Wlodawa {P} ghetto is liquidated and all Jews are deported to perish in the Sobibor gas chambers.

25   All Jewish males in Norway over sixteen years old are seized by the *Hirdmen* and deported to Auschwitz.

25/26   A Japanese attack on Guadalcanal is repulsed in a series of naval battles.

27   The Opoczno {P} ghetto is liquidated.

27/28   Nazis launch a second *aktion* in the Cracow ghetto: approximately 7,000 Jews are taken to Auschwitz and Belzec. The ghetto is split into two separate parts, with Part A for those with *arbeitscheine*, and Part B for the remainder.

27/31   Liquidation of the Przysucha {P} Jewish community: all 4,000 Jews are deported to Treblinka.

28   A transport of Terezin Jews sent to Auschwitz.

28   Final *aktion* takes place in the Pinsk {B/R SSR} ghetto. All of the ghetto's remaining 16,000 Jews, with the exception of 150 artisans, are killed within the next five days.

28   The Jewish National Committee and leaders of ZOB in the Warsaw ghetto secretly indict members of the *Judenrat* and the Jewish police suspected of collaborating with the *Gestapo*.

28   Liquidation of the Biala Rawska {P} ghetto.

28   *Aussiedlungsaktion* in Hrubieszow {P}: 2,000 Jews are deported to Sobibor.

29   Jacob Lajkin, second-in-command of the Warsaw *Juedischer Ordnungsdienst*, is assassinated by order of the ZOB.

29   An *aktion* in Sandomierz {P} sends over 3,000 Jews to Belzec.

29   A mass rally in London's Albert Hall voices protest of the Nazi treatment of Europe's Jews.

29   Japan begins withdrawing from Guadalcanal.

30 *IG-Farbenindustrie* opens an Auschwitz subcamp at Buna-Monowice (Auschwitz III) for the manufacture of synthetic rubber.

30 A *Hitachdut Olei Germania ve-Austria* (Association of German and Austrian Immigrants) Conference resolves to create a new political party, to be called *Aliya Chadasha*.

31 A massive *aktion* in the Tomaszow Mazowiecki {P} ghetto sends close to half (7,000) of its population to Treblinka to be murdered.

NOVEMBER

1 *Aeltestenrat der Juden in Wien* (the Council of Jewish Aldermen in Vienna), is established by order of the *Gestapo*. The Viennese *Israelitische Kultusgemeinde* (Jewish community) is officially dissolved.

1 Liquidation of the Plonsk {P} ghetto begins. Around 12,000 Jews are deported in four transports to Auschwitz (the last on December 5).

2 The Bilgoraj {P} ghetto is liquidated. All Jews are deported to Belzec.

2 The Bocki {P} ghetto is liquidated.

2 When the Ostryna {B/R SSR} ghetto is liquidated, all Jews are transferred to the Kelbasin {P} *Zwangsarbeitslager*. From there they are deported to Auschwitz.

2 The Wolkowysk {B/R SSR} *Judenlager* is established on the premises of a former prisoner-of-war camp.

2 Liquidation of the Augustow {P} ghetto.

2 Liquidation of the Tarnogrod {P} Jewish community: some 3,000 Jews are deported to Belzec.

2 *Umsiedlungsaktion* in Ruzhany {B/R SSR}: the entire Jewish community is deported to Volkovysk {B/R SSR}.

2 Some 2,500 Jews are deported to Belzec during the second *aktion* in Brody {Uk SSR}.

2/9 A series of *aktionen* in the Siemiatycze {P} ghetto sends thousands of Jews to their deaths in Treblinka.

2/11 The Bielsk {P} ghetto is liquidated and close to 5,000 Jews are deported to die in Treblinka.

3 The second *aktion* within four days liquidates the Tomaszow Mazowiecki {P} ghetto. Seven thousand Jews are deported to Treblinka, while 1,000 Jews deemed useful for the time are left behind. The ghetto changes to a *Judenlager*.

5 The second battle of El Alamein marks the beginning of an Allied counter-attack in North Africa.

5 During an *aussiedlungsaktion* in the Sokolka {P} ghetto, most Jews are deported to the Kelbasin {P} *Zwangsarbeitslager*.

5/6 Liquidation of the Stopnica {P} ghetto: 400 elderly Jews, the sick, and small children are taken to the cemetery, where they are killed; 1,500 of the select young men are sent to the Skarzysko-Kamienna {P} *Zwangsarbeitslager* and the remainder—about 3,000—are deported to Treblinka.

6 Over 1,000 Norwegian Jews, crammed on two German freighters, the *Donau* and *Monte Rosa*, are deported to Silesian coal mines for slave labor.

6 Vichy establishes a chair in Jewish history at the Sorbonne in Paris in order to study the "Jewish Question."

6 Second *aktion* in the Romarno {P} ghetto: most Jews are deported to Belzec.

8 Operation Torch, the Allied invasion of North Africa, begins. Vichy breaks diplomatic relations with the United States.

8 Jose Abulker, Jewish member of the Algerian underground, leads a revolt against Vichy forces, managing to hold Algiers until American forces land.

8 During liquidation of the Staszow {P} ghetto, hundreds of Jews are murdered during the *aktion*, while a handful manage to escape to the forests. All others are deported to Belzec.

9 Axis forces land in Tunisia.

9 Foreign Jews living in Vichy are forbidden to leave their place of residence without securing a special police permit.

9 Upon the final *aktion* in the Dzialoszyce {P} ghetto, the Nazis discover that most Jews have already fled.

10 A mass *aktion* in the Bochnia {P} ghetto leaves dozens of Jews dead as hundreds of others are deported to Belzec.

10 The Zionist Actions Committee approves the Biltmore Program.

10 Hitler, Laval, and Ciano discuss a military alliance between Axis and France during a conference in Munich.

10 The Archbishop of Canterbury, at the opening session of the House of Commons, once again deplores Nazi treatment of European Jewry.

10 The Radomsko {P} ghetto is established.

10 Nazis establish temporary ghettos in Sandomierz {P} and Szydlowiec {P} for thousands of Jews who had escaped from different *aktionen*, whom they lured back with the promise of "safety within the ghetto walls."

10 The Council of Jews and Christians is created in Australia to combat antisemitism.

11 Liquidation of the Ozery {B/R SSR} ghetto: all Jews are sent to the Kelbasim {P} *Zwangsarbeitslager* as a temporary measure and from there they are deported to Auschwitz.

11 Admiral Darlan orders the surrender of French North Africa to U.S. troops and he signs an armistice with Allies.

11 Nazis complete their occupation of France by invading the Vichy zone. Italy occupies eight French departments east of the Rhone.

11 A coalition of Norwegian churches protest Quisling's treatment of Norwegian Jews and send a letter to him denouncing the persecution of Jews as an illegal act. Bishops read the letter throughout Norway from their pulpits.

11 Liquidation of the Slutsk {B/R SSR} ghetto.

11 Eric Scavenius, a former pro-Nazi foreign minister of Denmark, forms a new Danish government. Nazification of Denmark increases.

12 Himmler orders over 100,000 Poles expelled from the Zamosc and Lublin regions.

15 Liquidation of the twin Dukla {P} *Judenlagern*.

15 Norwegian churches hold special prayer services for the Jews.

15 Some 3,000 Jews are deported to their death in the third *aktion* in the Tarnow {P} ghetto.

15 Vichy orders a census of all Jews in France.

18 Marshal Petain names Pierre Laval dictator of France.

18 Second *aktion* in Przemysl {P}: 4,000 Jews are deported to Belzec.

18 Germans order Jews in the Lvov ghetto to register. Those deemed fit for work in the *Wehrmacht* war industry receive special metal identifications stamped with W [*Wehrmacht*] or R [*Ruestungsindustrie*] (munitions industry). Around 5,000 Jews classified as nonessential are murdered.

18/19 The Jewish Agency for Palestine receives first-hand testimony on the mass killing of Jews by the Nazis.

19 The Soviet counter-offensive begins against the Third Rumanian Army in the Stalingrad region.

19 The Jewish community in Wyszogrod {P} is liquidated.

23 Nazis raid Tunisian Jews, arresting approximately 4,000 and deporting a number of them to perish in eastern Europe.

24 Soviet forces surround the German Sixth Army at Stalingrad.

24 The United States Under Secretary of State Sumner Welles confirms the Riegner cable. Dr. Wise is released from his pledge of silence.

24 The Mlawa {P} ghetto is liquidated with all Jews deported to Treblinka.

25 Norwegian deportations are renewed as some 770 Jewish women and children are deported to Auschwitz.

26 The Council for the Liberation of Yugoslavia established.

27 The French fleet is scuttled to prevent Nazi capture.

27 The National Council of the Polish government-in-exile in London meets in special session to protest the Nazi extermination of Polish Jewry and the fate awaiting those still alive.

29 Goering assures Hitler that the isolated German forces around Stalingrad can be supplied by air.

29 ZOB assassinates Israel Fuerst, the Warsaw ghetto *Judenrat* member responsible for deportations.

29 The Chief Rabbinate of Palestine declares a day of national mourning for European Jewry.

30 Liquidation of the Proskurov {Uk SSR} ghetto: all Jews are murdered during *aktion*.

30 An emergency meeting of *Asefat ha-Nivharim* deals with the rescue issue. The assembly declares three days of mourning and publishes a manifesto demanding Allied aid to rescue Jews.

30 The Jewish Agency creates the United Rescue Committee, headed by Yitzhak Gruenbaum.

DECEMBER

1 Admiral Francois Darlan, a Vichy sympathizer who defected to the Allies after Operation Torch, repudiates his allegiance to the Petain government and proclaims himself chief of state in North Africa.

1 A transport of Norwegian Jews is sent to Auschwitz.

1 The Stryj {Uk SSR} ghetto is established.

1   The Karczew {P} *Zwangsarbeitslager* is liquidated.

1   Final liquidation of the Sambor {Uk SSR} Jewish community.

1   Ethiopia declares war on Germany, Italy, and Japan.

1   Gasoline rationing is extended throughout the United States.

2   A few thousand Jews—some families or partial families, but mostly single people—are brought to Rzeszow {P} from places of incarceration in the region. The Rzeszow ghetto, subdivided from the ghetto *Ost*, is reopened as ghetto *West* and is nicknamed the *Schmelz* ghetto. Ghetto *Ost* is converted to a *Juedisches Zwangsarbeitslager*.

2   The Kallay government rejects German demands to massacre Hungarian Jewry.

2   The Jewish Agency for Palestine declares four days of official mourning and a fast day on behalf of Jewish victims of Nazism.

2   Jewish forced laborers become the official property of *SS*.

2   *Komitet Koordinacny* (the Coordinating Committee), an illegal organization, is established in the Warsaw ghetto to coordinate all underground activities.

2   American Jewish leaders declare an international day of mourning for European Jewry.

2   The *Histadrut* Executive calls for Jewish representatives on the United Nations committee to prosecute Nazi war crimes.

2   Jews in Latin America hold mass demonstrations protesting Nazi atrocities perpetrated on European Jews.

2   Bishops in Sweden denounce the Nazis for mistreating Jews not for any misdeeds, but solely because of their racial origin.

2   Enrico Fermi and other scientists at Chicago University are the first to split an atom.

3   The Podkamen {Uk SSR} Jewish community is liquidated.

4   *Rada Pomocy Zydom* [Zegota] (Polish Council for Aid to Jews), is organized by the government delegacy of the Polish government-in-exile in London.

4   A delegation from the Jewish Agency in London intercedes with the British Secretary of State for the Colonies on behalf of Jewish children from Bulgaria: 4,500 children must be saved.

4   Mainland Italy is bombed for the first time, when the U.S. Air Force raids Naples.

5 Dr. Yechezkiel Atlas, leader of a Jewish partisan unit, is killed during a battle with Nazis at Wielka Wola {P}.

5 The Lyubimovka labor camp outside Kherson {Uk SSR} is established.

6 Nazis destroy the 500-year-old Salonika Jewish cemetery.

6 The *SS* orders all German non-protected Gypsies, with the exception of ex-*Wehrmacht* soldiers, sent to Auschwitz.

8 The first Lodz ghetto coins are put into circulation.

8 American Jewish leaders meet with President Roosevelt to discuss the persecution of European Jewry.

10 The first transport of German Jews is sent to Auschwitz.

10 The Ministry of Foreign Affairs of the Polish government-in-exile sends an urgent note to the United Nations, bringing to their attention the extermination of Polish Jewry.

10 Hitler orders all Jews, Communists, and other enemies of the Third *Reich* arrested and deported from France.

10 Les Milles transit camp is closed down by Vichy France.

11 A law is published requiring identity cards for all French Jews stamped with *Juif*.

11 The International Federation of Trade Unions condemns German antisemitism.

11 The American Council for Judaism, an anti-Zionist organization, is established by a group of reformed rabbis.

11 Soviet forces isolate the German Sixth Army at Stalingrad.

12 Liquidation of the Nowy Dwor Mazowiecki {P} ghetto: some 2,000 Jews are deported to Auschwitz.

13 The Chief Rabbinate of the British Empire proclaims a day of fasting on behalf European Jewry under Nazism.

15 The Czech government-in-exile in London condemns extermination of Europe's Jews.

15 A *Judenlager* for 500 artisans in Chortkov {Uk SSR} is established.

16 The chief rabbi of Norway, Julius Isak Samual, is killed in Auschwitz.

17 The Ghetto at Baranowicze {B/R SSR} is liquidated in a final *aktion*. Close to 3,000 Jews are killed.

17 Allies issue a declaration in Moscow on German crimes against the Jews of Europe.

17 Anti-Jewish riots break out in Sandur, Iraq. Eight Jews are murdered.

17 Liquidation of the Vineta {P} *Judenlager*: some 3,000 Jews are deported to Auschwitz.

17 Liquidation of the Biala Podlaska {P} ghetto.

17 *Va'ad Leumi* and the Jewish Agency declare a thirty day mourning period for European Jewry to run from the fast of the tenth of *Teveth* (December 18, 1942) until the tenth of *Shevat* (January 16, 1943).

20 Liquidation of the Radzyn-Podlaski {P} Jewish community.

21 An earthquake in Turkey kills at least one thousand people.

22/24 The Jewish underground *he-Halutz ha-Lohem*, under the command of Aharon Liebeskind, attacks German military targets in Cracow. Liebeskind is killed in hand-to-hand combat when Nazis overrun his bunker headquarters.

23 The remaining 150 Jewish artisans in the Pinsk ghetto are taken to the Jewish cemetery where they are slaughtered. Pinsk is officially declared *Judenrein*.

23 *Va'ad Leumi* demands an exchange of German civilian prisoners in Allied hands for Jews in Nazi-occupied Europe.

24 The High Commissioner for North Africa, French Admiral Jean Louis Xavier Francois Darlan, is assassinated.

24 On General de Gaulle's orders, French Free Forces forcefully take over from Vichy the islands of St. Pierre and Miquelon.

25 Some 800 Jews from Chelmno {P} are deported to their deaths in Sobibor; the town famous for being the butt of Jewish folk-humor, is *Judenrein*.

25 An armed uprising occurs in Cracow ghetto.

27 General Andrei Vlasov, a Russian turncoat creates both the Smolensk Committee (Russian National Committee) and the Russian Liberation Army [ROA].

28 German Professor Karl Clauberg begins his "medical experiments" at the Auschwitz concentration camp, using prisoners as guinea pigs.

28 General de Gaulle urges a coalition of all French forces.

28 Gypsies are prohibited from traveling from one locality to the next within the *Generalgouvernement*.

29 The United Emergency Committee for European Jewry is established in Australia.

1943

JANUARY

1 The Hungarian Institute for Research into the Jewish Question is established in Budapest.

1 Dutch Jews are no longer permitted to possess individual bank accounts; all their balances are amalgamated into a single blocked account, from which the *Joodse Raad* is to receive monthly allocations.

3 Polish government-in-exile President Wladyslaw Raczkiewicz sends an urgent message to Pope Pius XII asking him to denounce German atrocities against the Jews. The Pope remains silent.

4 ZOB in the Czestochowa {P} ghetto engages in its first act of armed resistance.

5 Final liquidation of the Radomsko {P} ghetto: hundreds of Jews are murdered during *aktion* and the rest are deported to Treblinka.

5/7 During a mass *aktion* in the Lvov ghetto thousands are killed on the spot or deported to their deaths.

6 Liquidation of the Lubaczow {P} Jewish community: all Jews are deported to Belzec.

6 The American Jewish Conference is established.

6 The Synagogue Council of America and the Federal Council of the Churches of Christ in America meet and discuss the Jewish situation in Europe.

7 Liquidation of the Bilgoraj {P} *Judenlager*.

8 Hitler categorically forbids Field Marshal von Paulus to accept a Soviet offer of "honorable" surrender by the German Sixth Army.

9 *Reichsfuehrer-SS* Himmler visits the Warsaw ghetto.

10 The Kopernik {P} camp is liquidated. All its Jews are shot to death.

10 The short-lived Sandomierz {P} ghetto is liquidated and some 6,000 Jews are deported to Treblinka.

10 An armed uprising takes place in the Minsk Mazowiecki {P} ghetto.

11 The first in a series of deportations of Dutch Jews from Westerbork to Sobibor begins. Seven additional transports with Dutch Jews are dispatched, the last one leaving for Sobibor on February 23.

12 The first transport from a former Soviet army camp outside Zambrow {P} with some 2,000 out of 20,000 Jews kept there departs for Auschwitz. Subsequent transports of 2,000 are to follow nightly.

12 Battle of Voronezh.

12 Liquidation of the Volkovysk {B/R SSR} labor camp: all Jews are deported to Auschwitz.

13 Fifteen hundred Jews are deported from the Radom {P} ghetto to Treblinka.

13 KL Herzogenbusch (Vught), a *durchgangslager* and camp for Dutch Jewish diamond and textile workers, is established.

14 At a secret council meeting, Rabbi Menachem Ziemba of Warsaw urges the Jews in the ghetto to fight the Nazi evil.

14/24 Casablanca Conference.

15/23 Thousands of Poles are arrested in a series of mass roundups on the streets of Warsaw.

16 Iraq declares war on Germany, Italy, and Japan.

17/22 *Grossaktion* in the Grodno {B/R SSR} ghetto: over 10,000 Jews are deported to Treblinka.

18 Nazis begin a second wave of deportations from the Warsaw ghetto.

18 Himmler, in a directive to his Paris representative, Karl Oberg, orders 100,000 Frenchman from the Marseilles area deported to concentration camps in Germany.

18 With the murder of some 200 Jews in a shoe factory camp, Sokolka {P} is declared *Judenrein*.

18/21 "Small revolt" in the Warsaw ghetto.

20   Eichmann visits Theresienstadt.

20   Liquidation of the Ivye {B/R SSR} ghetto: all 1,100 remaining Jews are transferred to Borisow {B/R SSR} where they are murdered and the town is declared *Judenrein*.

22   Vichy rules that the small French *Karaite* community cannot be considered Jewish.

22   The Rabbinical Assembly of America attacks the American Council for Judaism.

23   Hitler reiterates that capitulation of the German Sixth Army is out of the question and orders the army to fight on to the last man.

23   *Faraynikte Partizaner Organizacje* [FPO] (United Partisan Organization) is organized in the Vilna ghetto. *Ha-Shomer ha-Zair*, Revisionists, General Zionists, *Bund*, and Communists participate.

23   The British army enters Tripoli.

26   The Jewish Council to Combat Antisemitism is established in Australia.

26   Members of the Swedish *Riksdag* ask the government to enact legislature to curb antisemitism.

26   Close to 1,000 Jews without *arbeitsscheinen* (labor permits) are caught in a raid and murdered by German and Polish police in the Stanislaw {P} ghetto.

27   Rabbi Leo Baeck, Paul Eppstein, and Philip Kotzover—the senior officials of the *Reichsvereinigung*—are deported to Terezin.

27   *Die Leitung* (the leadership), is established in Terezin with a three member board.

27   An all-party committee formed by members of both houses of the British parliament urges the government to take steps on behalf of European Jewry under the threat of the Nazis.

28   The Stalingrad defeat is viewed as a crippling blow to German morale, according to an SD report.

28   The *Gestapo* orders Berlin's Jewish community liquidated.

28/31   Liquidation of the Pruzhany {B/R SSR} ghetto: all 10,000 Jews are deported to Auschwitz in four successive transports of 2,500 each.

29   The University of Buenos Aires dismisses all pro-Axis faculty members.

30   ZOB expropriates 100,000 *zlotys* from Warsaw *Judenrat* safes.

31 Field Marshal Friedrich von Paulus, commander of the German Sixth Army, surrenders at Stalingrad.

31 Vichy founds the *Milice*, a French collaborationist paramilitary organization.

31 The American Jewish Committee publishes its Statement of Views declaring that, although an important factor, Palestine alone cannot solve the problem of postwar European Jewry.

FEBRUARY

1 Nazis plan to transfer a number of *SS* enterprises from the Warsaw ghetto to labor camps in Poniatow and Trawniki {P}.

1/2 Two thousand Jews from Buczacz {Uk SSR} are murdered at Fedor Hill, a short distance from town. The site is used for subsequent killings of large numbers of Jews.

2 Bulgaria agrees to hand over Jews to the *Gestapo*.

2 The last German forces in Stalingrad surrender.

4 At the annual meeting of the Council of Christians and Jews in London, the Archbishop of Canterbury condemns the mass extermination of Jews and others by Nazi hands.

5 Mussolini takes over the post of Italian foreign minister, held previously by Count Galeazzo Ciano since 1936.

5/12 First large-scale *aktion* in Bialystok ghetto takes place: over 10,000 Jews are killed on the spot, and the same number are deported to their deaths in Treblinka. ZOB offers armed resistance.

6 The Peresieka labor camp in Novogrudok {B/R SSR} is liquidated and all inmates are shot dead.

6 *SS-Sturmbannfuehrer* Alois Brunner and *SS-Hauptsturmfuehrer* Dieter Wisliceny come to Salonika to implement Nazi racial laws.

6 *SS* General Juergen Stroop is attached to the office of the HSSPF in Galicia.

6 Brazil joins the United Nations.

8 The *Gestapo* orders the Jewish Religious Congregation in Prague to reorganize as the *Aeltestenrat der Juden in Prag*.

8/26 A large-scale Nazi operation, *Aktion Hornung*, is aimed against Soviet partisans in the Pripyat Marshes.

9 The Lyons headquarters of the *Federation des societes juives de France* [FSJF] (Federation of Jewish Societies in France) are raided by the *Gestapo* and eighty of its members arrested.

10 Final liquidation of the Jewish community of Mainz {G}.

10 Mahatma Ghandi begins a twenty-one day hunger strike.

12 The yellow star is instituted for Jews in the Nazi zone of Greece.

12 Himmler visits Sobibor.

13 *SS-Sturmbannfuehrer* Amon Leopold Goeth becomes commandant of *Judenarbeitslager* Plaszow {P}.

13 German occupation authorities levy a ten million *franc* fine on Jews in Djerba, Tunisia.

14 The United States Office of War Information publishes a report on Nazi atrocities.

16 Himmler orders the Warsaw ghetto totally destroyed.

16 *SS-Obergruppenfuehrer* of the *Waffen-SS*, General Theodor Eicke, is killed on the Russian front.

16/17 Hundreds of Jewish women and children from Boryslav {Uk SSR} are driven to the town's local slaughterhouse, where with Nazi blessings Ukrainian gangs hack them to death.

18 Goebbels asks for a mandate for total war at the Berlin *Sportspalast* rally.

18 Liquidation of the Chryzanow {P} *Judenlager*.

18 Japan orders formation of the Shanghai ghetto for Jewish refugees in Manchuria.

19 The Allies halt the Axis drive in Tunisia.

19 Cambridge and London Universities hold a joint meeting at Guildhall to protest Nazi atrocities. Both institutions urge Britain to take appropriate steps.

22 Eichmann's office concludes an agreement with the Bulgarian Commissioner for Jewish Affairs on the deportation of the Jews from Bulgaria.

22 The Jewish Education Committee of New York in a solemn assembly proclaims a day of prayer for the safety of children in Nazi Europe.

22 Alfred Nossig, a member of the Warsaw *Judenrat*, is assassinated by the ZOB on strong suspicion of his close collaboration with the Nazis.

22   Liquidation of the Stanislawow {Uk SSR} ghetto. As in the first *aktion*, all remaining Jews are once again driven to the Jewish cemetery grounds and killed.

23   A transport of Jewish artisans leaves the Warsaw ghetto for Poniatow.

24   A Jewish ghetto is established in Salonika, Greece.

24   The Institute for the Study of the Jewish Question in Paris, is reopened as the *Institut d'Etude des Questions Juives et Ethno-Raciales*.

25   Von Ribbentrop complains to Mussolini about Italian lack of action in deporting Jews from Italy's occupied zone of France.

26   The French Jewish Representative Committee demands restoration of rights to the Jews of liberated North Africa.

26   The first transport of German Gypsies arrives in Auschwitz.

27/28   *Fabrikaktion* in Berlin: all German Jews working in German arms factories are abruptly deported to the East; those of *mischlinge* marriage are released after a violent demonstration by their aryan spouses.

29   Liquidation of the Kolomyya {Uk SSR} ghetto.

MARCH

1   The RAF initiates systematic bombing of the railway lines in Nazi occupied Europe.

1   A mass rally in Madison Square Garden under the joint auspices of the American Jewish Congress, the American Federation of Labor, and the Church Peace Union is attended by over 20,000 people, with an overflow crowd of more than 50,000 listening through amplifiers from the outside. The speakers include: Chaim Weizmann, Stephen S. Wise, Thomas E. Dewey, Fiorello H. LaGuardia, Robert F. Wagner, and William Green.

1   The Executive Committee of the Federal Council of Churches of Christ in America appeals to the American and British governments to offer financial aid to Jewish refugees from Nazism and Fascism.

1   The Union of Polish Patriots is established in Moscow.

1   A subcamp of Gross-Rosen, is established in Bukowiec {P}.

1   Liquidation of the Jewish Retraining Center in Paderborn {G}: all 100 German Jewish forced-laborers are deported to Auschwitz.

2   A heavy Allied air raid is inflicted on Berlin.

3   Eighteen hundred Jews from Kavalla, Macedonian Greece, are deported to the Polish extermination camps.

3 ZOB issues a warning to the Jews in the Warsaw ghetto to guard against self-complacency.

4/9 Four thousand Jews from Bulgarian Thrace are deported to Treblinka.

7 A conference of Socialist leaders from occupied countries in Europe opens in London.

7 Liquidation of the Radoszkowice {B/R SSR} ghetto: some fifty Jews succeed in escaping to the forests, but the rest of the community is slaughtered during *aktion*.

7/31 A number of Polish, Czechoslovakian, Yugoslavian, Hungarian, and Austrian Gypsies arrive in Auschwitz and are placed in specially designated "family camps."

8 A subcamp of Majdanek is established in Blizyn {P}. Some 10,000 victims Jews, Poles, and Soviet POWs will pass through the camp during its existence.

8 The New York State Senate and Assembly adopts a resolution calling for a Jewish state in Palestine.

8 *Wolna Polska* (Free Poland), a new Polish weekly published in Moscow, becomes the organ of the Union of Polish Patriots.

9 The first transport of Greek Jews from Salonika leaves for Auschwitz.

9 We Will Never Die, a pageant by Ben Hecht, is staged in Madison Square Garden.

9 An emergency meeting by the executive of the Canadian Jewish Congress is held in Montreal and a program of priorities for Canadian Jewry drafted.

9 The antisemitic South African Nationalist Party announces in parliament its intention to introduce a bill drastically limiting the number of Jews in the trades and professions.

10 The United States Congress condemns Nazi Germany for mass murdering European Jewry.

10 The Bolivian government instructs its consulates in Europe to grant 100 immigration visas to Jewish refugee children in Europe.

11 Over 7,000 Macedonian Jews are rounded up and assembled in Skopje, before they are deported to Treblinka.

12 The *SS* establishes its own industrial empire, *Ostindustrie GmbH* [OSTI], under the chairmanship and management of Oswald Pohl and Odilo Globocnik. The two plan to utilize all Jewish (and other) slave labor at their disposal from the vast network of their concentration camp system.

12 For the first time under a Fascist government, Italian workers stage a strike at the Fiat works in Turin.

13 Nazis place responsibility of the administration of Jewish properties in Salonika on the Jewish community council, who must, in turn, give full report to the German authorities.

13 Operation Flash, the code name for an attempt to kill Hitler by blowing up his personal aircraft, ends in failure.

13/14 Final liquidation of the Cracow ghetto: some 2,000 Jews from the Part A ghetto are taken to the Plaszow *Arbeitslager*; all Jews remaining in Part B of the ghetto are transported to the Auschwitz gas chambers.

14 French General Henri Giraud annuls Vichy racist laws, but reinstates the law that abolished the Cremieux Decree.

15 The first transport from Salonika to the East leaves with more than 2,000 Greek Jews. Additional transports follow every second or third day.

16 Over 1,000 Jews from the Lvov *SS* camp at 56 Czwartakow Street are taken to the "Sands" for execution.

19 During liquidation of the Braslav {B/R SSR} ghetto/camp, the Nazis meet with some resistance during *aktion*.

19 A Joint Emergency Committee for European Jewish Affairs is established by the American Jewish Committee, the American Jewish Congress, *B'nai B'rith*, and the Jewish Labor Committee.

20 The *Gestapo* executes 127 Jewish intellectuals in the Czestochowa {P} ghetto.

21 Twenty-three hundred Jews jailed in a temporary camp in the Monopol tobacco factory outside the town of Skopje {Y} are deported to their deaths in the Polish extermination camps. Two more transports with close to 6,000 Jews follow within the next two weeks.

23 Some 1,700 Polish Gypsies, sick with typhus, are gassed in Auschwitz-Birkenau.

25 Most of the Jews from Zolkiew {P} are massacred in the Borek forest.

31 Official date for an end to Jewish immigration to Palestine, as formulated in the 1939 White Paper.

31 Former French Prime Minister, Leon Blum, is imprisoned at Buchenwald.

APRIL

2 Final *aktion* and liquidation of the Zloczow {Uk SSR} ghetto.

2 At a plenary session of the Holy Synod, Metropolitan Stephan warns of the approaching danger threatening Bulgarian Jewry.

2 The Texas House of Representatives adopts a resolution urging that the United Nations find temporary havens of refuge for the persecuted Jews in Europe, and to remove all barriers on Jewish immigration to Palestine. The Texas State Senate concurs on April 16.

3 An armed uprising takes place in the Bedzin {P} ghetto.

7 The apostolic delegate to Slovakia expresses the Vatican's opposition to deportation of the remaining Jews.

7 American and British forces link up in Tunisia.

7 A Jewish history museum opens in Tomar, Portugal.

7 Bolivia declares war on the Axis states.

11 A Vichy-German agreement changes the status of French prisoners-of-war to laborers for Germany.

11/13 Hitler and Mussolini meet at the Brenner Pass to discuss war strategies.

12 Liquidation of the Brzezany {Uk SSR} Jewish community.

13 The Katyn Forest massacre is revealed. Nazis charge the Soviet Union with the murder of thousands of Polish officers.

13/14 The British Council of Churches passes a resolution condemning antisemitism in all forms and guises.

14 Both houses of the South Carolina legislature adopt a resolution urging the establishment of a Jewish homeland in Palestine.

14 A mass protest rally is held in Chicago Stadium to demand American intervention to save European Jews.

15 Hitler issues directive number six for Operation Citadel.

16 The Joint Emergency Committee for European Jewish Affairs submits a program to rescue European Jewry under Nazi rule.

16 Spain offers its good offices to conclude an honorable and speedy peace between the Allied and Axis belligerents.

17 Hitler and Horthy meet to discuss the deportation of Jews from Hungary.

17 The Jews are deported from Avignon {F}.

17 Liquidation of the Leshnev {Uk SSR} Jewish community.

19 The Warsaw ghetto uprising begins; Nazis liquidate the Gesia Street prison.

19/20 Belgian Jewish partisans intercept a transport on its way to Auschwitz and liberate the victims.

19/30 The Anglo-American Refugee Conference (Bermuda Conference) opens in Bermuda. The Jewish Agency, the Joint Emergency Committee for Jewish Affairs, the World Jewish Congress, and other organizations present their appeals to the Conference.

21 A number of Revisionists successfully escape from the Vilna ghetto and join partisan groups in the nearby forests.

22 All the Jews of Amersfoort {Ho} are taken to the Vught *Durchgangslager* and from there they are deported to their deaths in Auschwitz and Sobibor.

24 Rabbi Menachem Ziemba is murdered while crossing a street in the Warsaw ghetto.

25 The Polish government-in-exile in London breaks diplomatic relations with the Soviet Union over the Katyn incident.

273 Papal nuncio in Rumania, Monsignor Andrea Cassulo, visits Transnistria.

28 American labor leader, John L. Lewis, threatens a strike by 600,000 coal miners.

28 The Joint Distribution Committee allocates $1,000,000 for refugee aid and child-care work in Switzerland.

29 Anglo-Jewish relations become extremely strained when British police carry out a search in the recruiting office of the Jewish Agency in Tel Aviv.

30 Some 800 male Jews, part of the Hungarian-Jewish labor brigade sick with typhus, are burned alive in their Doroshich camp, a village near Zhitomir {Uk SSR}.

MAY

1 Liquidation of the Brody {Uk SSR} ghetto: all Jews are deported to Majdanek.

1 Liquidation of the Wegrow {P} *Judenlager*; all 100 prisoners are murdered.

2 Liquidation of the Miedzyrzec Podlaski {P} ghetto: some 4,000 Jews are deported to Treblinka while 200 Jews are left behind in a newly established forced labor camp.

2 Liquidation of the Lukow {P} ghetto: close to 4,000 Jews are murdered.

2 The United States seizes all coal mines whose workers are on strike.

5 The first transport of Jews from Croatia is sent to Auschwitz.

7 Liquidation of the Falenica {P} *Zwangsarbeitslager*; some 400 Jewish inmates are shot to death.

7 Over 7,000 Jews are killed during *grossaktion* in the Novogrodek {P} ghetto.

7 A joint resolution by the Senate and House legislature of the State of Pennsylvania calls for the establishment of a Jewish state in Palestine.

7/8 The Allies capture Tunis.

8 Mordechaj Anielewicz, ZOB commander, commits suicide in order not to be captured alive by the Germans. The ZOB headquarters falls into German hands.

9 Final *aktion* in Skalat {Uk SSR}: all of the remaining Jews are murdered except for about 400 who are left behind in a newly established labor camp.

12 The German army in Tunisia surrenders.

12/15 The Trident Conference is held in Washington, DC.

13 The last Axis forces in North Africa surrender and 150,000 prisoners-of-war are taken.

13 Szmul Zygelbojm, a member of the Polish National Council of the Polish government-in-exile, commits suicide to protest the gentile world's complete indifference to the Jewish predicament.

15 Stalin dissolves COMINTERN.

16 Dam Busters raid: the RAF raids the Ruhr dams.

16 After twenty-eight days of heroic fighting, Nazis finally manage to crush the Warsaw ghetto uprising. The Tlomackie Street synagogue is demolished as a symbol of Nazi victory.

18 The United Nations Relief and Rehabilitation Administration [UNRRA] is established.

18 A Japanese segregation order establishes Hongkew ghetto.

19   Berlin is declared *Judenrein*.

20   Italy establishes an internment camp for Jews and Slovenians on the occupied Yugoslavian island of Rab (Arbe).

21   Liquidation of the Brody {UK SSR} ghetto: some 3,000 Jews are deported to Majdanek, while hundreds of others are murdered during *aktion*.

21   The Drohobycz {Uk SSR} ghetto begins to be liquidated. Germans, with Ukrainian help, set fire to most of the ghetto houses in order to drive out the Jews hiding in the cellars and bunkers; most victims not killed on the spot or burned to death by the fires, are driven to the Bronica Forest, where they are machine-gunned to death and buried in giant pits.

22   One thousand Jews from the Stryj {Uk SSR} ghetto are murdered on the Jewish cemetery grounds.

23   *Grossaktion* in the Lvov ghetto: thousands of Jews slaughtered.

23   The Przemyslany {Uk SSR} ghetto is liquidated: all Jews are murdered and town is declared *Judenrein*.

24   Liquidation of the Czarny Dunajec {Y} camp.

25   Bulgaria orders the expulsion of its Jews from the cities to the countryside.

25   An armed uprising takes place in the Czestochowa {P} ghetto.

26   Nazi and Dutch police launch a major raid on the old Jewish quarter of Amsterdam.

26   London's Poles hold the Soviets responsible for the Katyn massacres.

27   Jean Moulin unifies the French underground with the creation of the *Conseil National de la Resistance*.

27   Liquidation of the Sokal {Uk SSR} ghetto: all remaining Jews are deported to Belzec and the town is declared *Judenrein*.

27   In a second large-scale *aktion* in Tolstoye {Uk SSR}, 3,000 Jews are driven to the Jewish cemetery grounds and murdered.

30   A French Committee of National Liberation is set up in Algiers. Generals de Gaulle and Giraud become co-presidents.

JUNE

1   Lvov's Jews attempt to resist during the ghetto's final liquidation. Three thousand Jews are murdered during *aktion*, and 7,000 Jews are transferred to the Janowska Street camp.

1 Jewish rescue activist Wilfrid Israel's plane is shot down by German fighters over the Atlantic, leaving no survivors.

1/6 Ten thousand Jews are sent to Auschwitz when the Sosnowiec {P} ghetto is liquidated.

3/23 *Aktion Cottbus*, a large-scale anti-partisan operation nets the Nazis some 5,000 Russian partisans killed.

5 A transport with close to 1,300 Jewish children under sixteen years old leaves from Vught, via Westerbork, to Sobibor.

6 The Death Brigade is established.

6 The Rohatyn {Uk SSR} ghetto is liquidated.

6 About 1,000 Jews are murdered during the final liquidation of the Tolstoye {Uk SSR} Jewish community.

8 The Zbaraz {Uk SSR} ghetto is liquidated and most of its remaining Jews are murdered.

10 The *Gestapo* confiscates the assets of the *Reichsvereinigung* and closes down its offices as punishment for the Baum group attack on the Nazi Soviet Paradise Exhibition. The Baum attack ends in failure, with most of the group killed. An additional 250 Jews are murdered as a reprisal for the five Nazis killed in the operation, with an equal number sent to Sachsenhausen.

11 Himmler orders final liquidation of Polish ghettos.

11 President Roosevelt meets with Chaim Weizmann in the White House. Roosevelt agrees to the need for an Arab-Jewish conference at which he and Churchill would be present.

12 All Jews remaining in the Berezhany {Uk SSR} ghetto are murdered when the ghetto is liquidated.

14 The Belgian government-in-exile estimates that the Nazis deported some 52,000 Jews from Belgium to date.

16 The *Gestapo* deports all "fully" Jewish members of the *Reichsvereinigung* to Terezin and Berlin is officially declared *Judenrein*.

18 Mass execution of Jews takes place in Liepaja {Lat SSR}.

20 A second large-scale *aktion* in Amsterdam affects more than 5,000 Jews.

20 Final liquidation of the Tarnopol {Uk SSR} ghetto.

21 Himmler orders all Russian ghettos liquidated.

21 Seventy-three Jewish men and thirty Jewish women are transferred from Auschwitz to the Natzweiler-Struthof concentration camp. After gassing them, their skeletons are to be used by Professor August Hirt, director of the Anatomical Institute at Strasbourg as a collection with Jewish characteristics with which to study race theory.

21 Moses Merin, *Judenaelteste* of the *Zentrale der Juedischen Aeltestenraete in Ostoberschlesien* (the chairman of the Central Office of the Jewish Councils of Elders in Eastern Upper Silesia), together with the other members of his council, is deported to Auschwitz.

22/27 The fifty-fourth convention of the Central Conference of American Rabbis opens with a call for Jewish unity.

23 Liquidation of the Chortkov {Uk SSR} *Judenlager.* Most of the prisoners are killed.

26 Liquidation of the Dabrowa Gornicza {P} ghetto.

26 ZOB leads a brief resistance during liquidation of the "small ghetto" in Czestochowa {P}.

28 The four new gas chambers and crematoria numbers II, III, IV, and V at Auschwitz-Birkenau become fully operational. The crematoria have the capacity to cremate 4,756 bodies per day.

29 Liquidation of the Podvolochisk {Uk SSR} *Judenlager.*

JULY

1 All of the remaining Jews in Germany are placed under exclusive jurisdiction of the *Gestapo* and are deprived of all recourse to court action; upon a Jew's death his or her estate is automatically forfeited to the *Reich*.

1 All non-Jews are ordered to be removed from Terezin.

1 A resolution by the Australian Council of Trade Unions condemns antisemitism in all its forms and manifestations.

2 The *SS*, under Alois Brunner, takes over the administration of the Drancy *Sammellager* from the French.

4 The prime minister of the Polish government-in-exile, General Wladyslaw Sikorski, dies in a plane crash over Gibraltar.

5 The greatest tank battle of World War II, the battle of Kursk, begins. The fierce fighting lasts through August 23, with German losses estimated at some 70,000 men killed, and more than 2,000 tanks and 1,300 aircraft destroyed.

8 Jean Moulin, French partisan leader, dies after extensive torture by *Gestapo* chief Klaus Barbie.

8 The Wittenberg affair in the Vilna ghetto begins. The *Gestapo* demands that *Judenaeltester* Jacob Gens hand over the Jewish Communist underground leader.

9/10 Operation Husky: the Allies invade Sicily.

10 Thousands of Jews from the Lvov district are taken to Kamenka-Bugskaya {Uk SSR} and murdered.

12 Allied Military Control in Sicily abolishes all Fascist enacted discriminatory laws.

12 *National Komitee Freies Deutschland* (National Committee for a Free Germany) is founded by German nationals in the Soviet Union.

13 The French Committee of National Liberation in Martinique joins the United Nations.

14 Stanislaw Mikolajczyk is elected prime minister of the Polish government-in-exile in London.

14/17 Krasnodar {RFSSR} trial: thirteen local Russian collaborators are tried by a Soviet court for their participation in the mass slaughter of some 7,000 Jews from Krasnodar and vicinity.

16 Vilna ghetto *Judenaeltester* Jacob Gens hands over FPO leader Yitzhak Wittenberg to German security police, but Wittenberg is freed by a group of FPO members before the Germans reach the ghetto gates.

16 The British advise the Jewish Agency that all Jewish refugees from Europe able to reach Turkey would be given permission to enter Palestine.

18 Liquidation of the Miedzyrzec Podlaski {P} forced labor camp: all 200 prisoners are shot to death and the town is declared *Judenrein*.

18/19 Hitler meets with Mussolini at Feltre in northern Italy.

19 Allied planes bomb Rome for the first time.

20 Five hundred Jews from the HASAG *Zwangsarbeitslager* are executed on the Jewish cemetery grounds in Czestochowa {P}.

20 Seventeen hundred Jews from Rhodes are deported to Athens.

24 Twenty-one members of the FPO escape from the Vilna ghetto; while nine are killed, the others join the Soviet partisans in Narocz forest.

25 Mussolini is forced to resign and Marshal Pietro Badoglio is installed as the head of the new government.

25 The Italian Foreign Ministry informs the Defense Ministry not to release Jews on Arbe unless the Jews themselves request it.

26 The Emergency Conference to Save the Jewish People opens in Washington, DC.

27/28 Operation Gomorrah: massive British air attacks on Hamburg begin, creating "fire storms" on Germany's second largest city. The operation lasts for ten full days before it ends on August 5.

28 Jan Karski, special courier in the Polish underground army, the *Armia Krajowa* [AK], gives a detailed report to President Roosevelt at the White House on the "Final Solution."

28 All Jews are murdered during liquidation of the Skalat {Uk SSR} labor camp.

AUGUST

1 The Nazis launch their plan for final liquidation of the remaining ghettos in eastern Upper Silesia.

1 Liquidation and uprising in the Sosnowiec {P} ghetto.

1 Operation Soapsuds: the United States Air Force bombs the Ploesti {Ru} oil fields.

1 Ismar Elbogen, Jewish historian, author, and scholar, dies in New York at age sixty-nine.

1/3 A revolt takes place in the Bedzin ghetto during its final liquidation.

2 Treblinka uprising.

2 Three hundred sixty-seven Salonika Jews with Spanish nationality are deported to Bergen-Belsen.

2 Lebanon is released from French mandate.

6 German troops begin occupying Italy.

6 One thousand Jews from Vilna are seized and deported to work camps in Estonia.

7 The last transport from Salonika leaves with some 1,200 Jews bound for Auschwitz. For all nineteen transports, close to 49,000 Jews are deported to their deaths in the Polish extermination camps.

9 The tiny Republic of San Marino repeals its racial laws.

9 *Kibbutz* Kefar Blum founded in the Huleh Valley.

10/24 Roosevelt, Churchill, and Mackenzie King confer in Quebec. Far Eastern operations are among the topics on the agenda.

14 Rome is declared an "open city."

14/24 The Quadrant Conference is held in Quebec, Canada.

16/20   Liquidation of the Bialystok {P} ghetto begins. Jewish defenders give strong resistance, and some succeed in breaking out and reaching the forests. Of the approximately 30,000 Jews left in the ghetto on the eve of liquidation, at least 25,000 are deported to their deaths in Treblinka, Auschwitz, or Majdanek.

17   U.S. forces capture Messina, ending the Sicilian campaign.

17   The United States Air Force stages massive daylight raids on Regensburg and Schweinfurt.

17   The first transport from Rhodes delivers 120 Jews to Auschwitz.

18   The Allies occupy the Azores islands with the Portuguese government's permission.

18   The Badoglio government begins negotiations with the Allies.

18   Jewish prisoners employed by *Sonderkommando 1005*, under *SS-Standartenfuehrer* Paul Blobel, begin the task of exhuming and cremating the thousands of corpses massacred at Babi Yar, in order to obliterate any traces of Nazi crimes.

18/19   The last transport of Jews from Bialystok arrives at Treblinka before the death camp is liquidated.

20   Revolt and liquidation of the Glebokie {B/R SSR} ghetto.

23   The Red Army liberates Kharkov.

24   Final liquidation of the Bialystok {P} ghetto: the last 5,000 Jews are deported to their deaths and Bialystok is declared *Judenrein*.

24   Himmler is named German Minister of the Interior.

24   Copenhagen is occupied by the *Wehrmacht*.

24   The French Committee for National Liberation in Algiers is recognized by the United States and Britain.

26   The Zawiercie {P} ghetto is liquidated and most of its Jews sent to Auschwitz. About 500 Jews are left behind in a newly established slave-labor camp.

27   Dora-Mittelbau is established as a subcamp of Buchenwald.

28   King Boris of Bulgaria dies soon after returning from a visit to Germany.

29   Danish government resigns under pressure from the active anti-Nazi resistance. Germans take over and declare martial law in Denmark.

29   The American Jewish Conference proposes a five-point rescue program for European Jewry: (1) the Allies must warn the Axis that perpetrators of crimes against Jews will be severely punished after the war; (2) temporary asylum should be given at once to Jews who are able to escape the Nazi dragnet; (3) those who make it to Palestine should be given legal residence; (4) neutral states should be given guarantees that any aid given to refugees will be compensated for and that the refugees would be resettled at the conclusion of hostilities; (5) that the United Nations should create a special intergovernmental agency to work with Jewish organizations to help supply them with arms and materials for self-defense in Nazi Europe.

SEPTEMBER

1 Gens refuses to actively cooperate with the *Gestapo* and the latter orders the Vilna ghetto sealed off; 5,000 Jews are caught in a massive roundup while the FPO stages an abortive uprising.

1 A small labor camp for Jews is established at Czarny Dunajec, outside Novy Targ {Y}.

1 The FPO partisan unit of Hirsh Glik, a Jewish poet-fighter famous for his Song of the Partisans poem *"Zog nisht keynmol az du gayhst dem letztn veg"* (Never say that you are going on your last journey), is captured during a confrontation with a German unit and deported to the Narva camp in Estonia.

1 The American Jewish Conference overwhelmingly endorses a Jewish commonwealth in Palestine.

2 A small group of Jews on a labor detail manage to escape from Treblinka by killing their Ukrainian guard.

2 The Hungarian parliament passes a law providing for expropriation of Jewish-owned property.

2 A large transport of Jews from France is deported to Auschwitz.

2 The last *aktion* is launched in the Tarnow {P} ghetto. Overwhelming force under the direction of Amon Goeth, commandant of Plaszow, squelches Jewish resistance during *aktion*. Seven thousand Jews are deported to Auschwitz and 3,000 to Plaszow; only 300 Jews are left in a one-building camp as a *Sauberungskommando*—to sort, clean, and pack all Jewish property.

2/3 A third mass *aktion* in Przemysl {P} almost depletes its Jewish community, with 3,500 Jews deported to Auschwitz.

3 *Aktion Iltis*: all Jews holding Belgian citizenship are rounded up and deported to the extermination centers in the East.

3   Operation Baytown: units of the British Eighth Army ferry across the Straits of Messina, landing on the Italian mainland near Reggio de Calabria.

3   Marshal Pietro Badoglio of Italy signs separate armistices with the Western powers.

4   Last deportation of Jews from Antwerp.

4   The Badoglio government closes down the Ferramonti di Tarsia camp and orders all Jews released.

8   The Nazis establish a temporary "family camp" in Auschwitz-Birkenau for some 5,000 Jews from the Terezin ghetto. Eventually, all are gassed.

8   A Jewish partisan unit on Rab Island {Y} with the help of Slovenes, takes over and liberates the internment camp.

9   Nazis occupy the former Italian zone of France. Thousands of Jews trapped in Nice are rounded up for shipment to the Auschwitz extermination camp.

9   Operation Avalanche: the U.S. Fifth Army lands at Salerno.

9   The Italian fleet leaves La Spezia to join the Allied fleet at Malta.

9   Iran declares war on Germany.

10   Germany occupies Rome.

10   *SS* General Jurgen Stroop, the "Conqueror of the Warsaw Ghetto," arrives in Athens to oversee the destruction of Greek Jewry.

11   One thousand Jews are discovered hiding in Przemysl {P} and are murdered by the Nazis.

11   The *Wehrmacht* starts evacuating from Sardinia.

11/14   Liquidation of the Minsk {B/R SSR} ghetto: all remaining Jews are murdered during *aktion*.

12   Shmerke Kaczerginski, *Yiddish* writer, poet, and FPO fighter, together with a group of other partisans escapes from the Vilna ghetto and joins the Voroshilov Brigade in the Naroch Forest.

13   *Operation Eiche* (Oak Tree): on Hitler's orders Benito Mussolini is rescued by German forces under Otto Skorzeny from his detention at a mountain-top hotel in the Gran Sasso d'Italia. Mussolini then becomes the nominal head of German-occupied northern Italy.

14   The *Gestapo* executes Jacob Gens, *Judenaelteste* of the Vilna ghetto.

15   Mussolini reorganizes the Italian Fascist Party.

17   The *Gestapo* raids a number of Jewish homes in Copenhagen.

17/19 Liquidation of the Lida {B/R SSR} ghetto: the Jews put up an organized resistance, but only a few manage to escape. Most Jews are deported to Majdanek.

18 Lieutenant Alexander Pecherski and Shelomo Lejtman, a Polish Jewish Communist leader, together with a group of Soviet Jewish POWs are transferred from the Shirakaya Street camp in Minsk {B/R SSR} to Sobibor.

19 All Jews remaining in the Dabrowa Tarnowska {P} ghetto are deported to Belzec when the ghetto is liquidated.

20 The *Gestapo* sets up a *Judenrat* in Athens under Moses Sciaki.

22 Wilhelm Kube, *Generalkommissar* for Belorussia, is assassinated by partisans in his Minsk headquarters.

23 Final liquidation of the Vilna ghetto: Abba Kovner, leader of the FPO, and a group of some 100 FPO fighters, make their way out from the ghetto by way of the city sewers and reach the Rudninkai Forest.

23 Abraham Asscher and all the other members of the *Joodse Raad* are sent to Westerbork.

26 *SS-Obersturmbannfuehrer* Hubert Kappler, commander of the SD in Rome, imposes a levy of 50 kg. of gold on Rome's Jewish community to be paid by September 28.

27 German troops occupy the Greek island of Corfu and institute a reign of terror for the 2,000 member Jewish community.

28 The last 5,000 Jews in Amsterdam are transferred to Westerbork, there to await transportation to Auschwitz.

28 A house-to-house roundup of Jews by Fascist militia and *Carabinieri* (state police) takes place in a number of localities in northern Italy; some Jews manage to escape after receiving warnings from friendly Italians.

28 Roman Jewry delivers 50 kg. of gold as ordered to *Gestapo* headquarters.

28 Members of the German army blow up the centuries-old synagogue in Vercelli, a town in northern Italy.

28 All adult Jewish males in Split {Y} are rounded up. The victims are taken to the Sajmiste concentration camp and murdered upon arrival.

29 A revolt is staged by the Jewish prisoners attached to the *Sonderkommando 1005-a* in the Syret camp (Babi Yar), but only about a handful of prisoners succeed in escaping.

29 The *Gestapo* raids the Jewish community's offices in Rome and confiscates all ancient archival materials.

29 The *Gestapo* announces that the *Joodse Raad* has been eliminated.

OCTOBER

1 The United States Fifth Army captures Naples {I}.

1 Two *Palmah* parachutists are dropped into Rumania.

2 A Nazi decree establishing *Standgerichte* (Exceptional Tribunals) legalizes the execution of hostages.

2 The *Gestapo* issues orders to deport Danish Jews.

2 A law to "combat anti-German activities" is promulgated by the HSSPF. *Judenbeguenstigung* (helping Jews) is considered an anti-German activity that falls under this law.

2 The Danes begin rescuing Jews threatened with deportation to death camps. Approximately 7,000 Jews reach the safety of Sweden.

2 The Cmielow {P} labor camp is established.

3 Bishops of the Danish Church issue a pastoral letter condemning Nazi actions.

3 The Emergency Committee on Zionist Affairs [AZEC] appeals to the U.S. government to secure abrogation of the 1939 British White Paper.

5 Corsica is liberated.

6 In a speech to a group of *SS* leaders at Posen, Himmler declares that the extermination of European Jewry was and is a patriotic and noble mission. The murder of a people "will constitute a page of glory in German history which has never been written and must never be written . . ."

6 Four hundred orthodox rabbis stage a demonstration in Washington, DC, to protest American apathy regarding the rescue of European Jewry.

7 *SS*-General Juergen Stroop orders all Jews in Athens to register, as a preliminary to their deportation to Auschwitz.

7 In a "declaration on world peace," 144 leading Jewish, Protestant, and Catholic religious leaders request equal rights for all minorities and oppressed people everywhere.

8 During liquidation of the Liepaja {Lat SSR} ghetto, all remaining Jews are transferred to the Kaiserwald {Lat SSR} concentration camp.

9 *Razzia* (roundup) against Jews in Trieste; a number of Jews are rounded up for deportation.

9 The American Federation of Labor at its convention in Boston adopts a resolution urging the United States to ensure that Britain abides by the terms of the Balfour Declaration and that the right of the Jewish people to a national home in Palestine is reaffirmed.

10 A "Day of Intercession" on behalf of European Jews is proclaimed by some 6,000 Protestant churches in America.

10 *Delasem*'s offices in Rome are closed by the *Gestapo*.

12 Portugal grants Britain facilities in the Azores.

13 Nazis plunder the Roman Jewish Community Library.

13 Italian co-belligerent forces declare war on Germany.

14 An uprising takes place in the Sobibor death camp.

14 Saul Tchernichovsky, Hebrew poet, physician, and translator of Shakespeare into Hebrew, dies in Jerusalem.

16 Black Saturday: the *SS*, under orders of Kappler and *SS-Hauptsturmfuehrer* Theodor Dannecker, begins to round up Roman Jews; 1,127 victims, 800 of them women and children, are sent to Auschwitz where they are gassed on October 23.

17 The slave-labor camp in Zawiercie {P} is liquidated.

30 During a conference in Moscow foreign secretaries of the Soviet Union, the United States, Britain, and the Chinese ambassador to Russia discuss and sign a four-power agreement on postwar treatment of the Axis powers.

19 The Nazis officially terminate *Operation Reinhard* after murdering approximately two million Jews during its twenty months' existence.

19 Jacques Helbronner, leader of the Jewish consistory in France, is arrested by Vichy gendarmes and deported to Auschwitz.

20 A *sonderkommando* of fifty Jewish prisoners from Treblinka is sent to Sobibor to dismantle the death camp. At least 250,000 Jews have been exterminated here during its twenty month existence. The Nazis try to obliterate all traces of the heinous crimes they committed here.

20 The United Nations War Crimes Commission [UNWCC] is established in Moscow.

20 American church leaders speak out against persecution of Jews in Denmark.

21 During the final *aktion* in Minsk {B/R SSR} ghetto, some 2,000 Jews are machine-gunned to death at the Maly Trostines extermination site.

21   Australia announces that henceforth "enemy aliens" who entered the country because of religious or political persecution, will be reclassified.

22   The Budzyn {P} *Judenlager* becomes a subcamp of Majdanek.

23   An unsuccessful revolt in the gas chamber at Auschwitz is led by 1,700 Jewish prisoners bearing foreign passports.

24   Mass rallies in many parts of the United States are called to protest British White Paper and demand its abrogation.

24   The American Jewish Committee withdraws from participation in the American Jewish Conference because of the Palestine resolution.

25   Liquidation of the Dvinsk {Lat SSR} ghetto: all remaining Jews are deported to the Kaiserwald camp.

26   Some 3,000 able-bodied Jews from the Kovno ghetto are deported to concentration camps in Estonia.

26   David Ben-Gurion resigns from the Jewish Agency Executive.

NOVEMBER

1   "Moscow Declaration" issued jointly by Roosevelt, Churchill, and Stalin; Germans are put on notice that they will be held responsible for their crimes against humanity; Allies also sign an agreement for the extradition of war criminals that would stand trial in the country (or countries) where they were responsible for or committed the crimes.

1   *Sonderkommando* made up of Jews and Soviet prisoners of war begins the digging up of the mass graves at the Ninth Fort and burns the bodies on giant pyres.

2   Final liquidation of the Riga Ghetto: most of the remaining 4,500 Jews are sent to Auschwitz, the rest are transferred to the Kaiserwald camp.

2   Tito's headquarters reports that Yugoslav partisans captured a large group of General Draza Mihailovic's men, who fought on the side of the Germans.

3   *Einsatz Erntefest*; code named "Harvest Festival," one of the last *grossaktionen* in the Lublin area, in their drive to totally eliminate Polish Jewry; some 42,000 Jews are machinegunned and thrown into mass graves.

3   Eighteen thousand Jews slaughtered in Majdanek in a single day, as part of *Einsatz Erntefest*; the day before victims are made to dig their own graves before being machinegunned to death.

3 As part of *Einsatz Erntefest*, Nazis liquidate Trawniki concentration camp, murdering some 10,000 Jews in prepared pits.

3 The Lublin-Lipowa {P} POW camp for Jews is liquidated. All prisoners are taken to Majdanek, where they are shot to death in front of prepared pits behind the crematorium.

3 Three hundred Italian Jews from Genoa are deported to Auschwitz.

3 In a very large daylight air raid, U.S. planes attack Wilhemshaven, a major German naval base and shipbuilding center.

4 Churchill announces in the House of Commons that special British forces are aiding anti-German guerrillas in Albania, Greece, and Yugoslavia.

5 The slave labor camp at Poniatow falls prey to *Einsatz Erntefest*: except for a small crew left for cleanup purposes, all Jewish inmates are slaughtered.

5 The first transport of Latvian Jews is dispatched to Auschwitz.

5 Four bombs are dropped over the Vatican City (State) by a single unmarked plane. Nazis point finger at the Allies, but they deny it.

5 The U.S. Senate votes 85 to 5 for a postwar international organization to replace the League of Nations.

5 Close to 500 Allied planes attack the industrial areas of Essen and Gelsenkirchen and the rail yards at Muenster during a daylight bombing raid.

6 *SS* squads round up 343 Jews in Florence, summarily executing 100 of them and deporting 243 to Auschwitz.

6 Kiev is recaptured by the Red Army.

6 *Sonderkommando 1005* begins operations in the Sajmiste {Y} area to eliminate all traces of Nazi crimes; some 80,000 corpses are exhumed and burned.

8 The Nazis discover an underground cell by stumbling on an almost completed escape tunnel in the Drancy camp. Robert Blum, the leader of the underground, is caught and deported with the note "return undesirable."

9 Chief Rabbi Adolfo Ottolenghi and a number of Jewish notables are among the first of some 200 Jews from Venice to be deported to Auschwitz.

11 *SS-Obersturmbannfuehrer* Arthur Liebehenschel takes over command of Auschwitz from Rudolf Hoess.

16   Liquidation of the Bodzechow {P} *Judenlager*.

18   A subcamp of Mauthausen is established in Ebensee {A}.

19   British Fascist leader Oswald Mosley, jailed since 1940, is released from prison on account of his failing health.

19/20   During a *Sonderkommando 1005* uprising in the Janowska Street (Lvov) camp, a small number of prisoners manage to flee to the forest, while most of the other inmates are murdered.

20   The Jewish prisoner "Death Brigade" in the Lesienice camp, outside Lvov, stages a revolt: a small group of Jews kill several *SS*-men and escape.

20   Liquidation of the Cmielow {P} labor camp.

20   A weapons search in *kibbutz* Ramat Hakovesh ignites clashes with British police.

22/27   In Cairo a conference is held between Roosevelt, Churchill, and Chiang Kai-shek. On the agenda is restoration of all Chinese territory, an independent Korea, and relinquishment of all Pacific islands seized by the Japanese.

25   Jan Karski's detailed report on the Nazi murder methods in Treblinka and Belzec is passed on to the British section of the World Jewish Congress.

26   Colombia declares war on Germany.

27   The London Polish National Council adopts a resolution protesting German crimes against Poland and especially against Polish Jews.

28   Roosevelt, Churchill and Stalin confer in Teheran. They agree on the timing for invasion of northern France, and advance plans for an Allied invasion of southern France. The Soviets will join in the war against Japan with defeat of Germany. The conference ends December 1.

29   The Anti-Fascist National Liberation Committee under Josip Broz Tito declares its intent to rule Yugoslavia, and in preparation for this, establishes a provisional government.

30   The *Yishuv* holds a mass protest demonstration demanding rescue actions for Polish Jewry.

DECEMBER

1   *Republica Sociale Italiana* (Italian Fascist Social Republic) is founded at Salo (northern Italy). A decree deprives Italian Jews of citizenship.

2   The first transport of Jews from Austria departs for Auschwitz.

4/6 During the second Cairo Conference, Roosevelt, Churchill and Ismet Inonu discuss Turkish plans to join the Allied war effort.

6 General Dwight David Eisenhower is appointed supreme commander of European operations.

8 British troops conduct a weapons search in Hulda and arrest a number of villagers for weapons possessions.

10 Liquidation of the Tarassiwka {P} camp: 500 Jews are killed during *aktion*.

10 Allied troops in Italy take Rocca d'Evandro, dislodging the Germans from the east bank of the Garigliano River.

10 Allied planes bomb the Bulgarian capital, Sofia.

11 Bulgaria, Hungary, and Rumania are warned by the U.S. State Department that they will suffer the consequences of defeat because they are part of the Axis.

11 Five hundred American planes participate in an air raid on Emden {G}.

13 All males fourteen years old and over are massacred in the Greek village of Kalavryta on the Peloponnesus by the German Sixty-eighth Infantry Division in reprisal for supposed guerrilla activity in the area. After the massacre the German troops burn down the village.

13 Liquidation of the Vladimir Volynski {Uk SSR} ghetto: some Jews who manage to escape during *aktion* are murdered outside by the *Armia Krajowa* [AK] or by Ukrainian peasants.

14 The Free Yugoslav radio reports heavy partisan fighting with German troops.

14/15 Final liquidation of the Cracow ghetto.

15 *Aktion Reinhard* headquarters in Lublin {P} submits an accounting to the WVHA—heir to all the belongings of the Jewish victims—of all valuables confiscated in Belzec, Sobibor, and Treblinka before sending them to be gassed.

15 The Red Army reports that it has cleared the Germans out from the right bank of the Dnieper River between Cherkassy and Kremenchug.

18 Jacob Edelstein, the former *Judenaeltester* from Terezin, is deported to Auschwitz where he and his family are shot to death on June 20, 1944.

20 A resolution creating a special agency to aid in the rescue of European Jewry passes the Senate, but bogs down in the House of Representatives.

20   Generalisimo Franco dissolves the Spanish *Falange*.

23   Liquidation of the Pinsk {B/R SSR} ghetto/camp: all of the remaining Jews are murdered.

24   Some seventy Jewish prisoners attached to *Sonderkommando 1005-b* to exhume and burn the bodies of the thousands of Jews murdered at the Ninth Fort in Kovno, successfully escape.

29   Polish Communists establish the *Krajowa Rada Narodowa*, the Polish National Council.

1944

JANUARY

1 General Mark Clark takes command of the U.S. Seventh Army.

4 Some 2,700 planes drop 3,000 tons of bombs during heavy Allied air raids over northern France and northwest Germany.

4 The Nazis announce the mobilization of German school children for the war effort.

4/5 Allied forces launch an attack on the Gustav Line between Naples and Rome.

5 The Polish government-in-exile calls on the Home Army [AK] to collaborate with the Red Army to liberate Poland.

6 The Red Army advances into Poland.

8 Count Galeazzo Ciano is tried for treason by a Fascist court at Verona.

9 *Rada Jednosci Narodowej*, the Polish Council of National Unity, is established.

10 The Soviets guarantee a strong and independent Poland, provided that the Polish government-in-exile agrees to abandon its eastern frontier demands and is ready to accept the Curzon line as the new Polish-Soviet border.

12 De Gaulle and Churchill meet in Marrakesh, Morocco.

12 Hermann Struck, artist, painter and etcher, dies in Haifa at the age of sixty-eight.

15   Berdichev {Uk SSR} is liberated by the Red Army.

15   Fifteen hundred people attend a rally against antisemitism at Carnegie Hall organized by the Federal Council of Churches of Christ in America.

15   The British Cabinet Committee under Clement Atlee proposes partitioning Germany.

15   The Red Army opens its Leningrad offensive.

16   U.S. Treasury Secretary Henry Morgenthau, Jr. accuses the State Department of gross neglect of the Jews trapped in Europe by not only failing to use government machinery for rescue purposes, but for actually using those facilities to hinder their rescue.

16   General Dwight David Eisenhower assumes his duties as the supreme commander of the Allied Expeditionary Forces.

17   The American Jewish Committee urges abrogation of the White Paper which restricts Jewish immigration to Palestine.

17   *Pravda*, the Soviet government newspaper, accuses Britain of planning a separate peace treaty with Germany, but the British Foreign Office denies any truth to the accusation.

20   Marshal Badoglio of Italy abrogates all anti-Jewish laws.

20   Britain's RAF drops 2,300 tons of bombs on Berlin.

22   President Roosevelt establishes the War Refugee Board.

22   Allied forces land in Anzio, Italy, but fail to advance toward Rome, thirty miles to the south.

23   Operation Shingle, an Allied offensive is launched northward along the Italian peninsula.

25   Governor General Hans Frank states that less than 100,000 Jews are left in the *Generalgouvernement*.

25   Allied bombing of the Schweinfurt ball-bearing factory severely damages the Nazi war machine.

27   The Soviets lift the siege of Leningrad after 870 days.

27   Two identical resolutions introduced in the House of Representatives demand that a free and democratic Jewish commonwealth is set up in Palestine.

27   Liberia declares war on the Axis.

27   The Western Allies protest Japanese treatment of prisoners of war.

29   The Polish underground makes an unsuccessful attempt to kill Governor General Hans Frank.

30/31 An extraordinary national conference of Orthodox Jewry meets in New York City, taking up the issue of rescue and calling for both abandonment of the White Paper and establishment of a Jewish commonwealth in Palestine.

31 U.S. forces land on the Marshall Islands.

31 The Australian government forms a commission to investigate Japanese war crimes.

FEBRUARY

2 A decree issued by the *Republica Sociale Italiana* (Republican Fascist government in Italy) orders the immediate arrest of all Jews at large and transfer of their property under the *Republica*'s jurisdiction in northern Italy.

2 Liquidation of the Cieszyna {P} *Judenlager.*

2 Stalin agrees to provide bases for American aircraft in the Soviet Union.

7 German troops begin their counteroffensive along the Anzio beachhead.

8 The *Gestapo* raids *Oeuvre de Secours aux Enfants* [OSE] (Children's Aid Society) headquarters in Chambery, France.

10 Salonika Jews incarcerated in Bergen-Belsen who hold Spanish citizenship are repatriated to Spain.

10 The Allies return jurisdiction of Sardinia, Sicily, and southern Italy to the Bagdolio government.

12 Horthy requests Hitler's permission to withdraw Hungarian troops from the Eastern Front.

12 IZL bombs British immigration offices in Jerusalem and Tel Aviv.

14 Hitler dissolves *Abwehr*, the German Foreign and Defense Intelligence Service.

14 Supreme Headquarters, Allied Expeditionary Force [SHAEF] are established by Eisenhower.

15 On orders of the Fascist government, the Jews of Alessandria {I} are sent to a holding camp in Carpi.

15 The Cassino Abbey is destroyed by heavy Allied air and artillery bombardment.

15 The Polish government-in-exile refuses to accept the Curzon line as the post-war Soviet-Polish frontier.

25 The last transport of Dutch Jews from Westerbork and a group of Portuguese Jews, are deported to Auschwitz and sent straight to the gas chambers.

26 IZL bombs the British tax offices in Jerusalem, Tel Aviv, and Haifa.

27 After a four month absence, Ben-Gurion rejoins the Jewish Agency Executive.

28 Iraq and Egypt complain to the American government about a statement issued by the U.S. Senate Committee concerning establishment of a Jewish state in Palestine.

MARCH

1 South African Nationalist Party deputies demand a halt to Jewish immigration into the country.

1 The Soviets launch a new offensive in the north, across the Narva River.

1 The Nazis indicate that there are at least 4,800,000 foreign forced laborers working in the *Reich*.

2 Jews are rounded up in droves in Nancy {F}) for deportation to Auschwitz.

3 A joint resolution by the House and Senate of Rhode Island calls on the U.S. to reaffirm its support for a Jewish commonwealth in Palestine.

4 The Soviets initiate their spring offensive in the Ukraine.

4 Some 1,500 American fighters and bombers make their first daytime raid on Berlin.

5 The Senate and the House of Representatives of Washington state hold a joint memorial to the Jewish victims of Nazism in Europe. In addition, they adopt a resolution urging the U.S. government to ensure that Palestine doors to immigration are kept wide open for the victims of Nazism.

7 When the *Gestapo* discovers Emanuel Ringelblum's hiding-place in Warsaw, the Jewish historian-archivist and his family are murdered.

7 In response to Iraqi and Egyptian complaints, the U.S. denies that it ever officially endorsed or approved a Jewish state for Palestine.

7/8 All Slovakian Jewish prisoners kept in the Auschwitz "family camp" are taken to the gas chambers.

9 KL Gusen II opens with approximately 10,000 prisoners of different nationalities.

9   Rabbis Abba Hillel Silver and Stephen S. Wise meet with President Roosevelt to discuss the Palestine situation.

11   All Jews in Split {Y} are deported to the Jasenovac {Y} concentration camp and murdered.

12   In a radio broadcast from London, the Czech government-in-exile calls upon Czech citizens to rise up against the German oppressor.

14   Josef Winniger, an *Abwehr* officer, warns Budapest's Jewish leaders of impending Nazi occupation of Hungary.

14   Antonescu agrees to the return of Jewish deportees from Transnistria to Rumania.

15   Cassino {I} is saturated by more than a thousand tons of bombs.

15   Liquidation of the Rogoznica {P} labor camp.

15   The Red Army crosses the Bug River.

17   During a Koldichevo {B/R SSR} slave labor camp uprising, some seventy-five Jews successfully escape and join the Bielski unit partisans.

18   Hitler summons Hungarian Regent Miklos Horthy to *Klessheim* Castle and gives him an ultimatum to dismiss the Kallay government.

18   The RAF carries out the heaviest air raid to date. Hamburg is hit with 3,000 tons of bombs.

19   *Einsatz Margaret*: Nazis occupy Hungary and arrest Horthy. Adolf Eichmann arrives at Gyor to serve as the head of a special column to deal with Hungarian Jewry.

19   Operation Strangle: a major Allied air effort to defeat German forces in Italy begins.

20   Eichmann orders a *Judenrat* for Hungarian Jews. The eight member council, under the leadership of Samu Stern, begins functioning the following day.

23   IZL destroys the British CID buildings in Jerusalem, Haifa, and Jaffa.

24   President Roosevelt warns Hungarians that they will receive retribution for crimes committed against Hungarian Jews.

24   The *Gestapo* traps 800 Greek Jews on the pretense that flour for baking Passover *matzoth* will be distributed at the Athens synagogue. Instead all 800 Jews are interned in a camp at Haidon and from there they are deported to Auschwitz on April 2.

24 Ardeatine Caves massacre: 335 Jewish and anti-Fascist prisoners are killed in retaliation for a partisan attack on German troops on Via Rasella in Rome.

26 A transport of Jews from the Kovno and Shavli ghettos arrives in Stutthof.

27/28 A *Kinderaktion* takes place in the Kovno ghetto. Two thousand Jewish children and a few older people are hunted down; most are slaughtered during *aktion*, the rest are deported to perish in Auschwitz.

29 The U.S. Congress approves $1,350,000,000 for the United Nations Relief and Rehabilitation Agency [UNRRA].

APRIL

1 *Zwangsarbeitslager* Blechhammer {P} becomes a subcamp of Auschwitz.

2 *SS* units murder eighty-six French civilians in the village of Asq in retaliation for resistance activity in the region.

2 Units of the Red Army cross into Rumania.

3 The United States Army Air Force bombs Budapest.

4 A heavy Allied bomber attack is aimed at Bucharest.

4 The Hungarian government orders the confiscation of 1,500 Jewish apartments in Budapest to house Christians whose residences were destroyed in the Allied air raid.

4 The *Wehrmacht* is forced to abandon rail traffic south of Florence, {I}.

4 General Charles de Gaulle is appointed head of the French armed forces and takes control of the Committee of National Liberation.

5 The yellow star is instituted for Jews in Hungary.

5 Rudolph (Rezso) Kasztner and Joel Brand, executive members of the *Vaadat ha-Ezra ve-ha-Hatzala* (Rescue and Relief Committee) in Budapest, meet Eichmann's aid *SS-Haptsturmfuehrer* Dieter Wisliceny for the first time. Kasztner and Brand will try to ransom Hungarian Jewry from the impending deportations to Poland.

6 The *Gestapo* under Klaus Barbie raids the orphanage at Isieux {F}.

6 The Hungarian General Assembly of the Reformed Church petitions the government to defer deportation of converted Jews.

6 The *SS Serpa Pinto* docks in Philadelphia with 280 mostly Jewish Canada-bound refugees.

7 Rudolf Vrba and Alfred Wetzler successfully escape from Auschwitz and reveal the horrors of the death camp to the Jewish underground in Slovakia.

7 A ghettoization decree is issued for Hungarian Jewry.

7 Hitler appoints Goebbels administrator of Berlin.

8 The Red Army approaches the Czech border.

10 Odessa is liberated.

10 Liberia joins the United Nations.

11 Laslo Endre is entrusted to handle the Jewish question in Hungary.

11 A subcamp of Mauthausen is established in Melk {A}. During its existence, over 5,000 prisoners perished, most of whom are Jews, Poles, Russians, and Yugoslavians.

14 The Doeme Sztojay government places 50,000 Hungarian Jews fit for work at Nazi disposal.

15 The previously arrested fifty-two children and their guardians at the Isieux orphanage, are sent by the *Gestapo* to be gassed at Auschwitz.

15 Thousands of Hungarian Jews are forced to move into newly designated ghetto areas.

15 Most Jewish prisoners attached to *Sonderkommando 1005-b* fail in their attempt to escape from Ponary {Lit SSR}: only about a dozen Jews survive.

17 The Nyirepyhaza {Hu} ghetto is established.

18 A transport of Jews held at the Vittel camp for people with Latin American papers are transferred to Drancy; most of them are later dispatched to perish in Auschwitz.

18 Nazis announce that they have solved the "Jewish problem in Croatia."

19 A mass rally at Madison Square Garden commemorates the first anniversary of the Warsaw ghetto uprising.

19 The American Jewish Conference adopts a resolution urging establishment of temporary safe havens in the free world for Jews who escape the Nazi dragnet.

20 The Polish government-in-exile in London creates the Council for the Rescue of the Jewish Population in Poland.

21 The "true meaning of Auschwitz" is secretly relayed by the Jewish underground in Slovakia to the Jewish community in Budapest to serve as a warning to Hungarian Jewry.

21/23 All Jews of Uzhgorod {Hu} and vicinity are ordered into a lumberyard and brick factory located outside the city which is to serve as a temporary ghetto/holding place. Within a month all 25,000 Jews are deported to Auschwitz.

25 Eichmann makes his first "blood for wares" offer to Joel Brand.

25/26 All remaining Jews from Backa and Baranja {Y} are deported to their deaths in the East.

27 A ghetto is established in Debrecen {Hu}.

28 The short-lived Hungarian ghettos begin to be liquidated; the first trainload of Jewish deportees leaves Kistarcsa for Auschwitz.

MAY

1/16 A conference of Dominion prime ministers opens in London.

2 The first transport of over 1,000 Hungarian Jews arrives in Auschwitz-Birkenau and its victims are immediately gassed. The number of Hungarian Jews murdered in Auschwitz eventually reaches 400,000.

3 The Jews in Cluj {Hu} and Dej {Hu} are ordered into temporary ghettos.

8 The Supreme Headquarters Allied Expeditionary Forces [SHAEF] in London decides on June 5th as D-Day for Operation Overlord, the Normandy invasion.

8 Wisliceny informs Kasztner on the Nazi decision to deport all the Jews of Hungary without exception.

8 De Gaulle asks the United Nations to recognize the National Liberation Committee as the legitimate government of France.

9 The Hungarian government threatens severe punishments for all who help Jews.

11 Munkacs {Hu} *aktion*: 33,000 Jews are deported to the Auschwitz gas chambers.

12 Close to a thousand bombers of the U.S. Eighth Air Force attack the German synthetic oil industry, beginning the Battle of Leuna.

12 The Hungarian Institute for Research into the Jewish Question is established.

12 Operation Diadem: Allied armies assault the German *Gustav* Line in Italy as they start their ground offensive toward Rome.

15 Deportations to Auschwitz begin for Jews in the Kosice {Slovakia/Hungary} ghetto; some 4,000 Jews are gassed immediately upon their arrival at the camp. Other transports with Hungarian Jews leave for Mauthausen and Buchenwald.

15 Enzo Sereni parachutes into Tuscany {I} and is almost immediately captured wearing the uniform of a British captain of a Palestine unit.

15 Angelo Rotta, the papal nuncio in Budapest, condemns deportations of Hungarian Jews.

15 The Germans begin the liquidation of the Kaszony {Hu} Jewish community.

17 Joel Brand and Bandi (Gyorgi) Grosz leave Budapest with a Nazi ransom offer, the controversial "blood for trucks" mission.

17 The (Hungarian) Assembly of the Reformed Church protests Jewish treatment in Hungary.

17 IZL attacks the radio station at Ramallah.

18 Cassino is captured by Polish troops under General Anders, opening the road to Rome.

18 The Turkish government imposes martial law against pro-Nazi groups.

19 Arthur Liebehenschel, the former commandant of the Auschwitz concentration camp, takes over as commandant of KL Majdanek.

20 The Allies stage massive air raids along a 150 mile strip from Brittany in France to Belgium. Six thousand planes saturate the area with 8,000 tons of bombs.

20 The Communist Political Association is formed in the United States.

23 Operation Buffalo: the Allied offensive from Anzio beachhead begins.

24 The American League for a Free Palestine is established in New York City.

24 Thirty-five hundred Jews from the Berehovo {Hu} ghetto are deported to Auschwitz.

24 Iceland votes for independence from Denmark.

25 The first of six transports of Jews from the Cluj {Hu} ghetto leaves for Auschwitz.

30 Mukachevo {Uk SSR} is declared *Judenrein*.

31 Latin American countries finally recognize passports held by Jews in the Vittel camp. However, most Jews (including the poet Itzhak

Katznelson), are now dead, having been gassed in the meantime at Auschwitz-Birkenau.

JUNE

3 Hitler authorizes *Wehrmacht's* withdrawal from Rome. *Generalfeldmarschall* Albert Kesselring proposes that Rome become an open city.

4 General Eisenhower postpones invasion of France by twenty-four hours.

4 The Fifth U.S. Army liberates Rome.

5 Stanislaw Mikolajczyk, representing the Polish government-in-exile, arrives from London for a week-long discussion with President Roosevelt and members of his administration.

6 D-Day: Allied forces land on the French coast between Cherbourg and Le Havre, opening the second front.

6 Nazis bomb and heavily damage the Florence synagogue.

6 A transport with 1,800 Greek Jews, 90 percent of the Jewish population from the island of Corfu, leaves for Auschwitz.

7 Hanna Szenes is arrested by Hungarian police as she crosses the border into Hungary shortly after parachuting into Yugoslavia.

7 Eichmann's emissary, Joel Brand, is arrested by the British at Aleppo, Syria.

9 The Emergency Refugee Shelter is established in Oswego, New York; 984 Jewish refugees are admitted.

10 *Waffen-SS* carry out a massacre of French civilians at Oradur-sur-Glane: 642 men, women and children are killed.

10 Soviet forces open their offensive against Finland.

11 The Swedish ambassador in Budapest offers to rescue 300 to 400 Hungarian Jews.

13 Germany begins a flying bomb (V-1) campaign against Britain.

15 The United States conducts its first B-29 air raid on Japan.

17 Denmark grants Iceland independence and the Icelandic republic is founded.

19 The Auschwitz Protocol—an abridged twenty-six page report describing in detail the process of annihilation in Auschwitz-Birkenau—is transmitted by underground courier to Switzerland by Rabbi Michael Dov Weissmandel of the *Pracovna Skupina* to Isaac Sternbuch, a Swiss

Jewish businessman, and Nathan Schwalb, *he-Halutz* representative in Geneva.

20 Jacob Edelstein, *Judenaelteste* of Terezin, is deported to Auschwitz and murdered.

22 The Polish Committee of National Liberation issues a manifesto guaranteeing equal rights to all citizens regardless of race, religion, or nationality.

23 Nazis resume deportations from the Lodz ghetto to Chelmno, after the Lodz ghetto is reconstituted in the former Waldlager.

23 The fifth annual convention of *Agudas Yisroel* opens in Ferndale, New York. Aid to European Jews is main topic discussed, but there is no demand for specific American action on the agenda.

23 The Red Army sweeps through Belorussia; by July 3 the entire region is liberated.

24 Jews remaining in Budapest are ordered to relocate to homes especially marked by a yellow Star of David.

25 Pope Pius XII sends an open telegram to Admiral Horthy asking him to stop the persecution of a large segment of the Hungarian population because of their race, but the Pope never mentions Jews *per se*.

26 The Budapest Jewish Council appeals to Horthy to intervene on their behalf. The Hungarian government approves limited emigration of Jews to neutral states.

26 The Operations Division of the U.S. War Department rejects as "impracticable" a request by leaders of the major Jewish organizations to bomb the approaches to Auschwitz.

26 Danish resistance declares a general strike that continues until July 3.

27 U.S. forces take Cherbourg {Fr}.

27 The Republican National Convention in Chicago unanimously adopts a platform favoring a Jewish commonwealth in Palestine and urges unrestricted immigration of Jews to Palestine and unlimited land ownership.

27 The U.S. government issues additional warnings to the Hungarian people and government regarding treatment of the country's Jews.

29 The Koldichevo {B/R SSR} camp is liquidated and some 22,000 inmates—Russians, Poles, and Jews—are murdered and buried in thirty-eight mass graves in and around the camp perimeter.

30 King Gustav V of Sweden cables Admiral Horthy to do everything in his power to save Hungarian Jews in the name of humanity.

30 To obliterate all traces of their crimes, Nazis burn the camp and mass extermination site to the ground at Maly Trostinets {B/R SSR}. At least 200,000 people, as many as 65,000 Jews among them, were murdered here.

JULY

1/2 Some 6,000 Jews from Kaposvar {Hu} and vicinity are deported to Auschwitz.

1/22 During the Bretton Woods Economic and Financial Conference, participants from forty-four nations meet at a resort hotel in New Hampshire and agree to establish an International Monetary Fund and an International Bank for Reconstruction and Development.

2 Laszlo Baky leads an abortive *coup* in Hungary.

2/3 The last 3,000 Jews from two working camps in Vilna are taken to Ponary and murdered. During its existence as an extermination site approximately 100,000 Jews perished here.

3 The British War Cabinet decides to approve the formation of a Jewish Palestine Brigade, instead of the suggested Jewish division. Brigadier Ernst Benjamin is appointed commanding officer, and the white and blue Star of David is officially approved as its standard.

4 Professor Karl Barth distributes a circular letter to Swiss clergy on the deportation of the Hungarian Jews.

4 The Koszeg {Hu} ghetto is liquidated with all Jews deported to Auschwitz.

5 The Red Army liberates Minsk.

6 *Judenlagern* in Poland that still exist begin liquidating; 4,000 Jews from Polish slave labor camps are brought to Dachau, while hundreds (perhaps thousands of others) are butchered outright.

6 A small labor camp for Jews opens in Wien-Fuenfhaus {A}.

7 The Archbishop of Canterbury appeals to the Hungarian government and people to stop the daily deportations of the country's Jews.

8 A labor camp for Jews opens in Wien-Meidling {A}.

8 Liquidation of the Kovno ghetto: thousands of Jews are killed during *aktion*, while thousands of others are force-marched toward Germany.

8 *Ungarnlager*, a camp for 1,684 Jews from Hungary, is set up in Bergen-Belsen.

8 Opening of the Wien-Loban {A} labor camp.

9 Raoul Wallenberg arrives in Budapest.

9 Opening of the Gerasdorf {A} labor camp.

10 Two hundred twenty-two Jewish inmates of Bergen-Belsen in possession of Palestine immigration certificates are released from the camp and arrive in Haifa.

11/15 An international anti-Jewish Congress convenes in Berlin.

13 Horthy informs the Western Allies that he is ready to release for emigration to Palestine 1,000 Jewish children under the age of sixteen accompanied by 100 adult chaperons, but offer is not taken up.

13 The Allied Military Government in Italy creates a commission to investigate claims to restore Jewish property, but the commission never gets off ground.

13 UGIF leaders in liberated Paris decide against voluntarily dissolving the German imposed organization, for fear of Nazi reprisals against Jews still under German occupation in France.

14 Eichmann attempts to dispatch a train with 1,500 Jews from Kistarcsa {Hu} to Auschwitz. Horthy intervenes and orders the transport halted before reaching the Polish border.

14 Vercors Plateau massacre near Grenoble {F}: the German army and *SS* slaughter thousands of French civilians and resistance fighters in a massive sweep through the plateau.

14 The Allies release news of Hungarian Jewish massacre.

16 The Red Army liberates Vilna.

16 The Allies broadcast an urgent appeal by the Swiss Evangelical Church Union to the Swiss *Bundesrat* and the International Red Cross to do everything in their power to help rescue those Jews in Hungary still alive.

16 Opening of the Wien-Floridsdorf {A} labor camp.

17 A small labor camp opens in Goestling {A}.

18 Horthy, under Allied pressure, announces that deportations of Jews to the East will be stopped.

19 Eichmann orders a round-up of Jews released from previous transport for re-shipment to Auschwitz.

20 An assassination attempt on Hitler fails.

20 Two thousand Jews from the island of Rhodes are deported to Auschwitz.

20 The *Gestapo* begins a mass deportation campaign of Poles from Warsaw; thousands are transferred to concentration camps in Germany.

20 The Democratic National Convention in Chicago adopts a platform that favors opening Palestine to unrestricted Jewish immigration and colonization.

20 The British press reveals the Joel Brand mission and calls it a Nazi attempt to blackmail the Allies.

21 Himmler assumes command of the German Replacement Army.

21 The Union of Polish Patriots and the Polish National Council create the Polish Committee of National Liberation.

21 U.S. Marines land on Guam.

21 The Democratic Party convention in Chicago nominates Franklin Delano Roosevelt for an unprecedented fourth term as President. Senator Harry S. Truman is nominated as the Democratic vice-presidential candidate.

21 The last transport of Gypsies arrives in Auschwitz.

21 Opening of the Laxenburg {A} labor camp.

22 The Polish Committee of National Liberation, the Lublin Committee, assumes administration of liberated Polish territory.

22 With the liquidation of the Shavli {Lit SSR} ghetto/camp, all surviving Jews are deported to concentration camps in Germany.

23 The International Red Cross visits Terezin. To fool the investigating committee, Nazis dress up the ghetto/camp to make it appear to be a fine resort.

23 Liquidation of the Deblin {P} *Judenlager* and the Pustkow {P} *Judenarbeitslager und Industriehof* (Jewish work camp and industrial court).

23 The Red Army liberates Lublin {P}.

24 Soviet forces liberate Majdanek. During its three year existence, some 500,000 victims from fifty-four different nationalities passed its portals. Of the 360,000 who perished, the majority were Jews.

25 Hitler appoints Goebbels *Reich* Plenipotentiary for Total War.

26 The Red Army reaches the Vistula River east of Radom.

27 A Pacific strategy conference is held in Honolulu between President Franklin D. Roosevelt, General Douglas MacArthur, and Admiral Chester W. Nimitz.

27 The Red Army liberates Lvov. Out of a prewar Jewish population of over 150,000, only about 800 Jews are found alive.

27 The Red Army liberates Bialystok and Dvinsk.

27 The Polish Committee for National Liberation in Lublin disbands the Polish collaborationist *Granatowa Policja* (Blue Police), who aided the Nazis in a number of ways.

28 Przemysl is liberated by the Red Army.

28 Nazis liquidate the Gesia Street labor camp in Warsaw. Over 4,000 Jewish inmates, mostly from Hungary and Greece, are force-marched to Kutno, 130 km. away. At least 1,000 victims die *en route*.

29 *SS-Hauptsturmfuehrer* Richard Baer becomes the new Auschwitz camp commandant.

29 Radio Moscow calls for an uprising of the civilian population in Warsaw. The outskirts of Warsaw are shelled by Soviet artillery.

31 The last transport of Jews from Drancy {F} leaves for Auschwitz. In all, a total of sixty-one transports with a thousand Jews each left the *durchgangslager* for Auschwitz, and three other transports with some 4,000 Jews left for Sobibor.

AUGUST

1 The Red Army liberates Kovno.

1 Raoul Wallenberg meets with Admiral Horthy and requests that the Regent permanently suspend deportation of Hungarian Jews.

1 Poles stage the Warsaw uprising. Approximately 1,000 Jews, former ZOB ghetto fighters who were hidden among Poles, take part in the fighting.

1 Liquidation of the HASAG Skarzysko-Kamienna {P} *Judenzwangsarbeitslager*. Hundreds of prisoners are killed on the spot, while 6,000 are transferred to Buchenwald. A total of some 30,000 victims passed through this forced-labor camp, and perhaps as many as 20,000 Jews perished from overwork, starvation, and disease during its existence.

1 The local Italian Fascist militia slaughter Giuseppe Pardo Roques, president of the Jewish community of Pisa, his family, and many Jews who sought refuge in his home.

2 Berlin reports that Field Marshal Erwin Rommel "met with an accidental death" on July 17.

2 Turkey severs diplomatic relations with Germany.

2 The Gypsy "family camp" at Birkenau is liquidated. Close to 3,000 German Romani Gypsies are gassed in Auschwitz and some 1,500 are transferred to Buchenwald.

2 The *Gestapo* closes the *Deutsche Strafanstalt* (the German penal institution) at 37 Rakowiecka Street, Warsaw, the scene of the tortures and executions of hundreds of Jews and Poles.

2 *Yishuv* holds elections to the Fourth *Asefat ha-Nivharim*; *Sephardim* and Yemenites boycott the elections.

3 The Ostrowiec {P} slave labor camp is liquidated and its inmates are deported to Auschwitz.

3 The Red Army crosses the Vistula River in Poland.

3 Wallenberg meets with the chief of the Hungarian police, Lieutenant Colonel Laszlo Ferenczy, on behalf of Hungarian Jewry.

4 Polish government-in-exile premier Mikolajczyk meets with Stalin in Moscow.

4 The *Gestapo* raids the Frank family hiding-place; Anne and her family are taken to Westerbork.

5 Antonescu meets with Hitler.

6 The British Eighth Army crosses the Arno River in Italy. Fighting takes place in Florence.

6 The first transport of Jews from Latvia leaves for Stutthof.

8 LEHI makes an unsuccessful attempt on the life of Sir Harold MacMichael, British high commissioner for Palestine.

10 A general strike is declared in Paris.

11 John Pehle of the War Refugee Board, in a Washington meeting with representatives of the major Jewish organizations, flatly rejects proposals to bomb Auschwitz or its rail approaches.

11 U.S. forces recapture Guam.

12 Churchill and Tito confer in Italy.

13 The Allies drop arms and ammunition to the beleaguered Polish insurrectionists in Warsaw.

15 Operation Anvil: joint Allied invasion of southern France begins.

15 Members of *Palmah* establish *kibbutz* Bet Keshet in the Eastern Lower Galilee.

15 Berl Katznelson, Zionist labor leader, dies.

17 Drancy is liberated. During its three year existence as a deportation center for Jews in France, some 65,000 French, Polish, German, Dutch, and Belgian Jews were deported from here to their deaths; at least another 5,000 perished from other causes.

17 The U.S. and Britain announce that they will undertake a joint effort to find a country of refuge for Hungarian Jewry.

17 The Red Army reaches the eastern Prussian border.

18 Roosevelt announces that the Allies have reached an agreement on military occupation of Germany.

19 An insurrection against Nazi occupation begins in Paris.

20 The Allies bomb eight German synthetic oil and rubber installations outside Auschwitz.

20 Liquidation of the HASAG-Granat *Zwangsarbeitslager* at Kielce {P}.

20 At the fortress of St. Genis-Laval, *Gestapo* chief Klaus Barbie orders 110 captured French resistance fighters, many of whom are Jews, handcuffed and machine-gunned to death.

21 Rudolph (Rezso) Kasztner, a representative of Hungarian Jews in Budapest, is sent under German escort to the Swiss frontier to act as an intermediary between *SS-Standartenfuehrer* Kurt Becher, a Himmler representative, and Saly Mayer, the Swiss representative of the JDC, to negotiate the price at which Nazis are willing to stop murdering Hungarian Jewry.

21 Neutral diplomatic legations in Budapest send an urgent note to the Hungarian government protesting resumption of its deportation schedule for Hungary's Jews.

21 Three hundred eighteen Hungarian Jews released from Bergen-Belsen as a Nazi gesture of good faith arrive in Basle, Switzerland.

21 The *Gestapo* destroys the Pawiak prison in Warsaw. About 65,000 people, mostly Poles, but also a number of Jews, passed through the prison during the Nazi period: approximately half of them were executed in its courtyards.

21 The American Palestine Committee urges President Roosevelt to ensure that Palestine is opened as a means of rescuing Hungarian Jewry.

21 The American Jewish Conference proposes that crimes against Jews be listed as a separate indictment in any postwar war crimes trials.

21 The "Big Three" (the United States, Britain, and the Soviet Union) hold a conference at Dumbarton Oaks in Washington, DC. They discuss ways for peaceful solutions to international problems in a postwar world. The conference closes September 28.

22 *Irgun* attacks the Tel Aviv-Jaffa district police station.

22 Bulgaria declares its desire to conclude peace with the Western Powers.

22 Florence {I} is liberated.

23 Ion Antonescu's government is overthrown during an anti-fascist uprising in Rumania. The country surrenders to the Red Army and Antonescu is arrested.

23 Under pressure Horthy informs Eichmann that he will not resume deportations of Hungarian Jewry.

24 By Nazi order the area of the Lodz ghetto diminished even further.

24 The Bulgarian Commissariat for Jewish Affairs is abolished.

24 The armored division of the French Free Forces enters Paris.

24 Opening of the Wien-Simmering {A} labor camp.

25 Rumania declares war against Nazi Germany after signing an armistice with the Soviet Union.

25 French Free Forces under General Charles de Gaulle liberate Paris.

25 The *Wehrmacht* reoccupies Slovakia.

26 Churchill and Pope Pius XII meet in Vatican City.

27 The U.S. Air Force drops millions of leaflets over Germany informing the Germans of the Nazi atrocities being committed daily against the Jews.

28 A Slovak national uprising begins.

28 The German-imposed *Association des Juifs en Belgique* votes to cease operations during its last meeting.

29 Horthy dismisses Hungarian Prime Minister General Doeme Sztojay.

30 A provisional government under General Charles de Gaulle is established in Paris.

31 Liquidation of the Natzweiler-Struthof concentration camp.

31 Soviet forces enter Bucharest.

31 British High Commissioner for Palestine Sir Harold MacMichael retires and is replaced by Field Marshal Lord Gort (John Standish Surtees Prendergast Vereker).

SEPTEMBER

2 Liquidation of the Plaszow {P} concentration camp: some 2,000 Jews sent to Auschwitz to be gassed, while Polish and other inmates are dispatched to other camps in Germany. A small group of Jews is left behind to work on obliterating all traces of Nazi crimes.

2 Anne Frank and her family are deported from Westerbork to Auschwitz.

2 The Finnish government asks Germany to withdraw its troops and accepts preliminary Soviet peace conditions.

3 Brussels is liberated by British troops.

3 Last transport is dispatched from Westerbork to Auschwitz with 1,000 Jews.

4 Antwerp is liberated by British troops.

4 Finland surrenders to the Soviet Union.

5 The Soviet Union declares war on Bulgaria.

5 The governments-in-exile from Belgium, The Netherlands, and Luxembourg integrate their economies and found the Benelux organization.

6 Greek Jews of the *sonderkommando* stage a revolt blowing up two of the four crematoria in Auschwitz.

6 The Vught *Durchgangslager* is closed. During its existence some 12,000 Jews passed through this transit camp via Westerbork to the Auschwitz and Sobibor extermination camps.

7 A French provisional government is set up in Paris under General Charles De Gaulle.

7 Hungary declares war on Rumania.

8 *Coup d'etat* by the Fatherland Front: Bulgaria switches sides and declares war on Nazi Germany.

8 The first V-2 rockets hit London.

8 Germany begins its offensive against the Slovakian uprising.

9 The Red Army enters Bulgaria and Nazi occupation collapses.

9 The new Soviet-sponsored Bulgarian Patriotic Front government abolishes all anti-Jewish laws and restrictions imposed on Bulgarian Jews.

9 The last transport of Latvian Jews leaves Riga for Stutthof and Latvia is officially declared *Judenrein*.

10 The French provisional government abolishes all Vichy legislation.

10 American forces liberate Luxembourg.

10/17 "Octagon," the second conference between Roosevelt and Churchill to finalize the strategy for defeat of Nazi Germany, opens in Quebec. Much consideration is given to the Morgenthau Plan to de-industrialize Germany after the war.

12 Rumania signs an armistice with the Soviet Union.

12 King Peter broadcasts an appeal from London for Yugoslav unity under Tito.

12 The Red Army begins its attack on Budapest.

13 The First Allied troops enter Germany near Aachen.

13 The U.S. Army Air Force bombs the *Buna-Werke* (Buna works) at Auschwitz.

15 Soviet airborne troops link up with Tito's partisans in Yugoslavia.

15 Soviet army units capture the Warsaw suburb of Praga.

16 Captured Soviet General Vlasov recruits an army of Russian collaborators from the ranks of prisoners of war to fight on the Nazis' side.

16 Bulgaria surrenders to the Allies.

16 The Soviet Union publishes report in Russian, Polish, English, and French on the Nazi atrocities and mass slaughter of hundreds of thousands of victims in the Majdanek camp system.

17 Operation Market-Garden: the Allies begin their airborne invasion of the Rhine basin.

17 The Dutch government voids all anti-Jewish legislation enacted during German occupation of Holland.

18 The Allies fail in an attempt to resupply the Warsaw rebels.

18 Marshal Ion Antonescu, prime minister of Rumania, and Mihai Antonescu, president of the Rumanian council, are arrested in Bucharest.

19 Some 3,000 Jews and over 100 Soviet prisoners of war are massacred by retreating German and Estonian guards during liquidation of the Klooga {Est SSR} slave labor camp.

19 *Hativa Yehudit Lohemet* (Jewish Brigade Group), the only independent Jewish military unit in the British army, is established.

19 Finland signs an armistice with the Soviet Union.

19   Germany disbands the Danish police and crushes the Danish general strike.

21   Haviva Reik, one of the thirty-five volunteer Palestine parachutists, is dropped on a mission near Banska Bystrica, Slovakia.

24   *Forces Francaises de l'Interieur*, the French resistance movement, is integrated into the French army.

27   IZL attacks British police stations at Haifa, Qalqilya, Katara, and Beit Dagon.

28   The Red Army liberates the Klooga {Est SSR} slave labor camp. Of the thousands who passed through this camp during its fifteen months of existence, less than 100 of its victims survived.

28   Most members of the *Pracovna Skupina* are arrested in an *SS* raid in Bratislava. Gisi Fleischmann is among those taken into custody.

29   The Red Army invades Yugoslavia.

30   A unit of the Ukrainian *Galicia Waffen-SS* division capture Haviva Reik, Chaim Hermesh, Zvi Ben-Yaakov, and Rafael Reiss, four of the Palestinian parachutists sent on a mission to Slovakia.

OCTOBER

2   In an official communique to the German foreign ministry, the International Red Cross finally inquires on the status of all foreign prisoners in Germany and the occupied countries.

2   *Armia Krajowa* [AK] (the Polish Home Army), surrenders in Warsaw. German military authorities depopulate the city.

3   Opening of the Gloggnitz {A} labor camp.

4   Operation Manna: British troops land in Greece.

4   A link-up between Tito's partisans and Soviet forces in Yugoslavia is reported.

5   The Italian government issues a decree regarding restitution of property confiscated by the previous Fascist government.

6   Soviet forces enter Hungary.

7   The Auschwitz-Birkenau *Sonderkommando* stages an only partially successful uprising, destroying one of the four crematoria.

7   Joel Brand is released in Jerusalem after he is sent by Eichmann to negotiate a "truck for blood deal" with the British.

7/8 Cservenka massacre: close to 1,000 Hungarian Jewish Labor serviceman are murdered in huge prepared pits near the Yugoslav-Hungarian border.

9/20 Churchill and Stalin meet in Moscow and discuss the future of Danubian Europe.

10 The Committee of Liberation is formed in Hungary.

10 A U.S. congressional debate resumes over the Jewish common-wealth in Palestine issue.

13 The Soviet army liberates Riga.

13 Members attending the biennial convention of the United Lutheran Church in America adopt a resolution to combat antisemitism.

13 The Chief Rabbi of Belgium issues a report on the fate of Jewish survivors in liberated territory.

14 Athens is liberated by British forces.

15 Horthy announces that he is requesting an armistice with the Soviet Union. The Arrow Cross Party assumes total power under Nazi protec-tion and brutal treatment of Jews intensifies. Horthy is arrested by the Germans and the Nazi-installed Szalasi government.

15 The Arrow Cross imprisons 6,000 Jews in the Budapest Dohany Street synagogue, the largest in Europe.

15 Gerasdorf {A} labor camp closes.

18 Eichmann's *Sondereinsatzkommando* returns to Budapest.

18 All German males from sixteen to sixty years old, who had not yet served in the *Wehrmacht*, are called up to serve in the *Volkssturm*.

20 Tito's partisans liberate Belgrade.

20 U.S. troops land at Leyte in the Philippines.

20 *Sondereinsatzkommando Eichmann* rounds up 22,000 Jews in Bu-dapest for deportation.

20 The British deport 251 *Irgun* and LEHI members to Eritrea.

23 The Allies recognize de Gaulle's French provisional government.

24 The last transport of Italian Jews bound for Auschwitz leaves from Bolzano.

27 Admiral Horthy abdicates.

28 A Slovak rebellion is crushed; thousands of Jews remaining in Slovakia are deported to Auschwitz, Terezin, and Sachsenhausen.

28 A Bulgarian-Soviet armistice is signed in Moscow.

29   Opening of the Wien-Favoriten {A} labor camp.

31   The *Centrala Evreilor* (the Jewish Center of Rumania), a *Judenrat*-like institution established by Antonescu, is officially closed.

NOVEMBER

1   Dora, a subcamp of Buchenwald, becomes an independent concentration camp.

1   *Wehrmacht* Arab units form an independent Arab Brigade.

2   Gassing ceases at Auschwitz.

4   Chaim Weizmann meets with Winston Churchill.

5   Hungarians begin handing Jews over to Nazis.

6   Middle East British Resident Minister Lord Moyne is assassinated in Cairo by two LEHI operatives, Eliahu Hakim and Ephraim Ben-Zuri.

7   Hanna Szenes, one of the thirty-two Palestinian parachutists dropped behind Nazi lines, is executed in Budapest.

7   President Franklin Delano Roosevelt is reelected to an unprecedented fourth term.

7   *Sonderkommandos* revolt at crematoria II and IV in Auschwitz-Birkenau.

8   Thousands of Jews from Budapest are taken on a death march.

9   The *SS* and Arrow Cross intensify the roundup of Hungarian Jewry. Hundreds of additional victims are brought to join the death marches.

12   The Szalasi government orders the so-called "protected Jews" (those holding passports from neutral countries) in Budapest, to move into the specially marked "yellow star" buildings.

16   Saengerhausen {G}, a subcamp of Dora-Mittelbau, opens.

16   The Provisional Committee for the Rehabilitation of Dutch Jews is established. The Committee publishes an appeal for help to reconstitute the Dutch Jewish community.

17   Australian Prime Minister Francis M. Forde rejects the Kimberley settlement proposal.

18   Enzo Hayyim Sereni, one of the thirty-two *Hagana* parachutists dropped behind enemy lines, is executed by the *Gestapo* in the Dachau concentration camp.

19   Soon after the Red Army liberates Kiev, a pogrom breaks out against the few remaining Jewish survivors who return to the city to reclaim their possessions.

20 Haviva Reik, together with three fellow *Hagana* parachutists, are executed by the *Gestapo* at Kremnica, Slovakia.

21 The death marches of Hungary's Jews are renewed on Eichmann's orders.

21 Gloggnitz {A} labor camp closes.

23 A labor camp for Jews opens in Wien-Neustadt {A}.

26 Opening of the Deutschkreutz {A} labor camp.

26/29 A ghetto is established in Budapest. All Jews remaining in Budapest, approximately 63,000 people, are herded into a small area containing 293 houses, or fourteen persons to a room.

27 Edward Stettinius becomes U.S. secretary of state on Cordell Hull's resignation.

29 General Enver Hoxha proclaims Albania's liberation from the Axis.

29 Himmler orders destruction of the Auschwitz-Birkenau gas chambers and crematoria.

DECEMBER

1 The Wien-Floridsdorf labor camp closes.

2 *SS-Hauptsturmfuehrer* Josef Kramer replaces Adolf Haas as commandant of Bergen-Belsen.

3 Clashes between Communist demonstrators and police in Athens and Piraeus lead to civil war in Greece.

8 The Red Army launches a new offensive, aiming to encircle Budapest.

8 Opening of the Hannersdorf {A} labor camp.

10 Eichmann orders the Budapest central ghetto sealed.

10 De Gaulle and Stalin sign the Franco-Soviet Treaty of Alliance in Moscow.

11 The U.S. Senate tables the Wagner-Taft resolution on Palestine.

12 Dr. Stephen S. Wise resigns as chairman of the Zionist Emergency Council; however, the Council refuses to accept his resignation.

15 A motion is introduced by U.S. Senator Guy Gillette stating that crimes against Jews will be considered war crimes.

16 *Einsatz Greif* forms the beginning of the failed German Ardennes offensive, Watch on the Rhine, or the Battle of the Bulge.

17 The U.S. Senate passes the Jewish Commonwealth Resolution.

24   Budapest is completely surrounded by the Red Army. Eichmann and his *einsatzkommando* hastily depart the city.

24   The Arrow Cross attacks Jewish children's home run by the International Red Cross. Many children are shot to death, and the survivors are driven into the icy Danube River to drown.

26   U.S. troops at Bastogne are relieved.

28   Abba Hillel Silver and Stephen S. Wise resign their co-chairmanship of the Zionist Emergency Council.

29   The Arrow Cross storm troopers attack "Swiss-protected" houses; a few dozen Jews are killed inside, and thousands of Jews are driven into the streets.

30   The Wueste-Guesdorf *Judenlager*, a subcamp of Gross-Rosen, is evacuated.

31   Deutschkreutz {A} labor camp closes.

31   The Lublin Committee declares itself the provisional Polish government.

1945

1 At the height of a bitter cold winter, thousands of victims from dozens of subcamps in Upper Silesia are relentlessly driven deeper into Germany and Austria, away from the approaching Soviet armies. The prisoners—men and women of many nationalities—are poorly dressed, their swollen feet wrapped in rags, with no food or water, drop like flies. Before the death marches are over, tens of thousands will perish.

1 The Lublin Committee declares itself the legitimate government of Poland.

1 The last major *Luftwaffe* attacks hit targets in France, Belgium, and Holland.

1 Hungarian Fascists murder Hungarian-Jewish leader, Otto Komoly.

2 The Danish resistance destroys a German V-2 components factory in Copenhagen.

2 The surrounded German garrison in Budapest goes on the offensive, counterattacking Soviet forces.

3 Dutch and Belgian governments sign a mutual agreement for repatriation of incarcerated civilians.

5 Five thousand Swedish "protected Jews" are driven from their "neutral houses" and marched into the Budapest central ghetto.

5 The last transport of Hungarian Jews is sent to Auschwitz.

5 The Soviet Union recognizes the Lublin Committee as the sole legitimate government of Poland, but the United States and Britain refuse to recognize the Lublin Committee.

6 Roza Robota, a member of the Jewish underground in Auschwitz, is executed by the *Gestapo* in connection with the unsuccessful *sonderkommando* revolt in the Birkenau crematoria.

7 During the Jokai Street massacre, members of the Arrow Cross terror squads attack Swedish "protective houses" in Budapest.

9 Operation Mike 1: U.S. forces land on Luzon.

11 The Red Army enters Warsaw.

11 The last transport of Italian Jews from the La Risiera camp leaves for Auschwitz.

12 Soviet forces begin their final Polish offensive.

14 Final liquidation of the Plaszow {P} *Zwangsarbeitslager*: all remaining inmates are sent to Auschwitz, More than 25,000 people passed through the camp (the majority of them Jews) and most of them perished there.

15 The first civilian ship since May 1940 leaves London for France.

16 Retreating *SS* liquidates the HASAG *Apparatenbau Juden-lager* in Czestochowa {P}. Approximately 6,000 victims passed through the camp during its existence, and over one-third of them died there.

16 The Soviet army liberates some 800 Jews in Lodz.

16 Kielce {P} is liberated by the Red Army. Only a handful of survivors from a prewar Jewish community of 20,000 come out from hiding.

16/18 The Red Army liberates Pest and 70,000 Jews of the Budapest ghetto are saved.

17 The devastated city of Warsaw is liberated and 200 Jewish survivors out of a 1939 pre-war Jewish population of 400,000 surface.

17 The four HASAG slave labor camps in Czestochowa {P} are liberated by the Red Army; 3,758 Jewish victims, whom the Nazis had left behind when they hastily departed only a day before, are freed.

17 Auschwitz is evacuated: some 66,000 prisoners are driven on foot (better known as the "death marches"), away from the fast-approaching Red Army.

17 The last forty-eight Jewish prisoners at Chelmno attached to *Sonderkommando 1005* revolt against the *SS*: only three survive. During the death camp's existence some 320,000 Jews were exterminated there.

17 Swedish diplomat Raul Wallenberg, saviour of tens of thousands of Hungarian Jews, is taken into custody by Soviets.

18 The Polish provisional government (the Lublin Committee) enters Warsaw.

19 The Althammer {P} *zwangsarbeitslager* is liquidated and some 400 Jews are taken on a death march.

19 *Armia Krajowa* (Polish Home Army) is dissolved.

19 Cracow, capital of the *Generalgouvernement*, liberated.

20 The Hungarian provisional government signs an armistice with the Soviet Union, the United States, and Britain.

20 President Franklin Delano Roosevelt is inaugurated for his fourth term.

21 Evacuation of the Blechhammer {P} concentration camp: about 4,000 prisoners are taken on a forced death march to Gross-Rosen; at least 1,000 Jews are murdered or die on the way.

21 Some 6,000 to 7,000 Jews on a death march from KL Stutthof satellite camps are driven into the Baltic Sea at Palmnicken and machine-gunned to death.

24 Hitler appoints Himmler commander-in-chief of Army group Vistula.

25 The Soviet army crosses the Oder River near Breslau.

25 The Provisional Hungarian government establishes people's tribunals for war crime trials.

25 Evacuation of the Stutthof concentration camp begins. Perhaps as many as 30,000 out of 50,000 Jewish prisoners die during the death marches.

26 One thousand Jewish women prisoners from the Neusalz {G} slave labor camp are taken on a death march to Flossenbuerg; 800 of the women die or are killed on the way.

27 Soviet troops liberate Auschwitz; some 7,000 prisoners of different nationalities - few of whom are Jews - are freed.

27 U.S. troops from General George Patton's Third Army enter Germany.

27 All of Lithuania is freed. Memel is liberated by Soviet troops.

28 Vidkum Quisling is received by Hitler in the *Reich* chancellery.

31 A pre-Yalta conference is held in Malta by the combined chiefs-of-staffs; Churchill, Edward R Stettinius, Jr., and Anthony Eden also attend.

FEBRUARY

1 Himmler orders 2,700 Jews released from Bergen-Belsen brought to Switzerland.

1 The U.S. Seventh Army reaches *Siegfried* Line.

2 The Mexican government approves immigration permits for 100 European Jewish children.

2 Wien-Neustadt {A} labor camp closes.

2 Soviet POWs stage an unsuccessful revolt in Block 20 in Mauthausen.

4 Belgium is cleared of all German resistance.

4/11 Yalta Conference: the last meeting between the original "big three" is held to discuss the final phase of the war.

4/24 Battle for Manila: Japanese forces offer stiff resistance.

5 A small transport of Jews from Terezin leaves for Switzerland with the help of the International Red Cross.

7 The Belgian government resigns.

8 Paraguay declares war on the Axis.

10 Thousands of exhausted prisoners evacuated from Upper Silesian camps arrive in Mauthausen {A}. Victims are forced to remain, stripped naked, for numerous hours in front of the "wailing wall" while awaiting to be integrated within the camp's system. A large number of the prisoners are beaten to death by "order-keeping" capos, or freeze to death.

11 A decree by the Polish Ministry of Public Administration creates the Organizing Committee of Jewish Religious Congregations in Poland.

11 Saly Mayer, Jewish representative of the JDC in Switzerland, meets with *SS-Obersturmbannfuehrer* Kurt Becher, at the Swiss border to negotiate the release of Jews in concentration camps to the International Committee of the Red Cross [ICRC]. Rudolph Kasztner also attends the meeting.

11 The German garrison in Budapest surrenders. The Soviet army takes at least 100,000 prisoners of war.

13 The U.S. Army crosses the Rhine River at Remagen.

13 Peru declares war on Germany and Japan.

13 The Red Army liberates KL Gross-Rosen. A total of some 125,000 prisoners of all nationalities passed through here during its existence. Approximately 40,000 perished during the height of its evacuation in the winter of 1945.

13 Henrietta Szold, founder of Hadassah and Youth *Aliya*, dies in Jerusalem.

13 ZOA radicals establish the American Zionist Policy Committee to support Abba Hillel Silver in his dispute with Stephen S. Wise.

13/15 The Allies carry out a massive air attack on Dresden. British incendiary bombs and American explosive bombs create a giant "fire storm" which destroys most of the city, with an estimated death toll between 35,000 and 100,000.

14 The Arab League Statute is presented in Cairo.

16 Hannersdorf {A} labor camp closes.

19 In one of the bloodiest battles fought in the Pacific, U.S. Marines land on Iwo Jima.

19 Count Folke Bernadotte meets with Himmler to negotiate release to the Swedish Red Cross of the small number of Jews still alive in the Nazi concentration camps.

19 The Inter-American Conference opens in Mexico City.

21 Laxenburg {A} labor camp closes.

22 Operation Clarion: 9,000 Allied aircraft attack central German rail and road communications.

23 Turkey declares war on Germany.

24 Egypt declares war on Germany and Japan. Premier Ahmed Pasha is assassinated.

27 Syria and Lebanon declare war on Germany.

27 The Soviet Union installs a Communist government in Rumania.

MARCH

1 Japanese forces in Corregidor surrender.

1 President Roosevelt reports to Congress on the Yalta Conference.

4 Finland declares war on Germany.

5 Wien-Favoriten {A} labor camp closes.

7 The Allies declare German Propaganda Minister Josef Goebbels and Foreign Minister Joachim von Ribbentrop war criminals.

7 Nazis execute 400 Dutch men in retaliation for the attempt on the life of local head of the German police.

7 The Federal People's Republic of Yugoslavia forms.

9 A U.S. air raid sets Tokyo ablaze.

10   The Soviet Union returns Transylvania to Rumania.

11   The Czechoslovak government-in-exile in London returns to Slovakia.

11   German Jewish refugees found *kibbutz* Even Yizhak.

12   Carl Burckhardt, the head of the ICRC, meets with the head of the *Reichssicherheitshauptamt* [RSHA], Ernst Kaltenbrunner, at the Arlberg Pass, near the Swiss border. The two plan to work out a deal for the ICRC to take over supervision of the Nazi concentration camps.

14   One thousand attacks against Nazis and Quislings are carried out by Norwegian resistance fighters in a single night.

14   American Jews mark a special day of mourning for slaughtered European Jewry.

16   Japanese resistance on Iwo Jima ends.

16   President Roosevelt assures Stephen S. Wise of Jewish participation at the San Francisco Conference.

16   The Germans pass peace overtures to the British embassy in Stockholm.

16   The last transport of Jews from the Protectorate is sent to Terezin. In all, 122 transports with more than 73,000 Jews from Czechoslovakia were sent to Terezin, and from there most of them were deported to their deaths in Auschwitz.

17   The Provisional Hungarian government repeals all anti-Jewish laws.

19   *Nero befehl*: Hitler orders the mass destruction of German factories, transportation services, communication systems, and supplies in order to prevent them from falling into enemy hands.

19   Wien-Simmering {A} labor camp closes.

21   Churchill announces that food shortages exist in Britain.

22   The Arab League forms in Cairo.

23   Operation Plunder: Allies cross the Rhine in the Ruhr basin.

23   Operation Varsity: the Allies invade the northern Rhine basin.

25   Fascist-oriented NSZ distributes leaflets declaring that the Poles' patriotic duty is to kill Jews.

27   The last transport of German Jews leaves Berlin for Terezin.

27   The last German V-2 rocket lands outside London. Close to 3,000 British civilians were killed as a result of the 1,100 rocket attacks.

27   Argentina declares war on Germany and Japan.

28 The Red Army reaches the Austrian border.

29 Frankfurt is captured by the American Third Army.

29 *Glowna Komisja Badania Zbrodni Hitlerowskich w Polsce* (Main Commission for Investigation of Nazi Crimes in Poland), is established by the Polish National Council.

30 The Red Army captures Danzig.

30 A group of women prisoners trying to escape from Ravensbrueck are captured and shot.

APRIL

1 U.S. forces invade Okinawa.

1 The *SS* begins evacuating KL Dora-Nordhausen. Thousands of prisoners are taken on a death march toward Bergen-Belsen.

3 Arthur Nebe, former commander of *Einsatzgruppe B*, is accused of participating in the failed plot to kill Hitler, is stripped of all of his *SS* ranks and powers, and is executed by hanging.

3 Wien-Laban {A} labor camp closes.

3/4 Some 30,000 Buchenwald inmates are taken on a forced death march, most of whom perish on the way; about 8,000 are massacred on camp grounds.

4 Himmler orders immediate evacuation of the Dachau and Flossenbuerg concentration camps.

4 American troops discover mass graves when they liberate Ohrdruf, a Buchenwald subcamp. Approximately 10,000 prisoners (Jews and others) perished there during its existence.

4 Hungary is cleared of the German army.

5 The Soviet Union renounces its non-aggression pact with Japan.

5 Generals Dwight D. Eisenhower, Omar N. Bradley, and George S. Patton view the horrors of the just-liberated Ohrdruf concentration camp.

6 Yugoslav partisans capture Sarajevo.

6 The *SS* dispatches a train with 2,400 Jewish prisoners from Bergen-Belsen to avoid their being liberated by the Allies.

6 Saengerhausen {G} concentration camp closes.

7 The Red Army enters Vienna.

7 Wien-Fuenfhaus {A} labor camp closes.

9 Admiral Wilhelm Canaris, former head of *Abwehr*, is hanged at Flossenbuerg.

9 American forces liberate the Dora-Nordhausen concentration camp. Thirty thousand prisoners of different nationalities lost their lives here building V-1 and V-2 rockets for Nazi Germany.

9 Evacuation of Mauthausen starts.

9/11 The Jewish Brigade establishes a bridgehead on the Sento River in northern Italy.

9/20 A committee of jurists from forty-four countries drafts a statute for an International Court of Justice.

10 Churchill announces that there were 1,126,802 armed forces war casualties in the British Empire and Commonwealth.

10 American Jewish organizations are invited to send special representatives to the opening of the San Francisco Conference.

11 KL Buchenwald is liberated by American troops from the Third Army, freeing 21,000 German, Russian, French, Polish, Italian, Czechoslovakian, and Jewish prisoners. During almost eight years of existence, a total of 238,980 inmates from thirty different countries passed through Buchenwald and its subcamps. Approximately 50,000 of them perished, mostly Jews.

11 Hundreds of evacuated prisoners from Mauthausen on their way to Ebensee, are shot death by their *SS* guards and their bodies are thrown into the Traun River.

11 Soviet-Yugoslav treaty signed.

12 Franklin Delano Roosevelt dies of a massive cerebral hemorrhage while vacationing at Warm Springs, Georgia. Harry S. Truman takes over the U.S. presidency.

12 An Allied bombing attack destroys the German Chancellery in Berlin.

13 Some 3,000 prisoners are driven into a large warehouse on the outskirts of Gardelegen {A}, which is incinerated and its prisoners burned to death. Those trying to break out are machine-gunned to death and only two prisoners escape.

13 Rehmsdorf, a subcamp of Buchenwald, is evacuated. Close to 4,500 Jewish prisoners are taken on a death march to Terezin; no more than 500 survive.

13 Goestling {A} labor camp closes.

14 The French army liberates Bordeaux.

14 Capture of Franz von Papen.

15 Bergen-Belsen is liberated by elements of the British Eleventh Armored Division: 28,000 women, 11,000 men, and 500 children are freed. The troops find thousands of dead bodies (perhaps as many as 30,000) strewn all over the camp grounds. Camp commandant Josef Kramer, some of his associates, and a number of *SS* guards are captured.

15 Close to 60,000 prisoners are force-marched westward from Sachsenhausen and Ravensbrueck concentration camps; thousands are murdered on the way.

15 The Jewish community is reestablished in Bratislava, Slovakia.

15 With the help of the International Red Cross, 400 Danish Jews imprisoned in Terezin are transferred to Sweden.

15 Wien-Meidling {A} labor camp closes.

16 The final Soviet Berlin offensive begins along the Oder and Neisse Rivers.

16 Hitler decrees that military commanders who give orders to German forces to retreat or surrender should be summarily executed.

17 The United States extends additional Lend-Lease agreements with the Soviet Union. President Truman, in a joint session of Congress, emphasizes his administration's continuation of Roosevelt's policies.

18 A transport of rescued Danish Jews from Terezin arrives in Sweden.

18 The Allies neutralize the Ruhr pocket: 370,000 Germans are taken prisoner and German Field Marshal Walther Model commits suicide.

19 Himmler plots to establish a new German government and to conclude an "honorable" peace with the Western Powers as soon as possible.

19 All inmates remaining at KZ Neuengamme are released to Danish volunteers and are brought to Denmark.

20 The U.S. Seventh Army captures Nuremberg.

20 Goering's faithful guards blow up the buildings of his *Karinhall* estate near Berlin as the Soviets approach.

20 Himmler secretly meets with the Swedish representative of the World Jewish Congress, Norbert Masur, agreeing to free 1,000 Jewish women from Ravensbrueck.

21 The Soviet Union signs a treaty with the Polish Lublin provisional government.

22 Hitler decides to stay in Berlin to the end.

22 One thousand desperate Serbian and Jewish prisoners stage an uprising at the Jasenovac {Y} extermination camp. Only a handful succeed in the attempted breakout: most are killed by the *Ustase* guards. During the camp's existence, approximately 600,000 victims were brutally murdered there, among them some 20,000 to 25,000 Jews.

22 Moshe Shertok reports to the Jewish Agency Executive in Jerusalem on his private audience with Pope Pius XII, informing them that the conversation led to nothing.

22/27 Himmler, through Swedish diplomat count Folke Bernadotte, attempts to conclude a separate peace with the Western Allies: the proposal is rejected on the 27th.

23 Hitler learns of Himmler's and Goering's treachery and, in a fit of rage, orders them immediately apprehended and imprisoned.

23 Seventeen thousand prisoners released from Nazi concentration camps, including some Jews, are moved from Denmark to Sweden with Himmler's permission.

23 U.S. troops cross the Po River. German resistance on the Italian front collapses.

23 American army units liberate 2,000 sick and starving inmates upon entering the Flossenbuerg {G} concentration camp.

24 A U.S. Congressional bipartisan committee arrives at Buchenwald for a first-hand look at the just liberated concentration camp.

25 War Crimes Commission delegates go on an inspection tour of liberated concentration camps to gather first-hand evidence.

25 U.S. and Soviet troops meet near Torgau on the Elbe River. The Red Army groups under Marshals Georgi K. Zhukov, Konstantin K. Rokossovski, and Ivan S. Koniev encircle Berlin.

25 Final evacuation of KL Stutthof: over 4,000 prisoners (40 percent of whom are Jews) are taken on a death march in no particular direction, and most of the victims perish on the way.

25 An organizational meeting of the United Nations organization opens in San Francisco with fifty member states attending. The session closes June 26.

26 Some 7,000 Jewish prisoners in Dachau are taken on a death march. Most of them are shot on the way, or fall dead from exhaustion, hunger, thirst, sickness or cold.

26 The French arrest Marshal Henri Phillipe Petain.

26 Italian partisans liberate Milan.

26 Aba Kovner, partisan and Hebrew poet, establishes the Organization of Eastern European Survivors; its goal is to help Jewish survivors reach the shores of Palestine.

27 *SS* guards massacre 1,000 Jewish slave laborers on their death march from Buchenwald.

27 American army units liberate KL Kaufering, a subcamp of Dachau. Thousands of bodies are discovered in giant pits, with hundreds of corpses strewn around the camp. About 28,000 victims—Jews and many other nationalities—passed through the camp during its existence, and the great majority perished there.

27 Red Army advance units overrun the Sachsenhausen concentration camp and liberate 3,000 sick prisoners. During its approximately ten years of existence, 200,000 prisoners—Jews, Soviet POWs, Poles, Czechs, and many other nationalities—passed through its gates, with perhaps as many as 30,000 dying within the camp.

28 Benito Mussolini and his mistress, Clara Petacci, are shot dead by Italian partisans near Lake Como while trying to escape to Switzerland. Their bodies are taken to Milan and hung on meat hooks for exhibition.

28 Hitler charges his brother-in-law, *SS-Gruppenfuehrer* Hermann Fegelein, with desertion and orders him executed.

29 Close to 32,000 survivors are liberated at Dachau by units of the U.S. Seventh Army. During its twelve years of existence 230,000 victims of about forty different nationalities passed through Dachau—from German criminals to Jehovah's Witnesses; from Soviet, American and British POWs, to Czech and Polish intelligentsia; from French and Italian citizens to Jews from all parts of Europe. Perhaps as many as 60,000 victims perished there.

29 The Red Army clears all German resistance in Slovakia.

29 The German armies in Italy sign an unconditional surrender at Caserta.

29 During the last few hours of his life in his Berlin bunker, Hitler dictates his final testament. Admiral Karl Doenitz is named as his successor and Propaganda Minister Josef Goebbels as *Reich* chancellor.

29 Soviet forces liberate 3,000 female prisoners at Ravensbrueck. During its existence over 100,000 women of different nationalities passed through its gates, among them some 15,000 to 20,000 Jews.

29 British forces liberate the Neuengamme {G} concentration camp. Out of the estimated 100,000 prisoners that passed through the camp and its seventy satellite camps during its existence, at least 55,000—among them large numbers of Hungarian and Polish Jews—perished.

29 Sixty thousand Jews attend a rally in New York City, demanding a Jewish commonwealth in Palestine.

30 Hitler commits suicide at 3:30 PM by firing a bullet through his mouth. Eva Braun, his mistress, commits suicide by taking a dose of cyanide.

30 Propaganda Minister Josef Goebbels follows Hitler's suit by ordering an *SS*-man to kill him and his wife; earlier, at Goebbels' request, a doctor injected his six children with poison.

30 The Soviet army reaches the *Reichstag* building in Berlin.

MAY

1 The Soviet Army hoists the Red Flag over the ruined *Reichstag* building in Berlin. In the battle for Berlin the Soviets suffer 300,000 casualties.

2 One hundred fifty thousand Germans surrender to General James Gavin's Eighty-Second Airborne Division.

2 Berlin surrenders to Soviet forces.

2 Close to 17,000 Terezin survivors are liberated by the Soviet army. Among the over 150,000 victims that passed through its gates between 1941 and 1945, close to 60,000 Jews perished—including about 15,000 children.

2 President Truman appoints Supreme Court Justice Robert H. Jackson as chief of counsel for the United States in the persecution of Nazi war criminals.

2 Ex-Vichy prime minister Pierre Laval is arrested in Barcelona.

2 Last RAF air raid on Germany.

3 Franz Ziereis, commandant of Mauthausen, flees the concentration camp just before its liberation by American military advance units. Members of the Vienna police department take over guard of the camp from the *SS*.

3 Hamburg is captured by British troops.

4 *OK Wehrmacht* agrees to surrender troops in Holland, Denmark, and northwest Germany.

4 Woebbelin, a transit camp for evacuated prisoners from areas overrun by the Allies, is liberated.

4 German troops in Denmark surrender to the Danish underground.

4 Gunskirchen *Lager* {A}, a Mauthausen subcamp, is liberated by units of the U.S. Seventy-First Infantry Division. Approximately 18,000 Jewish, Russian, Polish, French, Yugoslavian, Greek and prisoners of other nationalities—thousands of them on the verge of dying—are liberated.

4 KL Oranienburg {G}, a satellite of the Sachsenhausen concentration camp, is liberated by Soviet forces and units of the Polish Peoples Army.

5 Mauthausen is liberated by American forces. During its eight years of existence (1938-1945), at least 120,000 out of a total prisoner population of about 200,000—including 40,000 Jews—that passed through the camp, died.

5 KL Gusen {A}, a Mauthausen subcamp, is liberated. Forty thousand victims—Jews and others—perished in the camp during its existence.

5 Twenty-four hours before American advance units enter Ebensee {A}, Nazis try to persuade thousands of prisoners in the overcrowded camp to enter a number of tunnels, which the *SS* has previously mined in anticipation of the Allies over-running the camp. A prisoner committee refuses to follow orders.

5 The Vlasov army leads a revolt in Prague: Czechoslovak national sovereignty is restored in Prague.

5 The Red Army captures Peenemuende, an important German rocket development center.

5 The *Gestapo* camp in Amersfoort {Ho} is liberated.

6 KL Ebensee, a Mauthausen subcamp, is liberated by American troops. During its approximate eighteen months of existence 11,000 victims died in Ebensee, including a number of Jews.

6 During the San Francisco Conference, the United Nations suspends debate on Poland pending Soviet explanation of the arrest of Polish (London) leaders.

6 Syrians revolt against French rule.

7 At General Eisenhower's headquarters in Rheims, Field Marshal Alfred Jodl signs an unconditional surrender of Germany.

7 The Czechoslovak National Council dissociates itself from the Vlasov army.

8 V-E Day: German troops in Norway surrender.

8 Hermann Goering is captured by American soldiers in Berchtesgaden.

8   Arab nationalists riot in Algeria.

8   The *Rijksinstitut voor Oorlogsdocumentatie* (Netherlands State Institute for War Documentation), a research institute, archive, and library, is established in Amsterdam.

9   The Soviet army enters Prague.

9   German surrender is ratified in Berlin.

9   *SS-Obergruppenfuehrer* and former HSSPF in the *Generalgouvernement,* Friedrich Wilhelm Krueger, commits suicide.

10   The United States gives overall figures of American war casualties in Europe as 800,000 with 150,000 killed.

10   Operation Apostle: British forces land in Norway upon the Nazi collapse.

10   Vidkum Quisling and a number of his Norwegian Nazi collaborators are arrested.

11   Yemen joins the Arab League.

11   The mayor of Milan abrogates all anti-Jewish decrees.

13   The Western Allies oppose a Yugoslav administration of Trieste.

14   Austria declares its independence by reestablishing the Austrian Republic.

14   The *Oorlogspleepkinderenbureau* [OPK] (Office for Wartime Foster-Children), is set up in Holland.

17   The Hague reconstituted Jewish community reopens its synagogue.

20   Anti-French riots break out in Beirut.

22   President Truman reports to Congress on the Lend-Lease balance sheet.

23   *Reichsfuehrer-SS* Heinrich Himmler—once the most powerful figure in the Third *Reich* after Hitler—commits suicide.

23   Members of the OKW and acting German government officials are arrested at Flensburg.

23   Churchill resigns and forms a new caretaker government.

24   Repatriation of Allied POWs and civilian concentration camp victims begins.

25   *Irgun* attacks the Kirkuk-Haifa oil pipeline.

28   The German state of Bavaria is reconstituted.

28   Lebanese and Syrians battle French troops.

29   Belgian Socialists demand that King Leopold abdicate.

30 Persia demands the removal of Soviet, American, and British forces.

31 The War Crimes Commission Conference opens in London.

JUNE

3 French troops are evacuated from Beirut and Damascus.

5 The first meeting of the Allied Control Commission opens in Berlin and issues a declaration on defeated Germany: the country to be divided into four zones occupied by the four Allied powers, Berlin is to be jointly occupied.

5 The U.S. Marshall Plan is inaugurated.

5 France proposes an Allied conference on the Middle East.

7 King Haakon VII returns to Norway from his exile in Britain.

13 A French military court in Paris indicts Kurt Gerstein as a war criminal.

14 Joachim von Ribbentrop, former German foreign minister, is arrested by the British in Hamburg.

15 The Central Committee of Liberated Jews is founded in Germany by Jewish DPs.

15 The Allied Food Conference opens in London.

15 The United Jewish Appeal is reconstituted and unifies all American Jewish fundraising organizations.

18 Lord Haw Haw (William Joyce) is charged with treason for broadcasting propaganda from Germany and goes on trial in London.

20 An official delegation of the Palestine Jewish Brigade meets with representatives of the *She'erit ha-Peleta* in Germany.

21 The Allied Reparations Commission holds its first meeting in Moscow.

21 A new provisional government is formed in Poland.

22 President Truman commissions Earl G. Harrison to investigate and report on conditions in DP camps in the American zone of occupation in Germany.

25 The Allies announce occupation zones for Austria.

26 Representatives of fifty nations sign the United Nations Charter in San Francisco. The International Court of Justice begins operation.

26 The Austrian provisional government enacts the Constitutional Law on War Crimes and National Socialist Crimes.

28   The National Unity Government is formed in Warsaw.

29   Sub-Carpathian Ruthenia becomes part of the Soviet Union.

30   The U.S. military in Germany arrests Ilse Koch, the "beast of Buchenwald," to stand trial for her crimes.

JULY

1   Jewish DP representatives gather in Feldafing to create an official body to act as a voice for the *She'erit ha-Peleta*.

3   The Polish government announces that it will abide by the Yalta decisions and hold free elections by secret ballot.

4   Muslim anti-Jewish riots erupt in Tripoli, Libya.

5   The United States and Britain recognize the new Polish government.

5   Britain holds its first postwar elections.

7   The Four-power *Kommandatura* is established in Berlin.

12   American, British, and French military forces take control of their Berlin sectors.

12   The first DP *Yiddish* newspaper, *Unzer Shtime* (Our Voice), is published at Bergen-Belsen.

12   Japan asks the Soviet Union to mediate peace.

13   The Supreme Headquarters of the Allied Expeditionary Forces in Europe [SHAEF] goes out of existence.

15   Berlin's Jewish community is reconstituted.

15   The Berlin Municipal Council orders confiscation of all the properties of Nazi party members living in Berlin.

16   The first experimental atomic bomb explodes in Los Alamos, New Mexico.

17   The Potsdam Conference opens; Truman, Churchill (and later on Clement Atlee, the new British Prime minister), and Stalin meet to resolve and implement all previous wartime agreements on Germany and the Axis powers. The Conference closes August 2.

17   Fifteen hundred U.S. warplanes attack greater Tokyo.

25   Potsdam Declaration on Japan.

25   Representatives of the *Yishuv* and the *She'erit ha-Peleta* meet in Saint Ottilie {G}.

25   Kurt Gerstein commits suicide in a French prison by hanging himself.

26 The United States issues an ultimatum demanding Japanese unconditional surrender. Tokyo rejects the ultimatum on the 28th.

27 Clement Atlee forms a Labour government in Britain.

30 Japan rejects the Potsdam ultimatum.

31 Spain deports Pierre Laval to the American zone in Germany where he is arrested and handed over to the French.

AUGUST

1 Former Iowa senator, Guy Gillete, assumes the presidency of the American League of the Hebrew Committee.

1/8 The Zionist World Conference opens in London and demands that Britain open the gates of Palestine for all Jewish survivors languishing in the displaced persons camps.

6 The United States drops its first atomic bomb on Hiroshima. Eighty thousand Japanese are killed, with 60 percent of the city destroyed in the blast and firestorm that follow.

7 Nazi war criminal Karl Oberg is arrested by U.S. military police and handed over to French authorities.

8 The Soviet Union declares war on Japan.

8 The Charter of the International Tribunal is signed by the United States, the United Kingdom, the Soviet Union, and the provisional government of France.

9 The U.S. drops a second atomic bomb on Nagasaki, killing approximately 40,000 Japanese.

10 Truman threatens destruction of Japan, unless the country agrees to an unconditional surrender. Japan's Supreme War Council sues for peace.

11 An antisemitic pogrom takes place in Cracow.

12 Soviet forces occupy North Korea.

13 The World Jewish Congress requests that the British grant 100,000 immigrant certificates for Palestine.

13 A Dutch royal decree vests responsibility for war-orphaned children with a twenty-five member Committee for War Orphans.

14 Japan agrees to unconditional surrender terms.

15 V-J Day: General Douglas MacArthur is appointed Supreme Commander for the Allied Powers in the Pacific.

17 Poland's new western borders with Germany are established and recognized by the Soviet Union.

17   Indonesia declares itself an independent republic, free from Dutch rule.

18   Soviet forces occupy Manchuria.

19   Pogrom in Lublin.

21   Official beginning of the *Bricha*, the movement of Jewish survivors from eastern Europe southward and westward, preparatory to their repatriation to Palestine.

24   President Truman officially terminates Lend-Lease.

28   The *Mossad* ship *SS Dahlin*, with thirty-five *ma'apilim* aboard, runs the British blockade and lands on the coast near Caesarea.

30   The American Council for Judaism repudiates all Zionist claims to Palestine as a national home for the Jews.

31   Truman requests that Britain admit 100,000 Jewish DPs to Palestine.

SEPTEMBER

1/2   The Council of Jewish Religious Communities in Bohemia and Moravia established.

2   Japanese surrender is signed on the *USS Missouri* in Tokyo Bay. World War II officially ends.

5   Great Britain limits Jewish immigration to Palestine to 1,500 per month.

6   The British seize the Rheinish-Westphalian Coal Syndicate and arrest its forty-five coal-mine owners.

9   The Moscow Jewish community sends a *Rosh Hashana* message to Jews all over the world.

9   Japan signs the Chinese surrender terms.

14   The German state of Thuringia (in the Soviet zone of occupation) issues a law for restitution of Jewish property.

17   The "Bergen-Belsen" trial by a British military court begins at Luenburg {G}.

18   A number of Holocaust survivors reorganize the Jewish community of Hamburg.

20   The Allied Control Council officially abolishes all Nazi-promulgated discriminatory laws and declares the *Nationalsozialistische Deutsche Arbeiterpartei* [NSDAP], the Nazi party, an illegal organization.

20 Chaim Weizmann, on behalf of the Jewish Agency, submits memorandum to the Allied Powers demanding that Germany make restitution and pay reparations to the Jewish people.

20 OSS is dissolved.

20 The All-India Congress demands that Britain leave the country.

21 The Allied administration of Berlin classifies Jews as victims of Fascism.

23 Egypt asks for revision of the Anglo-Egyptian treaty.

24 Libelous accusations of well poisoning lead to a pogrom in Topolciany, Slovakia.

26/27 During a conference in Bergen-Belsen the Central Jewish Committee asks England to open Palestine to Jewish survivors.

29 The Harrison Report is published. The report is strongly critical of American army occupation in reference to Jewish displaced persons, and calls for 100,000 Jewish DPs to enter Palestine.

29 Representatives of the American Jewish Committee meeting with Truman ask for mass immigration to Palestine by Europe's Jewish survivors.

30 Eisenhower reports to President Truman that corrections have been made so that Jews in the DP camps are now being treated well.

OCTOBER

1 The American military lift a ban on fraternization between G.I.'s and German women.

2 General George S. Patton is removed from command of the U.S. Third Army because of his opposition to denazification.

5 The American Jewish Conference asks President Truman to find a solution to the Palestine problem.

6 The International Military Tribunal completes formal indictments against the major German war criminals.

9 The French execute Pierre Laval for Nazi collaboration.

10 A *Hagana* attack liberates *ma'apilim* at Athlit prison.

11 Renewed fighting breaks out in China between *Kuomintang* (Nationalists) and Communists.

14 Trials begin for Czech collaborators in Nazi-German crimes committed in Czechoslovakia.

15 The House of Commons extends wartime emergency powers to the British government for five years.

16 The United Nations creates the Food and Agricultural Organization [FAO].

17 U.S. military authorities in Berlin report seizure of the Nazi party master files listing eight million NSDAP members.

19 A seven-man military *junta* replaces the Venezuelan government in an army *coup*.

20 The Allied Council for Austria gives *de facto* recognition to Premier Karl Renner's Austrian government.

20 The Arab League is formed by Egypt, Syria, Iraq, and Lebanon to present a united front against establishment of a Jewish state in Palestine.

21 Communists win 26.4 percent of the vote in French elections.

24 Vidkum Quisling, Norwegian Nazi collaborator, is executed by hanging.

24 The United Nations Charter is ratified by twenty-nine member states.

24 Arab countries threaten economic sanctions against American oil companies if the United States persists in its campaign to open Palestine to Jewish immigration.

24 A mass demonstration in support of Palestinian Jewry is held in Madison Square Garden attended by an overflow crowd of 250,000 people.

25 Indicted Nazi Dr. Robert Ley commits suicide in the Nuremberg jail by hanging himself.

25 The Canadian government votes to maintain its discriminatory immigration regulations.

26 Senators Robert F. Wagner (NY) and Robert A. Taft (OH) introduce the Palestine Resolution. An identical resolution is introduced in the House by Congressman Joseph W. Martin (MA) on October 29.

29 Hitler's secretary, Martin Borman, is indicted in absentia by the International Military Tribunal at Nuremberg.

29 Hungarian war crimes trials begin.

30 A military *coup* in Brazil overthrows the government of President Getulio Vargas.

31 IZL blows up portions of the Palestine-Egypt railway.

NOVEMBER

1 Jewish resistance movements in Palestine—*Hagana, Irgun,* and *LEHI* launch major attacks on British coastal patrol launches and the rail lines.

2 Anti-Jewish disturbances break out in Cairo.

3 Hungary forms a coalition government.

4/7 Over 100 Jews are killed and hundreds injured during Arab riots in Tripolitania, Libya.

11 Tito's National Front wins Yugoslav elections.

13 Bevin announces his Palestine policy in the House of Commons: the new monthly quota for Jewish immigrants to Palestine is 1,500, but this number is contingent on Arab approval.

13 General Charles de Gaulle is elected president of the French Provisional Government.

13 Britain and America agree to a joint investigation committee on the Palestine question.

14 Anti-British riots break out in Tel Aviv.

15 The Soviet Military Government seizes all of Dr. Friedrich Flick's holdings with an estimated value at over $500,000,000.

15 The Dachau war crimes trial opens: forty former members of the camp's *SS* staff go on trial before an American military court at Dachau.

16 The United Nations General Assembly creates the United Nations Educational, Scientific and Cultural Organization [UNESCO].

16 The British Military Government seizes the entire holdings of Friedrich Krupp A.G. and its subsidiaries.

16/19 The forty-eighth annual convention of the Zionist Organization of America opens in Atlantic City, New Jersey attended by 1,000 delegates.

18 The Communist-controlled Fatherland Front wins the first postwar elections in Bulgaria.

19 Members of the Central Committee for Jewish Liberatees stage a hunger strike in protest of Bevin's statement on Palestine; a number of protesters are jailed by British military police.

20 Trial of major Nazi war criminals opens in the Nuremberg Palace of Justice. The International Military Tribunal [IMT] prosecution presents a 35,000 word indictment against the twenty-four top Nazi war criminals.

23 The American Jewish Committee rejects as totally inadequate the 1,500 monthly Jewish immigration certificates to Palestine granted by the British.

25 Night of the Radars: *Hagana* sappers demolish two British radar stations used to track *Aliya Bet* ships.

29 Yugoslavia is proclaimed a People's Republic.

30 All I. G. Farben assets are seized by the Control Council under the provisions of the Allied Control Council Law Number 9.

30 In the first Italian general elections since the demise of fascism, the Christian Democrats score a victory.

DECEMBER

2 A French decree officially reinstates government jobs to Jewish employees fired under Vichy racial laws.

2 The English Zionist Federation holds a "Palestine Crisis" demonstration at the Stoll Theatre in London.

4 The U.S. Senate approves America's participation in the United Nations.

10 The U.S. government announces that all Jewish refugees from Poland, once in the American zone, will be treated the same as other DPs.

12 Britain hangs former Bergen-Belsen camp commandant Josef Kramer and ten of his staff.

12 The U.S. Senate Foreign Relations Committee approves a congressional resolution on Palestine.

13 A U.S. military court sentences to death by hanging Martin Weiss, camp commandant of Dachau, and thirty-six of his staff.

15/17 A special convention of the United Jewish Appeal in Atlantic City, New Jersey hears representatives from the DP camps who express the wish of the *she'erit ha-Peleta* to live in *Eretz Israel*.

17 Both Houses of the U.S. Congress adopt a joint resolution favoring the establishment of a Jewish national home in Palestine.

20 The four Allied governments in occupied Germany enact Control Council Law Number 10, defining crimes committed by Nazi Germany as "crimes against humanity."

22 Truman issues a directive allowing for displaced persons and refugees from the American zone of occupation to immigrate to the United States.

22 The U.S. Department of the Interior designates the National Refugee Service with the relocation of the refugees from the Oswego shelter.

27 A series of explosions wreck the Palestine police headquarters in Jerusalem.

27 The *Mossad* ship *Hanna Szenesh* with 252 *ma'apilim* runs aground near Nahariya.

1946

1 The Arab League proclaims a boycott against "Zionist" products.

2 The head of the UNRRA operations in Germany, British General F. E. Morgan, charges that the exodus of Jews from Poland is a plot perpetrated by *Bricha*.

7 The Anglo-American Committee of Inquiry is established.

7 The Western Powers recognize Austrian independence with 1937 boundaries.

7 A truce is declared in the Chinese civil war in honor of visit by U.S. Secretary of State Marshall. The truce lasts through April 14.

10 The first session of the United Nations General Assembly opens in London; Belgian Foreign Minister Paul Spaak is elected president.

11 Communist-controlled assembly proclaims Albania a republic.

14 Chief Rabbi of the British Empire, Dr. Joseph Herman Hertz, dies.

17 In an address before the United Nations General Assembly Ernest Bevin declares Britain's intent to grant independence to Transjordan, an integral part of mandated Palestine.

17 The British Royal Navy captures the *Mossad* ship *SS Enzo Sereni* with 900 *ma'apilim* aboard.

20 Charles de Gaulle resigns as president of France.

24   The United Nations General Assembly creates an Atomic Energy Commission.

29   The Central Committee of Displaced Jews is formed in the American zone.

30   The British government decides to continue granting the monthly quota of 1,500 certificates for Jewish refugees to Palestine for three months.

FEBRUARY

1   Trygve Lie is elected as secretary-general of the United Nations.

3   *SS-Oberstgruppenfuehrer* and HSSPF Northern Army Group, Friedrich Jeckeln, together with six other Nazi war criminals, are tried by a Soviet military court at Riga. They are found guilty of mass murder and hanged the same afternoon on the grounds of the former Riga ghetto.

4   Five Jewish survivors in the Polish village of Parczew located in the Lublin district are killed during a pogrom initiated by soldiers of the *Armja Krajowa*.

7/13   The Anglo-American Committee of Inquiry visits Poland and takes testimony from Jewish survivors.

10   *Ha-rav* Isaac Halevi Herzog, the Chief Rabbi of Palestine, meets with Pope Pius XII.

11   Karl Schoengarth, *SS-Oberfuehrer* and commander of the SD in Cracow (1941-44), is sentenced to death by a British military court at Enschede {G}.

12   The International Refugee Organization [IRO] is created by the General Assembly of the UN as a specialized agency for refugees and displaced persons.

14   Britain nationalizes the Bank of England.

15   At the Nuremberg war crimes trial, Soviet prosecutor Smirnov states that as governor general of Poland, Hans Frank was responsible for the deaths of at least 3,000,000 Jews.

20   The *Palmah* destroys a British radar station on Mount Carmel, near Haifa.

20   The UN Economic and Social Council establishes the Special Committee on Refugees and Displaced Persons.

24   The Anglo-American Committee of Inquiry holds its hearings in Vienna.

24 Colonel Juan Domingo Peron is elected president of Argentina for a six year term.

29 The United Nations Economic and Social Council adopts a resolution creating the Commission on Human Rights.

MARCH

5 Winston Churchill delivers his "Iron Curtain" speech at Fulton, Missouri and exposes the "police states" of Eastern Europe.

5 The Allied Control Commission enacts the Denazification Law.

7/28 The Anglo-American Committee of Inquiry holds hearings in Palestine on the question of partition.

9 The Soviet Union returns North Transylvania to Rumanian administration.

10 Britain and France start evacuating from Lebanon.

19 Poles stage a pogrom against the few Jews who have returned to Lublin.

21 Australia announces that it will grant 2,500 immigration visas to former Jewish inmates of Nazi concentration camps who have relatives living in Australia.

24 Antisemitic outbreaks occur in Vienna.

26 The Royal Navy captures *Mossad* ship *Orde Wingate*, with 238 *ma'apilim* aboard. The Jews resist the British boarding party, resulting in the death of *Palmah* member Braha Fuld.

29 Armed German policemen accompanied by American MPs raid a Jewish DP camp in Stuttgart, killing one survivor.

29 Laszlo Endre, Hungarian antisemite and top government official largely responsible for destroying Hungarian Jewry, is hung as a war criminal.

APRIL

2 The Economic Council of the Central Jewish Committee announces plans to establish a number of Jewish cooperatives in Poland.

4 Hans Bothmann, former commander of the Chelmno extermination camp, commits suicide by hanging himself in prison while awaiting trial by a British military court.

7 Viennese Jews elect a thirty-six member *Kultusrat* (Community Council).

9 The German Radical Confessing Church admits guilt for not assisting Jews during the Nazi era.

9 The first "legal" transport of Jewish children in Bergen-Belsen leaves for Palestine.

10 The League of Nations' assembly dissolves itself.

17 French troops are withdrawn from Syria.

19 The UN International Court of Justice at The Hague officially absorbs the League of Nations Permanent Court in Geneva, Switzerland.

20 The Anglo-American Committee of Inquiry winds up its investigation on the partition of Palestine.

21 A uniformed band of the former Polish underground army, the *Armja Krajowa*, kills five young Jewish survivors in broad daylight near the town of Nowy Targ.

28 The Allied Control Council forbids Germans to engage in any kind of war research.

28 Riots break out in a number of Displaced Persons camps in Germany in and around Landsberg; U.S. troops restore order.

30 The Anglo-American Committee of Inquiry issues its report at Laussane, Switzerland, recommending that Britain admit 100,000 refugees into Palestine within one year pending a solution to the Palestine problem.

MAY

1 Attlee announces in the House of Commons that Britain's acceptance of the recommendations of the Anglo-American Committee of Inquiry depends both on the willingness of the United States to help maintain peace in Palestine, and disarmament of the Jewish underground.

3 The Tokyo International War Crimes Tribunal opens.

5 In a referendum French voters reject France's new constitution.

6 The Special Committee on Refugees and Displaced Persons holds hearings in London.

9 The Hungarian Reformed Church confesses its guilt by not doing enough to save Hungarian Jews from slaughter.

10 Acting Secretary of State Dean Acheson declares that the United States will first consult with Jewish and Arab leaders before giving its decision on the Anglo-American Committee of Inquiry report.

13 The British secret service instigates Italian police to arrest Jews at a *Mossad le Aliya Bet* camp in La Spezia. Adverse public opinion forces the British to grant immigrant certificates to all those arrested.

13 The *Mossad* ship *Max Nordau* with 1,666 *ma'apilim* aboard is captured by the British outside of Palestine's territorial waters.

15 The Institute of Arab-American Affairs condemns an Anglo-American Committee report.

16 Czechoslovakia promulgates the Law of Restitution.

17 Ion Antonescu is sentenced to death by a Rumanian court.

17 President Truman orders a government takeover of American railways dislocated by strikes.

20 *Marine Flasher* with the first 794 Holocaust survivors arrives in New York.

20 The Palestine mandatory government asks the Jewish Agency and the Arab Higher Committee to submit their views on the findings of the Anglo-American Committee of Inquiry.

22 Karl Hermann Frank, third *Reichsprotektor* of Bohemia and Moravia, is hanged in Prague.

24 The Palestine Arab Higher Committee rejects the recommendations of the Anglo-American Committee of Inquiry.

25 The kingdom of Transjordan is proclaimed by *Emir* Abdullah with British and American approval.

25 The Soviet Military Government orders the seizure of all businesses and industrial enterprises formerly owned by German war criminals or active Nazis.

25 General Lucius D. Clay orders suspension of all reparations deliveries to Russia from the American zone of occupation.

26 The Greek civil war begins.

28 The American Jewish Conference declines to give its views on the findings of the Anglo-American Committee of Inquiry.

JUNE

1 Former Rumanian dictator Ion Antonescu and his deputy Mihai Antonescu (no relation) are executed as war criminals.

2 Italians vote for a republic in a nationwide referendum.

2 The American Council for Judaism informs the American government that it endorses all the recommendations of the Anglo-American Committee of Inquiry.

2 The United States and Britain restore the Azores Islands to Portugal.

3 The British Zionist Federation calls on Britain to honor the recommendation of the Anglo-American Committee of Inquiry and immediately admit 100,000 Jewish DPs to Palestine.

4 The American Zionist Emergency Council declines to comment on the recommendations of the Anglo-American Committee of Inquiry.

6 Czechoslovakian President Benes resigns.

9 The Federation of Jewish Societies in France announces establishment of a special department to help Jewish refugees from Carpatho-Russia.

11 President Truman establishes a Cabinet Committee on Palestine and Related Problems.

12 A rally in Madison Square Garden sponsored by the American Zionist Emergency Council urges the admission of 100,000 Jews to Palestine.

14 The Baruch Plan: the U.S. proposes an international atomic development authority under the UN Atomic Energy Commission.

16 *Hagana* destroys all bridges into Palestine during a single operation.

17 The Council of Jewish Communities in Czechoslovakia is empowered to administer all heirless Jewish properties as of September 29, 1938.

19 Georges Bidault is elected president of the French provisional government.

24 French Jewry holds commemorative services for Jewish victims of Nazism in the *Rue de la Victoire* synagogue in Paris.

27 The *Josiah Wedgwood* with 1,259 *ma'apilim* aboard is intercepted by the Royal Navy off the coast of Haifa.

29 During Operation Agatha, nicknamed "Black Sabbath," the British raid the Jewish Agency and *Hagana*, arresting over 2,000 Jews, including all members of the Jewish Agency Executive then in Palestine.

JULY

2 The trial of former chief rabbi of Salonika, Dr. C. Koretz, and fifteen former members of the *Judenrat* accused of collaboration with the Nazis in the deportation of Greek Jewry, opens in Athens.

3 The League for Labor Palestine amalgamates with Labor Zionists of America-*Poale Zion*.

4 The United States grants independence to the Philippines; Raymond Magsaysay is elected the nation's first president.

4 A pogrom in Kielce {P} claims forty-two Jewish lives and seventy-five Jews are injured.

9 A Polish national tribunal in Poznan finds *SS-Gruppenfuehrer* Arthur Greiser, former *Gauleiter* and *Reichsstatthalter* of the Warthegau, guilty of war crimes and sentences him to death by hanging.

10 Sidney Hillman, American Jewish labor leader, dies at age fifty-nine.

11 In the aftermath of the Kielce pogrom, August Cardinal Hlond, Catholic Primate of Poland, accuses the victims—the tiny Jewish remnant in Poland—of causing their own misfortunes.

11 Nine Poles accused as the leaders of the Kielce pogrom receive the death sentence from a Polish court.

11 The United States and British German zones of occupation merge their economic administration.

12 The British return Jewish Agency Executive offices seized in Palestine back to the Agency.

16 The American League for a Free Palestine adopts a resolution to give active aid to Palestinian resistance against Britain.

17 The Yugoslav government executes Draza Mihailovic, former head of the *Chetniks*.

21 Britain introduces bread rationing because of a severe wheat shortage.

22 *Irgun* blows up British government and military headquarters in Jerusalem's King David Hotel; seventy-six people are killed and forty-six injured.

22 The World Health Organization is created as an agency of the United Nations general Assembly.

24 The *Mossad* ship *Hagana* sails from Yugoslavia with 2,678 *ma'apilim* and is captured by the British on July 29. The refugees on the *Hagana* become the first Jews deported to Cyprus.

26 The Anglo-American Committee for Palestine recommends a federalization scheme to be considered by their respective governments.

26 Czechoslovakia opens its borders for *bricha*.

29 The Peace Conference convenes in Paris. The twenty-one Allied nations who fought the Axis consider treaties proposed for Italy, Bulgaria, Hungary, Rumania, and Finland.

30 Poland opens its borders encouraging Jewish emigration.

30 Anti-Jewish outbreaks occur in Hungarian provincial towns.

31 The British parliament debates the Morrison-Grady Plan for Palestine.

AUGUST

1 The National Services to Foreign Born of the National Council of Jewish Women and the National Refugee Service consolidate into the United Service for New Americans, Inc.

2 General Vlasov, Soviet Nazi collaborator, is executed in Moscow.

12 Britain announces its policy of detention of "illegal" immigrants in Cyprus.

13 The British Colonial Office charges that American financial sources are responsible for "illegal" Jewish immigration to Palestine.

14 South African Prime Minister Jan Christian Smuts announces a new policy of increased immigration.

14 Thirteen hundred "illegal" Jewish immigrants bound for Palestine make up the first transport deported to Cyprus by Britain.

16 The Dutch Zionist Union sends a strongly worded protest letter to the British government, declaring that Jews are being sacrificed to Britain's imperialist interests.

19 The Czech ministry of the interior orders police to take all necessary measures against anti-Jewish outbreaks.

20 The Allied Control Commission officially dissolves the German *Wehrmacht*.

20 The American Jewish Committee announces its support for partition of Palestine.

SEPTEMBER

1 Greek citizens vote for a monarchy.

5 *SS-Hauptsturmfuehrer* Amon Goeth, commandant of the Plaszow *Judenzwangsarbeitslager*, is sentenced to death by a Polish court in Cracow.

7 U.S. General McNarney gives official recognition to the Central Committee of Liberated Jews in the American zone of occupation.

8 A plebiscite in Bulgaria overwhelmingly votes for a republican form of government.

13 Czechoslovakia issues the General Ruling on the Treatment of Jews.

15 The American Zionist Emergency Council declares Zionist intent to resist the British blockade against Jewish immigration to Palestine.

15 Bulgaria institutes a People's Republic.

26 The Great Synagogue in Turin {I} reopens.

29 French Jewry hold a commemorative service at Drancy, where about 70,000 Jews were deported to Auschwitz.

OCTOBER

1 The International Military Tribunal at Nuremberg passes judgment against the twenty-two major war criminals: twelve are sentenced to death, three to life in prison, four to various prison terms, and three are acquitted. Martin Borman is sentenced to death in absentia. Judgment is appropriately announced on *Yom Kippur*.

4 President Truman issues a *Yom Kippur* statement, urging Britain to immediately admit 100,000 Jewish DPs; rejects the Morrison-Grady Palestine partition plan.

4 *SS-Hauptsturmfuehrer* Siegfried Seidl, commander of the Terezin ghetto-camp and Bergen-Belsen, is sentenced to death by a People's Court in the Soviet sector of Vienna.

6 Eleven new settlements are established in the Negev over the course of one evening.

10 *SS-Standartenfuehrer*, SD commander for Belgium-Northern France, Helmuth Knochen is extradited to be tried in France after he was condemned to death by a British military court in Germany.

10 *SS-Brigadefuehrer* Karl Oberg after being sentenced to death by an American military court is extradited to France to stand trial for wartime crimes he committed as HSSPF in France.

13 A referendum approves the new French constitution.

14 The clandestine *Hagana* radio station *Kol Israel* resumes transmissions.

15 Hermann Goering commits suicide in the Nuremberg jail prior to his death sentence being carried out.

16 Ten major war criminals are hanged in Nuremberg jail by the International Military Tribunal; those hanged are: Alfred Rosenberg, Joachim von Ribbentrop, Alfred Jodl, Wilhelm Keitel, Ernst Kaltenbrunner, Julius Streicher, Hans Frank, Wilhelm Frick, Arthur Seyss-Inquart, and Fritz Sauckel.

20 *SS-Oberstgruppenfuehrer* Kurt Daluege, chief of the *Ordnungspolizei* in the Protectorate of Bohemia and Moravia and perpetrator of the Lidice massacre, is hanged for crimes committed in Czechoslovakia.

21 *Irgun* blows up the British embassy in Rome.

23 The United Nations General Assembly meets in New York.

27/28 The forty-ninth annual convention of the Zionist Organization of America rejects the Jewish Agency's partition plan, reaffirming its support of the Biltmore Program which calls for a Jewish commonwealth in the whole of Palestine; pledges full support for Jewish resistance in Palestine by responsible elements of the *Yishuv*.

NOVEMBER

3 Arabs attack Naoth Mordecai, a new settlement in Upper Galilee.

3 The twenty-seventh annual convention of the American *Mizrachi* Organization rejects partition of Palestine.

3 Ruling power in Japan is transferred from the emperor to an elected assembly.

4 The Republican Party wins 246 seats in U.S. Congressional elections while the Democratic party wins only 188.

6 Britain releases imprisoned Jewish Agency leaders from Latrun prison.

7 Juan Peron promises to personally take action in cases of discrimination against Jews seeking immigration to Argentina.

16 The Hebrew Committee of National Liberation sponsors a "Salute to Resistance" rally in Carnegie Hall in New York City.

16 The Board of Regents of the State of New York grants a charter to *Yeshiva* University, which then becomes the first all-Jewish university in the United States.

21 The Bulgarian government passes a decree ordering all properties confiscated by the authorities and transferred to third parties to be restored to the original owners.

21 International Military Tribunal "The Medical Case" begins; trial ends August 20, 1947.

25 Henry Morgenthau, American Jewish diplomat, dies at age ninety.

DECEMBER

1 The United Nations War Crimes Commission announces that 24,365 felons have been tried for war crimes by the United States, Great Britain, France, Poland, Greece, Czechoslovakia, and Norway.

3 *Mossad le-Aliya Bet* buys the *President Warfield*.

5 New York to become permanent United Nations headquarters.

9/24 The Twenty-Second World Zionist Congress meets in Basle, Switzerland and debates the Morrison-Grady plan for the cantonization of Palestine into Arab, Jewish, and neutral (international) areas. The upcoming London Conference is also discussed.

10 A four-power *kommandatur* approves a new city government for Berlin.

11 Spain is refused admittance to the United Nations.

11 The United Nations General Assembly approves the principles of Nuremberg.

11 The UN International Children's Emergency Fund [UNICEF] established by the General Assembly.

11 The Polish government enacts special legislation dealing with Nazi-German war crimes in Poland, based on the principle of the International Military Tribunal.

14 The International Labor Organization [ILO] becomes a United Nations specialized agency.

15 The UN General Assembly approves the International Refugee Organization's constitution.

16 David Ben-Gurion, Chaim Weizmann, and Stephen S. Wise defend the Palestine partition proposals and urge the World Zionist Congress to participate in the forthcoming London Conference.

16 Leon Blum forms a Socialist government in France.

20 The Citizens Committee on Displaced Persons [CCDP] is established in New York City.

20 International Military Tribunal "The Milch Case" begins; trial ends April 17, 1947.

24 The World Zionist Congress adopts a majority resolution not to participate in the upcoming London Conference.

29 In retaliation for the flogging of IZL prisoners, a British major is abducted near Netanyah and flogged.

31 United States hostilities with Japan are terminated by a presidential proclamation.

1947

JANUARY

1 Britain nationalizes its coal industry.

1 The United States and Britain merge their occupation zones in Germany.

3 Stephen S. Wise tenders his resignation from the World Zionist Organization.

5 Nazi war criminal, Karl Westphal, a former official of the German Ministry of Justice, commits suicide in the Nuremberg jail while awaiting trial.

7 U.S. Secretary of State James F. Byrnes resigns; General George C. Marshall to succeed him.

13 *SS* General Oswald Pohl is indicted by U.S. authorities in Nuremberg, together with seventeen other members of the *SS* Elite Guard.

14 The "Big Four" attend the London Conference which opens in Lancaster House. The main agenda is the drafting of peace treaties with Germany and Austria.

14 Two former female members of Euthanasia, Dr. Hilde Weroicke and nurse Helene Wieczorek, are guillotined in Berlin's *Lehrterstrasse* prison after they were found guilty of mass murder by injecting a death serum into hundreds of mentally ill patients in German hospitals.

16 Vincent Auriol is elected first president of the Fourth French Republic.

19 Stanislaw Mikolajczyk and his Peasant Party are defeated in Poland's first parliamentary elections since 1935.

21 Dr. Emanuel Neumann discloses that American Zionists are ready to finance "illegal" immigration to Palestine.

21 Siegfried Kabus, German neo-Nazi leader, is condemned to death by a U.S. Military Court in Stuttgart for the bombing of denazification courts the previous October.

24 British military administration in their German zone of occupation begin issuing DP passports to refugees without any valid identity papers.

24/26 The United Jewish Appeal National Mobilization Conference is held in Chicago.

25 The National Democratic Party of Germany, a new Right-wing group, is established in the U.S. zone of Germany.

25 A new Fascist organization, the Fasces of Revolutionary Action, surfaces in Italy after it explodes five bombs in Rome.

27 The United Nations Commission on Human Rights opens its first regular session in New York.

28 Britain agrees to admit 500,000 DPs, among them some 80,000 Jews.

31 The Allied Military Government orders seventy-six professors and lecturers suspended from the University of Heidelberg for having been active Nazis.

31 The High Commissioner for Palestine, General Allan Cunningham, issues orders for the immediate evacuation of all wives and children of British civilians residing in the country.

FEBRUARY

1 The Allied court in Rastadt sentences twenty-one members of the staff of the Natzweiler-Struthof concentration camp to death; twenty others are sentenced to prison terms of various duration.

3 The Palestine Mandatory Government gives an ultimatum to the Jewish Agency and the *Va'ad Leumi*, demanding that they urge the *Yishuv* to hand over "terrorists" to the British military.

3 The British Military Court in Hamburg issues death sentences to eleven staff members of the Ravensbrueck concentration camp.

4 Arabs categorically reject British plans for partition of Palestine. Anglo-Jewish talks end in deadlock the next day.

4 Franz von Papen is arrested to stand trial before a denazification court in Nuremberg.

4 Britain orders 1,000 Jews evacuated by February 6 from the Rehavia, Schneler, and German quarters in Jerusalem as Britain plans to use the area as a military security zone.

7 Josef Cyrankiewicz forms Poland's first legal postwar cabinet.

7 The British military court announces that it will clear 1,000,000 of the 1,500,000 Nazi suspects in its zone of occupation under a new policy "from punishment to rehabilitation."

8 The American Military Government [AMG] in Frankfort-am-Main indicts Friedrich Flick, *SS-Oberfuehrer* Otto Steinbrinck, Konrad Kaletsch, Bernhard Weiss, and Dr. Hermann Terberger for war crimes and crimes against humanity in exploiting slave labor.

9 The *Negev* with 650 refugees aboard is intercepted by the British outside Haifa. The *ma'apilim* are forcefully transferred to the ferry *Emperor Haywood* and deported to Cyprus.

10 A British Military Court in Jerusalem imposes the death sentence on three members of IZL, Dov Rosenbaum, Eliezer Kashani, and Mordechai Alkoshi, for possessing firearms. A fourth member, Chaim Gorovelsky, is sentenced to life in prison.

10 The UN Human Rights Commission establishes Freedom of Information and of the Press, and a Subcommittee on Prevention of Discrimination and Protection of Minorities.

10 Peace treaties ending World War II are signed in Paris between Italy and France, and between Rumania, Finland, and the Soviet Union.

11 The International Refugee Organization Preparatory Commission holds its first meeting in Geneva, Switzerland.

17 The International Military Tribunal "The Justice Case" begins; trial ends December 4, 1947.

18 In a speech at the House of Commons, Ernest Bevin announces Britain's intent to submit the Palestine problem to the United Nations.

20 An attack by IZL units on a RAF station near Hadera is repulsed by the British. In a second attack, IZL units blow up the Iraq Petroleum Company's pipeline in two places.

22 Poland closes its borders to Jewish emigration.

23   The Dutch Zionist Union resolves to ask The Netherlands government to support the Zionist cause when the Palestine question comes up before the United Nations General Assembly.

25   Bevin, speaking before the House of Commons, distorts the wording and true meaning of the original Mandate.

25   The blockade runner *Ben Hecht* departs France with 626 *ma'apilim*.

26   The Jewish Agency issues a statement attacking Bevin's speech before the House of Commons as utterly false and misleading.

28   The *SS Haim Arlosoroff* is captured at Bat Galim after a fierce battle with the Royal Navy.

MARCH

1   IZL and LEHI unleash a new wave of anti-British terror. *Irgun* blows up a British officer's club in Jerusalem.

2   Macmillan imposes martial law over large areas of Jewish Palestine.

3   United Zionist Revisionists of America urge a boycott of British goods and services.

4   A fifty year Anglo-French treaty of alliance against Germany is signed at Dunkerque.

7   British troops search and seize a large arms cache in Hadera.

8   The British navy intercepts the *SS Ben Hecht* near Haifa and deports its 600 *ma'apilim* to Cyprus.

9   ORT opens a maritime training school for young Jews in Marseille.

9   *SS-Standartenfuehrer* Harold Turner, who as military administrator in Serbia took part in the Belgrade ghetto massacre, is sentenced to death by a Yugoslavian court in Belgrade.

9   IZL carries out an attack on Citrus House, the British military headquarters in Tel Aviv.

10   The Moscow Conference of foreign ministers fails over the question of Germany.

10   International Military Tribunal "The Pohl Case" begins; trial ends November 3, 1947.

11   The trial of Rudolf Hoess, former commandant of KL Auschwitz, opens in Warsaw.

12   A two-pronged attack on the Palestine rail lines is carried out by the IZL: an oil-carrying train on the Tel Aviv-Haifa line is blown up, and a cargo train carrying supplies for the British garrisons is derailed on the Jerusalem-Jaffa line.

12   The Truman Doctrine of military and economic aid is publicized. U.S. foreign policy aims to combat communism throughout the world.

14   An Amsterdam court sentences Dutch Jewess Ans van Dijk to death for betraying sixty-eight Jews to the Nazis.

15   The UN General Assembly Economic and Social Council unanimously agrees on the need for an international convention outlawing genocide.

17   *Mossad le Aliya Bet* acquires *Pan Crescent* and *Pan York*.

17   The Palestine government lifts martial law.

18   The Jewish Agency Executive announces that it will not cooperate with British demands to hand over terrorists to the military, but that it will pursue its own policy to stop terror.

21   France and Italy sign an agreement providing for 200,000 Italians to immigrate to France within a year.

22   *SS-Gruppenfuehrer* Juergen Stroop, liquidator of the Warsaw ghetto and HSSPF in Greece, is sentenced to death by an American war crimes court at Dachau for shooting hostages in Greece. Stroop is later extradited to Poland where he is retried in Warsaw and executed, September 8, 1951.

23   Syria introduces a bill imposing the death penalty on any Syrian Jew illegally crossing into Palestine.

25   The U.S. Senate passes a resolution for America to join the International Refugee Organization [IRO].

26   The Dutch execute the collaborationist, Frederik H. Meyer, for betraying Jews to the Gestapo, who in turn paid him one *guilder* for each Jew handed over.

26   The American Fund for Palestinian Institutions launches a nationwide drive.

28   The American Jewish Conference urges the United States to intercede with Britain to halt the execution of the death sentence passed against four members of *Irgun*.

31   IZL sets fire to the Haifa oil refinery.

APRIL

1 A bill is introduced in Congress to allow 400,000 Displaced Persons to enter the United States during the coming four years.

2 A Polish court sentences Rudolf Hoess to death.

2 Britain submits a formal request for a special session of the UN General Assembly to deal with the Palestine problem.

4 The International Civil Aviation Organization [ICAO] is established and becomes a UN specialized agency on May 13, 1947.

12 Britain hands the Palestine issue to the United Nations.

15 Rudolf Hoess is taken to the place where he was responsible for the extermination of millions of innocent victims, and is himself hanged.

16 Dov Gruner, Yehiel Drezner, Mordechai Alkoshi, and Eliezer Kashani—the four members of the *Irgun Zvai Leumi*—are hung in Acre prison by the British.

16 Ex-President of Slovakia, Josef Tiso, is executed.

19 International Military Tribunal "The Flick Case" begins. Friedrich Flick, among others, is accused of employing some 40,000 slave laborers. The trial ends December 22, 1947.

21 General Lucius D. Clay bars newly arrived Jewish refugees entry to Displaced Person's camps in the American zone of occupation.

21 *Yeshurun*, a Hebrew/*Yiddish* weekly, organ of *B'rith Yeshurun*—a Jewish DP organization in Germany—premiers.

25 Meeting of Jewish survivors opens in Munich.

27 Hans Biebow, Nazi administrator of the Lodz ghetto, is hanged by sentence of the Polish court in Lodz.

28 A special United Nations session opens to deal with the Palestine issue.

30 *Irgun* stages a jail break at Acre prison and frees some 250 Jews and Arabs.

30 *Pan Crescent* nearly sinks in Venice harbor after a suspicious explosion on board.

MAY

3 A new Japanese constitution creates a limited monarchy.

3 Twenty-four top executives of I.G. Farben are indicted before the Military Tribunal in Nuremberg.

5 The United Nations General Assembly grants a hearing to the Jewish Agency for Palestine. David Ben-Gurion, Moshe Shertok, and Abba Hillel Silver testify.

7 The Jewish Museum opens in the former Warburg mansion in New York City.

7 Brazil outlaws the Communist party.

8 Abba Hillel Silver, chairman of the American section of the Jewish Agency, presents the case for an independent Jewish state in Palestine before the United Nations General Assembly.

13 The UN General Assembly selects an eleven-nation Special Committee on Palestine, excluding "the Big Five"—the United States, the Soviet Union, Great Britain, China, and France.

15 The UN General Assembly ends the Special Session on Palestine.

21 Austria promulgates the fourth Restitution Law.

23 Britain requests that United Nations members prevent transit or "illegal" departure of Jews attempting to enter Palestine from their ports.

26 The Special Committee of Inquiry begins studying the Palestine problem.

26 A new dictatorship is established in Nicaragua under General Anastasio Somoza.

30 The Seventh plenary session of the Canadian Jewish Congress opens in Montreal; closes June 2.

31 Communists seize power in Hungary.

JUNE

2 The German Economic Council is established.

2/3 The first conference of *B'rith Yeshurun* opens in Ferenwald {G} and cables a resolution to the United Nations requesting that it ensure that Britain opens Palestine to Jews.

4 U.S. Congressional hearings on the Straton bill begin.

5 The Marshall Plan for the European recovery is initiated.

7/8 The *Arbeitsgemeinschaft*, an overall body to coordinate the activities of the reconstituted Jewish communities in Germany, is founded during a two-day conference in Frankfort-am-Main.

10 The United Nations completes its first draft convention outlawing mass destruction.

11   Britain captures three members of *Irgun*—Absalom Habib, Meyer Nakar, and Jacob Weiss—and condemns them to death.

12   Canada agrees to admit 5,000 DPs. Approximately 1,000 Jews are eligible to immigrate to Canada under this agreement.

15   Arabs stage a two-day protest strike against the arrival of the United Nations Special Committee on Palestine [UNSCOP] in Palestine.

17   The U.S. Military Government in the American zone of occupation breaks up the I.G. Farben facilities into forty-seven independent units.

19   Britain gives notice to the Soviet Union that it will no longer follow its appeasement policy.

23   U.S. Congress passes the Taft-Hartley Act.

29   LEHI executes four British soldiers in retaliation for the death sentence issued by a British military court for three IZL members.

29   The World Jewish Congress meets in Buenos Aires.

30   UNRRA and the Intergovernmental Committee on Refugees [IGCR] cease their activities.

JULY

1   The International Refugee Organization [IRO] assumes formal responsibilities for displaced persons and refugees in Europe and Asia.

3   International Military Tribunal "The *Einsatzgruppen* Case" begins; trial ends April 10, 1948. Out of twenty-four indicted, fourteen receive death sentences, seven prison terms from ten years to life, one to time already served, and two are neither tried nor sentenced. Only four of the defendants are actually executed.

8   International Military Tribunal "The Hostage Case" begins; trial ends February 19, 1948.

11   The *President Warfield*, which changes its name to *Exodus 1947* while on the high seas, departs from the French port of Sete, near Marseilles, with 4,500 "illegal" immigrants on board bound for the *Yishuv*.

12   A Marshall Plan conference opens in Paris. Under Soviet pressure, East European governments reject the Plan.

12   *Irgun* members capture two British army sergeants to serve as hostages.

12   The British intercept *Exodus 1947* and bring it into Haifa harbor.

20   Australia is ready to admit 12,000 refugees, preferably from the Baltics. Jews are almost counted out.

20   A Dutch offensive attempts to recapture Indonesia.

20   The 4,500 *Exodus 1947 ma'apilim* are forcefully transferred aboard three British ships and taken back to Marseilles.

23   *Hagana* sinks a British prison ship in Haifa harbor.

26   The Central Intelligence Agency [CIA] is founded in the United States.

29   In retaliation for the hanging of Dov Gruner, the IZL hangs British Intelligence Corps sergeants Cliff Martin and Mervyn Price.

29   Refugees from the *Exodus 1947* aboard the British ships *Ocean Vigour*, *Empire Rival*, and *Runnymede Park* refuse to disembark at Marseilles.

AUGUST

1   The UN Security Council calls for cease-fire in Indonesia.

7   Nineteen former administration members of the Dora-Nordhausen concentration camp, including *SS-Obersturmfuehrer* Hans Karl Moeser, camp commandant, go on trial before a U.S. Military Tribunal.

14   International Military Tribunal "The I. G. Farben Case" begins; trial ends July 30, 1948.

15   Arab rioting breaks out in large areas of Palestine.

15   India is partitioned by Britain: India and Pakistan declare their independence.

17   The first-ever Jewish book month is celebrated in Buenos Aires.

19   An American military court at Nuremberg hands the death sentence to Dr. Karl Brandt, Hitler's personal physician, Viktor Brack, Rudolf Brandt, and Wolfram Sievers, who participated and raised funds to finance "medical" experiments.

19/27   The World Conference of *Agudas Yisroel* opens in Marienbad, Czechoslovakia.

21   The British deliver an ultimatum to *Exodus 1947* refugees that they disembark in Marseilles or face deportation to Germany.

21   Austria enacts *Wiedereinstellungsgesetz*, a law for the reinstatement of employees fired by the Nazis for political or racial reasons.

27 *SS-Brigadefuehrer* Dr. Joachim Mugrowski, chief of the *SS*-Health Institute, is sentenced to death at Nuremberg. The sentence is carried out June 2, 1948.

31 UNSCOP submits a report to the General Assembly calling for Partition of Palestine and creation of a Jewish state.

31 Communists win in Hungarian elections.

SEPTEMBER

2 An Austrian law guaranteeing favorable treatment to victims of Nazism goes into effect.

2 The Treaty of Rio de Janeiro is signed by nineteen nations.

3 The Zionist General Council meets in Zurich. The Palestine problem is foremost on its agenda.

3 The FBI uncovers a secret operation to smuggle arms from the United States to the *Yishuv.*

8 British troops forcibly remove *Exodus 1947* refugees on its arrival in Hamburg.

9 *Yishuv* holds a day of protest against the British for the forceful return to Hamburg of 4,500 Jewish Holocaust survivors aboard the *Exodus 1947.*

16 The UN General Assembly begins deliberations on the report and recommendations made by UNSCOP and sets up an Ad Hoc Committee to deal with the Palestine question.

16 The Arab League's Political Committee votes to supply men and weapons for Palestine's Arabs in the upcoming war with the Jews. The League threatens to attack the *Yishuv* if UNSCOP votes for partition.

17 International Military Tribunal "The Krupp Case" begins; trial ends April 10, 1948.

20 The British government decides to relinquish the Mandate and leave Palestine.

23 Bulgarian opposition leader Nikola Petkov is executed as a traitor by the communist-dominated government.

OCTOBER

2 Abba Hillel Silver testifies before the UN Ad Hoc Committee: the chairman of the Jewish Agency, American Section, tells the Committee that despite great sacrifices involved, he would recommend partition.

5 The Arab Liberation Army is founded by Fawzi al-Kaukji.

5 *Cominform*, the international Communist information bureau, is established in Warsaw.

7 The German Democratic Republic in the Soviet zone of occupation becomes a Communist state.

9 U.S. Secretary of Defense James Forrestal urges American business executives to speak out against "Zionist influence" in American foreign policy.

10 International Military Tribunal "The *Rasse- und Siedlungshauptamt* [RUSHA] Case" begins; trial ends March 10, 1948.

11 Ambassador Herschel V. Johnson informs the UN General Assembly that the United States will support the UNSCOP majority report.

12 The Jewish Agency Executive establishes *Va'adat ha-Matzav*, the emergency committee to prepare the *Yishuv* for statehood.

13 The Soviet Union endorses the UNSCOP partition plan.

15 The Rome Rabbinical College reopens under the leadership of Professor David Prato.

17/18 Moshe Shertok and Chaim Weizmann testify before the UN Ad Hoc Committee on Palestine.

19 Polish hooligans desecrate the Jewish cemetery in Szedliz.

19 The United Jewish Workers' Party, *Polaey Zion*, is created in Poland with the joining of the right and left wings of the Jewish Workers Socialist Party.

21 The UN General Assembly sets up a special committee on the Balkans.

29 Belgium, Holland, and Luxembourg ratify the Benelux customs union between all three countries.

30 The General Agreement of Tariffs and Trades, a UN-related agency, is established in Geneva.

31 Sixteen *SS* guards at the Sachsenhausen concentration camp are convicted of war crimes by a Soviet military court and sentenced to life in prison.

31 At a meeting in Warsaw the Polish Workers' Party takes up the activities of the reestablished Jewish communities in Poland.

NOVEMBER

3 *SS-Oberstgruppenfuehrer* Oswald Pohl, chief of the WVHA, is condemned to death at Nuremberg. The sentence is first carried out June 8, 1951.

10 The United States Military Government Law 59 on Restitution of Identifiable Property is published.

11 Golda Meir meets with Jewish Holocaust survivors imprisoned in Cyprus.

15 International Military Tribunal "The Ministry Case" begins; trial ends April 14, 1949.

19 Chaim Weizmann meets with President Truman in the White House.

22 A general conference of Jewish educators in Poland opens in Lodz.

22 A Polish court in Cracow issues the death sentence to *SS-Hauptsturmfuehrer* Professor Hans Hermann Kremer, who conducted the selections at the Auschwitz-Birkenau crematoria, Arthur Liebehenschel, commandant of Auschwitz from November 1943 to May 1944, and *SS-Hauptsturmfuehrer* Albert Schwarz, who kept the records of the Auschwitz gas-chamber selections.

25 The London Conference on Germany opens.

25 American Zionist leaders undertake an accelerated lobbying campaign to gain UN votes for the Palestine partition plan.

29 The UN General Assembly passes a resolution on the partition of Palestine into Jewish and Arab states.

30 Arab marauders attack Jewish buses on their way to Jerusalem. *Hagana* begins its first phase of operation against Arabs.

DECEMBER

1 An Arab mob attacks the Jewish quarter in Beirut, Lebanon.

1/4 The second national conference of the Revisionist-Zionist Party is held in Germany.

2 The Palestine Arab Higher Committee declares a three-day general strike, while an Arab mob attacks and burns Jerusalem's commercial center.

2 An Arab mob attacks the Jewish quarter in Aden.

4 Bulgaria establishes a Communist People's Republic.

5 The U.S. announces a total embargo on arms sales to the Middle East.

5 General strike is held in Lebanon in protest of the UN Palestine Partition Resolution.

6 Jewish defenders repel an Arab attack on Efal, killing eight of their antagonists.

9 The Jewish Agency Executive obtains from Austrian authorities the license necessary to transfer of Theodor Herzl's remains from Vienna to Jerusalem.

11 Arabs attack the Jewish quarter in the old city of Jerusalem; a Jewish convoy on the Jerusalem-Hebron road also comes under Arab fire.

12 *Hagana* forces take punitive action against the Arab village of Ramle.

15 Arab terrorists blow up the water pipeline to Jewish Jerusalem and attack a supply convoy from Tel Aviv to the children's village at Ben Shemen, murdering fourteen Jews.

17 A jury renders its decision in the court of honor against Abraham Asscher and David Cohen, finding both men guilty. Their punishments include a lifetime ban from the Jewish community.

22 A Polish court sentences twenty-one former Nazi officials at Auschwitz to death.

24 The Communist underground in Greece under general Markos Vafthiades proclaim a Free Greek Government in the northern part of the country. The Athens government outlaws the Communist party.

25 An Arab band ambushes a Jewish convoy to Jerusalem: seven Jews are killed.

25/25 Aliya Bet ships *Pan York* and *Pan Crescent* depart with 15,239 *ma'apilim* from Burgas, Bulgaria. By a prior agreement with the British, both refugee ships sail directly to Cyprus, arriving January 1, 1948.

30 Violence intensifies throughout Palestine.

30 The People's Republic of Rumania is created after King Michael is forced to abdicate.

30 International Military Tribunal "The High Command Case" begins; trial ends October 28, 1948.

1948

JANUARY

1 The *Aliya Bet* ship *Haumot Hameukhadot* (The United Nations) arrives in Nahariya.

1 *Pan York* and *Pan Crescent* arrive in Cyprus.

1 Italy adopts a new constitution.

1/30 Arabs commit forty individual attacks on Jews in Palestine, killing some ninety Jews.

9 Settlers in Kefar Szold repulse an attack by the Arab Liberation Army under the command of Fawzi al-Kaukji.

9 The five nation commission to supervise the transition of the British Mandate and the establishment of independent Jewish and Arab states holds its first discussion session.

10 The Arab Liberation Army invades Palestine.

13 The NKVD assassinates Shlomo Mikhoels, chairman of the Jewish Antifascist Committee.

16 Arab bands ambush and kill all thirty-five members of *Ha-lamed-he*, a Jewish unit of *Palmah*, on their way to reinforce the *Ezyon* Bloc.

18 Judge Joseph Meyer Proskauer, president of the American Jewish Committee, urges Truman to maintain support for the United Nations partition resolution.

21   Golda Meir arrives in Chicago on her first fundraising mission for the *Yishuv* in the United States; fifty million dollars is raised within three months for the war effort.

22   Arabs ambush and kill seven Jews outside the village of Yazur, then mutilate their bodies.

24   The death sentence issued by a Polish court in Cracow is carried out on former commandant of Auschwitz and Majdanek, *SS-Ober-sturmbannfuehrer* Arthur Liebehenschel.

26   The International Conference of Labor opens in Rome.

27   The Central Jewish Committee in Poland decides by a majority vote, to affiliate with the World Jewish Congress.

27   An official branch of *Hagana*-USA, Materials for Palestine [MFP], opens in New York City. Hundreds of items of a non-military nature are donated for the *Yishuv*.

30   Mahatma Ghandi is assassinated.

FEBRUARY

1   Elections to the Berlin Jewish *Gemeinde* (communal council) take place.

1   Arab terrorists with British help blow up *The Jerusalem Post*'s offices and press.

2   Truman presents a civil rights program to Congress.

3   Antisemites bomb the *Circulo Israelita* (Israelite Circle), the largest Jewish cultural institution in Santiago, Chile.

5   *SS-Oberfuehrer* Otto Rasch, who commanded *Einsatzgruppe C* in the Russian campaign and during the Babi Yar (Kiev) massacre, is declared unfit to plead in the *Einsatzgruppen* case.

5   The American Zionist Emergency Council holds a mass demonstration at Manhattan Center, New York City. Speakers deplore the policies of America's unsteady support for the Palestine partition resolution.

6   *SS-Oberstgruppenfuehrer* and HSSPF in Central Russia, Maximilian von Herff, is executed in Minsk {B/R SSR} by sentence of a Soviet court.

13   An Athens court hands down the death sentence to Inno Recanti and Vital Hasson, two Greek Jews accused of collaboration and betrayal to the *Gestapo* of fellow Jews during World War II.

16   The Arab Liberation Army attacks Tirath Zvi, but is defeated.

23 Ben-Yehuda Street explosion: Arab terrorist bomb kills fifty-five Jews in Jerusalem.

24 The United Nations Security Council begins to debate the use of force in Palestine.

25 President Benes yields to Soviet-inspired pressure to form a Czechoslovakian government with a Communist majority. Widespread purges under Klement Gottwald transform the country into a Soviet satellite.

26 Heavy Arab attacks are aimed at *Hadassah* Hospital and Hebrew University on Mount Scopus, Jerusalem.

27 The Action Committee for the Council of Jewish Religious Communities in Czechoslovakia forms.

27 The Allied Military Government nullifies all German court sentences passed between January 30, 1933 and May 9, 1945 on grounds of racial, political, and religious discrimination.

MARCH

5 British Forces begin to pull out from Palestine: the first 1,800 troops depart Haifa for Liverpool. Another transport with 2,000 soldiers is set to leave two days later.

8 The Hungarian Social Democratic Party agrees to fuse with the Communists.

11 An Arab bomb at the Jewish Agency building in Jerusalem kills thirteen Jews.

17 The Brussels Treaty is signed, forming a military alliance between Britain, France, Belgium, Holland, and Luxembourg.

18 Chaim Weizmann, in a private meeting with President Truman, pleads for continued American support for the Palestine partition plan.

20 The United States withdraws its support for the Partition Plan and instead proposes a temporary United Nations trusteeship regime for Palestine, until Arabs and Jews reach an agreement. Warren Austin's (the U.S. delegate to the UN) recommendations are in sharp contrast to Truman's assurances to Weizmann the day before that the United States would support partition.

20 The Soviets walk out of the Allied Control Commission for Germany.

21 Arabs ambush a Jewish bus on its way to Safed.

22 Jews manage to repulse an Arab attack on Nitzanim.

22   Abba Hillel Silver announces Zionist opposition to the American trusteeship plan for Palestine.

23   *Va'ad Leumi* warns that the *Yishuv* will oppose any attempt to prevent or postpone the proclamation of a Jewish state in Palestine after the expiration of the British Mandate.

24   Six hundred Jews picket the White House in opposition to America's trusteeship proposal for Palestine.

27   Arab Legion violence causes severe supply losses for a *Hagana* relief convoy for *Ezyon* Bloc.

29   Hungary nationalizes all of its major industrial plants.

31   The U.S. Congress passes the Marshall Aid Act.

31   Heavy fighting erupts between Jews and Arabs in Kastel.

31   The United Nations War Crimes Commission ceases operation.

APRIL

1   Soviet ground forces begin the Berlin Blockade.

1/25   Arabs accelerate their attacks on Jews in Jerusalem and its approaches.

3   *SS-Oberstgruppenfuehrer* and HSSPF in Holland, Hans Albin Rauter, is condemned to death by a special high court at The Hague.

3   *Hagana* launches Operation *Nachshon* in order to keep the road to Jerusalem open.

4   Al-Kaukji's forces launch an all-out attack on Mishmar ha-Emek, but they are repulsed and completely routed.

6   Czechoslovakia adopts an amendment to the restitution law.

6   The Soviet Union and Finland sign a treaty of mutual assistance.

6   The Zionist General Council establishes a thirty-seven member National Council to govern Palestine.

6   *Instytut Pamieci Narodowej* (Institute of National Remembrance) is created in Poland.

7   UN Security Council President Alfonso Lopez of Columbia opens Palestinian truce negotiations in New York with the Jewish Agency and Arab Higher Committee.

8   *Reichsbruderrat* (National Brethren Council of the Evangelical Church in Germany), issues a belated apology for Nazi Germany's crimes against the Jews and a manifesto against antisemitism.

9 *Hagana* recaptures Kastel; drives the Arab Liberation Army from Mishmar Ha'emek.

9 Chaim Weizmann tells President Truman the choice for Jews is either statehood or extermination.

10 The Arab League meets in Cairo.

11 Jewish forces destroy the Arab village of Kolonia outside Jerusalem.

11 Elections to the Jewish Community Council of Vienna: some 5,000 Jews cast their vote for the twenty-four member council.

13 Arab terrorists ambush a convoy of sixty-eight doctors, nurses, and academicians on their way to *Hadassah* Hospital on Mount Scopus.

13 IZL and LEHI forces capture the Arab village of Deir Yassin.

16 The United Nations General Assembly convenes in a special session. The American delegation submits, and then withdraws, Palestine Trusteeship proposal.

16 Jewish forces capture a Syrian army base at the village of Saris.

16 The Organization for European Economic Cooperation is established in Paris.

18 *Hagana* forces capture Tiberias.

18 Christian Democrats win Italian elections.

18 Social Democrats decide to join the Czechoslovakian Communist Party.

19 In the presence of many dignitaries from around the world assembled together in the Ghetto Heroes' Square, Polish Jewry commemorates the fifth anniversary of the Warsaw ghetto uprising with the unveiling of a monument to the heroic struggle, the work of sculptor Nathan Rappaport.

20 A Munich denazification court convicts former German-American Bund leader Fritz Kuhn in absentia to ten years imprisonment and confiscation of his property.

22 Operation *Misparayim*: Jewish forces capture Haifa. Most of city's 70,000 Arabs flee to Lebanon, despite urgings by *Histadrut* and *Hagana* that they remain.

22 A United States court in Nuremberg clears twenty-three I. G. Farben officials of crimes against humanity, but they are charged on crimes of plundering occupied countries.

23 The United Nations Security Council votes to establish a Palestine truce commission consisting of the United States, France, and Belgium.

23 Truman announces that the U.S. will support partition and recognize the state of Israel.

24   The British Royal Navy captures the *Mossad* ship *Nachshon*: the 553 *ma'apilim* aboard become the last refugees deported to Cyprus.

25   The Arab League prepares to invade the newborn Jewish state in Palestine.

25   *Irgun* begins a four-day attack on Arab Jaffa.

25   Vandals in Brazil burn down the Jewish communal institution in Porto Alegre.

26   Jewish forces capture Acre.

26   The *Va'ad Leumi* announces creation of a provisional cabinet in Tel Aviv.

26   *Hagana* forces capture the *Sheikh Jarrah* quarter in Jerusalem, but British troops force their withdrawal.

28   Czechoslovakia nationalizes all commercial and industrial businesses employing over fifty people.

29   *Hagana* forces launch a successful attack on the Arab-occupied Saint Simon Convent in the *Katamon* quarter of Jerusalem.

29   A Polish court in Danzig condemns Albrecht Foerster, *Gauleiter* for Danzig-West Prussia, to death by hanging for crimes against Jews.

30   The Organization of American States [OAS] Charter is signed in Bogota, Colombia.

MAY

1   The People's Committee of North Korea proclaims a People's Republic and claims authority over all of Korea.

1   Dean Rusk of the U.S. State Department asks Zionist leaders to postpone Israel's declaration of independence.

2   David Ben-Gurion issues a cease-fire order for the old quarter of Jerusalem pending negotiations of truce terms.

2   Britain sends Royal Marine commandos and additional army troops to reinforce its Palestine garrison.

2   *Hagana* forces capture the Katamon quarter of Jerusalem.

4   IZL captures the Arab village of Yahudia commanding the Tel Aviv-Lod airport highway.

4   In the name of the *Yishuv*, Ben-Gurion rebuffs the U.S. State Department request for any postponement.

4   The Soviet Communist Party charges Yugoslavia with deviating from orthodox Soviet Communism.

5 *Hagana* forces open an offensive against Arab strongholds in the Upper Galilee.

5 The Soviets tighten restrictions on the movement of goods between Berlin and the Western occupation zones.

6 A French High Court of Justice clears General Maxim Weygand of charges that he collaborated with the Nazis.

7 Winston Churchill urges creation of an assembly representing all European states.

8 Arab commanders order a cease-fire in Jerusalem.

9 The Czech parliament adopts a new constitution modeled after the Soviet Union.

10 Operation *Yiftach*: *Palmah* captures Safed in house-to-house fighting with some 3,000 Syrian and Iraqi troops.

10 Golda Meir takes a dangerous journey into Transjordan to secretly meet with King Abdullah.

12 Operation *Chametz*: Jewish forces secure Jaffa. Ninety-five percent of the city's 70,000 Arabs flee by the time the Arab Emergency Committee officially surrenders the next day.

12 The I. G. Farben trial ends after 152 trial days.

12 The Arab Legion makes its final assault on *Ezyon* Bloc.

12 The British army accelerates its withdrawal from Palestine.

12 *Hagana* units seize Bet-Shean.

12 Iraqi troops cut off Jerusalem's water supply.

12 Queen Wilhelmina of Holland announces her abdication, due to ill health.

13 The American League for a Free Palestine stages a mass rally at Madison Square Garden in New York City.

13 The Arab League in Damascus declares war on the *Yishuv*.

14 Fall of the *Ezyon* Bloc.

14 British High Commissioner Sir Allan Cunningham leaves Jerusalem. The British Mandate over Palestine is terminated.

14 David Ben-Gurion proclaims an independent Jewish state in Palestine; the combined Arab armies of the Arab League invade Israel; the United States of America recognizes the newly born state; elder Zionist statesman Dr. Chaim Weizmann is nominated as its first president.

Postscript: The World Since 1948

In a sense, May 14, 1948 represents the end of one era while also ushering in a new era. With the Second World War over and the Axis powers defeated, a new chapter of human history opened. Yet, the radical changes in Eastern and Central Europe during the late 1980s and early 1990s draw us inevitably back to the late 1940s.

Despite many high hopes, the destruction of the Axis did not result in the creation of an idyllic world. Violent confrontations, wars, and acts of political terrorism have continued, becoming increasingly costly and deadly. Although the world has been spared a direct military confrontation between the superpowers—which would inevitably lead to the destruction of all life as we know it in a massive nuclear apocalypse—a conflict of interests between the capitalist West and the Communist East did erupt. The first glimmerings of the Cold War were already visible in 1947 and 1948. Indeed, the traditional date for the beginning of the Cold War is April 1, 1948, when Soviet forces began a blockade on the parts of Berlin held by American, British, and French forces. The American-organized airlift saved West Berlin, but created the potential for a violent confrontation between Communist and non-Communist forces in Central Europe. In turn, this potential conflict spurred the creation of two military alliances: NATO and the Warsaw Pact, each attempting to gain the military and political edge over the other. As in the era before World War I, Europe was once again divided into two opposing camps, experienced a massive arms race, and prepared for war through contingency plans that included potential doomsday scenarios.

On two separate occasions the fulfillment of these doomsday scenarios appeared imminent. In 1962 U.S. Air Force reconnaissance aircraft discovered Soviet surface-to-surface ballistic missiles in Cuba. An American naval blockade convinced Soviet Premier Nikita S. Khrushchev to withdraw from the confrontation despite the suggestions by Cuba's Fidel Castro to launch an attack. Again, in October 1973, during the *Yom Kippur* War, rumors of imminent Soviet intervention to save the Egyptian Third Army from destruction brought about a massive American mobilization. This potential flashpoint for World War III was also avoided by diplomatic means.

This is not to imply that the Cold War did not, at times, spill over into direct military operations. The United States fought wars against Communism in Korea (1950-1953) and Vietnam (1964-1973). In addition, many of the wars for colonial freedom waged against Great Britain, France, and Portugal also played a role in Cold War politics, since almost invariably, the Soviet Union aided the rebel movements either directly or indirectly. Decolonization had two attractions for Soviet leaders: first, it won them new friends, thus increasing their prestige, and, second, the continuing defeats suffered by imperialist powers seemed to presage the eventual victory of Marxist-Leninist Socialism.

Two other series of wars that fall into this chronological framework were only indirectly influenced by the Cold War and imperialism. India and Pakistan—created by the partitioning of British Imperial India in 1947— have fought twice: over Kashmir (1965) and over Bangladesh (East Pakistan, 1970). Moreover, there is no guarantee that another Indo-Pakistani conflict will not break out in the near future. Similarly, the Holy Land has been the battlefield for six wars: Israel's War of Independence (1948-1949), the Sinai Campaign (1956), the Six-Day War (1967), the War of Attrition (1967-1970), the *Yom Kippur* War (1973), and Operation "Peace for Galilee" (1982). In addition, terrorist violence has been an almost daily experience for the Jewish state. Sadly, the state created as a haven and home for the tempest-tossed Jewish people did not know even one day's peace with its neighbors until 1977 when Egyptian President Anwar al-Sadat boldly traveled to Israel on a mission of peace. This brave act, which literally cost Sadat his life, has not, unfortunately, been followed up by any other Arab leader. The majority of Arab countries continue to follow the policy first enunciated at the Khartoum Conference of the Arab League in 1968: no recognition, no negotiation, and no peace with Israel.

The United Nations [UN] has been another great international disappointment as a peace-keeper. Planned as a successor for the League of Nations, the UN has not fulfilled its role as an agent of collective security. Unable to prevent any of the many wars that have been fought in the last forty-five years, the UN has also not fulfilled its moral role. Clearly, the nadir of morality was the 1975 "Zionism is Racism" resolution, designed to delegitimize the state of Israel and standing to this day as a libel against every Jew. The Iraqi invasion of Kuwait in August 1990, although not yet fully played out as of this writing, appears to presage a new UN, one which acts on the basis of morality rather than on the basis of might. At this stage the future of the UN cannot be gainsaid.

In the moral field, the fabric of the international community is less than favorable. Thousands of Nazi war criminals and as many or more of their collaborators have not been held accountable for their criminal deeds and are left to roam free forty-five years after the collapse of Nazism. Hundreds of thousands of documents detailing the misdeeds of those felons, are still crated and collecting dust in warehouses under the jurisdiction of the United Nations. Although the blood-soaked soil of Eastern Europe silently demanded justice, both the Western Powers and, to a slightly lesser extent, the Soviets and their satellites found it expedient to close their eyes to the perversion of justice. In some cases Nazis have been hunted down and belatedly brought to justice. The earliest of these was Adolf Eichmann, who was captured in Argentina by the Israeli Secret Service in 1961 and stood trial for crimes against the Jewish People in 1962. Indeed, the Eichmann trial did more to bring the Holocaust to the attention of an otherwise apathetic world than any single event until that time. Since then, the trial of Klaus Barbie in France and John (Ivan) Demjanjuk in Israel have again proved that justice has not yet been fully served. The crucial importance of such trials was proved by American President Ronald Reagan's trip to the Bitburg cemetery in Germany. Officially designed to symbolize Germany's political and moral rehabilitation, the Bitburg blunder actually lent a hand to those who would deny that the Holocaust ever happened.

Yet, writing in 1991 it is not possible to end on a note of caution. Although many dangers to humanity still exist, the student of history cannot fail to be effected by the massive changes in eastern Europe over the last two years. Where brutal Communist dictatorship once ruled, new fledgling democracies now are trying to emerge. In Hungary, Poland, and Czechoslovakia, reform movements that were once repressed, indeed were bloodily suppressed with the help of Soviet arms, the reform movements have now been embraced. If anything, these non-violent revolutions and the democratic reforms that have, in fits and starts, begun in the Soviet Union itself give cause for at least guarded optimism. Forty-six years after World War II, perhaps the idyll of a world at peace may yet come true.

Glossary

Abwehr: The German military intelligence and counter-espionage service.

Adler Tag: Day of the Eagle; term for the start of the German campaign to destroy the British Royal Air Force [RAF].

Aeltestenrat: Council of Jewish aldermen; a *Judenrat* in designated places, such as Austria or Bohemia and Moravia.

Afrika Korps [DAK]: German army corps in Africa, commanded by *Generalfeldmarschall* Erwin Rommel.

Agudas Yisroel: Union of Israel; non-Zionist Orthodox party founded in Katowice in 1912.

Ahdut ha-Yishuv: Unity of the Settlement; a Zionist and non-Zionist political association in Palestine.

Akademie fuer deutsches Recht: Academy for German Law, founded by Hans Frank in 1933.

Aktion/Aktionen: Anti-Jewish operation(s); roundup of Jews for deportation to extermination sites and/or slave labor camps.

Aliya: Immigration to Israel.

Aliya Bet: Immigration to Palestine without an immigrant certificate; "illegal" immigration.

Aliya Chadasha: The New Aliya; a political party of Central European Jews in Palestine established in 1942.

Allemane: Lit. "German"; a Nazi propaganda sheet in the French language.

Alliance Israelite Universelle: World Israelite Alliance; French based, world Jewish philanthropic and educational organization founded May 1860.

Altneu: The Old-New Synagogue in Prague built toward the beginning of the thirteenth century.

Altreich: The old Reich; pertaining to pre-*Anschluss* Germany.

A Magyar Nemzeti Szocialista Party: The Hungarian National Socialist Party, founded in 1937.

Annex: Building in Amsterdam where Anne Frank, her family, and friends lived in hiding until discovered by the *Gestapo*.

Anschluss: The unification of Austria with Germany on March 13, 1938.

Antisemitenbund: Antisemitic Association; an Austrian antisemitic organization.

Arbeitsamt fuer Judenarbeiter: Labor Exchange for Jewish Workers; Nazi imposed agency to draft German Jewish workers established in 1942.

Arbeitsdienst: Labor service; all aryans within Greater Germany were obligated to perform labor service for the state.

Arbeitseinsatz: A special work commando.

Arbeitserziehungslager(n): Work education camp(s); a camp category within the framework of the Nazi concentration camp system.

Arbeitsgemeinschaft: A committee to coordinate the reconstituted Jewish communities in post-Hitler Germany.

Arbeitslager(n): Labor camp(s); a camp category within the framework of the Nazi concentration camp system.

Arbeitspflicht: Work obligation; a Nazi decree imposing labor conscription for all Poles in the General Government.

Arbeitsscheinen: Labor permits; a sometimes temporary certificate of life for Jews in the eastern European ghettos.

Arbeitsschlacht: War on unemployment; an objective of Hitler.

Arisierung: Aryanization; the forceful takeover of Jewish enterprices and properties.

Armja Krajowa [AK]: Home Army; the underground of the Polish government-in-exile, officially established in 1942. AK had antisemitic overtones.

Asefat ha-Nivharim: Jewish legislative assembly of the *Yishuv* founded in 1922 and comprising seventy-one members.

Ashkenazi(m): Jews living in and originating from northern Europe.

Asocial: Category of prisoners in Nazi concentration camps which included homosexuals, prostitutes, pimps, thiefs, vagrants, drunkards, and persons unwilling to work; Gypsies were also included in this category.

Association des juifs en Belgique [AJB]: The Association of Jews in Belgium; a German imposed council established in 1941.

Ausbuergerungsliste: Denaturalization list that applied to eastern European Jews who had aquired German citizenship and who were denaturalized by Nazi law and put on a list for possible deportation.

Ausserordentliche Befriedungsaktion [ABA]: Extraordinary Tranquilizing Operation, applied to the Polish and Jewish intelligentsia.

Aussiedlungsaktion(en): Resettlement action(s); a Nazi term for the liquidation of Jewish communities and their deportations to specially built death camps or extermination sites.

Aussperrmauer: Lit. "outside wall"; the outside wall of a Nazi-created ghetto (usually in the larger communities) which separated the Jews from the rest of the population.

Avodath Hakodesh: Sacred Service; a musical composition for Reform temple service.

Beauftragter des Fuehrers: Representative of the *Fuehrer*; official ideologue of the NSDAP.

Befehl: An order or command.

Bene Israel: Sons of Israel; Cochin Jews or the Jewish community in India.

Berufsbeamtengesetz: German Law for the Restoration of the Professional Civil Service.

Beta Israel: *Falasha* Jewish community in Ethiopia.

Bet Ha-midrash: House of Learning; a place for study and prayer.

Betreibsfuehrer Erlass: General Manager Decree; a Nazi law replacing all Jewish-owned enterprises with aryan managers.

Bevollmaechtigte fuer den Arbeitseinsatz: Plenipotentiary for Labor Recruitment.

Bevollmaechtigte fuer die Bandenbekampfung in Osten: Plenipotentiary for the Combating of Bandits in the East.

Biuletyn Kroniki Codziennej: Daily Chronicle Bulletin; a Polish language news bulletin issued in the Lodz ghetto.

Blitzkrieg: Lightning war; a Nazi term for their rapid conquest of Europe utilizing armored forces with overpowering air support.

B'nai B'rith: Worldwide Jewish social organization founded in the United States, November 1, 1843.

Brennkommando (s): Arson squad(s); SD special detachment units whose main function was to incinerate and burn down synagogues and other Jewish communal institutions in Nazi-occupied eastern Europe.

Breslauer Judengemeindeblatt: Breslau Jewish community paper.

Bricha: Escape; a movement to foster "illegal" emigration of the remnants of the Jewish communities from eastern Europe, with the ultimate goal of bringing them to the Jewish national home in Palestine.

Brigadefuehrer: Major-General; an *SS* rank.

Brit ha-Biryonim: Lit. "Covenant of Terrorists"; a secret Revisionist Zionist organization in mandatory Palestine, the term derives from a group of Jewish terrorists in action against the Romans during Roman occupation of Judea (first century BCE).

Brith Trumpeldor [BETAR]: Activist Zionist youth movement associated with HA-ZOHAR, founded by Vladimir (Zeev) Jabotinsky in 1923.

Brit-Yeshurun: An organization of Jewish Displaced Persons in postwar Germany.

Buergerbrau Kellar: Lit. "Citizen-brewery Cellar"; a favorite Nazi tavern in Munich frequented by Hitler and top echelons of the NSDAP.

Bund: A worldwide German pro-Nazi party.

Bund: The General Jewish Workers Union of Lithuania, Poland, and Russia; the Jewish Marxist nationalist party founded October 4, 1897.

Bund Schweitzer Juden: Union of Swiss Jews founded in 1933.

Canton: A geographical and political unit; a state within the Swiss confederacy.

Causo Belli: A belligerent act.

Centralei Evreilor din Romania: Center for Jews in Rumania; a government-imposed council established in 1941.

Centralverein Deutscher Staatsbuerger Juedischen Glaubens [CV]: Central Organization of German Citizens of the Jewish Faith, founded in 1893.

Centralverein Zeitung: Newspaper published by the CV.

Centrici: Guerrilla unit established in 1941 by Yugoslav Colonel Draza Mihailovic, which eventually crystalized into the *Chetniks*.

Chef Oberkommando der Wehrmacht [OKW]: The High Command of the German Armed Forces.

Chelmner Naroonim: Lit. "the fools of Chelm"; a small Jewish community in Poland, famous for its folklore.

Clausenists: Pro-Nazi members of the Danish government.

Cominform: International Communist Information Bureau.

Comintern: Communist International.

Comisia Autonoma de Ajutorare: A refugee aid committee for Jews in Rumania founded in 1941.

Comite de Defense des Juifs: Jewish Defense Committee; a Belgian Jewish underground movement established in 1942.

Commissariat-General aux Questions Juives: General Commissariat for the Jewish Question; an office established in 1941 to deal with the Jewish question in Vichy France.

Commission Centrale des Organisations Juives d'Assistance [CCOJA]: Central Commission of Jewish Organizations for Assistance; a French Jewish umbrella organization established in 1940.

Conducator: Lit. "The Leader"; title of Rumanian dictator Ion Antonescu.

Conseil National de la Resistance: National Council of the French Underground established in 1942.

Consistoire Central des Israelites de France: Central Jewish Consistory of France; an organization responsible for overseeing Franco-Jewish religious life, founded in 1808.

Cortes: The Spanish parliament.

Cuzist: Rumanian Fascists, followers of Alexander Cuza.

Daf Yomi: Lit. "daily page"; an international movement for the study of the 39 tractates of the *Talmud*—a page a day.

Dak: The Irish parliament.

Das Sowjetparadies: The Soviet Paradise; an anti-Communist and anti-Jewish exhibit sponsored by Goebbels' propaganda ministry in Berlin.

De Geus onder Studenten: A Dutch student underground paper.

Der Emes: The Truth; a Soviet Communist *Yiddish* language newspaper.

Der Ewige Jude: The Eternal Jew; an antisemitic film and a Nazi anti-Jewish exhibition promoted by Julius Streicher.

Der Israelit: The Israelite; a journal of the Orthodox German Jewish party *Agudas Yisroel*.

Der Stuermer: Weekly Nazi newspaper published by Julius Streicher.

Der Tog: The Day; a Rumanian *Yiddish* daily newspaper.

Deutsch Amerikanische Wirtschaftsauschuss: German American Protective Alliance; a pro-Nazi organization, founded in 1933.

Deutsche Arbeitsfront [DAF]: German Labor Front; an NSDAP-affiliated organization founded in 1933 from the ranks of former labor unions, guilds, and professional associations led by Robert Ley.

Deutscher Suedwest-Bund: German South-West Association; a pro-Nazi party in South Africa, founded in 1937.

Deutscher Strafanstalt: German penal institution.

Deutsche Volkskirche: German People's Church; the official Nazi church, founded in 1937.

Die Bruecke: The Bridge; a German-language pro-Nazi newspaper published in the United States.

Die Deutsche Tribuene: The German Tribune; an anti-Nazi German language paper published in Sao Paulo, Brazil.

Die Leitung: Lit. "The Leadership"; a term for the Terezin {Cz} ghetto committee of three.

Die Rundschau: The Review; a Sudeten German pro-Nazi paper.

Diet: The Slovak parliament.

Difesa della Razza: Defense of the Race; an Italian journal on the racial question.

Durchgangslager(n): Transit camp(s); a camp category within the framework of the Nazi concentration camp system.

Eingegliederten Ostgebiete: Incorporated eastern territories.

Einikeit: Unity; a *Yiddish*-language periodical published by the Jewish Anti-Fascist Committee in the Soviet Union.

Einsatz des Juedischen Vermoegens: Decree Regarding Jewish Property, leading to complete aryanization.

Einsatz Erntefest: Operation Harvest Festival; a Nazi term for the liquidation and slaughter of the remaining Jews in the Lublin area slave labor camps that served as the headquarters for the *Einsatz Reinhard* campaign.

Einsatzgruppe(n): Mobile operational group(s) or task force(s) made up from units of the *Gestapo, Kriminalpolizei* (Criminal Police) and the *Sicherheitsdienst* [SD] (Security Service) of the *SS* entrusted to carry out the Final Solution in large areas of occupied eastern Europe. Each *Einsatzgruppe* was composed of up to six *Einsatzkommandos*.

Einsatzkommando(s): A detachment of an *Einsatzgruppe*.

Einsatz Reinhard: Operation Reinhard; a code name for the extermination of the Jews in the General Government (Poland), named after Reinhard Heydrich. For this operation three extermination camps—Belzec, Sobibor, and Treblinka—were established, and between March 1942 and November 1943 over 2,000,000 victims were dispatched by rail to these death camps at a constant pace. Some Jews from other parts of Nazi-occupied Europe were also brought there (especially to Sobibor) to be murdered.

Einsatzstab: Special Operational Staff.

Einsatzstab Reichsleiter Rosenberg [ERR]: The Operational Staff of State Leader Alfred Rosenberg, founded in 1940.

Einsatz Tannenberg: Operation Tannenberg; code name for the terror campaign against Polish intellectuals (Jews and non-Jews alike) in September 1939.

Emcol: The Jewish Emigration and Colonization Association.

Endeks/Endekcja: The Polish National Democratic party, founded in 1894.

Endloesung der Judenfrage: The Final Solution of the Jewish Question; a Nazi term for the physical destruction of the Jewish people in Europe.

Erbhoefe: German law regarding hereditary domains.

Ermaechtigungsgesetz: The Enabling Act.

14 F 13 Erlass: Nazi code name for the extermination of European Jewry.

Falange: A Spanish Fascist paramilitary organization.

Fall Gelb: Case Yellow; German plans for the invasion of the Low Countries.

Fall Gruen: Case Green; Hitler's plan for an attack on Czechoslovakia.

Fall Manstein: Case Manstein; the *Wehrmacht* operational plan for the attack on the West.

Fall Weiss: Case White; Hitler's plan for the invasion of Poland.

Faraynikte Partizaner Organizacje [FPO]: United Partisan Organization; the Jewish underground in Lithuania, founded in the Vilna ghetto in 1942.

Federatia Unionilor de Counitati Evreesti: The Union of Jewish Communities in Rumania, founded in 1910.

Federation des Societes Juives de France [FSJF]: Federation of Jewish Societies in France, established in 1913.

Forces Francaises de l'Interieur: French Forces of the Interior; the official name of the combined French resistance movements in 1944, led by Jean Moulin.

Forschungsabteilung Judenfrage: Research Department on the Jewish Question; a German agency founded in 1936.

Forteresse Juive: The Jewish Fortress; a rescue oriented Jewish underground movement in Nazi-occupied France, founded in 1940.

Freiheitsbund: Freedom Association; an Austrian Fascist and antisemitic paramilitary movement, founded in 1928.

Front Populaire: Popular Front; an anti-Nazi coalition government between French Socialists and Communists led by Leon Blum, established March 13, 1938.

Fuehrer: Leader: a term specifically applied to Hitler.

Garda de Fier: Iron Guard; a Rumanian Fascist organization, established in 1927.

Gau: District; a political and geographical unit in Nazi Germany.

Gauleiter: District leader; regional Nazi party boss.

Gazeta Polska: Polish Journal; semi-governmental newspaper, often publishing articles with an antisemitic overtone.

Gazeta Warszawska: Warsaw Journal; a major Polish daily.

Geheime Staatspolizei [Gestapo]: The Secret State Police established in 1933 by Goering. In 1939 the *Gestapo* became *Amt IV* of the RSHA.

Gelbe Flecke: Yellow badge; a term coined by Robert Weltsch, editor of the *Juedische Rundschau*, "Bear it with pride, the yellow badge!" A terminology for the yellow badge that Jews were ordered to wear in Nazi Europe.

Gemeinde: Communal council; a municipality.

Generalgevollmaechtigte fuer den Arbeitseinsatz: Plenipotentiary for Labor Recruitment.

Generalgouvernement: General Government; Administrative unit of those parts of occupied Poland not incorporated into the *Reich*.

Generalgouverneur: General Governor; title of Hans Frank, the head of the Nazi civilian administration in occupied Poland.

Generalkommissar: General Commissioner.

Generalleutnant: Lieutenant-General; a German military rank.

Generaloberst: Colonel-General; a German military rank.

Gerer Rebbe: *Hasidic* rabbi of Gur {P}, Rabbi Yitchok Meyer Alter.

Gericht: A court of law.

Gesamtaussiedlung: Total deportation.

Gesamtloesung: Total solution to the Jewish problem.

Gesetz gegen der Ueberfuellung von Deutscher Schulen und Hochschulen: Law for Preventing Overcrowding in German Schools and Institutions of Higher Learning.

Gesetz zum Schutze des deutschen Blutes und der deutschen Ehre: Law for the Protection of German Blood and German Honor.

Geto fun leben: Ghetto of life; a *Yiddish* term coined under the illusion that Jews working for the Germans would be allowed to live.

Geto fun toyit: Ghetto of death; this *Yiddish* term applied to numerous ghettos—large and small—where starved, cold, and sick Jews were kept awaiting deportation to the death camps or extermination sites.

Gettoverwaltung: The Nazi ghetto administration which oversaw the Polish ghettos.

Gleichschaltung: Coordination; Nazi term for the recasting of German society.

Glowna Komisja Badania Zbrodni Hitlerowskich w Polsce: Polish Government Commission to Investigate Nazi Crimes in Poland, established in 1945.

Granatowa Policja: Lit. "blue police"; the Polish police force that collaborated with the Nazis in occupied Poland, especially in connection with the roundup campaigns of single Jews or entire Jewish communities for extermination.

Grossaktion: Large Operation; Nazi term for the final liquidation of the larger east European ghettos.

Grossreich: Greater Germany; pertaining to Germany in its wartime borders.

Gruppenfuehrer: Lieutenant-General; an *SS* rank; most Nazi *Gauleiters* carried the rank of *Gruppenfuehrer*.

Gulden: Basic unit of Danzig currency.

Haavara: Transfer; agreement signed between Nazi Germany and the *Yishuv* in September 1933 to enable the transfer of a small percentage of Jewish capital to Palestine in the form of German goods.

Hachnasat Orechim: Hospitality Society for the Maintaining of the Needy.

Hachshara: Agricultural training programs for young immigrants to Palestine.

Hadassah: Women's Zionist Philanthropic Organization founded by Henrietta Szold in 1912.

Hagana: Lit. "defense"; the primary Zionist underground movement in Mandatory Palestine, founded in 1920.

Hagibor: The Mighty; a German Jewish sports organization.

Halacha: Law; religious law mandatory on all Jews.

Ha-Oved ha-Ziyyoni: The Zionist Worker; a General Zionist youth pioneer labor movement, founded in 1935.

Ha-Poel: Labor Zionist youth group.

Ha-Poel Hamizrachi: A religious Zionist labor movement, founded in 1921.

Haret El-Yahud: The Jewish quarter of Cairo.

Hasidim/Hasidic: Jewish mystical-pietistic religious movement arising in eighteenth-century eastern Europe.

Ha-Shomer ha-Zair: Young Watchmen; a Zionist Socialist party, founded in 1916.

Hatikvah: The Hope; the Zionist Jewish national anthem.

Hativa Yehudit Lohemet: Jewish Brigade Group; the only independent national Jewish military formation in World War II, established in 1944.

Hauptamt: Main Office; *e.g.* the *SS* administrative department.

Hauptsturmfuehrer: Captain; an *SS* rank.

Havlaga: Self-restraint; the defensive policy pursued by the *Hagana* during the 1930s.

Hazit Dor Bnei Midbar [HDBM]: Front of the Wilderness Generation; a Zionist youth movement in the Lodz ghetto, founded in 1940.

He-Halutz: Pioneer; Zionist pioneering youth movement associated with MAPAI.

He-Halutz ha-Lohem: The Fighting Pioneer; a Jewish underground in Cracow.

Heimwehr: Home Defense; an Austrian Fascist anti-Nazi militia, established in 1918.

Hilfsverein der deutschen Juden: Relief Organization of German Jews, established in 1901.

Hirdmen: Norwegian storm troopers, founded in 1934.

Histadrut: General Workers Union of Israel, founded in 1920.

Histadrut ha-Ovdim ha-Leumim: Nationalist Labor Federation, associated with HA-ZOHAR, founded in 1934.

Histadrut ha-Zionit ha-Hadasha [HA-ZACH]: The New Zionist Organization, created when HA-ZOHAR withdrew from the World Zionist Organization in 1935.

Hitahdut ha-Zionim ha-Revisionistim [HA-ZOHAR]: Union of Zionist Revisionist, founded by Vladimir (Zeev) Jabotinsky in 1925.

Hitachdut Olei Germania ve-Austria: Association of German and Austrian Immigrants, established in Palestine in 1932.

Hitachdut Olei Polonia: Union of Polish Immigrants; a Palestinian friendly society founded in 1936.

Hitlerjugend: Hitler Youth; a Nazi youth organization, founded in 1922.

Hlinka(s): Slovakian Fascist militia organized on the *SS* lines and named after its founder, Andrej Hlinka.

Hochschule fuer die Wissenschaft des Judentums: Graduate School for the Scientific Study of Judaism; a Reform rabbinical seminary in Berlin, founded in 1867.

Hoeherer SS und-Polizeifuehrer [HSSPF]: Higher *SS* and Police Leader; senior commander in a *Wehrkreis* (military district) and Himmler's liason with the *Wehrmacht*.

I. G. Farbenindustrie: A German chemical concern; large plants were established in the major concentration camps (especially in Buna or Auschwitz III) which took advantage of unlimited slave labor supplied by the *SS* administration for pennies a day.

Ifico: The Palestine Fund for Industrial Development, founded in 1934.

Ihud: Unity; a coalition of Socialist Zionist parties, established in 1942.

Il Duce: Official title for Benito Mussolini.

Il Popolo di Roma: The People of Rome; an Italian periodical.

Il Popolo Italiano: The Italian People; a major Italian daily newspaper.

Il Regime Fascista: The Fascist Regime; an Italian Fascist periodical.

Informazione Diplomatica: Diplomatic Information; journal of the Italian foreign ministry.

Institut der NSDAP zur Erforschung der Judenfrage: Nazi Institute to Research the Jewish Question, founded in 1939.

Institut d'Etude des Questions Juives: A French institute for the study of the Jewish question, established in 1941. It was replaced in 1943 by the *Institut d'Etudes des Questions Juives et Ethno-Raciales*.

Institut fuer deutsch Ostarbeit: Institute for German Work; a Nazi institution created in occupied Poland in 1940.

Instytut Pamieci Narodowej: Polish Institute of National Remembrance, established in 1948.

Integralistas: Brazilian pro-Nazi party.

Internationale Vereinigung Ernster Bibelforscher: The International Association of Serious Bible Researchers, better known as the Jehovah's Witnesses, its German branch was established in 1927.

Irgun Zvai Leumi [IZL]: National Military Organization; underground group that seceded from the *Hagana* in 1931, becoming fully independent in 1937.

Israelitische Kultusgemeinde: The Viennese Jewish community, founded in 1890.

Joodse Raad: Jewish Council; a Nazi imposed *Judenrat* in Holland, created in 1941.

Joodse Weekblad: The Jewish Weekly; the officially approved Jewish newspaper in Holland.

Jordan-Shaynen: A temporary "life-saving" certificate, 5,000 of these were handed out by the Jewish council in the Kovno ghetto.

Judenaeltester: Elder of the Jews; chairman of a *Judenrat* or *Aeltestenrat*.

Judenarbeitslager(n): Jewish work camp(s); up until 1944 most of the small Jewish labor camps in eastern Europe were not a part of the Nazi concentration camp system.

Judenbeguenstigung: "Be kind to Jews," lending a hand in whatever way to aid Jews, was a crime punishable by death.

Judenfrei/Judenrein(igung): Free of Jews; term applies to a given locality from which Jews were forcefully removed, usually to be killed or to perish in slave labor camps.

Judenrat/Judenraete: Nazi-imposed Jewish community council(s) in eastern Europe.

Judenstern: Jewish star; term applies to the yellow Star of David, identifying the bearer as a Jew.

Judenzwangsarbeitslager(n): Forced labor camp(s) for Jews.

Juedische Jugendhilfe: The agency overseeing Youth *Aliya*, established in 1933.

Juedische Kulturbund: Jewish Cultural Society; an association to promote culture and the arts among Jews in Germany, founded in 1933.

Juedischer Frauenbund: German Jewish Women's Association, founded in 1904.

Juedischer Ordnungsdienst: A term for Jewish police orderlies in the larger ghettos of eastern Europe.

Juedische Rundschau: Jewish Review; a German Zionist newspaper.

Juedischer Wohnbezirk: Jewish living quarter; a Nazi term for a ghetto.

Juedisches Nachrichtenblatt/Zidovske Listy: Jewish weekly in the Protectorate of Bohemia and Moravia, approved by the *Gestapo*, and printed in the German and Czech languages.

Jungreformatorische Bewegung: Protestant youth group founded in Germany by Martin Neimoeller in 1933.

Kamusay: The Turkish Grand National Assembly; parliament.

Karaite/Karaites: Sectarian Jews (identified by the Nazis as aryans), largely living in areas of the Soviet Union.

Kashrut/Kosher: Jewish dietary laws.

Katholic Bureau voor Israel: Catholic Office for Jews; a Belgian organization whose aim was to eliminate antisemitism.

Kehilla(s): The organized Jewish community, or the council running the community.

Kenkarte(n): Identification card(s).

Keren ha-Torah: Fundraising organization to foster religious education among American Jews, founded in 1942.

Keren Hayesod: Palestine Settlement Fund, founded in 1897.

Keren Kayemeth l'Israel [KKL]: The Jewish National Fund, founded in 1897.

Kibbutz: Zionist communal settlement(s) in Israel.

Kofer ha'Yishuv: Defense Fund; a voluntary tax in the *Yishuv* for the benefit of the *Hagana*.

Kolchoz(i): Collective farm(s) in the Soviet Union.

Kol Israel: The Voice of Israel; a clandestine *Hagana* radio station in mandatory Palestine.

Komitet Koordinacny [KK]: Coordinating Committee; a committee to coordinate all Jewish underground activities in the Warsaw ghetto.

Kommandatura: The four-power military government in Berlin.

Kommandobefehl: A Hitler decree for the immediate execution of captured Allied commandos.

Kommissarbefehl: Commissar Order; a document issued by the OKW on Hitler's specific orders (distributed to senior commanders only), entailing general instructions for the treatment of political commissars. This order legalized the Nazi slaughter of all Bolshevik agitators, saboteurs, partisans, Jews, and all those not considered worthy of life (according to Nazi ideology). In addition, the complete elimination of every active or passive resistance in occupied Soviet territories was officially approved.

Komunistische Partei Deutschland [KPD]: The German Communist Party.

Konzentrationslager(n) [KL]: Concentration camp(s).

Koumintang: Chinese Nationalist government under Chiang Kai-shek.

Kraft durch Freude: Strength Through Joy; a Nazi-controlled recreational organization, founded in 1933.

Krajowa Rada Narodowa: The Polish National Council; a Polish pro-Communist organization with quasi-governmental powers.

Kriegsakademie: The German military academy.

Krimchaks: Tatar-speaking Jews living primarily in the Crimea.

Kristallnacht: Night of the Broken Glass; the first systematic Nazi anti-Jewish pogrom throughout Germany and Austria on the night of November 9/10, 1938.

Krone(n): Basic unit of Slovakian currency.

Kultusrat: Community council.

Kurfurstendam: Berlin's main business district.

La Comite National de Secours aux Refugies: Central Committee for Aid to Refugees; a non-sectarian organization in France, established in 1933.

L'Action Catholique: The Catholic Action; a French Canadian anti-Jewish newspaper published in Quebec.

La Libre Belge: Free Belgium; a Belgian Catholic daily.

Landtag: The legislature of a German state.

Lebenshaynen: Life certificates; a valid working card, proof that one is usefully employed.

Lebensraum: Living space; the ideological justification for German expansion into eastern Europe.

Legion Kondor: The Condor Legion; a unit of the *Luftwaffe* operational in Spain during the civil war.

Lei: Basic unit of Rumanian currency.

Leibstandarte-SS Adolf Hitler: Hitler's *SS* bodyguard unit, founded in 1933 and expanded to a division of the *Waffen-SS* in 1940.

Le Pays Reel: Belgian Rexist antisemitic and racist party journal.

Lietuviu Aktyvistu Frontas: Lithuanian Activist Front; a nationalist, Fascist and antisemitic organization established in 1940.

Lietuvos Aidas: The Lithuanian government newspaper.

Lohamei Herut Israel [LEHI]: Fighters for the Freedom of Israel; a splinter group of the IZL, established in 1940, also known as the "Stern Gang."

Luftwaffe: The German air force.

Luxemburger Freiheit: Luxembourg Freedom; a pro-Nazi German language newspaper in the principality of Luxembourg.

Ma'apilim: Strivers; "illegal" Jewish immigrants to Palestine.

Maccabee: An international Jewish sports organization.

Machzike Hadas: International organization to strengthen the Jewish faith which also oversaw synagogues in Belgium, Holland, and Great Britain, founded in 1879.

Manifesto degli scienziatti razzisti: Manifesto of the Racial Scientists, an Italian antisemitic publication.

Masada: Nationwide American Zionist youth movement, founded in 1933.

Matzoh: Unleavened bread eaten on Passover.

Membres du Service d'Orde: Internal Jewish police force at Drancy {F} *durchgangslager*, established in 1942.

Messagero: Messenger; Judeo-Spanish daily published in Salonika.

Mifleget Poale Eretz Israel [MAPAI]: The Israel Labour Party, founded in 1930.

Milice: A French Fascist paramilitary organization which collaborated with the Nazis.

Mischling(e): Nazi term for persons of mixed Jewish and non-Jewish parentage.

Mit Brenender Sorge: "With Burning Sorrow"; a papal encyclical dealing with the Catholic Church in Germany.

Mizrachi: World union of religious Zionists, founded in 1902.

Mossad Bialik: The Bialik Institute; founded in 1934 to commemorate the Jewish national poet, Chaim Nachman Bialik.

Mosad le-Aliya Bet: Organization for Illegal Immigration, an *Hagana* rescue agency founded in 1937.

Nacht und Nebel Erlass: Night and Fog Decree; A Nazi policy designed to eliminate members of the resistance.

Nacion: Nation; a Spanish monarchist newspaper.

National Komitee Freies Deutschland: The National Committee for a Free Germany; a pro-Communist organization founded in Moscow, in 1943.

Nationalrat: The Austrian parliament.

National Socialiste Volken en Vaderland: Belgian Nazi antisemitic publication.

National Socialistisch Beweging [NSB]: The Dutch Nazi party, founded by Anton Mussert in 1931.

Nationalsozialistische Deutsche Arbeiterpartei [NSDAP]: The National Socialist (Nazi) German Workers Party, founded in 1920.

Nemzet Szava: Nation's Voice; official mouthpiece of Hungarian Nazis.

NKVD: People's Commissariat of Internal Affairs; the Soviet secret police.

Nyilaskeresztes Part: Arrow Cross; a Hungarian pro-Nazi Fascist party.

Oberfuehrer: Brigadier-General; an *SS* rank.

Obergruppenfuehrer: Lieutenant-General; an *SS* rank.

Oberjude: Head Jew; eldest of the Jews.

Oberstgruppenfuehrer: Colonel-General; an *SS* rank.

Obersturmbannfuehrer: Lieutenant-Colonel; an *SS* rank.

Obersturmfuehrer: First Lieutenant; an *SS* rank.

Oboz Narodowa Radicalny [NARA]: National Radical Union; a Polish antisemitic party, founded in 1934.

Oboz Zjednoczenia Narodowego [OZN]: Camp of National Unity; a Polish government bloc, founded in 1937.

Obshcheestvo Rasprostraneniya Truda Sredi Yevreyev [ORT]: Organization for Rehabilitation and Training; a worldwide Jewish vocational training and philanthropic organization, founded in 1880.

Oesterreichischer Beobachter: Austrian Observer; leading Austrian Nazi daily newspaper.

Olim: Persons who immigrate to Palestine.

Oorlogspleep-kinderenbureau [OPK]: A Dutch office for foster children in Holland.

Operation Chametz: Lit. "leaven"; a *Hagana* operation (that coincided with the feast of Passover, when *chametz* is eliminated from the Jewish diet) to isolate Arab Jaffa and to open a road to Lydda airport, which ended with the capture of Jaffa.

Operation Misparayim: Lit. "scissors"; a *Hagana* plan for the capture of the whole of Haifa.

Operation Yiftach: A *Palmah* plan to capture key positions in the Upper Galilee. The operation was named after the biblical Judge Jephtah.

Ordnungspolizei: Lit. "Order Police"; the German uniformed police, firemen, and certain other auxiliary services.

Organizacja Bojowa Zydowskiej Mlodziecy Chalucowej: A Zionist-oriented pioneering Jewish underground organization in Cracow, established in 1942.

Orhanizatsyia Ukrainskych Natsionalistiv [OUN]: Organization of Ukrainian Nationalists; an anti-Soviet Ukrainian movement founded in 1920.

Osservatore Romano: Roman Observer; the Vatican daily newspaper.

Ostindustrie GMBH [OSTI]: An *SS* conglomorate of industrial enterprises in Poland, exploiting thousands of (mostly) Jews through slave labor.

OZET: The organization for Jewish agricultural settlement in the Ukraine and Crimea, founded in 1924.

Palcor: Palestine Correspondents Agency, founded in 1934.

Peitsche und Zucker: The "Whip and Sugar"; Nazi policy against the Czech population in the Protectorate of Bohemia and Moravia.

Peluggot Mahaz [PALMAH]: Assault companies; *Hagana*'s mobile strike force, founded in 1940.

Perkonkrust: The Latvian Fascist and Antisemitic Party.

Pfarrernotbund: Pastors' Emergency League; a liberal anti-Nazi union of German pastors, founded in 1933.

Piaski: The "Sands"; a nickname for an execution site outside the city of Lvov, where thousands of victims were slaughtered.

Pidyon Shevuim: Redemption of Captives; a fund created by the *Va'ad Leumi* in 1939.

Poalei Agudas Yisroel [PAY]: Non-Zionist religious workers party founded in Lodz {P} in 1922.

Poalei Zion: The United Zionist Workers Party, founded in 1903.

Polizeihaftlager: Police internment camp; a camp category within the framework of the Nazi concentration camp system.

Polizeiliches Durchgangslager: Police transit camp, usually under *Gestapo* supervision; a camp category within the framework of the Nazi concentration camp system.

Polska Partia Robotnicza [PPR]: The Polish Workers Party; a cover name for the Polish Communist Party re-established as an underground group in 1942.

Polska Partia Socialisticzna [PPS]: The Polish Socialist Party, founded in 1892.

Pracovna Skupina: The Working Group; a Jewish semi-underground organization to help rescue Jews in Slovakia, founded in 1942.

Purim: Lots; Jewish springtime religious festival commemorating the victory of the Jews in the Persian Empire over the evil Haman who conspired to destroy them.

Quisling: A term for a traitor, a collaborator with the Nazis; term was adopted from the Norwegian traitor, Vidkum Quisling.

Rada Jednosci Narodowej: Polish council of national unity.

Rada Pomocy Zydom [Zegota]: Council for Aid to Jews; an organization established in Poland with the participation of the Polish government-in-exile in London.

Rasse-und Siedlungshauptamt [RuSHA]: *SS* Central Office for Race and Settlement; an office for racial purity in line with Nazi ideology.

Ratnizi: A Bulgarian pro-Nazi party.

Razzia: Lit. "raid"; a Fascist term for a roundup.

Reich: The State.

Reichsbank: The German National Bank.

Reichsbishop: The head of the Nazi church in Germany.

Reichsbruderrat: National Brethren Council of the Evangelical Church in Germany.

Reichsbuergergesetz: *Reich* Citizenship Law.

Reichsdeutsche: *Reich* German; a Nazi propaganda sheet.

Reichsfuehrer-SS und Chef der Deutschen Polizei: Leader of the *SS* and Chief of the German Police; Heinrich Himmler's title as of June 1936.

Reichsinstitut: Government-sponsored institutions.

Reichsinstitut fuer Geschichte des neuen Deutschlands: *Reich* Institute for the History of the New Germany; an institution with a primary aim to re-write the history of Germany in light of Nazi ideology and dogma, founded in 1935.

Reichskommissar: State Commissioner.

Reichskommissar fuer die Festigung des deutschen Volkstums [RKFVD]: Reich Commissioner for the Consolidation of German Nationhood; an office for the resettlement of German nationals in eastern European occupied areas, founded in 1939.

Reichskommissariat Ostland: German civil administration in occupied Russia, with the exception of the Ukraine.

Reichskulturkammergesetz: Law for the establishment of a state chamber of culture.

Reichsmark: Basic unit of German currency.

Reichsmarschall: State Marshal; rank of Nazi leader and *Luftwaffe* commander Hermann Goering.

Reichsprotector: Nazi regional leader in occupied territories.

Reichssicherheitshauptamt [RSHA]: State Security Main Office; an *SS* agency founded by Reinhard Heydrich in 1939, combining the *Sicherheitsdienst* [SD], *Gestapo*, and *Kripo*; it served both as the *Hauptamt* (Central Office) of the *SS* and the German Ministry of the Interior. Its major task was the implementation of the Final Solution.

Reichsstatthalter: District (*Gau*) governor, frequently identical to a Nazi Party *Gauleiter*.

Reichsstatthaltergesetz: Law concerning district governors in Germany.

Reichsstelle fuer Raumordnung: State Agency for Space Arrangement, established in Germany in 1933.

Reichstag: German parliament.

Reichsverband juedische Kulturbuende: *Reich* Association of Jewish Cultural Unions, established in 1935.

Reichsvereinigung der Juden in Deutschland: State Association of Jews in Germany; a Nazi-imposed communal organization, established in 1939.

Reichsvertretung der deutschen Juden: State Representation of Jews in Germany; a Nazi-imposed Jewish communal organization, established in 1933.

Reichszentralstelle fuer Juedische Auswanderung: State Control Office for Jewish Emigration, established by Adolf Eichmann in 1939.

Reprezentacja: Representatives of the Polish government-in-exile in London.

Rexist(s): Belgian Fascist Party, founded by Leon Degrelle in 1935.

Rijksinstitut voor Oorlogsdocumentatie: Dutch State Institute for War Documentation.

Riksdag: Swedish parliament.

Robotnik: Worker; a Polish Socialist party paper.

Rosh Hashana: The Jewish New Year.

Rozwoj: A Polish antisemitic organization.

Ruble(s): Basic unit of currency in the Soviet Union.

Ruestungsindustrie: The German armament industry.

Sammellager(n): Assembly camp(s); special camps where Jews were kept, after being rounded up, to await deportation to the death camps.

Sauberungsaktion(en): Purification action(s); the cleansing of Jews, Communist officials, and all other undesirables from occupied eastern territories in line with Nazi ideology.

Sauberungskommando(s): Cleaning commando(s); term applies to a small detail of Jews left behind (after the liquidation of a ghetto or Jewish community) to gather, sort, and bag the belongings of the victims for shipment (or Nazi distribution) to Germany.

Schutzbund: Defense Force; an Austrian Socialist paramilitary militia.

Schutzhaftbefehl: Protective custody warrant.

Schutzpolizei [Schupo(s)]: Protection police; the regular uniformed municipal constabulary. See *Ordnungspolizei*.

Schutzstaffel [SS]: Protection detachment; the most powerful organization within the NSDAP, a virtual state within the State.

Sejm: Lower house of the Polish parliament.

Sekretariat fuer das Sicherheitswesen: State Security Secretariat; a state security office in Nazi-occupied Poland, established in 1942.

Selektion(en): Selection(s) undertaken on the arrival of transports of Jews at any of the major concentration or extermination camps. The few whom the *SS* doctors thought could perform slave labor would be given a temporary reprieve—the rest would immediately be sent to the gas chambers.

Sephardi(m): Jews living in or originating from Spain.

Shas: The *Talmud*; the six orders of the *Mishna* (Oral Law) and the thirty-nine tractates of *Gemara* (*Talmudic* commentary on the *Mishna*).

Shavuot: The Feast of Weeks, a Jewish religious holiday.

Shechita: Jewish ritual slaughter.

She'erit ha-Peleta: The remnant; Jewish survivors of the Nazi horror who organized in postwar Europe for the social and political rehabilitation of the Jewish people.

Shevat: The eleventh month in the Jewish calendar.

Shtern: Star; Soviet *Yiddish* language daily newspaper.

Shuk: Arab marketplace.

Sicherheitsdienst [SD]: The security and intelligence services of the *SS*.

Sicherheitspolizei [SP]: Security police; the *SP* was composed of the *Gestapo* and *Kripo*.

Sicherheitspolizei Sonderkommandos: Security Police Special Units; special units of the *SS* to be used in Czech Sudetenland.

Social-Demokraten: Social Democrats; a Stockholm daily newspaper.

Solel Boneh: A *Histadrut*-owned construction company.

Sondereinsatzkommando(s): Special operational detachment(s) of the *SS* employed for political tasks.

Sonderkommando 1005: A special *SS* unit under the direction of Paul Blobel, charged with overseeing the exhumation and burning of thousands of corpses by a special group of Jewish laborers, in order to erase all signs of the heinous crimes the Nazis and their local collaborators committed at the numerous extermination sites in eastern Europe.

Sonderkommando(s) [SK]: Special commando(s); when used in the extermination camps, an *SK* referred to Jews selected to perform tasks in the murder process that the Nazis chose. *SK* also applied to a sub-unit of an *Einsatzgruppe*.

Sovinformbureau: Soviet Information Bureau, a precursor of the Cominform.

Sozialdemokratische Partei Deutschland [SPD]: German Social Democratic Party; a Marxist party founded in 1868.

Sperrgebiete: Prohibited areas.

Sportspalast: Sports Stadium in Berlin.

SS-Gericht: The *SS* court system, established in 1939.

SS-Sonderbataillon Dirlewanger: An *SS* special batallion composed of hardened criminals and commanded by Oskar Dirlewanger established in 1942.

SS-Totenkopfverbande: Death's Heads units of the *SS*; they were employed as concentration camp guards up until 1939, at the outbreak of World War II they became the nucleus of a *Waffen-SS* division.

SS-Verfuegungstruppe(n): *SS* Field Troops; militarized units founded by Himmler in 1940 that developed into the *Waffen-SS*.

Staatenlose: Stateless; persons without citizenship.

Staatsangehoerige: Subjects of the state; second-class citizenship status for all German non-aryans (*e.g.* Jews) after the Nuremberg Laws.

Staatszionistische Organisation: State Zionist organization; a German Jewish Revisionist-Zionist party, founded in 1934.

Stadttheater: States Theatre (in Zurich, Switzerland); site of the Twentieth World Zionist Congress.

Stahlhelm: A German nationalist right-wing veterans' organization founded by Franz Seldte in 1918 and absorbed by the *SA* in 1933.

Standartenfuehrer: Colonel; an *SS* rank.

Standgerichte: Exceptional Tribunals; special German courts that would provide "legality" to the execution of civilian or military hostages.

Straflager(n): Punishment camp(s); a camp category within the framework of the Nazi concentration camp system.

Statut des Juifs: Statute of the Jews; the Vichy French antisemitic legislation.

Studiengesellschaft fuer Geistesurgeschichte Deutsches Ahnen-erbe: The Society for Research into the Spiritual Roots of Germany's Ancestral Heritage, founded in 1935.

Stuka(s): Dive bomber(s).

Sturmabteilungen [SA]: Storm troopers; also known as Brown shirts (because of their brown uniforms as against the black uniforms of the *SS*)—the original shock troops of the NSDAP, established in 1921.

Sturmbannfuehrer: Major; an *SS* rank.

Sudetendeutsche: Ethnic Germans living in Czechoslovakia.

Sudetendeutsche Partei: The Sudeten German pro-Nazi party.

Sukkoth: The Feast of Tabernacles; a Jewish religious holiday.

Sztafieta: A Polish antisemitic daily newspaper.

Talmud: Rabbinic commentaries on the *Mishna* (the Oral Law), compiled between 300 and 500 BCE.

Tarbut: Lit. "Culture"; a Zionist oriented Jewish school system in eastern Europe.

Teveth: The tenth month in the Jewish calendar.

Tisha b'Av: The ninth day of the fifth month in the Jewish calendar; a Jewish fast day commemorating the destruction of both the first and second Temples in Jerusalem.

Totensonntag: Sunday of Death; a German term for the heavy loses the *Afrika Korps* suffered in one battle in North Africa.

Towarzystwo Ochrony Zdrowia Ludnosci Zydowskiej [TOZ]: Society for the Safeguarding of the Health of the Jewish Population; the major health organization for the Jews in Poland, founded in 1921.

Ullstein Verlag: House of Ullstein; one of Europe's largest publishing houses.

Umschlagplatz: An assembly point for deportation; usually located at a railroad spur.

Umsiedlungsaktion: The transfer of a Jewish community from one locality to another, or from one ghetto to another; in most cases as a preliminary to final deportation to a death factory or extermination site.

Union Generale des Israelites de France [UGIF]: General Union of Jews in France; a Nazi imposed Jewish council, established in 1941.

Unzer Shtime: Our Voice; a *Yiddish* DP newspaper in Germany.

Unzer Wort: Our Word; a *Yiddish* newspaper in the Soviet Union.

Ustasa/Ustase: Lit. "insurgents"; the Croatian *SS*.

Ustredna Zidov: Jewish Center; the government-imposed Jewish council of Slovakia, created in 1940.

Va'adat Hamatzav: The Emergency Committee to Prepare for Jewish Statehood in Palestine, established in 1948.

Va-ad ha-Poel ha-Zioni: Zionist Inner Actions Committee, established in 1897.

Va'ad Leumi: The National Council of Palestinian Jewry under the British Mandate, established in 1920.

Verband der Juedischer Front Soldaten: Association of German Jewish War Veterans, founded in 1920.

Verordnung zur Ausschaltung der Juden aus dem deutschen Wirtschaftsleben: Law to Eliminate Jews from the German Economic Life.

Vita Italiana: Italian Life; a Fascist periodical.

Voelkischer Beobachter: People's Observer; premier Nazi daily newspaper.

Volksdeutsche: Ethnic Germans.

Volksruf: Call to the People; an Austrian antisemitic paper.

Volkssturm: Peoples army; a militia created by Hitler in 1942 to include all Germans between the ages of sixteen and sixty.

Volkstag: The Danzig Senate.

Volksverwering: People's Defense; a Belgian antisemitic publication.

Waffen-SS [W SS]: The combat formations of the *SS* that replaced the *SS-Verfuegungstruppen* in 1941. *W SS* fielded some forty divisions in World War II, including non-German units.

Wehrmacht: The German armed forces.

Weltdienst: German antisemitic news service.

Wiedereinstellungsgesetz: Austrian law for the reinstatement of government employees fired by the Nazis.

Wirtschafts und Verwaltungshauptamt [WVHA]: Economic and Administration office; an agency established in 1942 to oversee the *SS* economic office.

Wojewodztwo: A geographical and political district in Poland.

Wolna Polska: Free Poland; a Polish weekly published in Moscow by the Union of Polish Patriots.

Yeshiva: Academy for the intensive study of *Talmud* and rabbinic lore.

Yiddish Buch Gezelschaft: *Yiddish* book company.

Yidisher Antifashistisher Komitet: Jewish Anti-Fascist Committee; a Soviet propaganda and information agency created in 1941.

Yishuv: The Jewish settlement in pre-state Palestine.

Yom Kippur: Day of Atonement; the most holy day in the Jewish calendar.

Yorde ha-Sira: A *Palmah* naval unit involved in seaborne operations in Lebanon in 1941.

Zentrale der Juedischen Aeltestenraete: Central Office of the Jewish Councils of Elders; a *Judenrat*.

Zentralstelle fuer juedische Auswanderung: Central Bureau for Jewish Emigration.

Zentralverein: Central Association of the Jews in Danzig.

Zidovska Ustredna Uradova pre Krajinu Slovenska [Ustredna Zidov]: The Jewish Central Office for the Land of Slovakia, founded in 1938.

Zionistische Vereinigung fuer Deutschland [ZVfD]: German Zionist Federation, founded in 1897.

Zloty(s): Basic unit of Polish currency.

Zwangsarbeit: Forced labor; millions of people from all over Nazi occupied Europe were forced to toil for Germany.

Zwangsarbeitslager(n): Forced labor camp(s); a camp category within the framework of the Nazi concentration camp system.

Zydowska Organizacja Bojowa [ZOB]: The Jewish Fighting Organization, founded in the Warsaw ghetto in 1942; it had branches in other ghettos, including Bialystok and Cracow.

Zyklon B: Prussic acid; poison gas used by the Nazis to murder millions of Jews in a number of extermination camps.

Bibliography

Abella, Irving and Harold Troper: *None is Too Many: Canada and the Jews of Europe 1933-1948*. New York: Random House, 1982.

Abitbol, Michel: *The Jews of North Africa during the Second World War*. Translated from the French by Catherine Zentelis. Detroit: Wayne State University Press, 1988.

Abramovici, Moscu: *Our Town Bivolari*. Haifa: Bivolari Immigrants Organization in Israel, 1981.

Abramovitch, Raphael (ed.): *The Vanished World*. New York: Forward Association, 1947.

Alperovitz, Yitzhak (ed.): *Gordz Book: A Memorial to the Jewish Community of Gordz*. Tel Aviv: The Gordz Society in Israel, 1980.

_____ (ed.): *Jaroslav Book: A Memorial to the Jewish Community of Jaroslav*. Tel Aviv: Jaroslav Societies in Israel, 1978.

American Jewish Year Book, The. Philadelphia: The Jewish Publication Society of America.

Amitai, Mordechai et al. (eds.): *The Jewish Community Rohatyn: A Town that Perished*. Tel Aviv: Rohatyn Association of Israel, 1962.

Arad, Yitzhak: *Belzec, Sobibor, Treblinka: The Operation Reinhard Death Camps*. Bloomington: Indiana University Press, 1987.

_____: *Ghetto in Flames: The Struggle and Destruction of the Jews in Vilna in the Holocaust*. New York: Holocaust Library, 1982.

_____, Shmuel Krakowski and Shmuel Spector (eds.): *The Einsatzgruppen Reports*. New York: Holocaust Library, 1989.

Aron, William: *The Jews of Hamburg*. New York: American Jewish Committee of Hamburg Jews, 1967.

Austri-Dan, Yeshayau (ed.): *Memorial Book of Czortkow*. Haifa: Irgun Yotzye Czortkow, 1967.

Avizohar, Meir: *National and Social Ideals as Reflected in Mapai—The Israeli Labour Party—1930-1942* (Hebrew). Tel Aviv: Am Oved Publishers, 1990.

Avni, Haim: *Spain, the Jews, and Franco*. Translated from the Hebrew by Emanuel Shimoni. Philadelphia: The Jewish Publication Society of America, 1982.

Ayalon, Ben-Zion H. (ed.): *Antopol (Antepolie) Yizkor Book*. Tel Aviv: The Antopoller Yizkor Book Committee in the United States, 1980.

Bachrach, Sh. (ed.): *Memorial Book to the Community of Proshnitz*. Tel Aviv: Proshnitz Landsmanschaft in Israel, 1974.

Bailey, Thomas A.: *A Diplomatic History of the American People*. Englewood Cliffs, NJ: Prentice-Hall, 1974.

Barker, E.: *Austria, 1918-1972*. Coral Gables, FL: University of Miami Press, 1973.

Baron, Salo W.: *The Russian Jew under Tsars and Soviets*. New York: Macmillan Publishing, 1976.

Bauer, Yehuda: *American Jewry and the Holocaust: The American Jewish Joint Distribution Committee, 1939-1945*. Detroit: Wayne State University Press, 1981.

_____: *Flight and Rescue: Brichah*. New York: Random House, 1970.

_____: *From Diplomacy to Resistance: A History of Jewish Palestine 1939-1945*. Translated from the Hebrew by Alton M. Winters. New York: Atheneum, 1973.

_____: *My Brother's Keeper: A History of the American Jewish Joint Distribution Committee 1929-1939*. Philadelphia: The Jewish Publication Society of America, 1974.

_____ and Nili Keren: *A History of the Holocaust*. New York: Franklin Watts, 1982.

Beller, Ilex: *Life in the Shtetl*. Translated from the French by Alastir D. Pannell. New York: Holmes & Meier, 1986.

Biderman, I. M. (ed.): *Kolbuszowa Memorial Book*. New York: United Kolbushover Society, 1971.

Black Book: The Nazi Crime Against the Jewish People, The. New York: Nexus Press, 1981.

Blakeney, Michael: *Australia and the Jewish Refugees 1933-1948*. Sydney: Croom Helm Australia, 1985.

Blond, Shlomo et al. (eds.): *Memorial Book of Tlumacz: The Life and Destruction of a Jewish Community*. Tel Aviv: The Tlumacz Society, 1976.

Blumenthal, Nachman (ed.): *A Memorial to the Jewish Community of Baranow*. Jerusalem: Yad Vashem, 1964.

_____ (ed.): *Rozwadow Memorial Book*. Jerusalem: Yad Vashem, 1968.

Bobe, M. et al. (eds.): *The Jews in Latvia*. Tel Aviv: Association of Latvian and Estonian Jews in Israel, 1971.

Bondy, Ruth: *Elder of the Jews: Jacob Edelstein of Theresienstadt*. Translated from the Hebrew by Evelyn Abel. New York: Grove Press, 1989.

Borkin, Joseph: *The Crime and Punishment of I. G. Farben*. New York: The Free Press, 1978.

Bracher, Karl D.: *The German Dictatorship: The Origins, Structure, and Effects of National Socialism*. Translated from the German by Jean Steinberg. New York: Holt, Rinehart and Winston, 1970.

Braham, Randolph L.: *The Politics of Genocide: The Holocaust in Hungary* (2 vols.). New York: Columbia University Press, 1981.

Breitman, Richard and Alan M. Kraut: *American Refugee Policy and European Jewry, 1933-1945*. Bloomington: Indiana University Press, 1987.

Browning, Christopher R.: *Fateful Months: Essays on the Emergence of the Final Solution.* New York: Holmes & Meier, 1985.

Brzezinski, Zbigniew K.: *The Soviet Bloc: Unity and Conflict.* Cambridge, MA: Harvard University Press, 1967.

Buechler, Y. R.: *The Story and Source of the Jewish Community of Topoltchany.* Jerusalem: Committee for the Commemoration of the Jewish Community of Topoltchany, 1976.

Calvocoressi, Peter and Guy Wint: *Total War: The Story of World War II.* New York: Pantheon Books, 1972.

Carlebach, Alexander: *Adas Yeschurun of Cologne: The Life and Death of a Kehilla.* Belfast: Mullan Pub., 1964.

Carmi, Israel (ed.): *Nadworna: Memorial and Records.* Tel Aviv: Nadworna Landsmanschaften in Israel and America, 1975.

Carmilly-Weinberger, Moshe (ed.): *Memorial Volume for the Jews of Cluj-Kolozsvar.* New York: The Author, 1970.

Carr, William: *A History of Germany 1815-1945.* New York: St. Martin's Press, 1979.

Cattell, David T.: *Soviet Diplomacy and the Spanish Civil War.* Berkeley: University of California Press, 1957.

Chamberlin, Brewster and Marcia Feldman (eds.): *The Liberation of the Nazi Concentration Camps 1945: Eyewitness Accounts of the Liberators.* Washington, D.C.: The United States Holocaust Memorial Council, 1987.

Chary, Frederick B.: *The Bulgarian Jews and the Final Solution 1940-1944.* Pittsburgh: University of Pittsburgh Press, 1972.

Chrust, Josef (ed.): *Keidan Memorial Book.* Tel Aviv: Keidan Association in Israel, South Africa and the USA, 1977.

Cienciala, A. M.: *Poland and the Western Powers 1938-1939.* London: Routledge & Kegan Paul, 1968.

Cohen, Richard I.: *The Burden of Conscience: French Jewish Leadership during the Holocaust.* Bloomington: Indiana University Press, 1987.

Cooper, Matthew: *The Nazi War Against Soviet Partisans 1941-1944.* New York: Stein and Day Publishers, 1979.

Danzig 1939: Treasures of a Destroyed Community. New York: The Jewish Museum, 1980.

Dawidowicz, Lucy S.: *The War Against the Jews 1933-1945.* New York: Macmillan Publishing, 1986.

Delarue, Jacques: *The Gestapo: A History of Horror.* Translated from the French by Mervin Savill. New York: William Morrow, 1964.

Dicker, Herman: *Creativity, Holocaust, Reconstruction: Jewish Life in Wuerttemberg Past and Present.* New York: Sepher-Hermon Press, 1984.

Dinnerstein, Leonard: *America and the Survivors of the Holocaust.* New York: Columbia University Press, 1982.

Druck, Samuel: *Swastika Over Jaworow: The Tragic Chronicle of the Jaworow Jewish Community.* New York: First Jaworower Independent Association, 1950.

Dziewanowski, M. K.: *Poland in the Twentieth Century.* New York: Columbia University Press, 1977.

Edelheit, Abraham J. and Hershel Edelheit (eds.): *Bibliography on Holocaust Literature.* Boulder, CO: Westview Press, 1986.

_____: *Bibliography on Holocaust Literature: Supplement*. Boulder, CO: Westview Press, 1990.

_____: *The Jewish World in Modern Times: A Selected, Annotated Bibliography*. Boulder, CO: Westview Press/London: Mansell Publishing, 1988.

Ehrlich, Elhanan (ed.): *The Staszow Book*. Tel Aviv: Irgun Yotzye Staszow in Israel, 1962.

_____ (ed.): *The Zdunska-Wola Book*. Tel Aviv: Zdunska-Wola Associations in Israel and in the Diaspora, 1968.

Eisenberg, Eliyahu (ed.): *Plotzk (Plock): A History of an Ancient Jewish Community in Poland*. Tel Aviv: Hamenora Publishing House, 1967.

Edmondson, C. Earl: *The Heimwehr and Austrian Politics 1918-1936*. Athens: The University of Georgia Press, 1978.

Ellwood, David W.: *Italy 1943-1945*. Leicester: Leicester University Press, 1985.

Engel, David: *In the Shadow of Auschwitz: The Polish Government-in-Exile and the Jews, 1939-1942*. Chapel Hill: The University of North Carolina Press, 1987.

Feingold, Henry L.: *The Politics of Rescue: The Roosevelt Administration and the Holocaust, 1938-1945*. New York: Holocaust Library, 1970.

Flannery, Edward H.: *The Anguish of the Jews: Twenty-three Centuries of Antisemitism*. New York: Macmillan Publishing, 1965.

Freeman, Michael: *Atlas of Nazi Germany*. New York: Macmillan Publishing, 1987.

Friedman, Philip: *Roads to Extinction: Essays on the Holocaust* (Edited by Ada June Friedman). New York/Philadelphia: Conference on Jewish Social Studies/The Jewish Publication Society of America, 1980.

Ganin, Zvi: *Truman, American Jewry, and Israel, 1945-1948*. New York: Holmes & Meier, 1979.

Garlinski, Jozef: *Poland in the Second World War*. New York: Hippocrene Books, 1988.

Gefen, Aba: *Hope in Darkness: The Aba Gefen Diaries*. New York: Holocaust Library, 1989.

Gelbart, M. (ed.): *Memorial Book Dobromil*. Tel Aviv: Dobromiler Societies in New York and Israel, 1963.

Gelber, Yoav: *Jewish Palestinian Volunteering in the British Army during the Second World War* (4 vols., Hebrew). Jerusalem: Yad Izhak Ben-Zvi Publications, 1979/1984.

Gilbert, Martin: *Auschwitz and the Allies*. New York: Holt, Rinehart and Winston, 1981.

_____: *Exile and Return: The Struggle for a Jewish Homeland*. Philadelphia: J. B. Lippincott, 1978.

_____: *The Holocaust: A History of the Jews of Europe during the Second World War*. New York: Holt, Rinehart and Winston, 1985.

_____: *The Macmillan Atlas of the Holocaust*. New York: Macmillan Publishing, 1982.

Goralski, Robert: *World War II Almanac 1939-1945*. New York: G. P. Putnam's Sons, 1981.

Graber, G. S.: *The History of the SS*. New York: Charter Books, 1978.

Grose, Peter: *Israel in the Mind of America*. New York: Schocken Books, 1984.

Grosser, Paul E. and Edwin G. Halperin: *Antisemitism: The Causes and Effects of a Prejudice*. Secaucus, NJ: Citadel Press, 1979.

Grun, Bernard: *The Timetables of History: A Horizontal Linkage of People and Events*. New York: Touchstone Books/Simon and Schuster, 1982.

Grunberger, Richard: *The 12-Year Reich: A Social History of Nazi Germany 1933-1945*. New York: Holt, Rinehart and Winston, 1971.

Guersen-Salzman, Ayse: *The Last Jews of Radauti*. Photographs by L. Salzman. New York: Dial Press, 1983.

Gumkowski, Janusz and Kazimierz Leszczynski: *Poland under Nazi Occupation*. Translated from the Polish by Edward Rothert. Warsaw: Polonia Publishing House, 1961.

Gutman, Israel: *Fighters Among the Ruins: The Story of Jewish Heroism during World War II*. Washington, D.C.: B'nai B'rith Books, 1988.

_____: *The Jews of Warsaw 1939-1943: Ghetto, Underground, Revolt*. Translated from the Hebrew by Ina Friedman. Bloomington: Indiana University Press, 1982.

_____ and Shmuel Krakowski: *Unequal Victims: Poles and Jews during World War II*. Translated from the Hebrew and Polish by Ted Gorelick and Witold Jedlicki. New York: Holocaust Library, 1986.

_____ (Editor in Chief): *Encyclopedia of the Holocaust* (4 vols.). New York: Macmillan Publishing, 1990.

_____ and Avital Saf (eds.): *The Nazi Concentration Camps: Proceedings of the Fourth Yad Vashem International Historical Conference*. Jerusalem: Yad Vashem, 1984.

_____ and Cynthia J. Haft (eds.): *Patterns of Jewish Leadership in Nazi Europe 1933-1945: Proceedings of the Third Yad Vashem International Historical Conference*. Jerusalem: Yad Vashem, 1979.

_____ and Efraim Zuroff (eds.): *Rescue Attempts during the Holocaust: Proceedings of the Second Yad Vashem International Historical Conference*. Jerusalem: Yad Vashem, 1977.

_____ and Livia Rothkirchen (eds.): *The Catastrophe of European Jewry: Antecedents —History —Reflections*. Jerusalem: Yad Vashem, 1976.

Gutteridge, Richard: *Open Thy Mouth for the Dumb: The German Evangelical Church and the Jews 1879-1950*. Oxford: Basil Blackwell, 1976.

Haesler, Alfred A.: *The Lifeboat Is Full: Switzerland and the Refugees, 1933-1945*. Translated from the German by Charles L. Markmann. New York: Funk & Wagnalls, 1969.

Halevi, Benjamin (ed.): *Rozhan Memorial Book*. Tel Aviv: The Rozhan Organization and Sigalit Publishing House, 1977.

Halperin, Samuel: *The Political World of American Zionism*. Detroit: Wayne State University Press, 1961.

Halpern, Henoch et al. (eds.): *The Tragic End of Our Gliniany*. Brooklyn, NY: The Author, 1946.

Handler, Andrew (ed.): *The Holocaust in Hungary: An Anthology of Jewish Response*. University: The University of Alabama Press, 1982.

Hausner, Gideon: *Justice in Jerusalem*. New York: Holocaust Library, 1968.

Heller, Celia S.: *On the Edge of Destruction: Jews of Poland between the Two World Wars*. New York: Schocken Books, 1980.

Heller, Mikhail and Aleksandr M. Nekrich: *Utopia in Power: The History of the Soviet Union from 1917 to the Present*. Translated from the Russian by Phyllis B. Carlos. New York: Summit Books, 1986.

Herzog, Willhelm: *From Dreyfus to Petain: The Struggle of a Republic*. New York: Creative Age Press, 1947.

Hilberg, Raul: *The Destruction of the European Jews* (3 vols., New Revised Edition). New York: Holmes & Meier, 1986.

Hochstein, Joseph M. and Murray S. Greenfield: *The Jews' Secret Fleet*. Jerusalem: Gefen Publishing House, 1987.

Holborn, Hajo: *A History of Modern Germany 1840-1945*. Princeton: Princeton University Press, 1969.

Holocaust and Genocide Studies. Oxford: Pergamon Press.

Hyman, Paula: *From Dreyfus to Vichy: The Remaking of French Jewry, 1906-1939*. New York: Columbia University Press, 1979.

Jelinek, Yeshayahu: *The Parish Republic: Hlinka's Slovak People's Party, 1939-1945*. New York: Columbia University Press, 1976.

Jews of Czechoslovakia, The (3 vols.). Philadelphia: The Jewish Publication Society of America, 1968-1988.

Joestem, Joachim: *Germany: What Now?* Chicago: Ziff-Davis Publishing, 1948.

Kagan, Berl (ed.): *Yizkor Book of Luboml*. Tel Aviv: Editorial Committee, n.d.

Kanc, Shimon (ed.): *Przedborz Memorial Book*. Tel Aviv: Przedborz Societies in Israel and America, 1977.

_____ (ed.): *Ripin: A Memorial to the Jewish Community of Ripin, Poland*. Tel Aviv: Irgun Yotzey Ripin, 1962.

_____ (ed.): *Yizkor Book in Memory of Wlodawa and Region Sobibor*. Tel Aviv: Irgun Yotzey Wlodawa, 1974.

Kaplinsky, Baruch (ed.): *Pinkas Hrubieshov: Memorial to a Jewish Community in Poland*. Tel Aviv: Hrubieshov Association in Israel and the USA, 1962.

Katz, Menachem (ed.): *Brzezany Memorial Book*. Haifa: Brzezany-Narajow Societies in Israel and the United States, 1978.

Katzburg, Nathaniel: *Hungary and the Jews: Policy and Legislation 1920-1943*. Ramat Gan, Israel: Bar-Ilan University Press, 1981.

Kedem, Menachem: *Chaim Weizmann in the Second World War* (Hebrew). Jerusalem: Maariv Books, 1983.

Klarsfeld, Serge: *The Children of Izieu: A Human Tragedy*. New York: Harry N. Abrams, 1984.

Klooz, Marie et al.: *Events Leading Up to World War II*. Washington, DC: Government Printing Office, 1944.

Knapp, Wilfrid: *A History of War and Peace 1939-1965*. London: Oxford University Press, 1967.

Koblik, Steven: *The Stones Cry Out: Sweden's Response to the Persecution of the Jews 1933-1945*. New York: Holocaust Library, 1988.

Kohn, Moshe M. (ed.): *Jewish Resistance during the Holocaust: Proceedings of the Conference on Manifestations of Jewish Resistance*. Translated from the Hebrew by Varda E. Bar-on et al. Jerusalem: Yad Vashem, 1971.

Korbonski, Stefan: *The Polish Underground State: A Guide to the Underground, 1939-1945*. Translated from the Polish by Marta Erdman. New York: Hippocrene Books, 1981.

Kowalski, Isaac (ed.): *Anthology on Armed Jewish Resistance 1939-1945* (3 vols.). Brooklyn: Jewish Combatants Publishers House, 1986

Kranzler, David: *Thy Brother's Blood: The Orthodox Jewish Response during the Holocaust*. Brooklyn: Mesorah Publications, 1987.

Krausnick, Helmut, Hans Buchheim, Martin Broszat, and Hans-Adolf Jacobsen: *Anatomy of the SS State*. Translated from the German by Richard barry et al. New York: Walker, 1968.

Kudish, N. et al. (eds.): *Seifer Stryj*. Tel Aviv: J. L. Peretz Publishing House for Former Residents of Stryj, 1962.

Kugelmass, Jack and Jonathan Boyarin (eds.): *From a Ruined Garden: The Memorial Book of Polish Jewry*. New York: Schocken Books, 1983.

Laqueur, Walter: *The Terrible Secret: Suppression of the Truth about Hitler's Final Solution*. Boston: Little, Brown, 1980.

Lask, I. M. (ed.): *The Kalish Book*. Tel Aviv: Kalish Societies in Israel and in the USA, 1968.

Lebeson, Anita L.: *Pilgrim People*. New York: Minerva Press, 1975.

Leoni, E. (ed.): *Wolozin: The Book of the City and of the Etz Hayyim Yeshiva*. Tel Aviv: Wolozin Landsleit Association in Israel and the USA, 1970.

Levin, Dov: *Fighting Back: Lithuanian Jewry's Armed Resistance to the Nazis, 1941-1945*. Translated from the Hebrew by Moshe Kohn and Dina Cohen. New York: Holmes & Meier, 1985.

Lewinsky, Yom-Tov (ed.): *The Book of Zambrov*. Tel Aviv: The Zambrover Society in Israel, the USA and Argentina, 1963.

Lichtenberger, Henri: *The Third Reich*. Translated from the French by Koppel S. Pinson. New York: The Greystone Press, 1937.

Lichtenstein, Kalman (ed.): *Slonim: Memorial Book*. Tel Aviv: Irgun Yotzey Slonim in Israel, 1979.

Liddell Hart, B. H.: *History of the Second World War*. New York: G. P. Putnam's Sons, 1970.

Lorch, Netanel: *One Long War: Arab Versus Jew Since 1920*. Jerusalem: Keter Publishing House, 1976.

Macartney, C. A.: *October Fifteenth: A History of Hungary, 1929-1945*. New York: Frederick A. Praeger, 1957.

Macdonald, John: *Great Battles of World War II*. New York: Macmillan Publishing, 1986.

Mamatey, Victor S. and Radomir Luza (eds.): *History of the Czechoslovak Republic, 1918-1948*. Princeton: Princeton University Press, 1973.

Manor, A. et al. (eds): *The Book of Sambor and Stary-Sambor*. Tel Aviv: Sambor/Stary-Sambor Societies, 1980.

_____ (eds.): *Sepher Lida: The Book of Lida*. Tel Aviv: Irgun Yotzey Lida in Israel, 1970.

Manvell, Roger and Heinrich Fraenkel: *The Incomparable Crime: Mass Extermination in the Twentieth Century*. New York: G. P. Putnam's Sons, 1967.

Marrus, Michael R.: *The Unwanted: European Refugees in the Twentieth Century*. New York: Oxford University Press, 1985.

_____ and Robert O. Paxton: *Vichy France and the Jews*. New York: Schocken Books, 1983.

Matley, Jan M.: *Romania: A Profile*. New York: Frederick A. Praeger, 1970.

Medoff, Rafael: *The Deafening Silence*. New York: Shapolsky Publishers, 1987.

Meiri, S. (ed.): *The Jewish Community of Wieliczka: A Memorial Book*. Tel Aviv: Wieliczka Association in Israel, 1980.

Mendelsohn, Ezra: *The Jews of East Central Europe between the World Wars*. Bloomington: Indiana University Press, 1983.

Meyer, Peter, Bernard D. Weinryb, Eugene Duschinsky, and Nicolas Sylvain: *The Jews in the Soviet Satellites*. Syracuse: Syracuse University Press, 1953.

Mikus, Joseph A.: *Slovakia: A Political History, 1918-1950*. Milwaukee: Marquette University Press, 1963.

Miller, Kenneth: *Government and Politics in Denmark*. Boston: Houghton Mifflin, 1968.

Mondry, Adele: *Wyszkowo, a Shtetl on the Bug River*. New York: Ktav Publishing House, 1980.

Morley, John F.: *Vatican Diplomacy and the Jews during the Holocaust 1939-1943*. New York: Ktav Publishing House, 1980.

Noakes, Jeremy and Geoffrey Pridham (eds.): *Documents on Nazism, 1919-1945*. New York: The Viking Press, 1975.

Novitch, Miriam: *Sobibor: Martyrdom and Revolt*. New York: Holocaust Library, 1980.

O'Brien, Conor C.: *The Siege: The Saga of Israel and Zionism*. New York: Simon and Schuster, 1986.

Ofer, Dalia: *Illegal Immigration during the Holocaust* (Hebrew). Jerusalem: Yad Izhak Ben-Zvi, 1988.

O'Neill, Robert J.: *The German Army and the Nazi Party, 1933-1939*. New York: James H. Heineman, 1966.

Page, Stanley W.: *The Formation of the Baltic States: A Study of the Effects of Great Power Politics upon the Emergence of Lithuania, Latvia, and Estonia*. Cambridge: Harvard University Press, 1959.

Patai, Robert: *The Vanished Worlds of Jewry*. New York: Macmillan, 1980.

Perlov, Yitzhak and Alfred Lipson (eds.): *Radom Book*. Tel Aviv: Radom Society in Israel and the USA, 1961.

Pitt, Barrie: *The Crucible of War: Western Desert 1941*. New York: Paragon House, 1989.

Poliakov, Leon: *Harvest of Hate: The Nazi Program for the Destruction of the Jews of Europe*. New York: Holocaust Library, 1979.

Polin: A Journal of Polish-Jewish Studies. Oxford: Basil Blackwell for the Institute for Polish-Jewish Studies.

Porat, Dina: *An Entangled Leadership: The Yishuv and the Holocaust, 1942-1945* (Hebrew). Tel Aviv: Am Oved Publishers, 1986.

Rabin, Haim (ed.): *Bielsk-Podliask: Book in the Holy Memory of the Beilsk-Podliask Jews Whose Lives Were Taken during the Holocaust between 1939 and 1944*. Tel Aviv: Bielsk Immigrants Association of Israel and the USA, 1975.

Rabinovitch, Jacob (ed.): *Lithuanian Jews: A Memorial Book*. Tel Aviv: Hamenora Publishing House, 1974.

Rabinowicz, Harry M.: *The Legacy of Polish Jewry: A History of the Polish Jews in the Interwar Years 1919-1939*. New York: Thomas Yoseloff, 1965.

Ran, Leyzer (ed.): *The Jerusalem of Lithuania: Illustrated and Documented* (3 volumes). New York: The Vilna Album Committee, 1974.

Reitlinger, Gerald: *The SS: Alibi of a Nation 1922-1945*. Englewood Cliffs, NJ: Prentice-Hall, 1981.

Rejwan, Nissim: *The Jews of Iraq: 3000 Years of History and Culture*. Boulder, CO: Westview Press, 1985.

Roth, Cecil: *The History of the Jews of Italy*. Philadelphia: The Jewish Publication Society of America, 1946.

Rothschild, Joseph: *East Central Europe between the Two World Wars*. Seattle: University of Washington Press, 1974.

Royal Institute of International Affairs: *Chronology of the Second World War*. London: The Institute, 1947.

Rundle, R. N.: *International Affairs 1939-1979*. New York: Holmes & Meier, 1982.

Sachar, Abram L.: *The Redemption of the Unwanted: From the Liberation of the Death Camps to the Founding of Israel*. New York: St. Martin's/Marek, 1983.

Schapiro, Leonard: *The Communist Party of the Soviet Union*. New York: Vintage Books, 1971.

Schechtman, Joseph B.: *The United States and the Jewish State Movement: The Crucial Decade, 1939-1949*. New York: Herzl Press, 1966.

Schleunes, Karl A.: *The Twisted Road to Auschwitz: Nazi Policy Toward German Jews 1933-1939*. Urbana: University of Illinois Press, 1970.

Schoenberner, Gerhard: *The Yellow Star: The Persecution of the Jews in Europe 1933-1945*. Translated from the German by Susan Sweet. New York: Bantam Books, 1979.

Seltzer, Robert M.: *Jewish People, Jewish Thought: The Jewish Experience in History*. New York: Macmillan Publishing, 1980.

Seton-Watson, Hugh: *The East European Revolution*. London: Methuen, 1961.

_____: *From Lenin to Khrushchev: The History of World Communism*. New York: Frederick A. Praeger, 1960.

Shaiak, G. (ed.): *Lowicz: A Town in Mazovia, Memorial Book*. Tel Aviv: Former Residents of Lowicz in Melbourne and Sydney, Australia, 1966.

Shedletzky, Ephraim (ed.): *Minsk-Mazowiecki Memorial Book*. Jerusalem: Minsk-Mazowiecki Societies in Israel and Abroad, 1977.

Shirer, William L.: *The Rise and Fall of the Third Reich: A History of Nazi Germany*. New York: Simon and Schuster, 1960.

Smolar, Hersh: *The Minsk Ghetto: Soviet-Jewish Partisans Against the Nazis*. Translated from the Yiddish by Max Rosenfeld. New York: Holocaust Library, 1989.

Shmulewitz, I. et al. (eds.): *The Bialystoker Memorial Book*. New York: The Bialystoker Center, 1982.

Shneiderman, S. L.: *The River Remembers*. New York: Horizon Press, 1978.

Snoek, Johan M.: *The Grey Book*. New York: Humanities Press, 1970.

Sohn, David (ed.): *Bialystok: Photo Album of a Renowned City and Its Jews the World Over*. New York: Bialystoker Album Committee, 1951.

Steinberg, Lucien: *Not as a Lamb: The Jews against Hitler*. Translated from the French by Marion Hunter. Farnborough, England: Saxon House, 1974.

Sydnor, Charles W. Jr.: *Soldiers of Destruction: The SS Death's Head Division, 1933-1945*. Princeton: Princeton University Press, 1977.

Tenenbaum, Joseph: *Underground: The Story of a People*. New York: Philosophical Library, 1952.

Thalmann, Rita and Emmanuel Feinermann: *Crystal Night: 9-10 November 1938*. London: Thames and Hudson, 1974.

Tory, Avraham: *Surviving the Holocaust: The Kovno Ghetto Diary*. Edited with an introduction by Martin Gilbert; textual and historical notes by Dina Porat; translated from the Hebrew by Jerzy Michalowicz. Cambridge, MA: Harvard University Press, 1990.

Tragic End of Our Gliniany. New York: Emergency Relief Committee for Gliniany, 1946.

Unger, Shabtai and Moshe Ettinger (eds.): *Kalusz: The Life and Destruction of the Jewish Community.* Tel Aviv: Kalusz Society, 1980.

Vinecour, Earl and Chuck Fishman: *Polish Jews: The Final Chapter.* New York: New York University Press, 1980.

Waagenar, Sam: *The Pope's Jews.* La Salle, IL: A Library Press Book/Open Court Publishing, 1974.

Walzer-Fass, Michael (ed.): *Remembrance Book Novy Targ and Vicinity.* Tel Aviv: Townspeople Association of Novy Targ and Vicinity, 1979.

_____ and N. Kudish (eds.): *Lancut: Life and Destruction of a Jewish Community.* Tel Aviv: Former Residents of Lancut Societies in Israel and the USA, 1963.

Wasserstein, Bernard: *Britain and the Jews of Europe, 1939-1945.* Oxford: Clarendon Press for the Institute of Jewish Affairs, London, 1979.

Watt, Richard M.: *Bitter Glory: Poland and its Fate 1918-1939.* New York: Touchstone Books/Simon and Schuster, 1979.

Weinreich, Max: *Hitler's Professors: The Part of Scholarship in Germany's Crimes against the Jewish People.* New York: Yiddish Scientific Institute - YIVO, 1946.

Werbell, Frederick E. and Thurston Clarke: *Lost Hero: The Mystery of Raoul Wallenberg.* New York: MacGraw-Hill, 1982.

Werth, Alexander: *Russia at War, 1941-1945.* New York: E. P. Dutton, 1964.

Wielun Memorial Book. Tel Aviv: Irgun Yotzey Wielun in Israel and the USA, 1971.

Wischnitzer, Mark: *To Dwell in Safety: The Story of Jewish Migration Since 1800.* Philadelphia: The Jewish Publication Society of America, 1948.

Wyman, David S.: *The Abandonment of the Jews: America and the Holocaust, 1941-1945.* New York: Pantheon Books, 1984.

_____: *Paper Walls: America and the Refugee Crisis 1938-1941.* Amherst: University of Massachusetts Press, 1968.

Yad Vashem Studies. Jerusalem: Yad Vashem.

Yahdut Zemanenu (Hebrew). Jerusalem: Magnes Press for the Institute of Contemporary Jewry, Hebrew University.

Yariwold, M. (ed.): *Rzeszow Jews: Memorial Book.* Tel Aviv: Committee of Rayshe Landsleite in Israel and America, 1967.

Yiddish Lodz: A Yiskor Book. Melbourne, Australia: The Lodz Center, 1974.

Yizkor Book of the Jewish Community in Dzialoszyce and Surroundings. Tel Aviv: Hamenora Publishing House, 1973.

Zaar, Isaac: *Rescue and Liberation: America's Part in the Birth of Israel.* New York: Bloch Publishing, 1954.

Zicklin, Jack (ed.): *Gombin: Life and Death of a Jewish Town in Poland.* New York: The Gumbiner Society of America, 1969.

Zuccotti, Susan: *The Italians and the Holocaust: Persecution, Rescue, Survival.* New York: Basic Books, 1987.

Name Index

Place Index

Subject Index

About the Authors

HERSHEL EDELHEIT, a Holocaust survivor, is a researcher and public speaker. He has collaborated with his son Abraham on three earlier bibliographies, *The Jewish World in Modern Times*, *Bibliography on Holocaust Literature* and its first *Supplement*.

ABRAHAM J. EDELHEIT is an Adjunct Professor of History, who has taught at Kingsborough Community College and Touro College.